The Knopf Collectors' Guides
to American Antiques

D0469999

A Chanticleer Press Edition

Quilts, Coverlets, Rugs & Samplers

Robert Bishop, William Secord and Judith Reiter Weissman

William C. Ketchum, Jr., Series Consultant

Alfred A. Knopf, New York

This is a Borzoi Book
Published by Alfred A. Knopf, Inc.

Copyright © 1982 by Chanticleer Press, Inc.
All rights reserved under International and Pan-American
Copyright Conventions. Published in the United States by
Alfred A. Knopf, Inc., New York, and simultaneously in
Canada by Random House of Canada Ltd., Toronto.
Distributed by Random House, Inc., New York.

Prepared and produced by
Chanticleer Press, Inc., New York.

Color reproductions by Nievergelt Repro AG, Zurich,
Switzerland. Type set in Century Expanded by Dix Type Inc.,
Syracuse, New York. Printed and bound by Kingsport Press,
Kingsport, Tennessee.

First Printing

Library of Congress Catalog Number: 82-47848
ISBN: 0-394-71271-4

Contents

Acknowledgments

Many people were kind enough to assist in the preparation of this book. My appreciation goes to all the collectors, dealers, and institutions that generously contributed to this project. In particular, Kate and Joel Kopp of America Hurrah Antiques, Jolie Kelter and Michael Malcé of Kelter-Malcé, and Tom Woodard and Blanche Greenstein of Thomas K. Woodard American Antiques and Quilts contributed unstintingly, both in making their collections available to us and in sharing their expertise. William Secord prepared much of the manuscript for the sections on quilts and coverlets; Judith Reiter Weissman wrote the portions of the guide dealing with rugs and miscellaneous bedcovers and reviewed other sections of the book; William C. Ketchum, Jr., read the entire manuscript and compiled the price guide; and Glee F. Krueger's far-reaching knowledge in the areas of needlework and samplers formed the basis for that section of this guide. Margaret Elliott assisted with the editing of the manuscript. Amelia Weiss and Kathleen Swan skillfully copy-edited the text.

Much of the credit for this book goes to Paul Steiner and his staff at Chanticleer Press. Special thanks are due to Gudrun Buettner and Susan Costello, who developed the idea for this series, and whose creative assistance added substantially to this volume. Carol Nehring supervised the art and layout, and Helga Lose and John Holliday saw the book through production. Most of all, I am indebted to Jane Opper, David Gibbin, and Mary Beth Brewer, who, with the help of Lori Renn, edited and coordinated this guide; and to Charles Elliott, Senior Editor at Alfred A. Knopf, for his encouragement and support.

About the Authors and Consultant

Robert Bishop
Director of the Museum of American Folk Art in New York City since 1976, Robert Bishop is a well-known author, lecturer, and teacher in the fields of American art and antiques. His more than 30 books include *America's Quilts and Coverlets*, *Treasures of American Folk Art*, and *American Decorative Arts, 1620–1980*. Dr. Bishop established the first master's degree program in folk art studies, at New York University, and is on the editorial boards of *Antique Monthly*, *Art & Antiques*, and *Horizon* magazines.

William Secord
William Secord recently served as the director of special projects at the Museum of American Folk Art and as a teacher in the folk art program at New York University. He is an associate curator of the traveling exhibition "American Folk Art: Expressions of a New Spirit." Currently he is the director of the Dog Museum of America in New York City.

Judith Reiter Weissman
Dr. Weissman is a freelance writer and lecturer whose specialty is American textiles. She was the guest curator of "Anonymous Beauty: Quilts, Coverlets, Bedcovers—Textile Treasures from Two Centuries" at the Museum of American Folk Art in 1981. She has also lectured on the subject at the Cooper-Hewitt Museum and New York University.

William C. Ketchum, Jr.
A member of the faculty of the New School for Social Research, consultant William C. Ketchum, Jr., is the author of 17 books, including *The Catalog of American Antiques*. Dr. Ketchum has also lectured on antiques around the country, and is a contributing editor of *Antique Monthly*.

Preface

Almost from the day it was finished, a quilt or sampler was admired and treasured. Little wonder, for the best handmade American textiles are not only masterfully executed and functional but are also considered works of art. Today the field of American textiles is one of the most popular and appealing in the antiques world, perhaps because collections can be as individual as the textiles themselves. This volume covers the most important and visually exciting categories of American textiles—quilts, coverlets, and other bedcovers, as well as rugs and samplers. Common types are emphasized, but exceptional historical pieces, important for an understanding of textiles, are covered as well.

Quilts
Interest in collecting quilts began in the 1920s. At first, specialists focused on the quality of the needlework, but in the 1960s the emphasis shifted to an aesthetic appreciation of quilts, as collectors began to value examples that could be related to modern art. Today attention is being lavished on such diverse forms as magnificent 19th-century appliquéd album quilts and simple pieced quilts made during the Depression years. Within the past 20 years, prices for quilts have escalated dramatically. Yet good buys remain, and the resourceful collector is sure to find handsome, reasonably priced examples.

Coverlets
Until recent decades, it was possible to acquire fine handwoven coverlets for very modest sums, often less than a hundred dollars. Although this is no longer true, coverlets remain among the most inexpensive American textiles. They are ideal collectibles: displaying a wonderful variety of patterns and designs, they are usually signed and dated.

Other Bedcovers
Serious collectors turn to such forms as stenciled spreads and bed rugs to understand the development of American textiles. These pieces illustrate the degree of artistry and skill achieved by gifted women in early America. Few people recognize the importance of many of these textiles—some of which are extremely rare and expensive.

Rugs
Hooked and braided rugs are only now beginning to command attention and substantial prices, with original designs most in demand. Rugs made from early stenciled patterns are still easy to find, inexpensive, and likely to appreciate in value.

Samplers and Needlework Pictures
In the 18th and 19th centuries, the mark of a well-trained young woman was recognized by the fine stitches and elaborate designs in her sampler. These are the same criteria by which the collector judges a sampler today. Although the most intricately stitched American samplers and needlework pictures are extremely high priced, less elaborate pieces are still available and, like other fine American textiles, a prime investment.

A Simple Way to Identify Textiles

Textiles are among the most diverse of American collectibles. Treasured in their own day for their beauty, utility, and craftsmanship, today they are perhaps even more highly regarded as documents of our American heritage. The finest examples are sought after throughout the world.

Even though quilts, coverlets, and other bedcovers, as well as rugs and samplers, have an immediate appeal, the inexperienced collector may have trouble evaluating them critically, at least in part because of their diversity. To help you identify, date, and assess the quality and value of handmade American textiles, we have assembled 343 representative examples for full picture-and-text coverage. These include the most common, reasonably priced pieces available, as well as some rare, costly examples that are important for a full understanding of American textiles. The examples range from fragile colonial bedcovers to textiles made in the 1980s. The color plates and accompanying text are organized by basic types in a visual sequence, so that beginners can find a similar textile quickly without knowing its pattern name, method of construction, or date. Each group of color plates is introduced by an essay that explains the history of the pieces covered and provides additional information on their construction.

Because it is impossible to illustrate every type of handmade American textile, this book is also designed to help you understand variations that are not shown. The supplementary guides to quilt and coverlet patterns, and to the stitches used on quilts, samplers, and needlework pictures, include examples not illustrated elsewhere in this book. An introductory essay explains how textiles are made, and illustrated color sections present the basic forms of each textile type. The Glossary defines specialized terms used in this book. Finally, the up-to-date Price Guide lists the many features that influence value and provides general price ranges and representative examples for each group. Using all of these tools, both the beginner and connoisseur will find it easier to understand American textiles and assemble a first-rate collection.

How Textiles Are Made

The most highly prized textiles are not only beautiful, they are also finely crafted. Some textiles involve just a few simple techniques that are easy to understand: quilts, for example, are either pieced or appliqued. Many coverlets, on the other hand, are woven in a process so complex that only a specialist can understand it. But not all woven textiles require such a complicated technique; in its simplest form, weaving is comprehensible to almost everyone. Familiarity with the basic techniques used in making textiles enables the collector to judge the quality of a piece.

Quilts

A quilt is made of three layers: the top, the filling, or interlining, and the back. The layers are usually held together by quilting stitches, but tufting is sometimes employed. Although only a few simple sewing methods are used to make most quilts, completing an elaborate example often took years, especially if it was sewn entirely by hand. The introduction of the sewing machine in about 1860 enabled women to stitch quilt tops by machine, yet the actual quilting was almost always done by hand.

Constructing the Quilt Top

The earliest quilt tops were built one piece at a time until the desired size was reached. But by the 1830s and 1840s, most quilts were constructed in a block-to-block fashion. Blocks were usually from 10 to 20 inches square, which made the work portable, and each was either pieced together or appliquéd. Sometimes sets, or narrow bands of fabric, were sewn on the completed top to hide the stitches that joined the blocks together. These sets also gave the quilt design a unifying grid. Some quiltmakers kept a rag-bag, in which they stored remnants of fabric until enough were accumulated to make a quilt. The use of scraps was ideally suited to patterns composed of many small geometric units, such as the One Patch. For other types of quilts, fabric was often specially purchased. To make both pieced and appliquéd quilts, templates, usually of cardboard or metal, were cut out in the shape of a pattern piece or motif. The template was placed on the fabric and traced with water-soluble ink. After the fabric pieces had been cut out, the seamstress would press down a uniform seam allowance and then stitch the pieces together.

Quilting

When the top was completed, it was joined to the back and the filling. This was generally done by quilting, or stitching, the three layers together. In preparation for the quilting, the layers were placed on a quilting frame, a rectangular unit made of four rods held together at the corners by clamps. First, the bottom layer, or back, was placed on the frame and stitched around the rods to hold it in place. Next, the filling was laid on the backing, smoothed down, and basted in place. Finally, the top was basted to the backing along all four sides. These steps ensured that the layers would remain taut during the quilting.

Before the quilting began, the quilting designs were marked on the top. Since careful quilting contributed greatly to the beauty of the quilt, the designs were rarely drawn freehand. Instead, templates were traced with chalk. For lines of parallel quilting, string was sometimes rubbed with chalk and then pressed down across the top. Occasionally tiny pinpricks were made in the fabric, which the quilters followed as they worked. The actual stitching was done from the outer edge of the quilt toward the center. As the work progressed, the finished parts were rolled tightly over the rods of the frame, bringing the next area within working distance of the quilters.

Quilting patterns varied greatly, ranging from simple motifs such as diamonds to elaborate wreaths and cornucopias. Highly skilled quilters could sew more than 12 to 14 stitches to the inch: the finer the stitches, the stronger and more elegant the finished quilt. Occasionally quilting patterns were stuffed after they were stitched, which added a third dimension to the design. The quiltmaker pried apart the weave of the backing and inserted small bits of cotton until the design was filled out.

Some quilts were tufted rather than quilted. Small lengths of thread or yarn were pulled from the bottom layer up through the quilt top and then knotted together.

Binding

By the time the quilting had been completed, the edges of the top and back were usually frayed from the tension of the frame. To hide the ragged edges and to seal the three layers together, binding was often added. After the quilt had been removed from the frame, bias tape or narrow pieces of cloth were stitched along the edges of the back and top. In some cases, the back was brought up over the top and hemmed, or the top and back edges were folded to the inside and stitched together.

Coverlets

Unlike the other bedcovers included in this book, coverlets were woven on looms. Woven fabric is composed of a warp and a weft. The warp threads remain stationary and run vertically, that is, parallel to the sides of the loom. The weft threads are woven horizontally back and forth through the warp.

The simplest loom has one harness—the device through which the warp is threaded. By changing the way in which the harness is threaded, the colors of the warp and weft, and the way in which the weft is passed through the warp, endless variations in pattern and texture are possible.

Early Home Looms

In colonial America looms usually had two or four harnesses. The harnesses were connected to treadles, which raised or lowered them. When a harness was raised, certain warp threads were raised as well. The weft, which was wound around a shuttle, was passed through the space between the raised warp threads and those that remained stationary; this space is called the shed. The harness was then depressed, lowering the raised warp threads, and the weft was again passed through the shed that had been created. The weaver had to carefully control the tension of the weaving. If he pulled the weft too tightly, the edges, or selvages, of the coverlet would be uneven.

After a length of fabric had been woven, it was wound around a beam, located at the front of the loom, which advanced the warp threads. Weaving continued until the desired length had been reached. Many early American coverlets have a border design woven on three sides or are fringed. Usually the top of the spread was simply hemmed, because it would be tucked under a pillow out of sight.

The earliest coverlets woven in America were made on two-harness looms. But four-harness looms soon replaced them. The loom would be set up in a common room of the home, or, if the family could afford it, in a loom shed separate from the main dwelling. Early home looms were very narrow, ranging from 28 to 48 inches in width. Consequently, coverlets were woven in two sections, each from 30 to 50 inches in length, and then sewn together.

By the early 19th century, when professional weavers gradually put an end to the home industry, six- and eight-harness looms were often used. These were operated by the weaver with the help of two apprentices or assistants.

Jacquard Patterns

Weavers usually relied on patterns that showed them how to thread the loom. Most patterns resulted in geometric designs. The introduction of the Jacquard attachment in the 1820s made it possible to weave complicated curvilinear patterns. Consisting of punched cards, which resemble the music rolls used on player pianos, the attachment controlled the movements of the harness and consequently the final pattern. Accomplished weavers could create their own patterns by punching new designs in cards. Many of the looms that used the Jacquard attachment were fully or partially mechanized and had as many as 40 harnesses.

Other Bedcovers

Most of the bedcovers included in this section of the book employ the same needlework techniques that are used to make floor rugs, samplers, or quilts. Relatively unusual construction methods are discussed below.

Bed Rugs

These bedcovers were almost always worked on a coarse foundation of wool homespun, although linen or silk foundations were occasionally used. Like floor rugs, their pile was formed by yarn that was knotted, sewn, or hooked through the foundation.

Stenciled Bedcovers

Generally stencils were cut out of oiled paper. For each design and color, an individual stencil was required. The maker would mark the placement of the various designs on a length of fabric—usually inexpensive, lightweight cotton—and then apply one dye through a stencil with a wad of cotton. Before another color could be applied, the first dye had to dry thoroughly.

Many of the dyes faded quickly, ran, or blurred around the edges of the designs. Choosing the dye and applying it carefully were as important to the appearance of a completed spread as the designs themselves.

Linsey-Woolseys

Made of homespun cloth, linsey-woolseys have a woolen weft and a linen warp. The top of the bedcover was seamed together from several widths of fabric and then sewn to a linen homespun or cotton backing. The top and back usually enclosed a thin layer of unwashed wool batting. Frequently the top was glazed, either by applying a solution of egg white and water or by rubbing it with a smooth stone. Like quilts, the layers of a linsey-woolsey were joined together by elaborate quilting, which was usually worked in thread that matched the color of the top.

Candlewick Spreads

Two techniques were used to make candlewick spreads, weaving and embroidery. In the woven spreads, raised designs were created as the fabric was woven. Embroidered candlewicks were stitched with cotton cording on cotton or linen. Outline, stem, and satin stitches and French knots were among the most popular raised stitches used. Often the same stitch would be done in different thicknesses of cotton cording. Heavy cording, called roving, resulted in large tufts, which were generally sheared.

Rugs
Most rugs were hooked, yarn-sewn, shirred, or braided. But occasionally they were woven, appliquéd, or embroidered, using standard weaving and sewing techniques.

Hooked Rugs
Narrow strips of cloth—generally wool, but also cotton, silk, nylon, or another fabric—were pulled through a foundation, usually burlap, to form the rug's pile. The narrower the cloth strips and the closer the loops, the tighter and more durable the rug. To produce a rough texture, the rugmaker could shear or clip the loops. Occasionally the rugmaker looped or clipped the pile in varying lengths, creating certain areas that were higher than others, producing a three-dimensional effect. This technique is usually associated with rugs made in Waldoboro, Maine.
Before a rug was hooked, its design had to be drawn on the cloth foundation. The earliest rug hookers often used the tip of a charred stick to do this. Women skilled at drawing sometimes furnished rug designs to others less talented, who then hooked the rugs themselves. Rugmakers with little drawing skill also turned to geometric designs, which could be traced from cups or plates, or worked along the lines of the foundation's warp and weft. After the introduction of stenciled rug patterns in about 1870, most rugs were worked on prepared foundations.

Yarn-Sewn Rugs
Resembling hooked rugs, yarn-sewn rugs were worked with a needle rather than a hook. The yarn was sewn through the foundation with a loose running stitch, and loops were left to form the rug's pile. In most, the loops were clipped.

Shirred Rugs
These rugs actually employed an appliqué technique. Long running stitches were sewn down the center of a narrow strip of cloth. The thread was then pulled tight, gathering up the fabric. This shirred fabric, or caterpillar, as it is often called, was then stitched at one edge to the foundation.

Braided Rugs
To fashion a braided rug, lengths of fabric were stitched into tubes, which were then turned inside out to hide the seams. Three tubes were braided together, then coiled into a round or oval shape and stitched together. Braided rugs were produced from whatever material was available, and most are fairly thick. Small, thin, delicate braids were sometimes used to make chair or table mats.

Samplers and Needlework Pictures
Both samplers and needlework pictures were executed with embroidery stitches. In early America, the stitches were done with silk, linen, cotton, or wool thread, usually on a linen ground. At certain times, wool, linsey-woolsey, and a sheer muslin called tiffany were also used as foundations. Later, canvas became popular. The foundation was usually held taut by a small frame, or hoop. The stitches ranged from simple stitches that could easily be worked by a child to complicated ones that only an accomplished needlewoman would attempt.

Quilt Types

There are 2 basic types of quilts: pieced and appliquéd. A pieced quilt is made of many fabrics that are sewn, or "pieced," together to form the quilt top. Most pieced quilts use regular geometric shapes, but some combine irregular forms. In an appliquéd quilt, cutout designs are sewn, or "appliquéd," to a cloth ground. The ground may be a single whole cloth or separate fabric blocks that are later sewn together. Most appliquéd designs, unlike pieced ones, depict realistic motifs such as flowers, leaves, and baskets. The piecing and appliqué techniques are often combined in a single quilt.

Pieced Quilt

Courtesy America Hurrah Antiques, New York City.

Pieced and Appliquéd Quilt

Courtesy America Hurrah Antiques, New York City.

Appliquéd Quilt

Courtesy America Hurrah Antiques, New York City.

Pieced and Appliquéd Quilt

Courtesy America Hurrah Antiques, New York City.

The Quilt Top

Most quilts consist of 3 layers: the top, the stuffing, and the backing. These layers are usually held together by quilting stitches. The finished quilt has a binding or hem around the 4 edges. Some pieced quilts are made of fabric blocks. A block consisting of 9 patches is called a nine-patch square, and a square made of a single patch is a one-patch square. In many quilts the central design is framed by a border or series of borders.

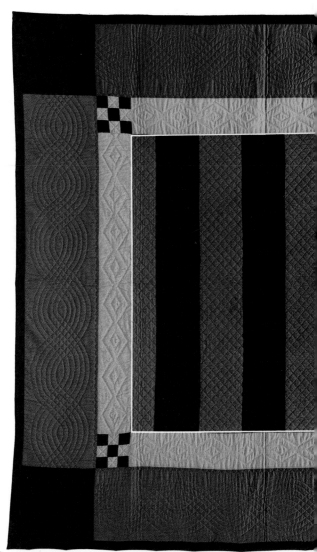

Courtesy America Hurrah Antiques, New York City.

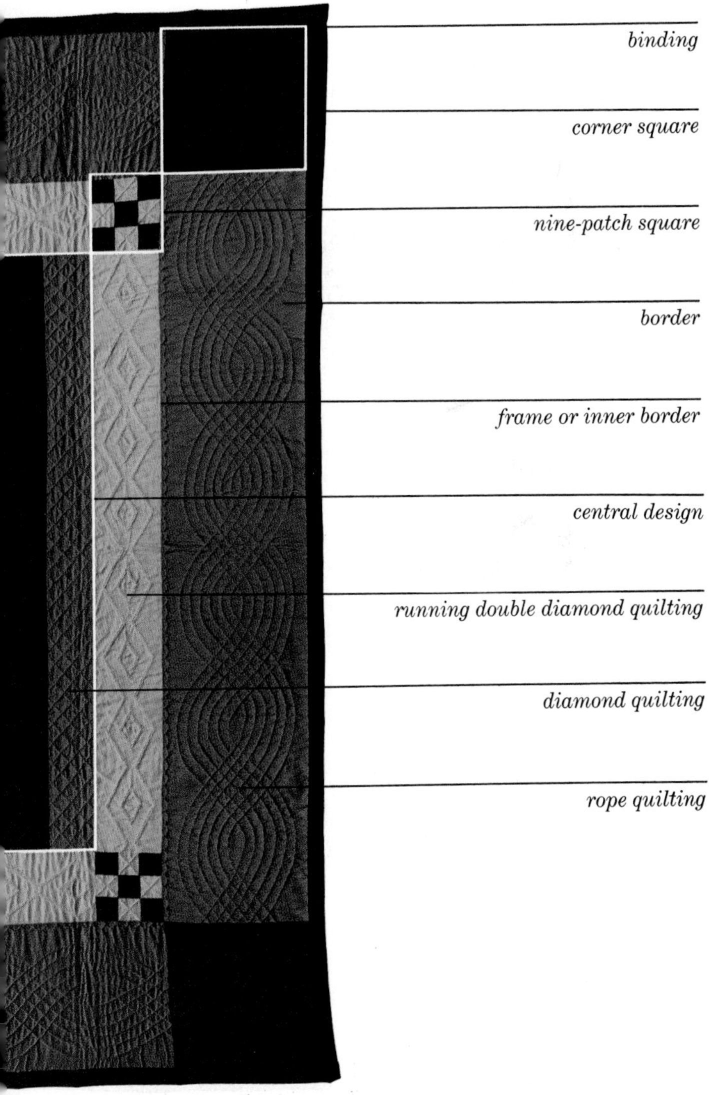

binding

corner square

nine-patch square

border

frame or inner border

central design

running double diamond quilting

diamond quilting

rope quilting

Coverlet Types

Coverlets are woven bedspreads, usually made of wool and cotton. The 4 basic types include the Overshot, Summer and Winter, Double Weave, and Jacquard. The Overshot coverlet is usually recognized by its loose weave. The Summer and Winter coverlet has a reversible pattern: one side is light and the other dark. The Double Weave also has a reversible pattern, but consists of 2 layers that are woven simultaneously and can be separated. All 3 types have geometric designs. In contrast, the overall pattern of a Jacquard coverlet is often composed of curvilinear motifs, such as flowers.

Summer and Winter Coverlet

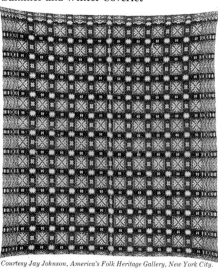

Courtesy Jay Johnson, America's Folk Heritage Gallery, New York City.

Jacquard Coverlet

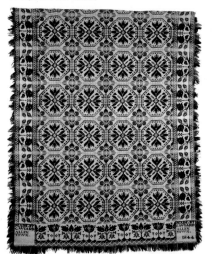

Courtesy Museum of American Folk Art, New York City.

Double Weave Coverlet

Collection of William C. Ketchum, Jr.

Overshot Coverlet

Courtesy Ruth Bigel Antiques, New York City.

Bedcovers

Few early bedcovers can be found today, and many surviving examples belong to museum collections. The bed rug, one of the first bedcovers used in the colonies, is a thick woolen textile that resembles a rug. The candlewick spread, most popular in the early 19th century, is an all-white bedcover with realistic raised designs that are either embroidered or woven with a heavy thread called candlewick. The stenciled spread, popular from about 1820 to 1840, utilized dyes and stencils to produce flowers, fruit, birds, and trees. Embroidered bedcovers date from the colonial period and continue to be made today.

Bed Rug

Courtesy The Brooklyn Museum, Brooklyn, New York.

Embroidered Bedcover

Courtesy Henry Ford Museum, The Edison Institute, Dearborn, Michigan.

Candlewick Spread

Courtesy Museum of American Folk Art, New York City.

Stenciled Spread

Courtesy Museum of American Folk Art, New York City.

Rug Types

There are 4 basic types of handmade rugs, and the hooked rug is
the most common. Using a special hook, narrow strips of cloth,
usually wool, are pulled through a cloth foundation to form the
rug's pile. The yarn-sewn rug involves a similar technique but
uses a needle to pull yarn, usually homespun, through a
foundation. The shirred rug is made of long strips of fabric that
are stitched down the center, gathered on a thread, and then
stitched to the top of a foundation. The braided rug, unlike the
other 3 types, is not worked on a cloth foundation. 3 narrow

Yarn-Sewn Rug

Courtesy America Hurrah Antiques, New York City.

Hooked Rug

Courtesy America Hurrah Antiques, New York City.

lengths of fabric are sewn into long tubes and braided. The braids are wrapped tightly in a coil and sewn together to form a round or oval rug.

Shirred Rug

Courtesy America Hurrah Antiques, New York City.

Braided Rug

Courtesy Museum of American Folk Art, New York City.

Sampler Types

The sampler is an embroidered textile, originally intended as a working "sample" of various kinds of stitches. Despite the great variety of designs, American samplers can be divided into 4 basic types: alphabet/verse, family record, map, and pictorial. The alphabet/verse sampler is the most common type. It generally contains letters of the alphabet, numbers, or verses, or some combination of these elements. The family record sampler is a genealogy that details the names, births, and deaths of family members. The map sampler was commonly used as a lesson in geography as well as embroidery. The pictorial sampler, unlike

Alphabet/Verse Sampler

Collection of Glee F. Krueger.

Map Sampler

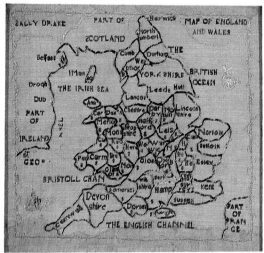

Collection of Glee F. Krueger.

the other types, usually has very little lettering, with most of the stitching devoted to a scene or several pictures of figures, animals, buildings, flowers, and fruit.

Family Record Sampler

Collection of Glee F. Krueger.

Pictorial Sampler

Courtesy Sotheby Parke Bernet, Inc., New York City.

How to Use This Guide

The major types of American textiles—quilts, coverlets, rugs, and samplers—are incredibly diverse. Each piece reflects the individuality of its maker, for no two handmade examples are alike. Yet most textiles can be loosely organized into groups according to their type and patterns. By following the simple steps listed below, you will be able to recognize types and patterns, as well as learn how to date textiles, evaluate their condition, and establish their worth.

Preparation

1. Turn to the Visual Key to become acquainted with the organization of this book. There are five major textile categories: quilts, coverlets, other bedcovers, rugs, and samplers and needlework pictures. Quilts are further divided into eleven subcategories and rugs into two. Within each category or subcategory, similar objects are grouped together.
2. Read the introduction to each category to learn the history of the type. Brief essays introduce the subcategories of quilts and rugs and provide additional historical and technical information.

Using the Color Plates to Identify Your Piece

1. Compare the textile you have found with the drawings in the Visual Key. Find the drawing that most closely resembles your textile, and then turn to the plates listed above the drawing. In choosing a drawing, look for a pattern that is similar to that found on your textile.
2. Continue the visual comparison by narrowing your choice to a single plate. Remember that each handmade textile is unique; look for general similarities between your textile and those featured.
3. Read the text to learn more about the textile you have selected. The information covered includes: the name of the textile's pattern or patterns; the techniques, materials, and stitches used; and when and where it was made.
4. Note that each entry concludes with a Price Guide Group. Turn to the group indicated within the Price Guide section. There you will find tips on what features are most valuable.

Developing Your Expertise

1. Begin by studying the color plates on pages 14 through 25, which illustrate the basic textile types.
2. Familiarize yourself with the terminology used in this book by reading the Glossary.
3. Learn the basic patterns and stitches by referring to the illustrated guides on pages 430 through 446.
4. Read the section How Textiles Are Made.
5. Consult the Bibliography, which lists some of the major books on textiles, and the list of Antiques Publications.
6. Learn which factors affect the price of textiles. The Price Guide describes the most desirable features for each type of textile, and provides information on collecting trends. Knowing about the marketplace will prepare you for shopping expeditions and will help ward off costly mistakes while making it easier to spot bargains.
7. Visit museum collections and antiques shops, one of the best ways of learning about textiles. Firsthand knowledge of the best examples available will enable you to develop a discerning eye and an ability to recognize outstanding pieces.

Information-at-a-Glance

Each color plate in this book is accompanied by a full text description. At a glance, you can recognize the type of textile you are looking at and then find the information you need to identify and date it.

Description
This covers the textile's most prominent features, including its method of construction and the patterns, motifs, and colors employed. The description is especially thorough to show you how to analyze the quality of a similar piece. Many details that are not visible at a distance or in a photograph, such as small prints or embroidery, are fully described. If a fabric is listed as a "red print" it often means that red is the predominant color. Technical terms are defined in the Glossary.

Materials and Dimensions
The materials used in the construction of the textile are given first; in the quilt section, the materials listed are for the quilt top. For both needlework and quilts, a detailed description of stitching is also included. Finally, the textile's dimensions are provided, with the largest given first.

Maker, Locality, and Period
This category indicates where and when the textile was made. Unless a piece is dated or thoroughly documented, the date is approximate and generally indicates when the type was most common. Remember that even dated examples must be evaluated carefully: Although a date on a sampler usually indicates exactly when the piece was completed, a rug may commemorate an event that occurred 50 years previously. "Locality" signifies the most likely provenance of each piece. When known, the name of the maker is provided.

Comment
The comment section provides a wealth of information about the textile's history and its pattern and motifs, as well as any alternate names. Additional information about the maker or how the textile is constructed may also be included. Design elements, such as color, are frequently discussed, making it easier to evaluate the success or failure of a textile's composition.

Hints for Collectors
These tips point out what to look for and what to avoid, how to detect repairs, what type of wear is acceptable, and the factors that influence price. Whether a textile is rarely or commonly found, whether it is overpriced or undervalued, and whether it is currently in vogue or out of fashion may also be covered here. In addition, there are hints on how to care for a textile once you have acquired it.

Visual Key

The textiles in this guide are divided into 16 groups: 11 groups of quilts, 1 of coverlets, 1 of bedcovers, 2 of rugs, and 1 of samplers and needlework pictures. A symbol for each group appears at the left, along with a description of the types of pieces within that category. Symbols of representative objects within the group are shown at the right, with plate numbers indicated above them. The group symbol is repeated on the opening page of the section concerning that group.

Quilts with Central Motifs (*Plates 1–12*)
Most of the quilts in this section have either Central Medallion designs or patterns based on that early 19th-century type. All are floral or foliate. Most made before 1850 are appliquéd; examples dating from after 1850 are pieced. One late example has floral motifs placed evenly across its surface.

Album Quilts (*Plates 13–24*)
Made of rows of blocks sewn together, usually by a group of women, most album quilts are appliquéd. Some are embellished with embroidery, crewelwork, stuffed work, or stenciling. The names of those who contributed the blocks are generally signed in ink or embroidery. Some examples have a grid that encloses the individual blocks. Many commemorate special occasions such as marriages or were gestures of friendship.

Quilts with Geometric Designs (*Plates 25–74*)
Geometric quilts are among the simplest to make, and, therefore, the most common. Their designs generally consist of many small, straight-sided pieces—or sometimes curved elements—that are sewn together to form overall patterns. This section includes several Amish quilts in such well-known, large-scale patterns as Bars or Diamond in Square.

1–2, 11   3–7   8–10   12

13–17   18–22   23–24

25–28   29–32, 68   33, 40–41   34–38, 44–48, 56, 61

39, 42–43, 70   49, 59–60   50–55   57, 65, 71–74

Quilts with Geometric Designs (*Plates 25–74*) (*continued*)

Log Cabin Quilts (*Plates 75–88*)
These quilts are named for the narrow strips, or "logs," used to construct them. The logs are pieced around a central square. The most popular patterns, named for their dramatic visual effect, include Light and Dark, Barn Raising, Courthouse Steps, Straight Furrow, Streak of Lightning, and Windmill Blades.

Quilts with Circular Designs (*Plates 89–112*)
Many quilts with circular designs fall into one of 4 general types: concentric circles, rows of separate circles, overlapping circles, or hexagonal shapes. Specific patterns include Mariner's Compass, Dresden Plate, Double Wedding Ring, and Grandmother's Flower Garden. Most are made either of curved elements or of straight-edged pieces carefully arranged to achieve a circular effect. Many were pieced, and only a few appliquéd.

Quilts with Star Designs (*Plates 113–134*)
Although star designs may have anywhere from 4 to hundreds of points, eight-pointed stars are the most common. Some bedcovers have just one large, radiating star; in others, dozens of smaller stars may be used, sometimes combined with appliquéd blocks, feathers, or elaborate quilting. Hundreds of star variations occur, and, all told, stars are probably the most common motif used on quilts.

Patriotic Quilts (*Plates 135–146*)
Patriotic motifs have been used on quilts for more than 200 years. Eagles and flags, or loosely arranged stars and stripes, are among the most common designs. Other quilts commemorate historical figures, such as George Washington and Abraham Lincoln, or important events, such as the end of the Second World War.

58, 62 *63–64* *66–67, 69*

75–76 *77–80* *81–83* *84–85*

86 *87–88*

89–92 *93–106* *107–108* *109–112*

113–118, 120,
128

119, 121–126,
129–132

127, 133–134

135–141 *142–144* *145–146*

Thematic Quilts (*Plates 147–160*)
The quilts in this section vary widely. Some show historic places or events. Others are personal, referring to important dates or depicting religious verses significant to the quiltmaker. A few, probably intended for children, illustrate the letters of the alphabet or simple poems. Also included here is a selection of contemporary quilts.

Leaf, Vine, and Basket Quilts (*Plates 161–180*)
The quilts included here depict plants, flowers, leaves, trees, and baskets. Often abstracted into repeating geometric patterns, these motifs are generally appliquéd to a quilt top or made of pieced blocks.

Representational Quilts (*Plates 181–192*)
These quilts incorporate motifs taken from everyday life: houses, people, ships, animals, and landscapes. Most of these representational designs were pieced together from small patches of fabric cut in geometric shapes. The individual blocks are usually contained within a grid.

Crazy Quilts (*Plates 193–202*)
Made of scraps of multicolored fabric, crazy quilts are usually stitched together into blocks or strips. They were particularly popular during the Victorian period, and many are made of rich fabrics such as velvet, satin, and silk. Most of the designs are abstract and kaleidoscopic, although some have pictorial elements such as flowers, fans, or houses. Several are organized into repeating patterns of squares, stars, and diamonds.

Coverlets (*Plates 203–232*)
These woven bedspreads, usually made of wool and cotton, have repeating geometric or floral designs, including stars, diamonds, snowflakes, leaves, roses, and medallions. In some, the border is executed in a different pattern than the central area of the textile. Many are reversible.

147–150	151–154	155–156	157–160

161–166	167–169, 173–174	170–172, 175–176	177–178

179–180

181–184	185	186	187–192

193–196, 199–200	197–198	201–202	

203–204	205–221	222–224	225–232

Other Bedcovers (*Plates 233–265*)
The bedcovers included in this section vary widely in materials, construction, and patterns. Bed rugs are early carpetlike textiles. Embroidered bedcovers have pictorial, linear, or geometric designs and were made during all periods. Stenciled examples, usually from the early 19th century, are decorated with dyed flowers, fruit, baskets, or trees. Linsey-woolsey bedcovers, which somewhat resemble quilts, are made of small geometric patches pieced together; others are glazed, quilted, and composed of large, solid-colored fabrics. Another early 19th-century type is the candlewick spread, which has a raised design.

Pictorial Rugs (*Plates 266–287*)
Most of the rugs in this section depict animals, houses, and landscapes. Although sometimes realistic, more often the subjects are simplified and primitive, like the folk paintings of the period. Almost all of these rugs were hooked.

Rugs with Floral and Geometric Designs (*Plates 288–317*)
Floral and geometric rugs are hooked, yarn-sewn, shirred, braided, and even appliquéd and embroidered. Floral rugs usually have large overall designs; geometric examples have small repeating or bold concentric patterns of lines, circles, and rectangles. Some rugs combine floral and geometric motifs.

Samplers and Needlework Pictures (*Plates 318–343*)
Samplers typically depict alphabets, verses, numbers, maps, or genealogies. Lettering may be combined with pictorial elements such as houses. Other samplers are primarily pictorial and include scenes with animals, buildings, people, trees, and flowers. Needlework pictures such as mourning scenes are related to pictorial samplers.

233–236	237–244, 253–254	245–250, 255	251–252

256–258	259–261	262–265

266–267, 269–278	268, 284–286	279–283	287

288–295	296–297	298–312	313–317

318–320	321–332	333–339, 342–343	340–341

Quilts

American quilts combine two ancient traditions—quilting and patchwork. No one knows when quilting began, but a small, carved ivory figure of an Egyptian pharaoh dating from 3400 B.C. wears what looks like a quilted garment. One of the earliest surviving quilted bedcovers, made in Sicily about 1400 A.D., depicts scenes from the legend of Tristan. The technique for making patchwork designs by sewing pieces of fabric together is thought by some historians to be of peasant origin.

Piecing and Appliquéing

The term "patchwork" includes two related techniques: piecing and appliquéing. In pieced quilts, many small, usually straight-edged pieces of fabric are sewn together to form a large cloth. In appliquéd quilts, small pieces of fabric are sewn onto a single block or a large ground. Appliquéd quilts are predominantly representational, for complex designs can be cut out and stitched down more quickly than they can be pieced together. Often the two techniques are combined in a single quilt.

Because there are no American quilts remaining from the 17th century, we do not know whether the appliquéd or the pieced quilt developed first, but it seems likely that both evolved simultaneously. The earliest known American appliquéd quilts were created by sewing designs cut from printed chintzes or imported calicoes onto white cotton or linen spreads, which were then quilted and embroidered. Popular throughout the 18th century, this technique, called broderie perse, enabled the housewife to salvage a worn coverlet or spread.

Early American Quilts

In England pieced quilts were fairly common by the end of the 18th century. The most popular form was probably the one-patch design, in which hundreds of identically shaped pieces of fabric were stitched together until an entire bedcover was created.

Detail of an appliquéd quilt. Courtesy America Hurrah Antiques, New York City.

It is likely that the first settlers brought quilts with them to America. Since materials of all types were scarce in the New World in the late 17th and 18th centuries, and imports when available were very expensive, the creation of patchwork quilts was probably a necessity.

The majority of American pieced quilts were composed of sections known as blocks, each individually constructed by sewing, or "piecing," together pieces of cloth in a pattern that was set beforehand or worked out as the sewing progressed. The finished quilt was usually named after the overall design or, in some cases, for the design repeated in each block.

Quiltmaking in America reached the height of its popularity in the mid–19th century. During the peak period of creative quilting, from about 1775 to 1850, the repertoire of quilt designs expanded greatly. Starting in the East, quilt styles and techniques moved westward with the settlers. Since many of the same patterns were used in several regions, it is nearly impossible to identify a quilt's origin simply by its design or colors. Quilts made in the Amish and Mennonite communities of Pennsylvania and the Midwest are exceptions. These distinctive quilts can easily be recognized by their bold geometric patterns and striking juxtaposition of colors, which range from soft grays and browns to brilliant purples, blues, and pinks. Few Amish quilts made before 1900 survive; most Amish and Mennonite quilts found today date from the 1920s and 1930s.

19th-century Quilting Bees

During the 19th century, quiltmaking was an important part of social life. Traditionally, before a young woman was married, she was supposed to make thirteen quilts—twelve for everyday use and a special bridal quilt to be displayed only on important occasions. This thirteenth quilt would be either an elaborate,

Detail of an appliquéd quilt. Collection of Rhea Goodman.

intricately stitched, appliquéd quilt or an all-white spread. The quilt tops remained unquilted until the young woman's engagement, at which time she would hold a quilting party, or "bee," where the quilts would be backed, interlined, and quilted. The bee became the equivalent of a public announcement of the engagement. Because the materials used for the quilt's backing and interlining were costly, most quilts were not finished until a wedding was certain. Many of these were carefully stored in a cupboard or trunk, and are still in good condition.

Quilts were also made for numerous other occasions. For example, Album quilts fashioned by several quiltmakers were offered as gifts of friendship, and Freedom quilts were presented to young men when they came of age or completed their apprenticeship.

Although many quilting bees took place in cities, they were probably more important in rural areas, where they were often one of a woman's few means of meeting with other women.

At the bee the completed quilt top was stretched on a wooden frame so that as many as twelve women could sew on it at a time. Only the best quilters would be allowed to work on the showpiece bridal quilt. In rural areas the guests would arrive early in the morning and stay all day, usually bringing a contribution to the communal meal. The quilting progressed very quickly, and several quilts were often finished by evening.

Quilting was never exclusively a woman's craft. In the 19th century, boys were taught to cut and sew patterns, and even today some men work on quilts. When they were boys, at least two future presidents, Calvin Coolidge and Dwight Eisenhower, helped their mothers piece quilts. Curiously, both quilts, which are now displayed in museums, are variations of the same popular pattern, Tumbling Blocks.

Detail of a pieced quilt. Private Collection.

Pattern Names

Once a pattern name was firmly established, it was handed down from one generation to the next. But as people moved about the expanding country, names were changed. A pattern known by one name in the East might be given a totally different name on the western frontier.

Several thousand quilt pattern names are recognized today. The names of many quilt patterns reflect regional folklore. Others indicate the religious beliefs of the quilter, with the Bible often serving as a source. Whatever the inspiration for the naming of a pattern, one can be certain that it was meaningful to the maker, for even the simplest quilt represented a considerable investment of time and energy.

Quilting in the Past Century

By the second half of the 19th century, crazy quilts of velvets, silks, and satins, overlaid with elaborate embroidery, became popular. Some of these quilts were small, decorative throws, frequently displayed over the arm of a parlor sofa as evidence of a woman's needlework skill.

Interest in making appliquéd quilts declined at the turn of the century, but revived again in the 1930s, when quilt kits with precut patterns became popular. At that time the depressed economy as well as a general emphasis on indigenous handicrafts encouraged a return to quiltmaking. Forty years later, during the Bicentennial celebration, interest in quiltmaking was reawakened. Quilts became the focus of museum shows and, for the first time, were appreciated as works of art, valued for their colors and designs.

Today people have once again turned to quiltmaking. However, contemporary quiltmakers use different materials and generally attempt to depict fresh and unusual themes.

Detail of a pieced quilt. Courtesy America Hurrah Antiques, New York City.

Dating Quilts

Unfortunately for the collector, dating a quilt is no easy task.
Identifying a pattern is of little use, since many patterns from as
early as 1830 are still being used today. As a rule, if no date or
other information came with a quilt when it was purchased, the
best guide to age is the fabric. Some fabrics, such as velvet and
satin, were not available until the late 19th century. Others, such
as chintz, were used after 1800. Synthetic fabrics are of course
products of the 20th century. Quilts should also be examined
carefully for other indications of age. Newspapers or letters that
were used as templates may have been sewn into a quilt to help
it retain its shape and to add insulation. The dates on these can
provide only a clue to a quilt's age, for collectors have found that
newspapers may have been saved many years before they were
used.

Quilts are rarely a standard size. The earliest beds were short
and wide, and many 18th-century quilts are as wide as they are
long. By the 19th century, however, both beds and their covers
had become longer. Most quilts found today date from the late
19th or early 20th centuries, so size is rarely an aid in dating
them.

While age is extremely important, it is not the final criterion for
choosing a quilt. Condition, design, colors, and other such factors
must also be considered. Some old quilts have been rejected by
collectors because their lackluster appearance and mediocre
craftsmanship make them questionable investments.

Preserving and Displaying Quilts

If you collect antique quilts, knowing how to preserve them and
display them is essential. Never expose a quilt to strong
sunlight, since its colors will quickly fade. A collection need not
be hidden away, but a judicious balance must be maintained

Detail of a crazy quilt. Courtesy America Hurrah Antiques, New York City.

between the requirements of proper preservation and the collector's desire to display a textile.

After sunlight, humidity and dampness are perhaps the second most damaging agents to antique quilts. Too many old textiles have been kept in basements, where they mildew and eventually deteriorate. A quilt or any other textile must be stored in a relatively dry place, preferably wrapped in cotton or tissue paper so that it can breathe. Plastic garbage bags are not suitable for this purpose since moisture forms inside them.

When the quilt is stored, it is wise to refold it every few months. Old fabrics become dry and brittle, and if folded in one position for too long either develop stains or become worn and begin to disintegrate. But handle the quilt as little as possible, since oil from the hands can leave stains that may darken with the passage of time.

Many collectors like to display quilts on the wall. In this case, the most important consideration, in addition to those of sunlight and possible soiling, is to avoid putting undue stress on any one part of the bedcover. Some collectors sew a sleeve of fabric onto the back of the quilt, and hang the quilt from a dowel placed inside the sleeve. Others sew a strip of Velcro onto the back of the edge of the quilt and glue a matching piece of Velcro to a strip of wood from which the textile can be hung. But both of these methods put stress on one side of the textile. Perhaps the best method for displaying a large quilt is to reback it with new fabric, leaving several inches overlapping around each edge. Then the quilt can be stretched over a wooden frame, much like the canvas of an oil painting. Although expensive, this technique distributes the weight evenly, and the frame may be turned and hung four different ways, insuring that the weight of the textile will not be concentrated on only one side.

Detail of a pieced quilt. Courtesy Thomas K. Woodard, American Antiques & Quilts, New York City.

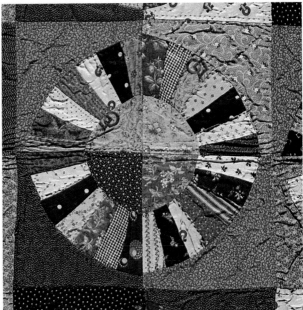

Quilts with Central Motifs

The technique of appliquéing or piecing bedcovers with large central motifs began early in the 18th century, when colonists began to import chintz palampores from India and block-printed spreads from England. At the time, imported cloth was very expensive and difficult to procure, so inventive American quiltmakers bought small yardages of these beautifully colored fabrics and then carefully cut out the motifs and stitched them onto a foundation cloth. This was known as the broderie perse method (3) and, although a time-consuming task, produced a finished bedcover comparable to an imported spread, but far less expensive.

By 1789, such American manufacturers as John Hewson were producing printed fabric similar in design to the imported cloths. Technical proficiency improved quickly, and in a matter of years American printed materials were comparable with European prints. Eventually, specially crafted fabric blocks were sold specifically as the central motif for a bedcover (5).

All the quilts in this section feature floral or foliate themes, with the earlier examples largely based on the Tree of Life pattern common on imported fabrics (1). By 1850, however, quiltmakers had incorporated many designs of American origin, including Oak Leaf Variation and Prairie Rose (7, 9). As cloth became increasingly available, methods such as broderie perse became unnecessary. And many bedcovers were pieced rather than appliquéd.

Most quiltmakers used simple color schemes when they experimented with new designs, but, as the designs became more widely used, elaborate quilting filled the ground, and motifs common to other types of quilts of the period, such as cats, palm trees, and hearts, were added (8).

In the late 19th and early 20th centuries, quiltmakers' interests in central floral themes began to wane; however, the presence in this section of at least one 20th-century quilt made from a kit suggests that the design still held some sway among quiltmakers (12).

Central floral motifs were among the most popular design elements ever employed by American quiltmakers, and there are many fine examples available to today's collector.

1 Tree of Life

Description
Appliquéd quilt. Central design of faded green Tree of Life motif serves as perch for 6 red and 2 yellow birds, all with faded green wings. Crowned by hanging faded green vine bearing red berries and wreath. Foot of tree rests on oval wreath of leaves flanked by 2 plants bearing red berries. White ground. Border consists of inner and outer alternating red and faded green oak and maple leaves.

Materials, Quilting, and Dimensions
Cotton. Ground quilted in diamond motif. Leaves of tree, wreaths, and border oak and maple leaves have stitched veins. 82″ × 72″.

Maker, Locality, and Period
Maker unknown. Connecticut. c. 1870.

Comment
This bedcover, with its red and green color scheme, was possibly meant to suggest the Christmas season, and given as a gift. The overall design might well have been inspired by a palampore imported from India. These rich cotton textiles usually reproduced the Tree of Life pattern and were printed in brilliant colors.

Hints for Collectors
The green in this quilt appears to have faded considerably, and the white ground is slightly discolored. Although unfaded textiles are far more desirable, the intricate one-of-a-kind design of this quilt makes it eminently collectible.

Price Guide Group: Floral Quilts.

Courtesy America Hurrah Antiques, New York City.

Description

Appliquéd quilt. Central bouquet of flowers and fruit held by white bow, surrounded by 6 smaller treelike plants, each alternately bearing fruit and flowers; plant at bottom has 2 red birds. White stuffed work depicting wide variety of motifs, including equestrian statue of Henry Clay, flowers, and farm animals. Predominantly green and red. Framed by green trailing vine with red and yellow flowers and grape clusters. Handmade lace fringe binding.

Materials, Quilting, and Dimensions

Cotton with stuffed work. Red birds executed in crewel embroidery; many appliqués laid down with fine crewel embroidery. 92″ × 78″.

Maker, Locality, and Period

Maker and locality unknown. c. 1840.

Comment

This bedcover is an extraordinary work of art combining beautiful motifs and a balanced design equaled by few other quilts. While it is very difficult to determine attribution, experts have isolated the work of several 19th-century quiltmakers. The top of this bedcover is reminiscent of the work done by Virginia Ivey, a mid-19th-century quiltmaker known for her exceptionally fine work.

Hints for Collectors

A masterpiece like the one shown here is a considerable responsibility. It should be cleaned only by a professional restorer and not displayed in the light for any length of time as the colors will quickly fade.

Price Guide Group: Floral Quilts.

Courtesy America Hurrah Antiques, New York City.

3 Central Medallion

Description

Appliquéd quilt. Central design of patterned chintz depicting floral urn and 2 hovering butterflies. Urn surrounded by alternating frames of white stuffed work and fruit and floral appliqués. Stuffed work frames include floral sprays, fruit, and feathered vine. White ground. Printed chintz sawtooth border. No binding.

Materials, Quilting, and Dimensions

Cotton and chintz. White stuffing includes grapes on vines, stitched flowers, and feathered vine motif. Diamond quilting in outer white border. 122″ × 120″.

Maker, Locality, and Period

Maker unknown. Paducah, Kentucky. c. 1830.

Comment

The appliqué technique used in this bedcover, in which cutout chintz designs are sewn to another piece of cloth, is sometimes called broderie perse, which means Persian embroidery. Pieces of English block-printed textiles or printed chintzes from India were often salvaged from older bedcovers or curtains that had particularly fine designs. With imported fabrics so expensive and difficult to obtain, reusing them was a necessity.

Hints for Collectors

Bedcovers with such extraordinary quilting and stuffed work are extremely rare and valuable. They were often made as gifts or in honor of special occasions, and no 2 are ever the same.

Price Guide Group: Floral Quilts.

Courtesy America Hurrah Antiques, New York City.

4 Central Medallion

Description
Pieced and appliquéd summer spread. Central medallion with floral urn surrounded by variety of multicolored birds. Six-petaled blossoms found in 4 corners of central medallion, framed by scrolled floral prints with printed fabric sawtooth outer edge. Enclosed by multiple frames: birds in flight; red, purple-and-white flowers connected by vine of black-and-white dotted fabric; and rows of nosegays and birds. Predominantly red, brown, and black. White ground. Signed and dated. Scalloped outer border created by printed fabrics of brown, blue, and red that has leaves and single stemmed flower. Brown floral printed sawtooth binding.

Materials, Quilting, and Dimensions
Cotton and linen. Unquilted. 84″ × 74″.

Maker, Locality, and Period
Ann Daggs. Rochester, New York. May 1, 1818.

Comment
Although this textile is from the early 19th century, the stylized central medallion has the feeling of American printed fabrics from the last decades of the 18th century. The piecing and appliqué work are particularly fine, as is the choice of fabrics.

Hints for Collectors
It is particularly rare to find an early quilt in such good condition, especially a signed and dated one. This kind of documentation, besides adding historical interest, inevitably increases the value of a bedcover by firmly establishing its origin.

Price Guide Group: Floral Quilts.

Courtesy America Hurrah Antiques, New York City.

5 Framed Center Quilt

Description
Appliquéd quilt. Central urn of flowers in chintz print
symmetrically surrounded by appliquéd butterflies, floral sprays,
and small birds. Central ground with stuffed feathered vine and
flower medallions, enclosed by square of floral printed chintz in
brown, gold, blue, white, and green. Further surrounded by
white stuffed work in chain and flower patterns, and enclosed by
border of same printed chintz. Predominantly red, green, gold,
and blue. White ground. Initialed. Wide white stuffed work
outer border meandering vine with flower and plant motifs.
White fringe binding on 3 sides, plain white binding on 4th.

Materials, Quilting, and Dimensions
Cotton and chintz with stuffed work. Extensively quilted.
116⅓″ × 112¼″.

Maker, Locality, and Period
Initialed EvC. Chintz prints by John Hewson. Philadelphia.
c. 1745–1821.

Comment
John Hewson arrived in America from England in 1773 and by
1774 had established a textile bleaching and printing business in
Pennsylvania. Hewson's textiles quickly became comparable in
quality to European imports. He sold not only printed fabrics but
also squares of fabric specifically designed for the central portion
of quilts.

Hints for Collectors
The collector should be wary of American quilts that integrate
English or European fabrics. There is a loose, awkward quality
to the Hewsons; their European counterparts are much more
refined.

Price Guide Group: Floral Quilts.

Courtesy the St. Louis Art Museum, St. Louis, Missouri.

6 Central Medallion

Description
Pieced and appliquéd summer spread. Central diamond in square surrounded by concentric frames. Printed floral chintz appliqués depict large stylized plant with multicolored bird in center, flanked by 2 small plants bearing blue and yellow flowers. Surrounded by printed fabric in red, yellow, and white creating checkerboard field; framed by floral print in pink-and-white and green-and-white; further framed by pieced blue, printed, and white triangles creating pinwheel pattern frame. Inner border of pink-and-brown running diamond pattern with black-and-green ground. 3-sided outer border, with triangular printed fabric alternating with diagonally set chintz squares. Tan print binding.

Materials, Quilting, and Dimensions
Cotton and chintz. Unquilted. 78″ × 70″.

Maker, Locality, and Period
Maker unknown. Maryland. c. 1820.

Comment
Lavishly decorated with brightly colored flowers, chintz was first used in the 18th century for wearing apparel. Today the term is broadly used to describe printed and solid color glazed cottons. This quilt's appeal lies in the wide variety of fabrics employed and their skillful integration into the overall design.

Hints for Collectors
Indian chintzes from the 17th century characteristically had a central medallion surrounded by a wide border, a pattern that continued to be popular throughout the 18th century and into the early part of the 19th century. This format helps to identify a textile made before 1850.

Price Guide Group: Floral Quilts.

Courtesy America Hurrah Antiques, New York City.

7 Oak Leaf

Description
Appliquéd quilt. Symmetrical pattern of red and green oak leaves with varying numbers of leaves and leaf clusters set within green and red border creating Diamond in Square pattern. Outer border of red oak leaves on white ground. Green binding.

Materials, Quilting, and Dimensions
Cotton. Ground quilted in diagonal lines. 86″ × 86″.

Maker, Locality, and Period
Maker unknown. Connecticut. c. 1860.

Comment
The quiltmaker who designed this bedcover was successful in creating a complex visual effect with a traditional design motif. A wide variety of oak leaf patterns appear on bedcovers from the mid–19th century, but its use on the quilt shown here is very unusual: the oak leaf appears throughout the quilt, making only one color change—from green to red. The symmetrical design is a testament to the seamstress's ability to create a variation that never becomes tedious or uninteresting.

Hints for Collectors
White areas of quilts often have small stains acquired through years of use. Never attempt to bleach these, for the amateur will often damage the colored fabrics in the process. If you wish to undertake this type of restoration, consult a professional conservator.

Price Guide Group: Floral Quilts.

Courtesy America Hurrah Antiques, New York City.

8 Hearts and Cats

Description
Appliquéd quilt. Circular motif encloses large red and green stylized floral design, with alternating red and green doughnut shapes; 6 stems, 4 with heart-shaped buds and 2 with crocuses, emanate from central motif. Birds, hearts, flowers, cats with calico eyes, and abstract palm trees appear across surface of quilt. Bordered with vine incorporating red crocuses and large red tulips at each corner. Top and bottom of quilt have green hearts decorated with small flowers and inner design in red. White ground. Red binding.

Materials, Quilting, and Dimensions
Cotton. Ground quilted in parallel lines throughout; hearts have diamond quilting. Crocuses contain interior outline stitching. Cats' eyes appliquéd in yellow calico with contrasting embroidered whiskers. 88″ × 84″.

Maker, Locality, and Period
Maker unknown. New York State. c. 1850.

Comment
Because quilts were often given as gifts, quiltmakers sometimes incorporated personal messages into the motifs that seem meaningless to the modern viewer. The wealth of personal details in this quilt plus some traditional motifs, such as hearts and flowers, suggest that this may have been a wedding quilt.

Hints for Collectors
Before trying to wash a quilt, test its dyes by placing a few drops of water on a small section of the textile and pressing it with a white blotter. If the color holds, repeat the test with detergent and water. Should the blotter pick up any color, the quilt must be professionally cleaned.

Price Guide Group: Floral Quilts.

Courtesy America Hurrah Antiques, New York City.

9 Prairie Rose and Pineapple

Description
Appliquéd quilt. Central red, pink, and yellow rose surrounded by 8 red carnations, enclosed by green printed vine with red and yellow flowers. Pineapples with green printed stems and 3 red and yellow flowers surround central motif. White ground. 8 red and pink roses with green printed stems crowned by 3 rose buds border bedcover. 4 carnations placed in border echo central motif. Yellow binding.

Materials, Quilting, and Dimensions
Cotton. Appliqués have very fine buttonhole stitches. Floral and leaf quilting on ground. 100″ × 90″.

Maker, Locality, and Period
Maker unknown. Maine. c. 1860.

Comment
The carnation motif appeared early in the history of American textiles and was a popular part of the Tree of Life design, included on imported Indian palampores during the late 17th and early 18th centuries. The motif also appeared on bed rugs. The pineapple was a popular symbol of hospitality, seen not only on textiles but also as a decorative element on architecture, furniture, and household accessories.

Hints for Collectors
Because floral motifs were very popular with quiltmakers, they are among the most common motifs seen on quilts in galleries and antiques shops. Look for good condition, clarity of design, and precise cutting and stitching when shopping for this type of appliquéd bedcover.

Price Guide Group: Floral Quilts.

Courtesy America Hurrah Antiques, New York City.

10 Floral

Description
Appliquéd quilt. Central yellow, red, and green flower surrounded at top and bottom by 2 hanging blossoms; central oval incorporating floral motif composed of blue, white, and green bands, the green band appliquéd with yellow circles. Central oval enclosed by green flowering vine with large abstract floral designs and large white, red, and blue blossoms at corners; small blossoms randomly float on yellow ground. No consistent border.

Materials, Quilting, and Dimensions
Cotton. Large leaf and floral quilting with parallel lines. Leaf and floral motifs have interior and exterior outline quilting. Ground around central motif has chevron and floral quilting. 96″ × 87″.

Maker, Locality, and Period
Maker unknown. Pennsylvania. c. 1860.

Comment
Unusual for its bold floral designs, this appliquéd quilt is reminiscent more of Hawaiian quilts than of the quilts made by the Pennsylvania Germans. These German immigrants—erroneously referred to as the Pennsylvania Dutch—came to Pennsylvania in successive waves in the late 17th and early 18th centuries. Pennsylvania German quilts are characterized by small images and colors that are not very bold.

Hints for Collectors
This bedcover has the naive look of a good piece of folk art, a quality much sought after by contemporary collectors. Its excellent condition, original design, and unique colors all contribute to making it a fine example of the quiltmaker's art.

Price Guide Group: Floral Quilts.

Courtesy America Hurrah Antiques, New York City.

Basket of Flowers

Description
Appliquéd pillow sham. Yellow latticework basket holds red, yellow, and pink rosebuds, roses, and tulips. White ground. Meandering vine border in 2 shades of green printed fabric accented with red flower buds. No binding.

Materials, Quilting, and Dimensions
Cotton. Ground with floral motif and feathered circle quilting. Meandering vine border has outline quilting. 42″ × 28″.

Maker, Locality, and Period
Maker unknown. Pennsylvania. c. 1855.

Comment
The rectangular shape of this small textile makes it likely that it was a pillow sham, probably designed to match a quilt. Many pillow shams can be categorized with quilts, as their surface is often extensively stitched and they may be stuffed and backed. Whatever its use, this example has the bold, naive quality associated with the best folk art.

Hints for Collectors
The small size and the shape of pillow shams make them especially suitable for framing. They are, however, very rare and consequently quite expensive. Such rarities are probably best bought by the expert collector, one who has seen and examined hundreds of quilts, rather than the novice, whose likes and dislikes are still subject to change. Collectors should also be aware that damaged quilts are occasionally cut down and presented as crib quilts or pillow shams.

Price Guide Group: Floral Quilts.

Courtesy America Hurrah Antiques, New York City.

12 Water Lilies

Description
Appliquéd quilt. Quilt center has red, pink, blue, purple, rust, and yellow water lilies on green lily pads with surrounding cattails. White ground. Border on sides of water lilies linked by stylized connecting vine. Border on top and bottom has 2 water lilies linked by stylized vine, lily pads without lilies float between them. Pink binding.

Materials, Quilting, and Dimensions
Cotton. Center lily pads have outline quilting. Borders have diamond stitching. Petals of each water lily in border have exterior and interior stitching. 86″ × 78″.

Maker, Locality, and Period
Maker and locality unknown. c. 1925.

Comment
Other quilts in this pattern exist, identical even in their border treatment, indicating that this quilt was probably made from a kit. Kits began to appear in the late 19th century and increased in popularity during the late 1920s and early 1930s, when they were advertised extensively in women's magazines.

Hints for Collectors
In the early years of quilt collecting, 20th-century quilts were generally disregarded. That attitude has changed dramatically, however, and the better examples from the 1920s and 1930s have recently become quite popular. Although made from a kit, this piece is enhanced by imaginative quilting and pleasing colors, which make it a fine example of a Depression-Era quilt.

Price Guide Group: Floral Quilts.

Courtesy America Hurrah Antiques, New York City.

Album Quilts

Most album quilts were created through the cooperative effort of a group of women. Each quilter designed and made a block that was later included in the bedcover. The blocks were almost always appliquéd, although some sampler albums consist almost entirely of pieced work or combine the two methods. After the individual blocks were appliquéd, they were frequently embellished with embroidery, crewelwork, stuffed work, or stenciling. Album quilting parties were then arranged so that the finished top could be joined with the filling and backing. The final arrangement of the individual blocks lay either with the woman who had suggested making the quilt, or with a particularly talented seamstress noted for her sense of design. Although most album quilts were cooperative efforts, in a few cases one woman executed all the blocks and then finished the quilt by herself. These quilts are distinguished by their uniform needlework and consistent design.

Album quilts were usually created for special occasions. Some marked the impending marriage of a young woman (15). Others, called Freedom quilts, celebrated either the 21st birthday of a young man or the date when he finished his apprenticeship. Often an album quilt was made as a token of appreciation for the efforts of a minister in a local community (21) or as a gesture of friendship (16), perhaps for a beloved friend who was moving away from the community. Most often each block was signed, which further personalized the work. Some signatures are executed in pen and ink, others in embroidery. When men signed blocks that had been designed and sewn by women, they almost always used pen and ink. In some cases, one woman was chosen to embroider the names of all those who had contributed to the bedcover, or of those who were especially dear to the recipient.

Most album quilts can be dated from the first half of the 19th century. A particularly remarkable group of quilts was made between 1840 and 1860 by a group of women living in and around Baltimore. Today these Baltimore Albums, as they are called, are considered some of the most beautiful quilts made in America (14, 20). It is generally believed that two women were responsible for these masterpieces: Achsah Goodwin Wilkins, who created many of the designs, and Mary Evans Ford, who made them into finished quilts. Baltimore Album quilts have several characteristic design elements, including overflowing baskets of fruit or flowers, cornucopias, animals, and Baltimore monuments. Most are large and exhibit superior craftsmanship.

13 Circular Album

Description
Appliquéd quilt. 20 designs, each enclosed by double circle in blue and orange; all circles interlock. Motifs include cornucopias, baskets of fruit, flower bouquets, wreaths of flowers, a peacock, a house, and horse and rider. Predominantly green, orange, red, and yellow. White ground. Pieced meandering vine border with flowers, leaves, fruit, and birds. No binding.

Materials, Quilting, and Dimensions
Cotton. Very fine edge stitching. Embroidered details. Unquilted. 101″ × 90″.

Maker, Locality, and Period
Maker unknown. New England. c. 1835.

Comment
This extraordinary example of appliqué quilting is very rare because circles in quilts are difficult to execute successfully. Note how skillfully this seamstress has integrated 20 circular motifs into the overall design. The appliqués are finely cut and intricately stitched. During the early 19th century, sailors returning from east Asia brought detailed stories of the exotic landscape, which may account for the intriguing palm tree motif (fourth row, left).

Hints for Collectors
Circular Album bedcovers are virtually unattainable by the average collector. The few examples on the market are only available through dealers, who reserve them for their best customers. Interested collectors should gain the confidence of a reputable dealer.

Price Guide Group: Album and Sampler Quilts.

Courtesy America Hurrah Antiques, New York City.

Baltimore Album

Description
Appliquéd quilt. 16 printed and plain fabric blocks with variety of motifs, including floral cornucopias, floral urns and baskets, floral wreaths, hands, red, blue, and yellow banners, and brown ship with yellow sails flying American flag. 3 blocks display eagle motifs; 1 blue eagle contained within wreath with 4 flags; 2 other blue eagles act as base of wreaths enclosing stenciled fountains— 1 inscribed "Fountain of Health" and other inscribed "Fountain of Life." Predominantly red, green, and blue. White ground. Pen and ink inscriptions. Dated. White muslin at edges. Blue binding.

Materials, Quilting, and Dimensions
Cotton and silk. Embroidered details. Unquilted. 72½" × 72½".

Maker, Locality, and Period
Maker unknown. Maryland. May 5, 1847.

Comment
This type of bedcover is known as a Baltimore Album quilt because the design was popular in and around Baltimore during the 1840s and 1850s. Of particular interest is the uncommon use of the hand motif, found in pink and blue on either side of both the red and yellow fountains enclosed by wreaths, and the silk ribbons appliquéd to form a basketlike vase (second block from bottom, left side).

Hints for Collectors
Because of their delicate appliqués, album quilts are particularly difficult to conserve and display—many have faded or deteriorated with use. In this quilt white muslin has been sewn along the borders; the muslin is attached to aid in displaying the quilt, and in no way alters its value.

Price Guide Group: Album and Sampler Quilts.

Courtesy Kelter-Malcé Antiques, New York City.

15 Betrothal Album

Description
Appliquéd quilt top. Blocks of printed and plain fabric with naturalistic motifs, including racehorses and riders, domestic and wild animals (ostriches, peacocks, and a rooster), trees, and flowering vines. Central block with multicolored bird inscribed "Bird of Paradise" in pen and ink. Several horses have names, including "Ivory Black" and "Black Hawk" in panel above elephant named "Hanible." Figure of woman at top right. Predominantly red and green. Off-white ground. No consistent border, with motifs around edge of bedcover. No binding.

Materials, Quilting, and Dimensions
Cotton, wool, silk, and velvet on muslin. Embroidered details. Unquilted. 84½″ × 69⅝″.

Maker, Locality, and Period
Maker unknown. Near Poughkeepsie, New York. c. 1860.

Comment
This quilt was discovered along with a photograph of a woman and a group of pattern templates cut from newspapers published in the Albany area between 1858 and 1863. The photograph is believed to be of the quiltmaker. One template outlining a woman matches the female image that appears in the top row of quilt blocks. A template figure of a man is believed to have been her betrothed, but his figure was not incorporated into the quilt.

Hints for Collectors
Templates were often cut from cardboard, newspapers, or tin to provide a model from which a design could be traced. Few, however, were as detailed or naturalistic as those used to make the Betrothal Album illustrated here.

Price Guide Group: Album and Sampler Quilts.

Courtesy Museum of American Folk Art, New York City.

16 Friendship Album

Description
Appliquéd quilt. Central portion has floral designs interspersed with floral urns and baskets, wreaths, red, white, and blue banners, and a pineapple. Top border has grapevine with red grape clusters; bottom border has shorter vine of same design. Predominantly red, yellow, and green. Embroidered signatures on several blocks. Dated. No binding.

Materials, Quilting, and Dimensions
Cotton. Border has leaf quilting on sides. Some embroidered details. 90¼″ × 75″.

Maker, Locality, and Period
Maker unknown. New York, Connecticut, or Pennsylvania. November 1, 1861.

Comment
The block construction of this quilt is typical of Friendship Album bedcovers. Along with traditional designs, there are some original touches: the presence at the top and bottom of a continuous flowing vine, red stockings and green button shoes, green "button grapes" in the border, and a block devoted to a pineapple.

Hints for Collectors
Although this bedcover was completed by several quiltmakers, not all of them have signed their individual blocks. In general, album quilts that have been signed are of far more interest to collectors than those that have not. This is particularly true if the signatures refer to important historical figures or even individuals who can be identified.

Price Guide Group: Album and Sampler Quilts.

Courtesy Museum of American Folk Art, New York City.

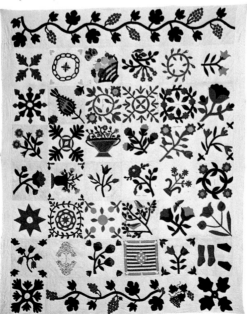

17 Album

Description
Appliquéd quilt. 49 blocks with many popular designs, including flower baskets, floral wreaths and sprays, oak leaves, cornucopias, horses, birds, hearts, fruit, a pineapple, a star, and an American flag surrounded by wreath. Block with pen and ink inscription. Several distinctive motifs, including green and red parrot and yellow butterfly and green and blue peacock. Predominantly red, yellow, green, and gold. Pen and ink signatures. Red binding.

Materials, Quilting, and Dimensions
Cotton, wool, and velvet. Embroidered details. Unquilted. 92″ × 88″.

Maker, Locality, and Period
Several quiltmakers. New York State. c. 1860.

Comment
This unusual quilt has a surprising unity for a bedcover stitched by several different makers. The wealth of individualistic detail adds to its charm, including the inscribed block in the upper left corner. Folk legend claims that an eccentric member of the family created a secret code for this pen and ink block.

Hints for Collectors
The numerous popular motifs on this bedcover are characteristic of mid-19th-century American quilts. Unusual details—the intricately stitched flying birds, cherries over the head of a blue horse, and the blue and gold pineapple—give the quilt its own distinct appeal.

Price Guide Group: Album and Sampler Quilts.

Courtesy America Hurrah Antiques, New York City.

Description
Appliquéd summer spread. 49 blocks with floral, basket, bird, heart, fruit, and star motifs. 9 central blocks; 5 feature patriotic motifs, including flags, an emblem, and American eagle. Predominantly red, green, and blue. White ground. White binding.

Materials, Quilting, and Dimensions
Cotton and silk. Embroidered details. Unquilted. 88⅜″ × 88⅛″.

Maker, Locality, and Period
Maker unknown. New York State. c. 1860.

Comment
Wreaths, hearts, patriotic emblems, and fruit were favorite motifs of 19th-century American quiltmakers. This summer spread was never intended to be filled or quilted, and, because individual blocks were worked on separately, had the advantage of being easier to stitch than most appliquéd quilts. It served as a decorative bedcover, allowing the maker an opportunity to vary motif design.

Hints for Collectors
Summer spreads were usually used less than other bedcovers and hence may be in better condition, bringing a higher market price. Some collectors back, fill, and bind quilt tops that the maker never intended to be backed or interlined. This decreases the worth of the quilt and should only be done when the top has deteriorated and backing is necessary to strengthen the fabric.

Price Guide Group: Album and Sampler Quilts.

Courtesy Museum of American Folk Art, New York City.

19 Album

Description
Appliquéd quilt top. 16 blocks with floral motifs. 4 central blocks feature variations of flower baskets; outer blocks include wreaths, thistles, and the acorn and oak leaf. Predominantly red, green, and yellow. White ground. Border has meandering flower vine in green and red. No binding.

Materials, Quilting, and Dimensions
Cotton. Unquilted. 88″ × 88″.

Maker, Locality, and Period
Maker unknown. Pennsylvania. c. 1855.

Comment
Comparing the designs of album quilts can be very informative. Those that are the strongest visually often have an enclosed grid. In this example, intense reds and vibrant greens, colors favored by Pennsylvania German quiltmakers, dominate the entire surface of the quilt. This bedcover was probably a bride's quilt that was never completed; the heart and arrow in the block with the lyre and wreath often appeared on brides' quilts and sometimes on babies' quilts.

Hints for Collectors
Album quilts may have as few as 9 blocks or as many as 49; number, to some extent, determines the size and the amount of detail on individual motifs. Large designs executed in primary colors give quilts a distinctly naive quality, a characteristic much valued among collectors. The ingenious choice of printed fabrics seen in the appliquéd baskets and urns adds further to the value of this quilt.

Price Guide Group: Album and Sampler Quilts.

Courtesy America Hurrah Antiques, New York City.

Description
Appliquéd quilt top. 16 blocks depicting flower urns and baskets, floral wreaths with birds, a heart, a building, a fire engine, and a monument surmounted by bright red bird. Predominantly red, green, blue, and yellow. Red grid separates blocks; grid enclosed by red sawtooth frame. Off-white ground. Border of floral sprays and garland pattern enclosed by green sawtooth design. Dated. Red binding.

Materials, Quilting, and Dimensions
Cotton. Embroidered details. Unquilted. 107″ × 106″.

Maker, Locality, and Period
Maker unknown. Baltimore, Maryland. 1852.

Comment
Of special interest in this quilt is Baltimore's monument honoring George Washington (bottom row, left). Built earlier than the one in Washington, D.C., the monument was a source of pride and, along with the Seaman's Bethel Mission, was a frequent motif in quilts from this region. Flying 2 American flags and crowned by a rose vine, the 19th-century fire engine (bottom row, right) rarely appears as a quilt motif.

Hints for Collectors
Baltimore Album quilts are currently highly prized collectibles. They have several general characteristics: they are assembled in block style with a different design in each block, frequently rely on realistic motifs, tend to be larger than other quilts, and exhibit superb craftsmanship and color sense.

Price Guide Group: Album and Sampler Quilts.

Courtesy America Hurrah Antiques, New York City.

Description
Pieced and appliquéd quilt. 72 blocks separated by pink grid. Motifs include variations of basket design, star pattern, floral design, and patterns based on square. One of central blocks contains Christian cross, surrounded by red stars and hearts, surmounted by golden crown. Right column contains modified American flag. Predominantly pink, green, red, and yellow. Pen and ink signatures. Dated. Pink binding.

Materials, Quilting, and Dimensions
Cotton. Parallel and diagonal line and diamond quilting. Some block motifs with outline quilting. Some embroidered details. 100″ × 90″.

Maker, Locality, and Period
Several quiltmakers. Maine. 1862.

Comment
This type of quilt is known as a Friendship Album quilt because each block was made and signed by a different person, and the finished quilt was presented as a gift. The quilt pictured was made for the Reverend David Libby of Maine; ministers were often the recipients of early American quiltmakers' efforts. In Friendship Album quilts from Maine individual blocks were usually pieced or appliquéd, stuffed, and then quilted before all the blocks were sewn into a full-size quilt.

Hints for Collectors
Baltimore Album quilts and fine album quilts in general command greater prices than simpler pieced or appliquéd quilts. Because tiny pieces of fabric were used to create individual blocks, a quilt of this type should be carefully scrutinized to insure that original materials remain intact.

Price Guide Group: Album and Sampler Quilts.

Courtesy America Hurrah Antiques, New York City.

Description
Pieced quilt. 85 full and 24 half blocks set on diagonal. Large variety of traditional patterns, including Sunburst, Log Cabin, Flower Basket, and Eight-Pointed Star. Several block designs original to quiltmaker. Predominantly pink, red, green, and brown. Blocks separated by brown-and-white printed fabric bands. Small square of printed fabric in red, brown, and black on band at corner of each block. Inner pink-and-white printed fabric sawtooth border on green ground. Outer border brown-and-white printed fabric. Pink-and-white binding.

Materials, Quilting, and Dimensions
Cotton. Inner border has modified shell and circular quilting; some blocks have diagonal quilting. Outer border has rope design quilting. 88″ × 87¾″.

Maker, Locality, and Period
Salinda W. Rupp. Lancaster County, Pennsylvania. c. 1870.

Comment
Many of the traditional designs found in this bedcover may have been based on patterns published in *Godey's Lady's Book*, a popular 19th-century women's periodical. It was not uncommon, however, for the quiltmaker to design her own patterns, as our seamstress has done here. Quilt design was a creative outlet for thousands of women in rural America.

Hints for Collectors
Be careful when dating a quilt based on the materials used. Quiltmakers often kept fabrics for many years, and sometimes handed them down from mother to daughter.

Price Guide Group: Album and Sampler Quilts.

Courtesy America Hurrah Antiques, New York City.

Description
Pieced and appliquéd quilt. 60 blocks depicting birds, floral sprays and wreaths, and one pictorial element. Central motif 4 times larger than surrounding blocks and composed of double wreath. Many different pieced and appliquéd blocks with traditional designs, including Birds in Flight, Pinwheel, Wild Goose Chase, Bride's Bouquet, and an Eight-Pointed Star. Unusual motif (top row, 4th block) illustrating crowning of Charlemagne. Wide range of fabrics and colors. Off-white ground. Pen and ink signatures. Off-white sawtooth border on 3 sides.

Materials, Quilting, and Dimensions
Cotton and chintz. Chintz appliquéd in the broderie perse method. Diamond quilting on white and off-white areas. 102″ × 96″.

Maker, Locality, and Period
Several quiltmakers. New England. c. 1850.

Comment
It was fashionable in colonial and federal America to decorate with imported printed cotton. When these fabrics became worn out, the parts that were still bright were salvaged and used as appliqués. The method in which individual design motifs were cut from printed fabrics and stitched onto a quilt became known as the broderie perse method.

Hints for Collectors
It is possible to restore the discolored white areas of this quilt as well as the frayed fabrics and several damaged red-and-white blocks. Consult your local museum curator for the name of a competent conservator.

Price Guide Group: Album and Sampler Quilts.

Courtesy America Hurrah Antiques, New York City.

Description
Pieced quilt. Many irregular blocks of fabric including a variety of English and French glazed chintzes. Chintz motifs depict stripes, floral sprays, and meandering scroll-like motifs. 57 blocks surrounded by white borders. Large central medallion of floral printed fabric in pink, green, and tan. Tan-and-white floral printed border with white corner squares; surrounded by 2nd border of printed fabrics also with white corner squares; 3rd brown geometric border with floral printed corner squares. Above central medallion, long rectangle (asymmetrically inserted) of floral printed fabric. Blue-and-tan printed fabric border. Handloomed tape binding.

Materials, Quilting, and Dimensions
Glazed cotton chintz. Unquilted. 101″ × 99½″.

Maker, Locality, and Period
Maker unknown. Maine. c. 1825.

Comment
Made predominantly of English and French glazed chintz fabrics, this bedcover is American in origin. Imported fabrics, even as late as the early 19th century, were particularly expensive. This quilt was doubtless made from scraps of fabric intended for other uses. Notice the handloomed binding tape, which was often used in the late 18th century.

Hints for Collectors
Bedcovers like this are significant because they help the historian determine the range of materials imported from England into America. But most collectors still prefer quilts made from American fabrics.

Price Guide Group: Album and Sampler Quilts.

Courtesy Kelter-Malcé Antiques, New York City.

Quilts with Geometric Designs

The simplest and most basic quilt designs are geometric. Any moderately skilled seamstress can make a pieced quilt based on squares, rectangles, triangles, or curvilinear shapes. Straight-edged forms are the easiest to cut and stitch, for fabric cut into curved forms stretches out of shape very easily.

Basically there are three ways of using geometric designs to make a pieced, or patchwork, quilt. In one method, small straight-edged forms, often hundreds or even thousands, are pieced into an overall pattern; many bedcovers made this way use variations of the one-, four-, or nine-patch patterns (31). In another method, straight-edged and curved elements, used by themselves or in combination, are joined together into individual blocks. When the blocks are sewn together, they create a design that is repeated across the bedcover to form the desired visual effect (40). Some patterns, such as Drunkard's Path (45), work so effectively that it is difficult to distinguish where the individual blocks begin and end. Since both of these methods rely on small pieces of fabric, they provided an economical way to use bits of leftover material. In addition, women could easily carry quilting projects about, working on them as they visited with neighbors or watched over their children.

Patterns such as Bars (26) and Diamond in Square (55) also employ basic geometric shapes, but they do so on a grand scale. Typically one or two simple shapes—for example, bars or a diamond—cover almost the entire surface of the quilt. These bold designs were especially popular among the Amish, although non-Amish bedcovers occasionally employed similar design elements.

Amish quilts can generally be characterized by the use of geometric designs, rich colors, and wide, extensively quilted borders. These simple, large-scale patterns reflect the austere religious beliefs of the Amish, which prohibited the use of printed fabrics and the use of representational forms. Although the patterns themselves are plain, Amish quilts are embellished with extraordinary stitching, including waffle grids, scallops, roses, feathers, hearts, and intricately detailed wreaths (25). Until about 1930 Amish quilts were made almost exclusively in natural fabrics, and today these pieces are some of the most prized and sought after textiles available. After 1930 the Amish began to use synthetic fabrics, and unfortunately their needlework lost much of its former power.

25 Bars

Description
Amish pieced quilt. 7 central bars, 5 wide and 2 narrow, in black, brown, and tan, enclosed by green frame with nine-patch corner squares in black and green. Wide border brown with large black corner squares. Black binding.

Materials, Quilting, and Dimensions
Wool. Central bars have diamond quilting. Frame quilted in running pattern of double diamonds with narrow row of scallops. Nine-patch squares with single X motifs. Border with wide rope quilting. 82″ × 82″.

Maker, Locality, and Period
Maker unknown. Lancaster County, Pennsylvania. c. 1890.

Comment
The Amish and Mennonites, often referred to as "the plain people," frequently used combinations of colors that today seem very contemporary. Patterned fabric was almost never used by the Amish on the surface of a bedcover, especially on a traditional Lancaster County quilt like this one. It was relegated to the back of a quilt, if used at all.

Hints for Collectors
To display an antique bedcover, be sure to keep it from direct sunlight, and if it is to be hung, keep any strain on the fabric to a minimum. Antique textiles should never hang for extended periods of time. The exposure to light, dust, and dirt, and the tension on the edges of the fabric, will all contribute to shortening its life.

Price Guide Group: Amish and Mennonite Quilts.

Courtesy America Hurrah Antiques, New York City.

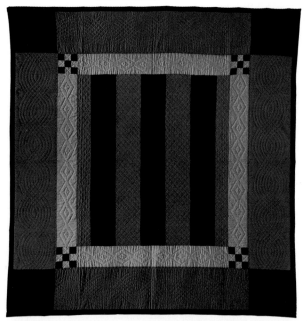

Description
Amish pieced quilt. 7 central bars, alternating blue and red.
Wide border olive-green with red corner squares. Magenta
binding.

Materials, Quilting, and Dimensions
Wool. Swag motif quilted on red bars; chevron and flower motifs
on blue bars. Small scallop design quilted on inner edge of
border. Floral and diagonal quilting on red corner squares.
Green border at top and bottom has floral motifs and feathered
quilting; border at sides has large rope design. 80″ × 74″.

Maker, Locality, and Period
Maker unknown. Lancaster County, Pennsylvania. c. 1890.

Comment
Although bedcovers with bars as their central motif were known
elsewhere in the Northeast during the 19th century, this design,
called simply Bars, is most commonly associated with Amish
quilts. Many variations on the theme were made—among them
patterns called Joseph's Coat of Many Colors and Rainbow—but
the basic pattern, seen in the example illustrated, was by far the
most popular. Note the wide border, the deep, subtle colors, and
the intricacy of the stitching—all typical of Amish quilts of the
period.

Hints for Collectors
Before you purchase an outstanding quilt, such as the piece
illustrated, read as much as you possibly can about the type, see
examples in museums, and make your interest known to a
reputable dealer. Many dealers are willing to share their
expertise with collectors.

Price Guide Group: Amish and Mennonite Quilts.

Courtesy America Hurrah Antiques, New York City.

Description
Amish pieced quilt. 19 central bars of various colors and widths enclosed by turquoise frame with pink corner squares. Wide border deep purple with bluish-purple corner squares. Dark blue binding.

Materials, Quilting, and Dimensions
Wool. Bars have alternating floral and diamond quilting. Pink corner squares are each stitched with a single bloom. Border has feathered quilting. Blue corner squares each have feathered wreath. 80″ × 80″.

Maker, Locality, and Period
Maker unknown. Lancaster County, Pennsylvania. c. 1910.

Comment
The intense colors in this quilt are typical of Amish work done between 1910 and 1920. Until about 1900 the Amish usually used homemade dyes, which resulted in subdued browns and grays; after the turn of the century, they were more likely to buy their fabrics, and they chose brightly colored wools and cottons. The Split Bars pattern seen here was in common use in the early 20th century; the simpler Bars pattern was found more often in the 19th. Note the irregularity of the blue binding in the upper right-hand corner of this quilt; this may mean that the seamstress had run out of fabric.

Hints for Collectors
With as many as 20 quilting stitches per inch, this quilt is the work of an accomplished seamstress. Such exceptionally fine needlework always adds to the value of a quilt.

Price Guide Group: Amish and Mennonite Quilts.

Courtesy America Hurrah Antiques, New York City.

Square

Description
Amish pieced quilt. Red central rectangle framed by 4 intersecting red stripes that form 2nd rectangle. Dark blue ground. Red binding.

Materials, Quilting, and Dimensions
Wool. Elaborately quilted. Concentric rings of feathered wreaths and flowers radiate from central flowers. Feathered wreaths at corners of central rectangle. Border has running feathered quilting. 85″ × 70″.

Maker, Locality, and Period
Maker unknown. Midwest. c. 1900.

Comment
Although graphically simple, Amish quilts were often embellished with extensive quilting, as in the example illustrated. Sometimes the stitching patterns were drawn freehand, but more often templates were used to loosely sketch in the design on the quilt top. After the quilting was completed, the quilt would be laundered, and all traces of the drawn design would disappear.

Hints for Collectors
Like the example illustrated, many fine quilts are in museum collections. If you are seriously interested in antique quilts, never hesitate to write a museum requesting to see specific examples in its collection. The best way to learn to recognize quality and to appreciate the subtle variations in color is by seeing many fine textiles. Museum registrars and curators are often booked far ahead, however, so always call or write well in advance.

Price Guide Group: Amish and Mennonite Quilts.

Courtesy Museum of American Folk Art, New York City.

Description
Mennonite pieced quilt. Maroon center square surrounded by gold, navy-blue, and maroon frames that radiate outward and form concentric squares. Inner border navy-blue. Outer border gold. No binding.

Materials, Quilting, and Dimensions
Cotton. Borders quilted in diagonal lines. 82″ × 82″.

Maker, Locality, and Period
Maker unknown. Pennsylvania. c. 1890.

Comment
The traditional Log Cabin pattern may have inspired this simple, unusual quilt, pieced in a stark geometric pattern that resembles the Op Art of the 1960s. In fact, 20th-century artists like Grant Wood and Charles Sheeler were among the first to appreciate the abstract qualities of American quilts. They began to collect them and were influential in elevating American needlework to the status of an art form.

Hints for Collectors
Do not be put off by the new appearance of many Mennonite quilts. The crisp, fresh colors seen here may simply indicate that this quilt was reserved for special occasions, a common practice among the Amish and Mennonites. Quilts in such fine condition are particularly desirable. To keep them in good condition, avoid displaying textiles in full light; they fade easily, which diminishes both their beauty and their value.

Price Guide Group: Amish and Mennonite Quilts.

Courtesy America Hurrah Antiques, New York City.

Description
Pieced quilt. Long, thin strips form multicolored concentric squares that radiate outward from a blue center square. Predominantly red, blue, brown, pink, and red-and-white checked gingham; also several printed fabrics, including gold-and-brown print. 6 long, thin strips of fabric added across top. Red binding.

Materials, Quilting, and Dimensions
Wool challis. Unquilted. 80″ × 76″.

Maker, Locality, and Period
Maker unknown. Pennsylvania. c. 1880.

Comment
Although not strictly a Log Cabin design, this bedcover was constructed by the same method. Long strips, or logs, of fabric have been pieced together edge to edge, like those in the individual blocks of a Log Cabin quilt. Presumably to make it long enough for her bed, the quiltmaker added 6 strips of wool challis to the top of the bedcover, lengthening it and defining the head of the bedcover at the same time. Wool challis is a soft, plain-weave fabric that was often printed in small patterns and used for women's dresses.

Hints for Collectors
Log Cabin bedcovers were often tufted rather than quilted. In many cases the individual blocks were first sewn to backing squares and then brought together to form the quilt—thus eliminating the need for additional stitches to hold the quilt layers together. Some Log Cabins have layers of cotton filling between the top and backing.

Price Guide Group: Other Geometric Quilts.

Courtesy America Hurrah Antiques, New York City.

31 Trip Around the World

Description
Pieced quilt. Concentric squares radiating outward and constructed of hundreds of small solid and printed square patches set diagonally. Black center square surrounded by 4 red squares and 8 blue squares printed with white stars. Predominantly red, pink, yellow, and blue fabrics printed with nautical designs. Border of pink squares. White binding.

Materials, Quilting, and Dimensions
Cotton. Quilted in parallel lines. 75″ × 62″.

Maker, Locality, and Period
Maker unknown. Pennsylvania. c. 1940.

Comment
Trip Around the World, a variation on the most basic pieced quilt pattern—the one-patch—is made by piecing together hundreds of tiny squares of fabric that are exactly the same size. Usually the squares are placed so they are parallel to the sides of the quilt; in this example, however, they are set on end to create a diamond effect. The nautical motifs of the printed fabric, in particular the tiny white anchors on the small red squares, suggest that this bedcover may have been intended for a child's room.

Hints for Collectors
The revival of interest in quiltmaking reached a peak in the 1930s and 1940s. Quiltmaking competitions were held across the country, often sponsored by women's magazines, and prizes were offered for the best bedcover. At the beginning of the war, however, interest in quiltmaking declined, not to be renewed until the 1970s.

Price Guide Group: Other Geometric Quilts.

Courtesy Kelter-Malcé Antiques, New York City.

32 Four-Patch Variation

Description
Pieced crib quilt. Combination of four-patch blocks, checkerboard blocks, and rectangular strips. Central section of smaller and larger squares, surrounded by strips, with checkerboard blocks in each corner. Strips coral-red and blue-and-white prints. Frame in blue-and-white print. Border coral-red. Black-and-white printed binding.

Materials, Quilting, and Dimensions
Cotton. Unquilted. 42″ × 38″.

Maker, Locality, and Period
Maker unknown. New Jersey. c. 1890.

Comment
This crib quilt is especially interesting not only for its unique combination of patterns but also because it suggests the American flag. A bedcover like this, which would have been relatively easy to make—it has no curved lines and no quilting—might have been the work of a child. Young boys as well as girls were taught to sew, the most well-known example probably being the young Dwight D. Eisenhower.

Hints for Collectors
With the increase in popularity and rising prices of 19th-century crib quilts, they have sometimes been faked by cutting down full-size bedcovers and rebinding them with old fabric. Designs that seem out of scale and binding or stitching that looks new are both clues that a piece was probably cut down.

Price Guide Group: Crib Quilts.

Courtesy Thomas K. Woodard, American Antiques and Quilts, New York City.

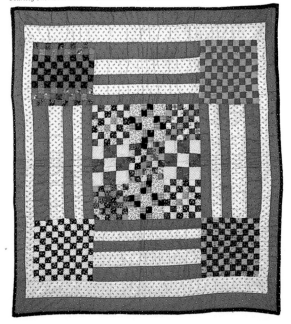

Description
Amish pieced quilt. 16 large multicolored nine-patch squares divided by turquoise grid. In large squares, red blocks alternate with small multicolored nine-patch blocks. Framed by alternating dark gray triangles and dark green diamonds with turquoise corner squares. Wide border fuchsia with turquoise corner squares. Red binding.

Materials, Quilting, and Dimensions
Wool. In central section, blocks quilted in diamonds, turquoise grid and corners in star and chevron motifs. Diamond-shaped patches of frame quilted in diamonds with flowers. Border has feathered vine and wreath quilting, and each large corner square has feathered horseshoe that connects with feathered wreaths of border. 82″ × 82″.

Maker, Locality, and Period
Maker unknown. Lancaster County, Pennsylvania. c. 1900.

Comment
The Nine-Patch pattern was an especially popular one, for it was a good way to use up every small scrap a needlewoman might own. By the end of the 19th century, however, Amish women began purchasing fabrics for clothing and quilts at special stores that catered to the Amish trade, and the use of salvaged materials diminished substantially.

Hints for Collectors
This quilt's bold colors and the traditional wide outer border are clues that it is a genuine Amish piece. One seldom finds such deep borders on non-Amish quilts. The feathered quilting is also characteristic of Amish work.

Price Guide Group: Amish and Mennonite Quilts.

Courtesy America Hurrah Antiques, New York City.

Description
Amish pieced quilt. 12 large nine-patch blocks, set diagonally, alternate with purple blocks, also set diagonally. In large nine-patch blocks, 4 small orange squares alternate with small nine-patch blocks in various colors. Frame bright yellow diamonds on pale purple ground, with dark purple corner squares. Wide border red with large purple corner squares. Binding 2 shades of purple.

Materials, Quilting, and Dimensions
Wool. Large nine-patch blocks quilted in squares; purple blocks have circular quilting pattern. Frame with floral and chevron designs. Border quilted in running feather and shells, with feathered horseshoe in each corner. 82″ × 74″.

Maker, Locality, and Period
Maker unknown. Lancaster County, Pennsylvania. c. 1910.

Comment
Although one might not expect the Amish to use such bright colors in their textiles, it should be remembered that the Amish rules of conduct did not necessarily apply to quiltmaking, and design prohibitions differed greatly from community to community.

Hints for Collectors
Do not be misled by the slight difference in color of the binding at the top of this bedcover. Quilts often wore out first at the head of the bed, and housewives would have to replace the binding there. If such a repair was made while the quilt was still in an Amish home, the value of the quilt would not be much affected.

Price Guide Group: Amish and Mennonite Quilts.

Courtesy America Hurrah Antiques, New York City.

35 Nine Patch

Description
Amish pieced quilt. 30 nine-patch blocks, set diagonally, alternate with solid-color blocks, also set diagonally; blocks surrounded by sawtooth edge. Predominantly browns, blues, and reds. Frame coral. Wide border deep plum. Olive-green binding with pale brown at bottom edge.

Materials, Quilting, and Dimensions
Wool. Nine-patch blocks quilted with crosses of parallel lines; solid-color blocks quilted in diamonds; blue triangles with shell quilting. Frame quilted in rope design. Border with running feather, floral, and shell motifs. 78″ × 64″.

Maker, Locality, and Period
Maker unknown. Miflin County, Nebraska. c. 1900.

Comment
This particular Nine-Patch variation is typical of quilts from the Amish community in Miflin County, known for its conservative religious practices. Note that the blue and brown nine-patch blocks appear only down the center of the quilt, and that the dark red, gray, and brown nine-patch blocks on the left and right are framed by nine-patch blocks in 3 shades of brown at the top.

Hints for Collectors
Amish quilts of this period have become very rare, and as textile classics, bring high prices in the marketplace. The subtle, rich color scheme and the elaborate stitching make this quilt an extraordinary example.

Price Guide Group: Amish and Mennonite Quilts.

Courtesy America Hurrah Antiques, New York City.

36 Four-Patch Check

Description
Pieced quilt. 24 full and 16 partial blocks, set diagonally, made of smaller four-patch squares. Various prints and solids; predominantly red, black, white, blue, and dark green. Blocks separated by red-and-white printed grid. Small four-patch square at each corner of grid and at center of each large block. Frame red-and-white print. Black printed border. Red binding.

Materials, Quilting, and Dimensions
Cotton. Quilted in parallel lines. 85″ × 78″.

Maker, Locality, and Period
Maker and locality unknown. c. 1860.

Comment
Undoubtedly made from salvaged materials saved over a long period, this quilt is typical of thousands of late 19th-century bedcovers. It is primarily a utilitarian quilt, but despite its unpretentiousness, the design is a pleasing combination of colors and shapes. Although the printed fabrics may at first appear randomly distributed, they do in fact reflect a sophisticated color sense and are evenly balanced throughout the quilt. Bedcovers such as this were made for everyday use. Since they were often used until they wore out, it is surprising that so many quilts of this type are available today.

Hints for Collectors
Although quilts such as the one shown here do not bring a large price in the marketplace, many collectors prefer their naive charm. Everyday quilts are excellent starting points for the beginning collector.

Price Guide Group: Other Geometric Quilts.

Collection of Donna and Ken Fadeley.

37 Double Nine Patch

Description
Pieced quilt. Large nine-patch blocks, set diagonally, alternating with printed squares of equal size, also set diagonally. Large nine-patch blocks composed of small pink squares alternating with small nine-patch blocks in printed fabrics. Triple border: 2 blue-and-white printed bands enclose narrow band of pink. Pink printed binding.

Materials, Quilting, and Dimensions
Cotton. Central portion quilted in straight lines; border in diagonal lines. 83″ × 63″.

Maker, Locality, and Period
Maker and locality unknown. c. 1840.

Comment
There are many variations of the Nine-Patch pattern, and almost all were popular with quiltmakers in the Northeast and Midwest, including members of the Amish and Mennonite communities. The term "nine-patch" refers to the division of a block into 9 pieces, as a starting point from which to develop a design. The Double Nine-Patch pattern seen here also has several variations, but most often each block is constructed of 5 small nine-patch blocks and 4 squares of solid color.

Hints for Collectors
This quilt retains its original backing, but the collector should always check a quilt carefully to make sure the backing material is consistent with that of the top. Many tops were pieced but not actually assembled into a quilt until much later, or not at all. Many rural church groups today make bedcovers using old quilt tops to raise money for their churches.

Price Guide Group: Other Geometric Quilts.

Collection of Mr. and Mrs. Michael D. Hall.

Wild Goose Chase

Description
Pieced quilt. Pink-and-white printed blocks set diagonally on white ground, forming checkerboard. Printed blocks divided into 4 triangles by white grid. Bands of grid enclose multicolored triangles, creating Wild Goose Chase pattern, and small square of green-and-yellow print at grid intersections. Pink-and-white printed binding.

Materials, Quilting, and Dimensions
Cotton. White diamonds quilted in feathered medallion and diamond motifs. Pink-and-white triangles with square quilting. Ground at borders quilted with diagonal lines. 95″ × 80½″.

Maker, Locality, and Period
Maker unknown. New England. c. 1830.

Comment
The triangles, or "geese," of the Wild Goose Chase pattern can easily be arranged in many different designs. This quilt, which appears to be of rural origin, is especially pleasing because of its use of color.

Hints for Collectors
Without documentation, the origin of a quilt in a standard pattern like this is uncertain since such quilts were produced not only throughout the northeastern United States but in eastern Canada as well. Quilts identified as being from New England may well be Canadian imports, possibly brought into this country many years ago. Although Canadian quilts may be of comparable quality, a quilt known to have been made in the United States will generally be worth more in the marketplace; American collectors prefer American quilts.

Price Guide Group: Other Geometric Quilts.

Collection of Mr. and Mrs. Donald Morris.

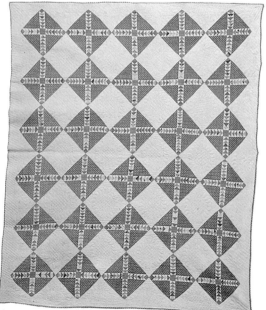

39 Storm at Sea

Description
Pieced quilt. 30 blocks of blue-and-white dotted and solid white fabric cut in triangular, rectangular, and diamond shapes. Each block composed of central blue-and-white diamond on white square, surrounded by blue-and-white triangular and diamond patches. Pieced together, the 30 blocks create whole as well as partial circular motifs. Blue-and-white dotted binding.

Materials, Quilting, and Dimensions
Cotton. Outline, parallel, and diamond quilting. 83″ × 68″.

Maker, Locality, and Period
Maker unknown. Maine. c. 1870.

Comment
The Storm at Sea pattern has many variations. The same name may refer to entirely different designs, which are also known by such diverse names as Weather Vane, Indian Trail, Winding Walk, and Prickly Pear. The naming of quilts is a particularly hazardous procedure, for not only do different quiltmakers give the same name to different designs, but books on quilts and quiltmaking often disagree about even the most basic designs.

Hints for Collectors
In this quilt an optical illusion is created, and the circlelike designs seem to merge into one another, blurring the distinction of where one ends and the other begins. The piecing has been done very meticulously.

Price Guide Group: Other Geometric Quilts.

Collection of Mr. and Mrs. Donald Morris.

40 Jacob's Ladder

Description
Amish pieced quilt. 30 blocks, each with large black geometric form constructed of small squares and triangles on cream-colored ground, and small black square in 2 opposite corners. Aquamarine grid with four-patch block in cream and black at each intersection. Black border. Black binding.

Materials, Quilting, and Dimensions
Cotton. Blocks with teacup quilting. Grid with concentric arcs. Four-patch blocks and border with diamond quilting. 98″ × 84″.

Maker, Locality, and Period
Maker unknown. Probably Ohio. c. 1920.

Comment
This bold and graphic interpretation of the Jacob's Ladder pattern is particularly striking because of the contrast between the black and the cream and aquamarine. Probably this quilt was made by the Ohio Amish; by the 1920s Ohio communities were using more black than the Amish of Pennsylvania. However, the black forms are stitched with white thread, an unusual feature that is not typical of either the Ohio or the Pennsylvania communities.

Hints for Collectors
By the 1920s it was difficult to distinguish between Pennsylvania Amish quilts and those made by their midwestern counterparts. The Amish had slowly become less insular, and as a result, their quilt designs often appear less distinctively Amish. Since one pays more for the Amish attribution, go to a dealer who can document this identification.

Price Guide Group: Amish and Mennonite Quilts.

Courtesy Kelter-Malcé Antiques, New York City.

41 Cross and Crown

Description
Pieced quilt. 20 squares, each with modified Cross and Crown motif in orange on light green printed ground. Squares framed by darker green printed grid, with orange crosses in light green blocks at each intersection. Grid continues to form inner border. Outer border dark green print. Orange binding.

Materials, Quilting, and Dimensions
Cotton. Parallel and diagonal line quilting. 84½″ × 70″.

Maker, Locality, and Period
Maker unknown. Indiana. c. 1880–1900.

Comment
One of several variations, all called Cross and Crown or sometimes Crowned Cross, this pattern was not particularly common. It was, however, one of many geometric quilts with a biblical name. Here the crosses in the grid and blocks are clear, and the pointed elements in each block represent the crowns.

Hints for Collectors
Although one can learn a good deal about quilts by reading and looking at reproductions, the quality and age of any bedcover can only be determined by close and careful examination of the actual textile. Look for fabrics that are typical of a particular period, signs of wear that might indicate age, and quilt patterns known to have been particularly popular at a certain time. In many cases, tracing the history of a bedcover's ownership may help determine its period and authenticity.

Price Guide Group: Other Geometric Quilts.

Collection of William C. Ketchum, Jr.

Description
Amish pieced crib quilt. 12 blocks, each composed of a pale pink square set in a light green diamond on dark green ground, with pale pink chevron at each corner of square. Chevrons surround dark green squares. Frame light green. Wide border dark green. Dark green binding.

Materials, Quilting, and Dimensions
Cotton. Central section and frame quilted in diamonds. Outer border with rope quilting. 43″ × 36″.

Maker, Locality, and Period
Maker unknown. Indiana. Early 20th century.

Comment
This quilt might have been quilted at a bee, where women from the community gather to finish one woman's quilt as well as visit with each other. Since most Amish communities do not have churches or meetinghouses, members of the congregation meet every other Sunday at each other's homes. Consequently many houses are designed with large rooms that can accommodate sizable gatherings and are well suited for quilting bees.

Hints for Collectors
It is almost impossible to distinguish Amish and Mennonite quilts made in America from those made in Canada. Because Amish quilts of this period were usually made from fabrics purchased especially for the project, and because Canadians often bought American-manufactured yardage, even tracing the history of the materials used may prove inconclusive.

Price Guide Group: Crib Quilts.

Courtesy Museum of American Folk Art, New York City.

43 Unnamed Design

Description
Amish pieced quilt. Blue and black squares and triangles arranged in diagonal intersecting chains. At each intersection, larger nine-patch squares, also blue and black. Between the diagonal chains large black squares, surrounded by purple triangles. Frame blue. Wide border black. Blue binding.

Materials, Quilting, and Dimensions
Wool. Central section quilted in diamonds. Intersecting clamshell quilting in frame; modified triple clamshells in border. 72″ × 41″.

Maker, Locality, and Period
Maker unknown. Lancaster County, Pennsylvania. Late 19th century.

Comment
An Amish quilt in a single-bed size, like the one illustrated, is sometimes referred to as a "hired hand's quilt." It is most likely that this example was cut down from a larger bedcover and given a new border. The design is not typical of Lancaster County Amish quilts and may be the result of the quiltmaker's contact with non-Amish neighbors.

Hints for Collectors
This rare hired hand's quilt, with its unique design, is of interest as an atypical example of Amish artistry. Midwestern Amish quilts, and those from other Amish communities outside Lancaster County, were made in a much wider variety of patterns and generally are less expensive than Lancaster County examples.

Price Guide Group: Amish and Mennonite Quilts.

Courtesy America Hurrah Antiques, New York City.

Double Irish Chain

Description
Pieced quilt. 3 chains of squares that together form bands of diagonal grid, enclosed by frame. Center chain of squares and frame blue-and-brown print. Outer chains red-and-white print. White ground. Wide border white. Blue-and-brown printed binding.

Materials, Quilting, and Dimensions
Cotton. Central white areas quilted in feathered medallions and diamonds. Frame and binding with parallel quilting. Border with diamond quilting and rope design. 86″ × 86″.

Maker, Locality, and Period
Maker unknown. New York State. c. 1850.

Comment
There are many variations of the Irish Chain. The simplest is a single chain of small squares placed diagonally across a quilt. The Double Irish Chain, a somewhat confusing name, consists of 3 chains of small squares set diagonally on the quilt. The term "double" comes from the 2 rows on either side of the single chain, which are frequently pieced in a darker fabric. A Triple Irish Chain has 4 diagonal chains. Other variations on the design include the Double Nine Patch and Burgoyne Surrounded.

Hints for Collectors
Although the Irish Chain pattern was very common in the late 19th and early 20th centuries, many of the surviving bedcovers are in poor condition. Quilts in this pattern were generally made for everyday use, and over the years many have deteriorated from frequent washings and exposure to sunlight.

Price Guide Group: Other Geometric Quilts.

Courtesy America Hurrah Antiques, New York City.

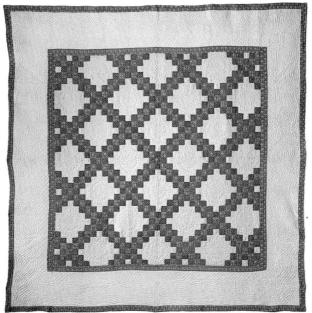

Description
Pieced quilt. 64 blocks in blue and white. 32 white blocks with
blue quarter-circles at corners alternate with 32 white blocks
having central blue pinwheel design to create Drunkard's Path
pattern. Blue and white sawtooth frame. Wide white border.
White binding.

Materials, Quilting, and Dimensions
Cotton. Central area with diamond quilting. Border with running
feather and diamond quilting. 76″ × 76″.

Maker, Locality, and Period
Maker unknown. Midwest. c. 1930.

Comment
It is easy to imagine the origin of the name Drunkard's Path.
Even with a sober eye, it is difficult to trace the outlines of the
pieced fabrics. The meandering blue diagonals resemble the path
of an inebriated person. Curved patterns, although very popular,
are extremely difficult to piece. The Drunkard's Path pattern is
created by the ingenious use of 2 different blocks.

Hints for Collectors
Drunkard's Path was especially popular during the late 19th
century and again in the 1930s, when a revival in quiltmaking
spread across America. Quilts in this pattern are very common,
and often can be purchased at garage sales or country auctions.
The quilt illustrated is greatly enhanced by its fine piecing and
stitching.

Price Guide Group: Other Geometric Quilts.

Courtesy America Hurrah Antiques, New York City.

Puss-in-the-Corner

Description
Pieced quilt. Tan blocks alternate with nine-patch blocks constructed of 4 tan and 5 dark blue squares; dark blue squares link together to form diagonal grid. Tan binding.

Materials, Quilting, and Dimensions
Hand-dyed indigo cotton patches on homespun linen. Diamond and chevron quilting. 87½″ × 81⅜″.

Maker, Locality, and Period
Maker unknown. Probably New England. c. 1820.

Comment
Indigo dye was extracted from the stems and leaves of the plants *Indigofera tinctoria* and *Indigofera anil*, or from woad plants. An ancient dye stuff, indigo was used extensively for cotton, wool, and silk before the development in the 19th century of a synthetic indigo dye made from coal tar products. Because indigo was so strong, it sometimes caused the material it was used on to disintegrate slowly.

Hints for Collectors
After the mid–19th century, few quilts were made with a linen foundation, although linen continued to be used for patches on quilts until at least the late 1800s. With the invention of the cotton gin by Eli Whitney in the 18th century, and the mass production of cotton fabric, it could be purchased at the general store for less money than it cost to make it at home. When dating a quilt on the basis of its materials, it is important to remember that fabrics were often saved for many years before they were used in a quilt.

Price Guide Group: Other Geometric Quilts.

Courtesy Museum of American Folk Art, New York City.

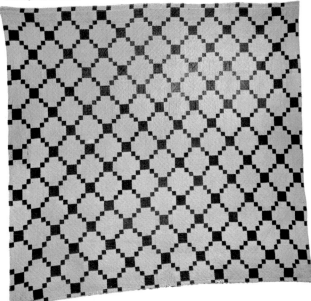

47 Ocean Waves

Description
Mennonite pieced quilt. Deep red diamonds, each surrounded by 4 rows of blue and gold triangles, forming Ocean Waves pattern. Border deep red. Green-and-yellow printed binding.

Materials, Quilting, and Dimensions
Cotton. Diamonds quilted in squares. Border quilted in rope design. 82″ × 82″.

Maker, Locality, and Period
Maker unknown. Pennsylvania. c. 1890.

Comment
Mennonite needlewomen are known for their intricate quilting patterns, like the rope design seen here, almost all of which are stitched by hand. Among the most common motifs are diamonds, waffles, grids, scallops, fish scales, stylized roses, tulips, feathers, and wreaths. The characteristic wide borders are usually decorated with feathers, cables, tulips, or baskets. The bold, striking colors are also typical of Mennonite quilts of the 19th century. Unlike the Amish, the Mennonites occasionally used printed fabric on the surface of their bedcovers. Its presence can help establish that a quilt is Mennonite rather than Amish.

Hints for Collectors
Collectors are always willing to spend more for a Mennonite bedcover that has been hand quilted. The piecing of a Mennonite quilt is usually done by machine, but the quilting is usually done by hand, substantially increasing a quilt's value.

Price Guide Group: Amish and Mennonite Quilts.

Courtesy America Hurrah Antiques, New York City.

48 Ocean Waves

Description
Amish pieced quilt. Dark blue diamonds, each surrounded by 4 rows of variously colored triangles, creating Ocean Waves pattern. Triangles predominantly blue and cream-colored, interspersed with light green and deep purple, orange, and yellow. Narrow frame light green. Wide border dark blue. Red binding.

Materials, Quilting, and Dimensions
Cotton. Diamond quilting in squares; triangles with outline quilting. Frame quilted with halves of teacup design. Border with rope motif. 84″ × 80″.

Maker, Locality, and Period
Ann Yoker. Honeyville, Indiana. c. 1930.

Comment
Although this is a 20th-century quilt, and made in one of the less traditional Amish communities of the Midwest, it is nevertheless distinctively Amish. Still, the quilt pattern and color range seen here are common only in midwestern Amish quilts of the period. Even as late as 1930, it is unlikely that a piece like this would have been made by the stricter Pennsylvania Amish.

Hints for Collectors
One of the best ways to determine the age of a quilt is to trace its movements from collection to collection. Without this kind of documentation, it is virtually impossible to give it a firm date. Even though most collectors want to know how old a bedcover is before they purchase it, other factors, such as originality and clarity of design, and fine craftsmanship, are equally important in assessing the worth of a textile.

Price Guide Group: Amish and Mennonite Quilts.

Courtesy Museum of American Folk Art, New York City.

Description
Pieced quilt. Large triangles of blue-and-brown printed fabric alternate with large triangular sections constructed of 9 smaller triangles in white and various red, brown, and blue prints. Triangles form Birds-in-the-Air pattern. Wide pink and white striped border. No binding.

Materials, Quilting, and Dimensions
Cotton. Central section loosely quilted in diamond pattern. 94″ × 92″.

Maker, Locality, and Period
Maker unknown. Massachusetts. c. 1840.

Comment
The 2 dominant colors of this quilt, blue and pink, contrast sharply to create a glowing effect. The "rainbow fabrics" of the smaller triangles, so named for their subtle gradations of color, were made by roller-printing, a technique that had been invented early in the 19th century. The overall design of the bedcover is less well thought out, especially at the bottom corners, where the pattern of triangles seems awkward. The triangles used in this pattern and a number of others were traditional quilt symbols for birds.

Hints for Collectors
A bedcover this old and rare should never be used every day. If antique quilts are used, be sure to rotate several different ones, to prolong the life of all of them. If possible, a quilt should be hung from a different side each time it is displayed.

Price Guide Group: Other Geometric Quilts.

Courtesy America Hurrah Antiques, New York City.

Geometric Design

Description
Pieced quilt. Triangular, rectangular, and square patches form
overall design of Diamond in Square. Various prints and solids;
predominantly brown, beige, purple, and red. Center eight-
pointed star in circle, set in diamond within 2 concentric squares.
Sawtooth border of beige and black printed triangles.

Materials, Quilting, and Dimensions
Cotton. Unquilted. 81″ × 80″.

Maker, Locality, and Period
Maker unknown. Northeast. c. 1880.

Comment
The quilt illustrated is an excellent example of how traditional
19th-century designs could be modified to create a unique
pattern. Although the overall design is based on the Diamond in
Square pattern and the triangular motifs are reminiscent of the
Flying Geese or Wild Goose Chase patterns, the novel
arrangement of the many patches makes this a strikingly original
piece.

Hints for Collectors
Pieced quilts such as the example illustrated are very rare,
because they vary so much from traditional designs. Since they
do not easily fit a category, they are very difficult to assess and
dealers must rely on their own taste in establishing a purchase
price. In general, original designs bring more on the marketplace
than standard designs, especially when they ingeniously combine
several common patterns, as this one does. And, of course, fine
craftsmanship always increases worth.

Price Guide Group: Other Geometric Quilts.

Courtesy Museum of American Folk Art, New York City.

Sunshine and Shadow

Description
Amish pieced quilt. Central section with hundreds of small squares radiating outward in concentric diamonds from a pink center square. Predominantly white, gray, black, green, blue, lavender, red, maroon, and turquoise. Central section framed with wide band of turquoise. Wide border dark green. Turquoise binding.

Materials, Quilting, and Dimensions
Wool. Central squares with diamond quilting. Frame quilted with 4-petaled flowers enclosed by triple diamond grid. Wide border lavishly quilted with scallops, double running feather, and a feathered medallion in each corner. 80″ × 80″.

Maker, Locality, and Period
Maker unknown. Lancaster County, Pennsylvania. c. 1895.

Comment
A design classic, this quilt embodies many of the qualities collectors have come to associate with Amish bedcovers: fine stitching, striking colors, and traditional designs. Most Amish quilts are based on 3 simple geometric shapes—the square, the triangle, and the rectangle. Using these, the Amish created a few basic patterns on which variations were made.

Hints for Collectors
Quilts like the example illustrated are relatively rare. For at least the past decade, they have been highly sought after by major collectors and consequently bring very high prices. Yet dealers often have such quilts, and some, in fact, have a number of them. Do not expect, however, to find one on your own easily, and be prepared to pay for their rarity.

Price Guide Group: Amish and Mennonite Quilts.

Courtesy America Hurrah Antiques, New York City.

Diamond in Square

Description
Amish pieced quilt. Tan central diamond framed by light blue border with tan corner squares. Central diamond on purple ground framed by turquoise border with tan corner squares. Outer border maroon with large tan corner squares. Deep purple binding.

Materials, Quilting, and Dimensions
Wool. Lavishly quilted. Central diamond has eight-pointed star inside feathered wreath. Blue frame and tan corner squares quilted in floral motifs. Purple square quilted in roses and tulips; turquoise frame with rope motif. Border with running feather design. Tan corner squares of border with feathered horseshoes. 80″ × 80″.

Maker, Locality, and Period
Maker unknown. Lancaster County, Pennsylvania. c. 1910.

Comment
Diamond in Square variations were popular with the Amish in parts of eastern Pennsylvania. Many of these quilts were made in Lancaster County, the first Amish settlement in America. For the Amish, quilting motifs generally reflect their faith. The diamond, for example, is a symbol of Christ, the cornerstone of human experience, and the tulips are a variation of the lily motif, used by Christians to represent purity and immortality.

Hints for Collectors
Fine examples in this pattern are becoming increasingly rare today. The extraordinary stitching and the juxtaposition of colors make this quilt particularly desirable.

Price Guide Group: Amish and Mennonite Quilts.

Courtesy America Hurrah Antiques, New York City.

53 Sawtooth Diamond in Square

Description
Amish pieced quilt. Light brown center diamond with light purple sawtooth edge set against purple square enclosed by sawtooth frame in lighter purple. Wide border light brown with sawtooth edge and purple corner squares. Binding 2 shades of purple.

Materials, Quilting, and Dimensions
Wool. Diamond quilted with eight-pointed star in feathered wreath and tulips. Quilted flowers in sawtooth frame. Border quilted with running feather motif, and each corner square with single basket. 82″ × 82″.

Maker, Locality, and Period
Maker unknown. Lancaster County, Pennsylvania. c. 1900.

Comment
In the Amish community, quilting was one of the few areas where individual creativity was allowed to flourish, but still within certain limits. Printed fabrics, as well as pieced or appliquéd natural forms, were generally not permitted on a quilt top. Some Amish women used printed materials for backing their bedcovers, and simple naturalistic motifs often appear in the quilting.

Hints for Collectors
If one part of the binding is a slightly different color from the rest, check the texture of that piece to see if it feels similar to the rest of the binding. Although the quiltmaker may simply have run out of fabric, the difference may also indicate that part of the binding has been repaired or replaced.

Price Guide Group: Amish and Mennonite Quilts.

Courtesy America Hurrah Antiques, New York City.

54 Sawtooth Diamond in Square

Description
Amish pieced quilt. Rust-colored center diamond framed by
yellow diamond set on rust-colored square. Yellow frame. Border
rust. All edges sawtooth except outer edge of border. Yellow
binding.

Materials, Quilting, and Dimensions
Wool. Lavishly quilted with diamonds and feathered medallions.
Yellow diamond with rope motif. Diamond quilting and feathered
medallions in rust square. Frame with square quilting; outer
border with rope pattern. 80″ × 80″.

Maker, Locality, and Period
Maker unknown. Lancaster County, Pennsylvania. c. 1890.

Comment
On this bedcover some of the patterns, like the rope motif in the
yellow diamond and outer border, were quilted by first laying
templates on the quilt top and tracing their outlines.

Hints for Collectors
With the rapid growth of interest in Amish quilts over the past
10 years or so, period bedcovers like this one are increasingly
hard to find. The fine condition of this piece suggests it was
probably kept in storage and taken out only for special occasions.
On an early quilt, some colors, brown in particular, tend to
deteriorate more quickly than others—a result of iron in the
mordants used to set the dyes. In general, the truer the colors of
a quilt, the more desirable it is. An early example without any
change in color or other deterioration is extremely rare and
valuable.

Price Guide Group: Amish and Mennonite Quilts.

Courtesy America Hurrah Antiques, New York City.

55 Diamond in Square

Description
Amish pieced quilt. Lavender center square surrounded by purple diamond. Both enclosed by lavender diamond, with purple bar at each side. Purple ground. Framed by 2 concentric lavender squares. Lavender binding.

Materials, Quilting, and Dimensions
Cotton. Center square and corners of lavender diamond quilted in floral medallion. Rest of central diamond quilted with modified chain stitch. Ground with diagonal quilting. Borders with modified running scroll. 76½" × 76¼".

Maker, Locality, and Period
Maker unknown. Indiana. c. 1910–30.

Comment
The unusual coloring and design of this quilt are typical of Amish settlements in Indiana. Religious strictures were less oppressive in these communities, and quilts tended to be brighter and less formal in design. For example, in the quilt shown here, side bars have been added to the classic Diamond in Square pattern. Both the pale color and the light weight of this quilt suggest that it was intended for summer use.

Hints for Collectors
At a time when prices for Pennsylvania Amish quilts have become very high, quilts made by the midwestern Amish offer an attractive investment to the collector. These quilts are usually less expensive, particularly those in lighter shades, such as pale purple, pink, or yellow. However, prices for these bedcovers are beginning to rise, and now is a good time to buy them.

Price Guide Group: Amish and Mennonite Quilts.

Collection of William C. Ketchum, Jr.

Double Square

Description
Mennonite pieced quilt. Rows of squares, placed diagonally, each with red center square surrounded by a dark frame, a red frame, and a second dark frame that forms an overall grid. Narrow triple border black, red, and black. Red binding.

Materials, Quilting, and Dimensions
Wool. Unquilted. 84″ × 82″.

Maker, Locality, and Period
Maker unknown. Pennsylvania. c. 1885.

Comment
Mennonite quilts are known for their rich use of color and their bold, intricate patterns. The Mennonites developed complicated quilt designs much earlier than the Amish. Amish quilts of the same period often had only a simple central diamond or vertical bars.

Hints for Collectors
On close inspection, one can see that several of the bars that make up the dark diamond patterns are actually brown or blue rather than black. Although this may have been intended, it is more likely that the bars were composed of different black fabrics, some of which simply faded over the years. It is important to inspect such a quilt closely to see if older materials were combined with newer ones when the quilt was made—or to determine that newer materials are not original but the result of repairs done later. Repairs, of course, lessen the value of a quilt.

Price Guide Group: Amish and Mennonite Quilts.

Courtesy America Hurrah Antiques, New York City.

Capital T

Description
Mennonite pieced quilt. Alternating dark blue and red T-shaped patches. Enclosed by triple border: red sawtooth inner border, smaller red-and-blue sawtooth middle border, and wide dark blue outer border. Blue binding.

Materials, Quilting, and Dimensions
Cotton. Central portion quilted in diagonal lines and semicircles, inner sawtooth border in chevrons, and outer border in rope pattern. 83" × 78".

Maker, Locality, and Period
Maker unknown. Pennsylvania. c. 1890.

Comment
Between 1890 and 1900 the Mennonites were far more adventurous in their quilt designs than the Amish. Amish examples from the same period are usually based on large geometric shapes, such as bars, diamonds, and squares. But by 1910, the Amish had also begun to make quilts in more complex designs, which consequently are often confused with Mennonite examples.

Hints for Collectors
The clarity of design, fine condition, and age of this quilt make it very rare. The T-shape, which also appears in non-Mennonite bedcovers, is used here with great skill, so that the red and blue T designs create a positive-negative effect. A very graphic quilt like this, with strong primary colors, is almost always worth buying, provided it is in good condition.

Price Guide Group: Amish and Mennonite Quilts.

Courtesy America Hurrah Antiques, New York City.

Bittersweet XII

Description
Pieced quilt. 9 large blocks, each in an original design and each constructed of a large diagonal red, blue, or purple strip surrounded by thin multicolored strips and a thin black strip on either side. Widest strip partially covers center square. Narrow diagonal strips, perpendicular to large strip and in various solid colors, complete each block. Blocks placed to create overall abstract design. Wide border blue. Red binding.

Materials, Quilting, and Dimensions
Cotton-polyester broadcloth. Blocks quilted in diagonal lines outlining pieced strips. Border quilted in broad, incomplete triangles enclosing finely stitched parallel lines. 88″ × 82″.

Maker, Locality, and Period
Strip pieced and marked by Nancy Crow. Baltimore, Ohio. Hand quilted by Velma Brill. Cambridge, Ohio. 1980.

Comment
This quilt is an especially fine example of Nancy Crow's highly original work because it combines brilliant use of color, fine design, and careful execution. Like several other contemporary quiltmakers, the maker designed and marked her quilt for piecing but had someone else do the actual quilting. Splitting up the work between women is, in fact, in keeping with the 19th-century tradition of the quilting bee.

Hints for Collectors
Contemporary quilts like the one shown here are particularly appealing to admirers of contemporary paintings and are often exhibited in fine arts galleries rather than craft shops.

Price Guide Group: Other Geometric Quilts.

Courtesy Museum of American Folk Art, New York City.

59 Flying Geese

Description
Pieced quilt. Diagonal rows of triangles in various prints,
forming Flying Geese pattern, alternate with diagonal rows of
finely printed rose, pink, and white-and-blue floral fabric. Border
with triangles in predominantly red and yellow prints.
Multicolored printed binding.

Materials, Quilting, and Dimensions
Cotton. Diagonal and chevron quilting. 88″ × 86″.

Maker, Locality, and Period
Maker unknown. New England. c. 1840.

Comment
The Flying Geese pattern, of which there are many variations,
all using triangles, is more commonly found with the triangles in
lines parallel to the edge of the quilt, or in repeating blocks. The
version illustrated here is particularly fine and contains a variety
of typical mid-19th-century printed cottons. Note especially the
delicate balance of colors achieved by the careful choice and
arrangement of the prints. The triangles used on the border are
quite unusual. Generally the borders are plain. Unique features
like this add to the value of a bedcover, especially when they are
incorporated as effectively as they are in the quilt illustrated.

Hints for Collectors
Always examine the fabric carefully on both the quilt top and
backing. Broken quilting stitches or tiny holes will lessen a
quilt's value.

Price Guide Group: Other Geometric Quilts.

Courtesy America Hurrah Antiques, New York City.

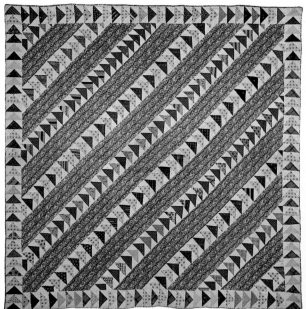

60 Flying Geese

Description
Pieced crib quilt. 8 vertical rows of blue-and-white calico triangles divided by vertical strips of blue-and-white calico, on a white ground. Blue-and-white calico frame. Border white. White binding.

Materials, Quilting, and Dimensions
Cotton. Central section has diagonal quilting. Border quilted in undulating wave motif. 40″ × 36″.

Maker, Locality, and Period
Maker unknown. New York State. c. 1885.

Comment
Crib quilts have become some of the most desirable and collectible of all 19th-century textiles. Their small size enhances their appeal, especially to the modern apartment dweller who lacks the wall space to display larger pieces. As was the case with most 19th-century crib quilts, this one is a scaled-down version of a larger quilt.

Hints for Collectors
With crib-size quilts, just as with full-size examples, the novice collector should seek expert advice, read widely, and look at the finest pieces in both private and public collections. Many small museums have very fine collections of antique quilts, and several historical societies throughout the country also have interesting holdings. Special exhibitions are particularly instructive, for they generally bring together a number of examples of one type for study and comparison.

Price Guide Group: Crib Quilts.

Courtesy Thomas K. Woodard, American Antiques & Quilts, New York City.

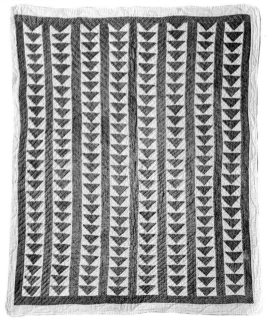

Birds-in-the-Air

Description
Pieced and appliquéd quilt. Central section with thousands of tiny triangles forming Birds-in-the-Air pattern. Predominantly red and brown prints and solids. Border crowded with appliquéd motifs in yellow, brown, green, and red, on white ground. Name "HARRIET J. DISHONG" appliquéd in top border. Corner blocks have large yellow, brown, and red flower and other appliqués, enclosed by brown sawtooth border. Sawtooth edge around entire outer border. Red binding.

Materials, Quilting, and Dimensions
Cotton. White border areas quilted in parallel lines and stitches that echo shapes of appliquéd motifs. Embroidery on many appliqués. 94″ × 88″.

Maker, Locality, and Period
Harriet J. Dishong and Mary E. Dishong. Pennsylvania. 1875–90.

Comment
This quilt of more than 22,000 tiny triangles is an extraordinary interpretation of a traditional design. The dove, cross, and heart motifs suggest that it was intended as a bridal quilt.

Hints for Collectors
This quilt not only has a large range of appliquéd motifs, beautiful piecing, and fine embroidery, it is also signed and dated. Quilts that are both aesthetically pleasing and well documented are quite rare and consequently highly prized by collector and historian alike.

Price Guide Group: Other Geometric Quilts.

Courtesy America Hurrah Antiques, New York City.

Streak of Lightning

Description
Pieced quilt. Hundreds of uniformly shaped rectangular bars arranged diagonally in rows, forming zigzag Streak of Lightning pattern. Predominantly prints of red, yellow, blue, green, and white arranged in contrasting light and dark colors. White print binding.

Materials, Quilting, and Dimensions
Cotton. Unquilted. 87½″ × 77″.

Maker, Locality, and Period
Maker and locality unknown. c. 1860.

Comment
The consistently uniform pieces of fabric on this bedcover suggest that it was made with the aid of a template. A rectangular piece of cardboard or tin was placed on the fabric and its shape traced. Each piece of fabric was cut about ¼″ wider so that the edges could be tucked underneath when pieced together. Some quiltmakers used templates made of newspaper. The fabric was often sewn around the newspaper to give the quilt shape and added warmth. The dates on these newspapers, however, are usually unreliable indicators of the quilt's age—old newspapers could easily have been used and the bedcover made 10 or 20 years after.

Hints for Collectors
The current vogue of country antiques has created very high market prices for quilts. Always look for the best quality you can afford. Good pieces, despite changing fashions and trends, will maintain their value. Never buy a quilt that is extensively damaged or restored.

Price Guide Group: Other Geometric Quilts.

Courtesy America Hurrah Antiques, New York City.

63 Stairway to Heaven

Description
Amish pieced quilt. Block-shaped motifs, each constructed of 3 diamond-shaped patches, arranged diagonally in rows to form 3-dimensional chevron design. Overall arrangement creates Stairway to Heaven pattern. Each block in 3 shades of a color, including lavender, pink, black, brown, blue, and green. Pale green binding.

Materials, Quilting, and Dimensions
Cotton. Loose outline quilting. 98″ × 86″.

Maker, Locality, and Period
Maker unknown. Holmes County, Ohio. c. 1935.

Comment
This 3-dimensional design was obviously influenced by the Art Deco movement, although it is hard to know how midwestern Amish quilters became aware of it. Possibly they were inspired by Art Deco posters and other forms of advertising that they found in their local stores.

Hints for Collectors
The traditional tumbling block motif is most often arranged in the simpler Baby's Blocks or Pandora's Box patterns, and only rarely in the chevron design pictured here, a pattern that typifies early 20th-century design. Unlike most block variations, this bedcover has been quilted; generally the top, filling, and backing are tied together with yarn. Found only rarely, the Stairway to Heaven pattern would probably bring more in the marketplace than other, less graphic, block variations.

Price Guide Group: Amish and Mennonite Quilts.

Courtesy America Hurrah Antiques, New York City.

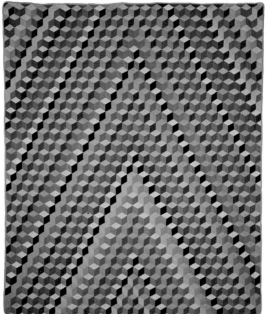

Tumbling Blocks

Description
Pieced quilt. Overall design of thousands of tiny diamonds pieced together to form blocks in vertical chains. Arrangement of light and dark fabrics creates 3-dimensional effect known as Tumbling Blocks. Solid colors and prints; predominantly rose, green, and blue. Green binding.

Materials, Quilting, and Dimensions
Silk. Unquilted. 86″ × 68″.

Maker, Locality, and Period
Maker unknown. New York State. c. 1850.

Comment
While attempts at establishing a silk industry, including the cultivation of silkworms and the mulberry trees to feed them, were made in the late colonial period, most silks were imported until the end of the 19th century. Even then, imported goods far exceeded those produced in the United States. Because it was so precious, silk fabric was reused until it wore out, and many of the fabrics in this bedcover were probably salvaged from old clothing. The Tumbling Blocks design appealed to both male and female quilters. Both Calvin Coolidge and Dwight D. Eisenhower are known to have made bedcovers in this pattern.

Hints for Collectors
Silk is a particularly fragile material, and many mid-19th-century silk bedcovers are severely damaged. Be certain to check the condition of any silk bedcover, for having a silk quilt repaired can be very expensive. If an example is especially charming or graphic, it may be worth repairing, provided most of the pieces are strong. Professional framing under glass or Plexiglas is a good way to prevent further deterioration.

Price Guide Group: Other Geometric Quilts.

Courtesy America Hurrah Antiques, New York City.

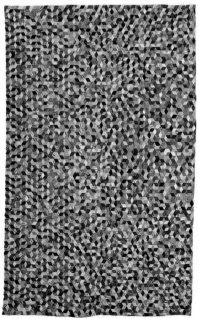

Ocean Waves

Description
Pieced quilt. 110 full and partial blocks, each constructed of 8 rows of tiny triangles, all facing one direction within block; direction of triangles alternates from block to block. Predominantly browns and pinks, with red triangles at corners of each block arranged to create bow-tie or pinwheel motif. Outer triangles form sawtooth border. Pale blue binding.

Materials, Quilting, and Dimensions
Cotton. Unquilted. 88" × 80".

Maker, Locality, and Period
Maker unknown. New England. c. 1880.

Comment
In this extraordinary example of piecing, not only has the quiltmaker made a quilt out of literally thousands of tiny patches, she has also originated a pattern that creates a very subtle optical illusion. The point of departure is the traditional triangular Ocean Waves pattern. The placement of the very small triangles gives the illusion of much larger squares, all set on the diagonal and centered with tiny red bow ties or pinwheels. The colors and prints are also very well balanced to produce the overall effect—except for those in the lower right corner, where there is a mixture of colors, possibly the last block to be done.

Hints for Collectors
Bedcovers like this one are very rare. Although most women in late 19th-century America were avid quiltmakers, few had the ingenuity or patience for such an ambitious project.

Price Guide Group: Other Geometric Quilts.

Courtesy America Hurrah Antiques, New York City.

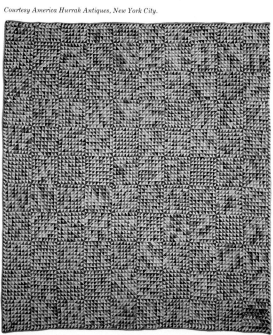

Postage Stamp

Description
Pieced quilt. Thousands of tiny squares organized in nine-patch blocks, in prints and solid colors, predominantly pinks, browns, and blues. Blocks arranged to create irregular pattern of light and dark across the surface. White binding.

Materials, Quilting, and Dimensions
Cotton. Unquilted. 84″ × 84″.

Maker, Locality, and Period
Maker unknown. New York State. c. 1880.

Comment
This painstakingly pieced bedcover creates an unusual visual effect reminiscent of the work of the French pointillist painters of the late 19th century. It is remarkable not only for its tiny squares, which resemble postage stamps, but also for their careful arrangement, each one lining up exactly with the other. On most such quilts, the arrangement of the stamps is more irregular, and many, in fact, are made of pieces too large to make the name appropriate.

Hints for Collectors
When choosing a Postage Stamp quilt, the quality of the piecing and the size of the individual stamplike squares are equally important. In both cases the smaller the better. Such bedcovers were rarely quilted, so the absence of quilting in no way diminishes value. Postage Stamp quilts were made in the 19th and 20th centuries, and dating them depends primarily on being able to date the fabrics used.

Price Guide Group: Other Geometric Quilts.

Courtesy America Hurrah Antiques, New York City.

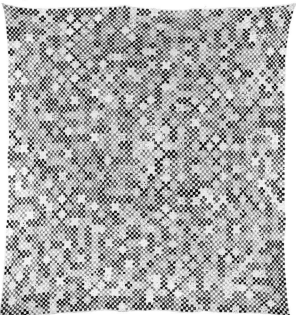

67 Framed Four Patch

Description
Pieced quilt. Central area of small four-patch and one-patch blocks arranged to form diagonal chains surrounded by 8 rows of one-patch blocks interrupted by narrow red frame. Blocks predominantly pink, brown, and red prints and solids. Border red. No binding.

Materials, Quilting, and Dimensions
Cotton. Squares quilted in diamonds, with X in center of each square. Frame with zigzag motif; border quilted in diamonds. 82″ × 82″.

Maker, Locality, and Period
Maker and locality unknown. Late 19th century.

Comment
The one-patch quilt was an ideal way to use up all the old scraps of material that almost every 19th-century housewife saved. Here the varied sizes of the scraps probably made it necessary to use both one-patch and four-patch blocks, resulting in an interesting and original design. One-patch patterns were especially popular in rural areas and wherever fabric was scarce. Easy to cut and stitch, they were also good beginners' patterns.

Hints for Collectors
It is often difficult to date quilts by their materials alone: fabrics were generally accumulated over a long period of time, and many bedcovers, like the one shown here, probably contained scraps saved for 20 years or more. Quilt patterns, fabric designs and colors, the type of binding, and the history of its ownership, if known, all help determine the age of a quilt.

Price Guide Group: Other Geometric Quilts.

Courtesy America Hurrah Antiques, New York City.

Description

Pieced quilt. Rectangles radiate from nine-patch center block with blue square at its center, and form a bricklike pattern. Blue squares form large X across quilt surface. Predominantly blue, red, and yellow solid and printed fabrics. Noncontinuous triple border of 2 narrow blue bands surrounding narrow band of blue, red, and white print. White binding.

Materials, Quilting, and Dimensions

Cotton. Unquilted. 76″ × 64″.

Maker, Locality, and Period

Maker unknown. Ohio. c. 1920.

Comment

A unique interpretation of the Brick Wall pattern, this quilt adds a large blue X to the usual straight rows of rectangles. Traditionally, this pattern is constructed of variously colored rectangles of fabric in alternating light and dark shades that cover the entire surface of a bedcover. In the bedcover illustrated, the width and placement of the rectangles, or bricks, vary throughout the quilt. Very likely made from pieces of fabric saved by the frugal housewife for just such a project, this scrap-bag cover, as these quilts were called, foreshadows the widespread use of fabric scraps during the Depression years.

Hints for Collectors

Neither sophisticated nor elegant, this bedcover has the charm and utilitarian beauty that many collectors prefer to the refined aesthetic of more graphic designs.

Price Guide Group: Other Geometric Quilts.

Courtesy America Hurrah Antiques, New York City.

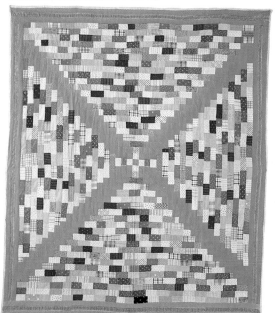

Description
Pieced and appliquéd quilt. Central area of 30 alternating red and tan blocks appliquéd with a variety of motifs, including hearts, flowers, crosses, arrows, ovals, circles, stars, and a hand. Small cross where 4 corners meet. Appliqués predominantly red, gold, pink, green, and pale blue. Triple border pale blue, pink, and deep green. Pale blue binding.

Materials, Quilting, and Dimensions
Cotton. Inner and outer bands of border quilted with diamond motif; middle with rope design. 80″ × 71¾″.

Maker, Locality, and Period
Maker unknown. Probably Pennsylvania. Late 19th century.

Comment
Although motifs are repeated in several of the blocks, no 2 blocks are identical. Some quiltmakers actually used cookie cutters to mark the fabrics from which they cut their appliqués. The shape of the cookie cutter was transferred to the material by rubbing the cutter with soap and pressing it down on the cloth.

Hints for Collectors
It is often necessary to rebind the frayed edges of a quilt, and it is usually the edge at the head of the bed that wears out first. While restoration should be avoided whenever possible, repairs that are well done are acceptable and will have only a small effect on the market value of the quilt. There are, however, collectors who will buy only untouched quilts, unless the repaired example is exceptionally rare or very old.

Price Guide Group: Other Geometric Quilts.

Courtesy America Hurrah Antiques, New York City.

Description
Mennonite pieced quilt. 25 red squares, 10 with olive-green diamonds and 15 with black diamonds, alternate with 24 olive-green squares. Frame of red bars with black bar at top. Narrow olive-green border with wider corner blocks. Red binding.

Materials, Quilting, and Dimensions
Wool. Central area with shell quilting. Border and frame with diagonal quilting. 80″ × 78″.

Maker, Locality, and Period
Maker unknown. Ohio. c. 1890.

Comment
The quilts of the Mennonites and the Amish appear strikingly modern today, and it is hard to understand that they were considered "plain" designs. In their isolated communities, Amish and Mennonite women created bold graphic designs that bear virtually no relationship to other quilts of the period. By about 1890, when this bedcover was made, most other quilts followed complicated Victorian designs.

Hints for Collectors
When choosing a Mennonite quilt, look for richness of color and fine stitching, which characterize the best of both Mennonite and Amish quilts. The Mennonites tended to be more adventurous in their designs and their choice of colors than the Amish. Amish bedcovers made around 1890 were usually much simpler than the Mennonite example illustrated here. Mennonite quilts are very much in demand today and prized for their rarity.

Price Guide Group: Amish and Mennonite Quilts.

Courtesy America Hurrah Antiques, New York City.

71 Geometric Design

Description
Pieced quilt. Triangles of printed and solid color fabrics form 80
blocks of varied geometric designs. Predominantly prints and
solids of blue, brown, and beige. Border narrow strips of fabric
set perpendicular to each side. No binding.

Materials, Quilting, and Dimensions
Cotton. Loosely stitched diamond quilting. 74¾″ × 61″.

Maker, Locality, and Period
Maker unknown. Pennsylvania. c. 1880.

Comment
This is an original quilt pattern, of which there are relatively
few. While parts of the quilt have a geometric progression of
triangles, in other areas the design is broken by triangles set in
the opposite direction. The quilt blocks appear to have 2
triangles, but each triangle is actually constructed of several
very thin rectangles placed parallel to each other, a process that
required great care and accuracy. In some cases the triangles
have been pieced so precisely from scraps of the same fabric that
they re-create the overall pattern of the fabric exactly.

Hints for Collectors
An incredible number of quilts were made in America in the late
19th century, as they provided an economical and attractive
solution to the ever-present need for bedcovers. Of the hundreds
of thousands that were made, however, most were variations of a
relatively small number of traditional patterns, and quilts with
one-of-a-kind designs are difficult to find.

Price Guide Group: Other Geometric Quilts.

Description
Pieced cradle quilt. Blocks composed of 4 equal triangles, mostly in brown prints, arranged to form Bow Tie pattern. Bordered on left and right with columns of rectangles in brown prints. Brown printed binding.

Materials, Quilting, and Dimensions
Cotton. Tufted with blue string. Unquilted. 41″ × 31″.

Maker, Locality, and Period
Maker unknown. New York State. c. 1840.

Comment
The cradle was especially popular in homes before the introduction of central heating, for its high sides and wooden bonnet protected the infant from drafts. Cradle quilts, made especially to fit these small beds, tend to be longer than crib quilts. In this example, each block was tufted and tied through all 3 layers with blue string, a technique also used for crazy quilts in the Victorian period. The name Bow Tie for this pattern first became popular in the late 19th century, even though the design appears on quilts of a much earlier date.

Hints for Collectors
Cradle quilts are very rare, and like crib quilts are popular among collectors who like to frame or hang textiles for display in their homes. While the warm earth tones in this quilt are very appealing, most collectors prefer more vibrant colors. For that reason, textiles with bright, rich colors almost always command higher prices in the market.

Price Guide Group: Crib Quilts.

Courtesy Museum of American Folk Art, New York City.

Broken Dishes

Description
Pieced crib quilt. Rows of brightly colored square blocks, each made of 2 triangles. Triangles arranged to form a light-dark pattern diagonally across surface. Predominantly yellows, blues, pinks, greens, browns, and reds. Border with plum-colored triangles, creating sawtooth edge. No binding.

Materials, Quilting, and Dimensions
Silk. Double-shell quilting. 42″ × 42″.

Maker, Locality, and Period
Maker unknown. New York State. c. 1920.

Comment
Crib quilts have been popular in America almost as long as full-size ones. The earliest specific reference to a child's quilt appears in the late 17th century. Most crib quilts were made of washable cotton, and a silk one, even from the 1920s, is quite rare. Silk was generally reserved for parlor throws, covers made for display and only occasionally used. Few silk bedcovers from the late Victorian era were quilted.

Hints for Collectors
Crib quilts have recently enjoyed an extraordinary surge of popularity with collectors. Because of their size, crib quilts can easily be framed like paintings or simply stretched and hung. In the example shown, the use of triangles in the border, emphasizing the triangular piecing, is evidence of the quiltmaker's excellent design skill. Touches like this add to a quilt's value.

Price Guide Group: Crib Quilts.

Courtesy America Hurrah Antiques, New York City.

Pinwheels and Hexagons

Description
Pieced quilt. Central section blue, beige, cream, green, and blue-and-white checked hexagonal patches surrounded by small one-patch squares in brown, blue-and-white, black, and purple with sawtooth edge. Framed by square of small pinwheels with sawtooth edge in same colors. Very wide border of large pinwheels in yellow, brown, green, blue, and black, outlined with very narrow sawtooth edge in various colors. Brown binding.

Materials, Quilting, and Dimensions
Silk. Unquilted. 84″ × 82″.

Maker, Locality, and Period
Maker and locality unknown. c. 1850.

Comment
Silk bedcovers, made of bits of dress silk, ribbon, and men's ties, became very popular in the second half of the 19th century. Most were parlor or lap throws; they were not quilted or lined and were made in a smaller size than bed quilts (usually about 60–70″, square or rectangular). The larger dimensions of this piece and its unique design combine to make it an interesting and unusual example.

Hints for Collectors
A silk bedcover should always be examined with great care. As it ages, silk has a tendency to turn brittle and tear. Condition is crucial because repairing silk requires an expert restorer and is expensive. If much of a silk bedcover needs repair, it is probably not worth buying.

Price Guide Group: Other Geometric Quilts.

Courtesy America Hurrah Antiques, New York City.

Log Cabin Quilts

 Log Cabin quilts are named for their method of construction. To begin the design, a central square, often in red to symbolize a glowing chimney, is sewn onto a larger block of fabric. A narrow strip, or "log," is then pieced to the edge of the center square. Subsequent strips are added, each perpendicular to the previous strip until the center square is entirely bordered by logs. Additional strips are added until the block reaches the size desired—generally anywhere from 12 to 14 inches. These blocks are pieced together and the backing added.

Because the individual piecing of the logs is strong enough to hold the layers of the quilt together, Log Cabin bedcovers are rarely quilted. Instead, most are tufted: several lengths of thread or yarn are pulled through the backing and top at regular intervals and then the protruding threads are knotted on the surface of the quilt.

Using contrasting light and dark fabrics, the quiltmaker can create many variations of the Log Cabin design. In light-and-dark variations, each block is divided into two triangular sections; one section is executed in dark fabric, the other in light fabric. By manipulating the final placement of the individual blocks, the quiltmaker can create dramatic visual effects. Some of the most interesting variations include Straight Furrow, Barn Raising, and Courthouse Steps (84, 77, 81).

By 1850 the Log Cabin design had become one of the most popular quilt types, and literally thousands of Log Cabin quilts were created. These early bedcovers were made of sturdy woolens, but were quickly followed by lightweight cottons that featured small-scale prints. The Victorians used lush silks, satins, brocades, and velvets to create their Log Cabin quilts. Most of these Victorian pieces are decorative spreads, intended more for the parlor than for the bedroom (200). With the revival of quilting in the 1930s, Art Deco colors were used, including turquoise, shocking pink, and brightly colored prints, often set against a black ground.

The best Log Cabin quilt designs create marvelous optical illusions. As they are looked at in different ways, they surprise the viewer by revealing striking new patterns.

75 Light and Dark

Description
Mennonite pieced quilt. 144 blocks, each with center gray square surrounded on 2 sides by red bars, on other 2 by black bars. Blocks divided on color diagonal. Overall effect of pattern is that gray squares float over red and black diamond ground. Red border. Red binding.

Materials, Quilting, and Dimensions
Wool. Yellow thread diamond stitching on border. 78″ × 78″.

Maker, Locality, and Period
Maker unknown. Pennsylvania. c. 1880.

Comment
At first glance it is difficult to determine how this quilt is constructed. The Log Cabin pattern encompasses a wide range of variation, and, after some scrutiny, the basic pattern always appears. Here we have a central gray square surrounded by rectangular "logs" of red and black that are pieced together to form a square block. This example is Mennonite, with typically strong colors and restrained design. Non-Mennonite quilts of the same period often employed printed fabrics; hence they were visually more complicated. Notice that only 3 colors are used in this quilt.

Hints for Collectors
With their strong, deep colors and simple designs, Mennonite quilts are actively sought by collectors. They are considerably more expensive than their non-Mennonite counterparts.

Price Guide Group: Amish and Mennonite Quilts.

Courtesy America Hurrah Antiques, New York City.

Light and Dark

Description
Mennonite pieced quilt. 64 blocks, each with center beige square surrounded on 2 sides by maroon bars, on other 2 by blue bars. Blocks divided on color diagonal. Overall effect of pattern is that beige squares float over blue and maroon diamond ground. Maroon binding.

Materials, Quilting, and Dimensions
Wool. Unquilted. 82″ × 82″.

Maker, Locality, and Period
Maker unknown. Pennsylvania. c. 1880.

Comment
The Amish and Mennonites were fond of the Log Cabin pattern and its many variations, at least in part because it gave them the opportunity to experiment with the use of color. In the best of their Log Cabin quilts, subtle optical illusions are created by the interplay of the light and dark bars. Although these bedcovers are rarely worked with the handsome, intricate stitches for which Amish and Mennonite quilts are famous, their strikingly original use of color justifiably makes them among the most sought after of American textiles.

Hints for Collectors
Both old and new Amish and Mennonite quilts are still available on a limited basis from the Pennsylvania Germans. One woman usually serves as an agent for several quiltmakers from the community, selling others' quilts on a commission basis. Newer bedcovers, including those using old designs, lack subtlety of texture and color and are of little interest to the serious collector.

Price Guide Group: Amish and Mennonite Quilts.

Courtesy America Hurrah Antiques, New York City.

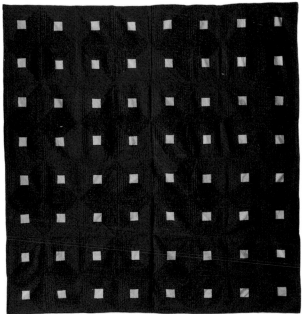

77 Barn Raising

Description
Pieced quilt. 100 blocks, each with central black square surrounded by either red and green, pink and dark green, or brown bars or a combination of 2 of these groups. Bars create a pattern of concentric diamonds typical of Barn Raising variation. Dark green binding.

Materials, Quilting, and Dimensions
Wool and cotton velvet. Unquilted. 76″ × 76″.

Maker, Locality, and Period
Maker unknown. Ohio. c. 1880.

Comment
The well-planned design, with wide brown areas at the corners balanced by the large brown diamond in the middle, and the unorthodox color scheme—pink against red, green and red against brown—suggest that this bedcover may be of Amish origin. No matter who its maker was, it has a subtle and sophisticated design.

Hints for Collectors
A popular misconception is that the older a quilt is, the higher the price, regardless of quality. In fact, Amish quilts created with great technical skill and sophisticated color schemes in the 1920s are far more valuable than a poorly conceived and shabbily executed example from the early 19th century. Attributing a date to a bedcover is very difficult unless it has been embroidered, stenciled, or stitched somewhere on the textile. And, remember, a date assigned without documentation is often nothing more than an educated guess.

Price Guide Group: Log Cabin Quilts.

Courtesy America Hurrah Antiques, New York City.

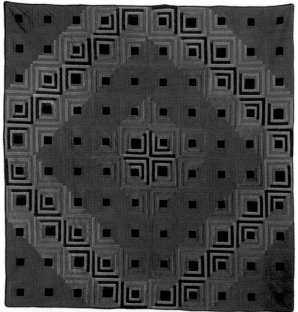

Barn Raising

Description
Amish pieced quilt. 64 blocks, each with center red square surrounded by strips of colored fabrics, including black, green, pink, blue, brown, red, orange, and purple. Pattern arranged to form concentric diamonds typical of Barn Raising pattern. Wide red border. Blue binding.

Materials, Quilting, and Dimensions
Cotton. Borders have parallel line and running chevron quilting. 76″ × 74″.

Maker, Locality, and Period
Maker unknown. Centre County, Pennsylvania. c. 1890.

Comment
The Log Cabin pattern and its many variations became popular throughout America in the latter part of the 19th century. Women's magazines highly recommended them as a way of creating a work of art using bits of treasured fabrics. The Amish adopted the Log Cabin pattern because it was well suited to their desire for simple yet bold designs. Based on small geometric shapes, it made thrifty use of fabric remnants.

Hints for Collectors
A border that is irregular in size may indicate that the quilt has been cut to eliminate badly worn areas and then rebound. The top and bottom borders of this quilt are equally wide, as are the sides, an indication that they are probably original to the bedcover.

Price Guide Group: Amish and Mennonite Quilts.

Courtesy America Hurrah Antiques, New York City.

79 Barn Raising

Description
Pieced quilt. 64 blocks, each with center square surrounded by variety of colored plain and printed fabric bars, including bright red plaid, blue-and-white, brown-and-white, and black-and-white pinstripes, and black-and-white check; plain fabric in reds, blues, greens, and black. Bars arranged to form concentric diamonds, or Barn Raising pattern. Wide black-and-brown striped border. Black binding.

Materials, Quilting, and Dimensions
Pieced velvet, satin, chintz, taffeta, and velvet and satin ribbon. Unquilted. 67⅛″ × 66⅞″.

Maker, Locality, and Period
Mrs. Elihu M. Dwight. Connecticut. c. 1875.

Comment
Quilts often became an informal family history, incorporating scraps of fabric from treasured garments or using motifs that represent events in the maker's life. From a note pinned to this bedcover we know it was made from pieces of the maker's own wedding dress and her daughter's first silk dresses. The success of the Barn Raising pattern depends entirely upon the selection of colors and fabrics.

Hints for Collectors
Because silk is almost impossible to repair successfully, few late 19th-century silk quilts are in good condition today. Because of the special meaning it held for its owner, the quilt illustrated here was probably used infrequently and is in surprisingly good condition.

Price Guide Group: Log Cabin Quilts.

Courtesy Museum of American Folk Art, New York City.

Log Cabin

Description
Pieced quilt. 100 blocks, each with center red square surrounded by 2 pink and green bars. Other bars are brown, white, blue, or yellow printed fabric. Colors and pattern create reverberating diamond motifs that radiate from 4 center blocks arranged to form cross. 4 corners echo cross motif. Pink print binding.

Materials, Quilting, and Dimensions
Cotton. Unquilted. 84″ × 84″.

Maker, Locality, and Period
Maker unknown. New York State. 1885.

Comment
At first this pattern appears to be a variation of the Barn Raising, Log Cabin design, but it is not. The Barn Raising pattern is designed so that solid diamonds of fabric radiate from the central diamond shape. Although this design might be viewed that way, the diamond effect is only an optical illusion created by color. This visual effect is further heightened by the manipulation of rows of striped fabrics in contrast to rows of unstriped fabrics, which gives the whole quilt a sense of intense movement. The dark brown bars actually combine with the yellow bars to form a cross. Rather than continue the diamond illusion off the edge of the bedcover, the quiltmaker has terminated the pattern with the cross motif at each corner.

Hints for Collectors
The use of contrasting colors makes this an extraordinarily vibrant quilt. Abstract patterns are particularly striking when installed against a neutral backdrop.

Price Guide Group: Log Cabin Quilts.

Courtesy America Hurrah Antiques, New York City.

Description
Mennonite pieced quilt. 90 blocks, each with center square in
shades of red and green surrounded by bars in shades of purple,
blue, green, gold, black, white, brown, plum, and maroon, and in
various printed fabrics. Prints include checkerboard, pinstripe,
stars, circles, and floral designs. Bar placement creates illusion of
steps advancing or receding from center square. Red-and-green
striped border. No binding.

Materials, Quilting, and Dimensions
Wool challis. Unquilted. 92″ × 84″.

Maker, Locality, and Period
Maker unknown. Pennsylvania. c. 1870.

Comment
Wool was the first material used for Log Cabin quilts in the
1850s. The design was a perfect vehicle for using up old scraps of
fabric; exact pattern and color matches were not necessary for
the successful bedcover as the design was largely dependent on
the placement of light and dark bars, rather than carefully
matched or contrasting fabrics.

Hints for Collectors
Mennonite Log Cabin quilts from this period are relatively rare.
In the example illustrated, plum and maroon fabrics add
consistency to the overall design. Like most Log Cabin
bedcovers, this one was not quilted. Instead, tufting was used to
hold the top, back, and filling together.

Price Guide Group: Amish and Mennonite Quilts.

Courtesy America Hurrah Antiques, New York City.

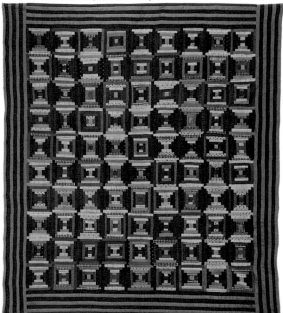

Description
Pieced crib quilt. 100 blocks, each with center square of red-and-beige printed fabric surrounded by bars of calico and other prints. Small bars create step pattern around central square. Predominantly red, green, orange, and beige. Orange paisley binding.

Materials, Quilting, and Dimensions
Cotton. Unquilted. 42″ × 42″.

Maker, Locality, and Period
Maker unknown. New England. c. 1880.

Comment
This truly extraordinary crib quilt has been cut and pieced using very small fabric bars. It was probably made to match a larger quilt and used in the crib next to a parent's bed. In the 19th century it was common practice for children to sleep in the same room as their parents or servants, and crib quilt designs often complemented or matched patterns found in larger bedroom furnishings.

Hints for Collectors
Many collectors prefer to frame crib quilts, both to protect them and to provide a convenient way to display them. Although expensive, a shallow Plexiglas box serves this purpose well (ultraviolet Plexiglas, which helps screen out damaging sunlight, is preferable to the nontreated variety). The quilt should never touch the sides of the box. Do not hang a textile in direct or reflected sunlight, because fading depreciates its aesthetic and monetary value.

Price Guide Group: Crib Quilts.

Courtesy Thomas K. Woodard, American Antiques & Quilts, New York City.

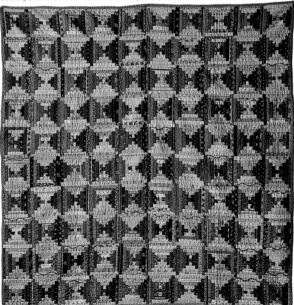

83 Courthouse Steps

Description
Pieced crib quilt. 64 small blocks, each with center square of predominantly brown, blue, or beige printed fabric, surrounded by bars of red, green, orange, brown, blue, yellow, and beige checks, stripes, and dotted fabric. Effect of design is advancing or receding steps, achieved by placement of dark and light bars. Narrow green-and-white printed border. Brown paisley binding.

Materials, Quilting, and Dimensions
Cotton and cotton calicos. Unquilted. 39″ × 36″.

Maker, Locality, and Period
Maker unknown. Pennsylvania. c. 1880.

Comment
Although many crib quilts were made by children, it is doubtful that this complicated design could have been executed by anyone of a very young age. Made of calico skillfully pieced in a harmonious arrangement, the quilt's pattern creates an optical illusion of advancing and receding steps. The finely printed green border acts as a unifying device. More often the border is a solid color fabric.

Hints for Collectors
Crib quilts are known to have existed in America since the latter part of the 17th century, but the vast majority that remain today date from the late 19th century. Because so many were made to be compatible with full-sized bedcovers, one can easily find parallel designs.

Price Guide Group: Crib Quilts.

Courtesy Thomas K. Woodard, American Antiques & Quilts, New York City.

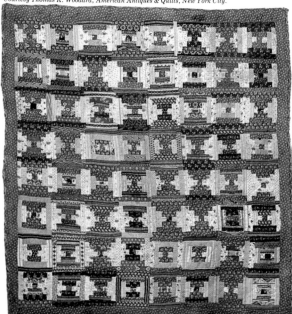

Straight Furrow

Description
Amish pieced and appliquéd crib quilt. 169 blocks, each with center square that is usually maroon but may also be red, blue, and gray; surrounded by light and dark bars of solid plum, red, tan, blue, brown, and green, as well as brown-and-white print, and black-and-white check. Bar arrangement creates jagged diagonal bands known as Straight Furrow design. Plum border embellished with appliquéd meandering blue, brown, orange, and tan ribbon. Tan binding.

Materials, Quilting, and Dimensions
Wool. Border ribbon machine stitched. 33¾″ × 33½″.

Maker, Locality, and Period
Maker unknown. Pennsylvania. c. 1860.

Comment
This crib quilt is very complicated and must have been difficult to execute on such a small scale. The variation of colors among the individual strips has not distorted the overall light and dark pattern. Note the interesting border; not only has the quiltmaker varied the color of the winding ribbon, but she has added a whimsical touch in the lower right—an unfinished dark blue diamond—that is missing in the other corners.

Hints for Collectors
In the past 10 years crib quilts have become very popular. Their association with children accounts for some of their wide appeal, but they are also easily displayed and cared for. It is rare to find such detailed design in an Amish bedcover with so early an attribution.

Price Guide Group: Crib Quilts.

Courtesy America Hurrah Antiques, New York City.

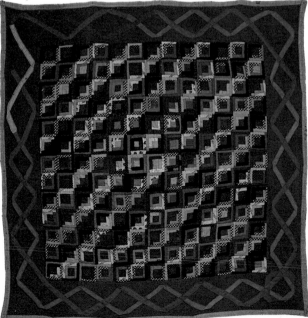

Pineapple

Description
Amish pieced quilt. 99 Log Cabin blocks, each with large black-and-white or purple-and-white printed center square surrounded by solid brown, rust, light and dark green, beige, and pink bars. Light and dark pattern creates Pineapple design. Narrow beige frame. Purple border.

Materials, Quilting, and Dimensions
Wool. Diagonal quilting on frame and border. 78″ × 68″.

Maker, Locality, and Period
Maker unknown. Ohio. c. 1885.

Comment
This is an atypical example of the Log Cabin design. The center squares that ground each quilt block are unusually large, and, while they are the same 2 colors throughout the bedcover, the quiltmaker has placed the black-and-white and purple-and-white print centers in a random manner. Also note that while the logs of the design are usually pieced parallel to the sides of the interior square, in this example rust triangles have been inserted at the corners of each series of concentric squares. Their placement remains consistent, however, throughout the quilt, adding visual strength to the overall design of the bedcover.

Hints for Collectors
Although it is tempting to assume that a quilt was made near the area in which it is found, this is not always the case. Oral history or written documentation of a bedcover's provenance are far more trustworthy.

Price Guide Group: Amish and Mennonite Quilts.

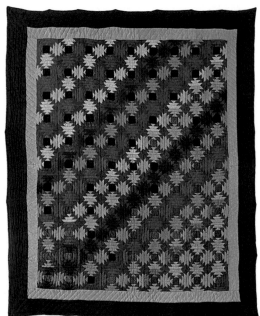

Streak of Lightning

Description
Pieced quilt. 100 blocks, each with center square created by red and black triangles pieced together, surrounded by printed fabric bars that are predominantly blue, black, red, brown, and gray. Fabric patterns include plaids, checks, florals, and geometric designs. Colors arranged in jagged horizontal bands forming Streak of Lightning, or Herringbone, pattern. Gray binding.

Materials, Quilting, and Dimensions
Cotton. Unquilted. 80″ × 68″.

Maker, Locality, and Period
Maker unknown. East or Midwest. Late 19th century.

Comment
The Log Cabin pattern provides an infinite variety of overall visual effects. The pattern name is derived from the arrangement of the bars, or logs, on the quilt top. Generally, a pattern was created and named; when variations began to appear, quiltmakers often adopted the variation's name for common usage. Although Streak of Lightning was a popular design, most quiltmakers preferred the Barn Raising or the Courthouse Steps variations.

Hints for Collectors
Because Log Cabins are rarely quilted, color choices become very important in selecting a bedcover. The particular arrangement of colored fabrics influences and articulates the design—the basic construction never changes. It is fascinating to compare several quilts done in one variation of the Log Cabin pattern. Even though they are based on the same design, they often appear almost totally dissimilar because of their use of color.

Price Guide Group: Log Cabin Quilts.

Courtesy Kelter-Malcé Antiques, New York City.

87 Windmill Blades

Description
Pieced quilt. 25 blocks, each with green-and-white printed center square enclosed by yellow printed diamond that sits on larger, printed square. Surrounded by printed bars in predominantly green, yellow, brown, gray, white, blue, pink, and red. Light and dark areas form contrasting arms that vibrate from center square of each block. Illusion reversible. Green-and-white print binding.

Materials, Quilting, and Dimensions
Cotton. Unquilted. 80″ × 80″.

Maker, Locality, and Period
Maker unknown. Pennsylvania. c. 1880.

Comment
Because the Windmill Blades variation demanded such exact piecing in comparison with the other Log Cabin designs, it was quite rare. This windmill effect was created by piecing the dark bars on the diagonal. When the individual blocks were sewn together, these diagonal bars helped create the feeling of swirling motion.

Hints for Collectors
Early Log Cabins were made of thick woolens; by the 1860s and 1870s a wide variety of cotton prints and challis came into use. The late Victorian period favored rich velvets and silks, satins, and brocades. However, it is particularly difficult to date Log Cabin quilts according to fabric. For example, the quilt illustrated here was made of cotton, but dates from the Victorian period when richer fabrics were more commonly used.

Price Guide Group: Log Cabin Quilts.

Windmill Blades

Description
Amish pieced crib quilt. 4 blocks, each with center diamond surrounded by bars of yellow, light and dark green, beige, and aqua. Contrasting light and dark bars create blades of windmill. Rectangular patches of yellow, green, brown, orange, and shades of blue make up border. Pale green binding.

Materials, Quilting, and Dimensions
Cotton. 4 white buttons sewn onto common edges of central blocks. White thread chevron quilting in colored rectangles of border. 34″ × 33″.

Maker, Locality, and Period
Maker and locality unknown. c. 1910.

Comment
Unlike most crib quilts, which are scaled-down versions of full-size designs, this bedcover uses 4 large blocks of the Windmill Blade variation to create an unusual, somewhat overstated effect. In the 20th century, Amish quilts frequently contained white material. This was previously frowned upon for both practical and religious reasons—white represented the purity of Christ and was considered inappropriate for a bedcover.

Hints for Collectors
Like many Amish quilts, this bedcover has a wide border composed of a simple alignment of blocks enclosing carefully stitched motifs. It is unusual, however, for the quilting to be done in a contrasting color as it was on the border of this bedcover. Pennsylvania quiltmakers found the Windmill Blades variation too flamboyant for their standards. This pattern generally is found in the Midwest.

Price Guide Group: Log Cabin Quilts.

Courtesy Museum of American Folk Art, New York City.

Quilts with Circular Designs

Circular designs became increasingly popular in the 1840s as quilting became a widespread pastime in America. By this time quilting techniques had reached a high level of sophistication, but quiltmakers were still confronted with the difficulties of piecing curvilinear patches so that they would not buckle. To avoid this problem, most circular designs were pieced with straight-edged fabric patches, creating such well known patterns as the Dresden Plate (99) and Wagon Wheels (106). With the exception of the Mariner's Compass quilts, the Bull's Eye, and some unique designs, all the quilts included in this section are pieced.

Most of the examples illustrated here date from the late 19th and early 20th centuries when printed fabrics were widely used. Rectilinear borders and frames were also common, both because they contained the central circular design, and because they afforded the quiltmaker an opportunity to incorporate other non-circular motifs such as fruits, vines, and animals. Frames were also advantageous in that they avoided the problem of a border with a curved edge.

Of particular interest in this section are the Wedding Ring designs, which became popular for a short time during the Civil War and were later reintroduced in kit form in the early 20th century.

Kits, many of which contained instructions for quilts with circular motifs, were very popular in the 1920s. Sold through the mail, they generally included a precut pattern with suggested fabrics and color schemes. The more expensive ones offered not only precut patterns, but also precut fabrics in many colors. To finish a quilt, all the seamstress needed to do was stitch her quilt top according to instructions and add the stuffing and backing. Among the patterns that came in kit form were the Dresden Plate, Wagon Wheels, Grandmother's Flower Garden, and the Fan.

Art Deco enthusiasts created an abundance of Fan quilts. These were usually designed with bold colors set against a contrasting dark ground (105).

Collectors should always carefully examine a quilt with a circular pattern to insure that the piecing is accurate, as the success or failure of a circular design depends on good proportions and excellent craftsmanship.

Description
Pieced and appliquéd quilt. Stylized six-pointed star of 3 red and 3 blue-and-white anchor-printed arms. Each arm created by pieced hexagonal patchwork. Star enclosed by narrow blue circle surrounded by red triangular pieces of fabric and 2 concentric circles of small blue triangles. Beige sawtooth border. Border created by interlocking red and white triangles and blue-and-white squares on 3 sides, beige and red triangles and blue-and-white squares at top. Off-white ground. Red binding. Embroidered initials.

Materials, Quilting, and Dimensions
Cotton. Large blue-and-white squares in border quilted in double five-pointed stars; sawtooth border corner patches have similar five-pointed stars. Outline stitching on all other patchwork. 83⅜" × 83⅛".

Maker, Locality, and Period
Initialed BB. Maine. c. 1885.

Comment
Quilt designs often evolved from the experiences of their makers' everyday lives. The quiltmaker who created this bedcover may have lived in a coastal town in Maine or been married to a sailor, for a nautical theme is evident not only in the pattern but also in the selection of fabrics.

Hints for Collectors
Unique quilts are almost always more in demand than those that follow a standard pattern. When they are beautifully conceived and skillfully executed, like the example illustrated, they are especially valuable.

Price Guide Group: Circular Geometric Quilts.

Courtesy Museum of American Folk Art, New York City.

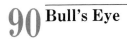

90 Bull's Eye

Description
Pieced and appliquéd quilt. Red and green central circle surrounded by 8 pieced pink, white, red, and green broken triangular and diamond-shaped concentric circles. Dark blue ground. Appliquéd red, yellow, and green floral vase in each corner. Signed. Dark red border. Red binding.

Materials, Quilting, and Dimensions
Cotton. Ground quilted with flowers, stars, and hearts. Border stitched with rope quilting. 85½″ × 84½″.

Maker, Locality, and Period
Alverba H. Herb. Lancaster County, Pennsylvania. c. 1920.

Comment
Many quilt patterns are based on the circle. However, few quiltmakers would have filled the surface of a quilt with one large circular design, as this quiltmaker has done, for the design would have been difficult to piece together, and one small miscalculation would have destroyed the unity and symmetry of the pattern. Although accuracy in cutting and sewing is important in any pattern that is based on small geometric components, it is vital when one large design covers the surface of the bedcover. Only an accomplished seamstress could successfully execute a quilt like the one shown here.

Hints for Collectors
Until recently few collectors specialized in quilts from the 1920s and 1930s. Today they are becoming popular, in part because of the increasing scarcity of 19th-century quilts. Furthermore, most 20th-century quilts are in good condition, which enhances their desirability. Many older quilts are almost unmarketable because of their fragility.

Price Guide Group: Circular Geometric Quilts.

Courtesy Museum of American Folk Art, New York City.

91 Compass

Description
Pieced and appliquéd quilt. Center compass motif in red, green, and yellow printed fabrics surrounded by colored band and 3 sawtooth bands in green, yellow, red, and orange. Compass motifs recur in each corner, with 2 half compasses at top and bottom of bedcover. 4 green, yellow, and red floral blooms, 4 pairs of green, yellow, and red tulips, and 4 green and yellow lighted candles are arranged symmetrically around circles. Red and yellow diamond frame, with green squares at corners. White border. White ground. White binding.

Materials, Quilting, and Dimensions
Cotton. Central ground has diamond and feathered scroll quilting. Top and bottom of border stitched with feathered vine; side borders quilted with intertwining feathered vine. 92″ × 86″.

Maker, Locality, and Period
Maker unknown. Pennsylvania. c. 1860.

Comment
The example illustrated here has 4 small candle motifs integrated into the central design. Quiltmakers often embellished their designs with motifs of a highly personal nature, thereby creating an individual statement.

Hints for Collectors
This design is rare, but it is not unique—4 similar quilts are known. When attempting to trace the origin of a particular design or ascertain its rarity, consult a dealer who is familiar not only with the current market but also with what has passed through it over a number of years.

Price Guide Group: Circular Geometric Quilts.

Description
Appliquéd summer crib quilt. Pink central circle surrounded by 10 triangles of pink-and-white paisley fabric, enclosed by 10 red-and-white printed modified T shapes. Circles, ovals, and modified T shapes arranged around central field. At each corner, five-pointed star composed of printed and solid fabrics with pink circle placed on white ground. Predominantly white-and-pink printed border cut away to form crenellated inside border. White-and-pink print binding.

Materials, Quilting, and Dimensions
Cotton. Unquilted. 33¾" × 33¼".

Maker, Locality, and Period
Maker unknown. Probably Pennsylvania. c. 1845.

Comment
As with most appliquéd quilts, the design motifs on this quilt are composed primarily of rounded shapes, in contrast to pieced quilts, most of which are made of straight-edged forms. This bedcover exhibits a pleasing and sensitive balance of color, ranging from white through pastel pink and bright red, and was probably made in expectation of the birth of a girl.

Hints for Collectors
Appliquéd quilts are generally more difficult to name than pieced ones because the designs are less apt to be in recognizable patterns. To make their inventory more desirable, inventive dealers often create names to serve as sales tools for patterns that were originally unnamed.

Price Guide Group: Crib Quilts.

Courtesy America Hurrah Antiques, New York City.

93 Floral Sunburst

Description
Pieced and appliquéd quilt. 4 circular motifs; center of each composed of yellow, white, red, and faded green flower. Enclosed by yellow band with faded green hanging leaves, surrounded by circle of red triangles placed side by side; each triangle point touches thin yellow circular band. Faded green leaves between triangle points. Faded green trees and red and green grape clusters sprout from yellow circular band. Central portion of quilt accented with 1 full and 8 partial yellow and red flowers. White-and-green printed fabric ground. Faded green frame. Border composed of faded green meandering vine with green-and-red grape clusters.

Materials, Quilting, and Dimensions
Cotton. Ground quilted with diamond stitching. Frame with chevron quilting. Grape clusters stuffed. 88″ × 84″.

Maker, Locality, and Period
Maker unknown. Pennsylvania. c. 1885.

Comment
Note how the green fabric used for the frame and grapevine is faded in subtle gradations—from green to ochre—suggesting that the fabric was faded before it was used in this quilt. Its skillful addition enhances the visual effect of the design.

Hints for Collectors
Be certain to examine quilts with stuffed designs thoroughly, for 3-dimensional areas show wear much more quickly than the ground areas do.

Price Guide Group: Circular Geometric Quilts.

Courtesy America Hurrah Antiques, New York City.

Mariner's Compass

Description
Pieced and appliquéd quilt. 11 full and 12 partial orange, green, pink, and blue compass motifs. Narrow appliquéd olive-green frame. Border filled with appliquéd motifs, including variety of pink, orange, green, and blue horses, cows, bulls, birds (many different species), pears, palm trees, and a ram. White ground. Olive-green binding.

Materials, Quilting, and Dimensions
Cotton. Diagonal and floral quilting on white ground. 96″ × 83″.

Maker, Locality, and Period
Maker unknown. New York State. c. 1855.

Comment
It is not unusual to find a quilt where both piecing and appliqué techniques have been employed. It is rare, however, to find a bedcover of such distinction. The motifs in the border provide a playfulness that is unusual for quilts of this period. Note in particular the intricately detailed running horses and various species of birds.

Hints for Collectors
Appliquéd farm animals, such as horses, cows, bulls, and sheep, always add substantially to a quilt's value. The quilt illustrated here, with its unique and endearing use of appliquéd figures, is highly desirable in spite of the fact that portions of it have faded. Many quilts have faded, either because of repeated washings or overexposure to sunlight; unless they have exceptional details, as this one does, they usually command less in the marketplace.

Price Guide Group: Circular Geometric Quilts.

Courtesy America Hurrah Antiques, New York City.

95 Mariner's Compass

Description
Pieced quilt. 18 blocks of white-and-yellow and blue-and-yellow printed fabric compass motifs; separated by white grid with small squares at each intersection. Sawtooth frame. Border has white and print Streak of Lightning pattern. Squares at 3 corners are diagonal bands of fabric halting Streak of Lightning pattern. Several irregularities, including fabric strip border with small white square at top of quilt; lower left corner block has pieced irregular cross. Binding in same printed fabric as motifs.

Materials, Quilting, and Dimensions
Cotton. Outline stitching on compass motifs and within both Streak of Lightning patterns. Parallel stitching on white bands. 77½" × 44".

Maker, Locality, and Period
Maker unknown. Virginia. c. 1860.

Comment
It is difficult to explain why the piecing of this bedcover was completed in such an irregular manner. For instance, each corner is treated differently. Perhaps this quilt was intended for a bed situated in a corner, where only 2 sides of it would have been visible.

Hints for Collectors
Quilts such as this were made by the thousands throughout the 2nd half of the 19th century, for it is simple in design and roughly executed. Its appeal lies in its attractive printed fabric.

Price Guide Group: Circular Geometric Quilts.

Courtesy Kelter-Malcé Antiques, New York City.

Description
Pieced quilt. 9 white blocks with brown fanlike designs at each corner; blocks divided by grid of green elongated diamonds placed side by side. Grid contains brown twelve-pointed star at each junction. White ground. Brown and green border on 2 sides; border on other 2 sides green, brown, and green. Brown binding.

Materials, Quilting, and Dimensions
Cotton. 3 center blocks quilted and stuffed with 4 flowers emanating from center bloom. Blocks on left and right sides quilted and stuffed with basket motif filled with 3 flowers and center bloom. Grid quilted in parallel and diagonal lines as well as outline stitching. Border quilted in parallel and diagonal lines and herringbone pattern. 86″ × 70″.

Maker, Locality, and Period
Maker unknown. Texas. c. 1850.

Comment
This quilt has a remarkable sense of design. When placed on a bed, the stuffed floral motifs on the right and left sides hang in an upright position. The quality of the stitching is distinguished but varies from block to block, so it is likely that more than one seamstress participated in the quilting.

Hints for Collectors
Although small sections of brown fabric appear to have been replaced with a beige textile, it is more likely that the beige is original to this quilt and that it has faded over time.

Price Guide Group: Circular Geometric Quilts.

Courtesy America Hurrah Antiques, New York City.

Description
Pieced quilt. 12 Mariner's Compass motifs in red-and-white, yellow-and-red, blue-and-white, and pink printed fabrics. White ground. Border red, white, and gray bands. Gray band patched in upper left with dark blue fabric. Red binding.

Materials, Quilting, and Dimensions
Cotton. Central ground stitched with floral motifs; border stitched with diamond quilting; and corners stitched with large chevrons. 78″ × 68″.

Maker, Locality, and Period
Maker unknown. Ohio. c. 1890.

Comment
Quilts with irregular designs are often prized by collectors because they illustrate the 19th-century quiltmaker's belief that a perfect quilt would be an affront to God, for only He was capable of creating a perfect object. This quilt would have a special attraction for such collectors because of the portions that have been made deliberately irregular, including pink rather than red piecing of certain compass motifs and a section of the gray border that has been patched with dark blue fabric.

Hints for Collectors
Although this bedcover has been extensively quilted, the stitching is not as fine as that found on some quilts. To learn how to recognize skillful needlework, compare and contrast the stitching on various quilts and study the intricacy of the stitches.

Price Guide Group: Circular Geometric Quilts.

Courtesy America Hurrah Antiques, New York City.

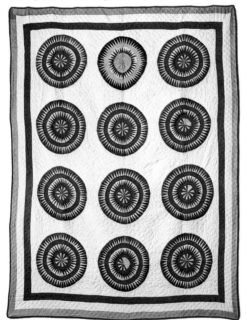

Friendship

Description
Appliquéd quilt. 30 red circular patches with white reverse appliquéd petals. Each petal has embroidered signature, and signatures appear around circumferences of circles. White ground. White border. Red binding.

Materials, Quilting, and Dimensions
Cotton. Diamond pattern stitched between red circles. White border stitched with diagonal lines. Embroidered signatures. 64″ × 56″.

Maker, Locality, and Period
Maker unknown. Akron, Ohio. c. 1850.

Comment
A Friendship quilt was created by women of a community as a practical gift for the wife of a teacher, merchant, or minister who was about to leave the community. Quiltmakers often added names, dates, and geographic locations to their bedcovers to personalize them for the recipient of the gift. There is no standard pattern for signed bedcovers; each was determined by the individual whim of the quiltmaker. In some Friendship quilts, the design of each block is different. In others, such as the one shown here, only the signatures vary.

Hints for Collectors
It is a rare pleasure to discover a bedcover that has identifying marks. And if a quilt is by a known historical figure or a particularly distinguished seamstress, it may increase the price of the bedcover dramatically.

Price Guide Group: Circular Geometric Quilts.

Courtesy America Hurrah Antiques, New York City.

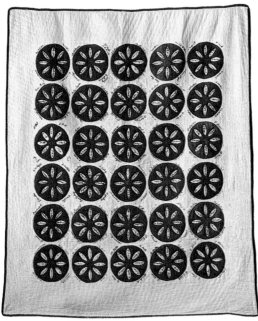

99 Dresden Plate

Description
Pieced and appliquéd quilt. 30 Dresden Plate motifs pieced with many almost identical patterns of printed fabric. Predominantly pink, green, blue, mauve, and red. Large red dots decorate center of each plate and ground between plates. White ground. Narrow blue frame. White inner border with red dots. Narrow blue outer border. No binding.

Materials, Quilting, and Dimensions
Cotton. Dresden Plates have outline stitching. Red dots in central field quilted in floral motifs. Blue frame and border quilted with rope motif; white border quilted with concentric heart and bell motifs. 84″ × 72″.

Maker, Locality, and Period
Maker unknown. Ohio or Michigan. c. 1930.

Comment
The Dresden Plate design has been popular throughout the 19th and 20th centuries. The large red dots on this bedcover provide a vibrant quality to the design that most Dresden Plate patterns lack. The prevalence of pastel colors illustrates how readily available these colored fabrics were in the early 20th century. Note that the red dots in the central portion of the quilt line up in roughly parallel lines, and the border dots relate not to the center but to the dots opposite them in the border.

Hints for Collectors
Collectors searching for unusual patterns often overlook traditional ones. This can be a mistake, for a creative seamstress can transform a simple design into a unique quilt.

Price Guide Group: Circular Geometric Quilts.

Courtesy America Hurrah Antiques, New York City.

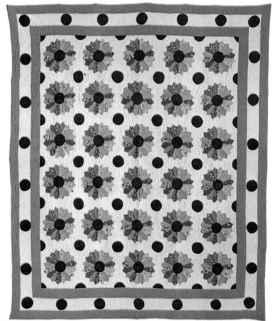

Circle

Description
Pieced Amish quilt. 288 small square blocks make up 72 circles in red, maroon, green, and 3 shades of blue. Black ground. Blue frame. Wide black outer border. Dark blue binding.

Materials, Quilting, and Dimensions
Cotton. Outline stitching within circles. Inner border and outer border stitched in loose shell quilting. 78″ × 74″.

Maker, Locality, and Period
Maker unknown. Ohio. c. 1920.

Comment
Ohio and Indiana Amish quilts differ significantly from their Pennsylvania Amish counterparts (the Ohio and Indiana groups usually exhibiting more non-Amish influences). For the most part, the Pennsylvania Amish lived in close-knit and geographically contained communities, and the Ohio and Indiana Amish lived outside their church districts, where they had non-Amish neighbors. This fluid environment introduced less conservative design elements into their quilts.

Hints for Collectors
Although the late 19th-century Lancaster County, Pennsylvania, Amish quilts are by far the most sought after as collectibles, midwestern quilts are becoming increasingly popular among quilt collectors. When looking at Amish quilts, remember that the Pennsylvania Amish rarely used black as extensively as their Ohio counterparts did.

Price Guide Group: Amish and Mennonite Quilts.

Courtesy America Hurrah Antiques, New York City.

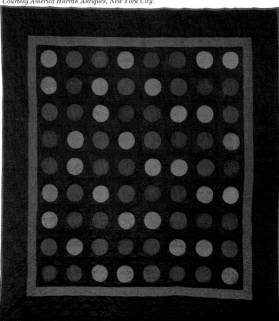

101 Snowball

Description
Pieced quilt. 20 Snowball blocks of printed and solid color fabrics, dominated by blue-and-white checked gingham. Peach frame surrounded by red-and-white printed fabric frame, with cream strip pieced on top and bottom. Pink border of polka-dot and doughnut-shape print in red, yellow, green, and white. Strip of dark blue-and-white printed fabric pieced on border at right and left sides. Pink binding.

Materials, Quilting, and Dimensions
Cotton. Quilted with wide parallel lines and some outline stitching. 82″ × 71″.

Maker, Locality, and Period
Maker unknown. Arizona. c. 1935.

Comment
During the Great Depression quilting became very popular with housewives, who turned to traditional means of making ends meet. As in the past, quilt patches were made from scraps of dresses and other clothing; patches were easy to cut, the stitching minimal, and the overall effect was often charming rather than sophisticated. This unpretentious bedcover is a very good example from the 1930s. The design, like many from the period, was widely reprinted in women's magazines and newspapers; this particular design appeared in the *Kansas City Star* in 1934.

Hints for Collectors
Quilts similar to the example illustrated are still widely available because they were produced by almost every American middle-class housewife in the 1930s.

Price Guide Group: Circular Geometric Quilts.

Private Collection.

Moon and Stars

Description
Pieced Mennonite crib quilt. 24 colored full and half circles, each with 4 or 8 pie-shaped wedges, in solid shades and prints of red, blue, black, purple, gray, and brown on light brown ground. Individual blocks divided into 2 triangles, each with 2 pie-shaped pieces in opposite corners. Dark brown printed border. Blue binding.

Materials, Quilting, and Dimensions
Wool. Loose outline stitching within each pie-shaped motif and around moon design. Quilted diagonal lines in outer brown border. 34″ × 34″.

Maker, Locality, and Period
Maker unknown. Pennsylvania. c. 1890.

Comment
Pieced patterns such as this tested the skill of a needlewoman. Slight irregularities in stitching resulted in an uneven design—in this case, the irregular circumference of the circles. Unlike the Amish, Mennonites were free to use printed fabrics like those seen here.

Hints for Collectors
Because crib quilts were generally made for everyday use, they often lack refined design and quilting. Nevertheless, many collectors prefer them because of their naive charm. In recent years crib quilts have become very popular, and the price levels have risen steadily. Although romantic names for quilt patterns, like Moon and Stars, may appeal to the novice, they do not affect the commercial value of a quilt.

Price Guide Group: Crib Quilts.

Courtesy America Hurrah Antiques, New York City.

103 Robbing Peter to Pay Paul

Description
Pieced Amish quilt. 99 small blocks in variety of pastel blues and purples. Each four-patch block is circle created by piecing alternating white, blue, and purple patch next to reverse color creating circle. Pale blue frame. Wide white border. Blue binding.

Materials, Quilting, and Dimensions
Cotton. Central motifs have outline stitching. Blue frame with chain quilting. White border quilted in abstract leaf motif. 88″ × 76″.

Maker, Locality, and Period
Maker unknown. Ohio. c. 1940.

Comment
Robbing Peter to Pay Paul was published widely in popular ladies' magazines of the late 19th and early 20th centuries, and existed in many variations. Probably because the curves surrounding the pieced circles appear to be constantly in motion, this has been a widely used pattern. Although modern admirers of antique quilts cling to the notion that materials for bedcovers were often salvaged scraps, close attention to the colors used in this textile show that they were chosen and purchased especially for its creation. There are only a few quilts—some of the crazy quilts being the best examples—that were actually made entirely from scraps.

Hints for Collectors
The light pastel hues on a white ground are typical of Ohio and midwestern Amish quilts of the 1930s.

Price Guide Group: Amish and Mennonite Quilts.

Courtesy America Hurrah Antiques, New York City.

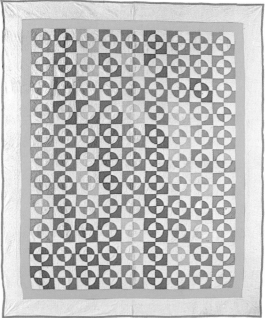

Description
Pieced quilt. 30 full and 6 half blocks, each with central pinwheel design of blue and red printed fabric. Surrounded by an orange-and-white printed fabric circle placed on pink and dark green pinwheel block. No binding.

Materials, Quilting, and Dimensions
Cotton. Simple outline stitching throughout. 84″ × 76″.

Maker, Locality, and Period
Maker unknown. New York State. c. 1870.

Comment
Quilt names can be very confusing; even the example illustrated is a variation on what is believed to be the traditional Pinwheel pattern. The quiltmaker who made this textile was an innovative designer, for in addition to the blue and red pinwheel at the center of each block, there is another pinwheel formed by the green and pink fabrics.

Hints for Collectors
Bedcovers may have been cut down or altered through the years. It is important to consider that 19th-century quilts were primarily practical, and aesthetic importance was secondary. Consequently, when a quilt became so badly worn around the edges that even rebinding could not rejuvenate it, a seamstress might cut it down substantially to form a child's quilt or slightly to eliminate the worn areas. The bedcover illustrated here has an incomplete design at the left. Although it may have been cut down when one side became worn, it is more likely that it was intended for a specific bed, and the incomplete motifs were meant to hang unseen next to a wall.

Price Guide Group: Circular Geometric Quilts.

Courtesy America Hurrah Antiques, New York City.

105 Fan

Description
Pieced Amish quilt. 36 blocks, each with pieced Fan pattern in yellow, rose, white, red, and 2 shades of blue stitched onto black ground. Wide black border. Black binding.

Materials, Quilting, and Dimensions
Polished cotton. Black ground quilted in diagonal lines. Border quilted in herringbone pattern. 74" × 74".

Maker, Locality, and Period
Maker unknown. Holmes County, Ohio. c. 1920.

Comment
The Fan pattern first appeared in the mid–19th century, was immensely popular by the 1880s, and experienced a resurgence in the 1920s and 1930s during the Art Deco period. Its initial popularity may be linked to the increasing awareness of Oriental design brought about by the objects displayed in the Japanese Pavilion at the Philadelphia Centennial in 1876. Oriental motifs appealed to the Amish love of abstract design, evident here not only in the Fan pattern but also in the herringbone quilting on the border.

Hints for Collectors
Many old Amish quilts look new because of their bold patterns and bright colors. When in doubt about a quilt's age, inspect the thread, for it can help to date a bedcover: 3-ply cotton thread was used throughout the 19th century until about 1920; 6-ply cotton thread began to be used in about 1840 and is still in use today.

Price Guide Group: Amish and Mennonite Quilts.

Courtesy America Hurrah Antiques, New York City.

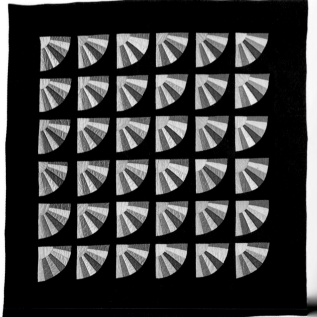

Wagon Wheel

Description
Pieced crib quilt. 9 circles made from variety of printed fabric strips. Colors include yellow, red, blue, black, green, brown, and shades of gray. Ground for Wagon Wheel pattern made from 4 squares of dissimilar printed fabric cut to create scalloped edge. Wide border of red-and-black printed fabric. No binding.

Materials, Quilting, and Dimensions
Cotton. Chevron quilting in border. 42″ × 38″.

Maker, Locality, and Period
Maker unknown. Pennsylvania. c. 1890.

Comment
The Wagon Wheel pattern is thought to be a design inspired by everyday objects, although by the time this quilt was created, the pattern had been widely published. Note that in this example the light and dark ground fabrics have been arranged to create a sense of motion. Contained within their dark borders, the wheels seem to spin in imitation of their namesakes.

Hints for Collectors
One should be very careful about laundering antique textiles, especially embroidered bedcovers or quilts with very dark prints. Textiles are often irreparably damaged by harsh detergents or improper drying methods. Bedcovers may also be professionally dry-cleaned, but if at all fragile, antique bedspreads should be taken to a professional antique-textile restorer.

Price Guide Group: Crib Quilts.

Courtesy Thomas K. Woodard, American Antiques & Quilts, New York City.

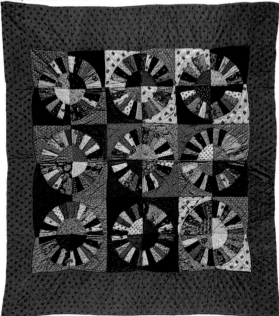

Double Wedding Ring

Description
Pieced Amish quilt. 18 full and 13 partial circles create Double Wedding Ring pattern. Circles pieced from blue, mauve, green, yellow, orange, and red fabrics. Black ground. Blue binding.

Materials, Quilting, and Dimensions
Cotton. Diamond quilting throughout. 84⅝" × 67".

Maker, Locality, and Period
Maker unknown. Pennsylvania. c. 1920.

Comment
The Double Wedding Ring pattern first became popular after the Civil War, but it did not achieve wide use until the early decades of the 20th century, when quilting kits were made available for mail-order distribution. Some of these kits supplied patterns and instructions. The more expensive generally included precut fabrics as well. It is unusual to see an Amish quilt in this pattern, for designs based upon rectilinear forms were usually preferred by Amish seamstresses.

Hints for Collectors
Most early Amish quilts were made of wool and predate those made of cotton. Because natural dyes cause fabric to "burn," or disintegrate, with time, many wool quilts have not survived. If an all-wool quilt and an all-cotton quilt of comparable design, craftsmanship, and color were matched, the wool quilt would probably sell for roughly 25 percent more. The cotton fabric and vibrant colors in the example here indicate that it was made in the 20th century.

Price Guide Group: Amish and Mennonite Quilts.

Courtesy Museum of American Folk Art, New York City.

Double Wedding Ring

Description
Pieced quilt. 28 full and 17 partial circles create Double Wedding Ring pattern. Pieced from solid-color and printed fabrics, mostly in pastel hues, including blue, pink, and green. Yellow ground. Scalloped edge follows contours of overall design. Blue binding.

Materials, Quilting, and Dimensions
Cotton. Ground quilted in unusual modified cross; each arm of cross ends in quilted plant form. Wedding rings have outline stitching. 84″ × 76″.

Maker, Locality, and Period
Maker and locality unknown. c. 1930.

Comment
This is an unusual variation of the Double Wedding Ring design. Notice the presence of 4-pointed stars at the intersections of the double wedding rings; that unfinished circular designs have resulted in 2 pointed corners; and that the quilt has a scalloped edge. All these elements are uncharacteristic of a quilt worked in the Double Wedding Ring pattern. Since so many quilts exist in this pattern, unique touches are especially appealing.

Hints for Collectors
The fabrics employed in this textile are typical of the early 20th century when pastels were very popular. It is possible to date a quilt from its fabrics, but that date can never be earlier than the newest textile used. Many quiltmakers collected fabrics for years before assembling them into a quilt.

Price Guide Group: Circular Geometric Quilts.

Courtesy America Hurrah Antiques, New York City.

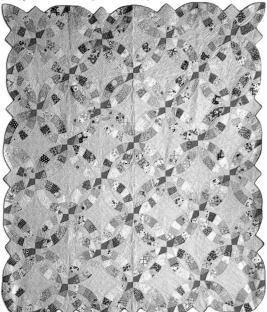

109 Honeycomb

Description
Pieced quilt. 67 complete and partial hexagonal cells create Honeycomb pattern. Each cell made of concentric hexagons pieced from print fabric. Cells defined by grid of dark brown-and-red floral print fabric. Frame of fabric printed with red-and-green nosegays and floral urns on gray ground. Border has same color floral design on tan ground. White binding.

Materials, Quilting, and Dimensions
Cotton. White hexagonal pieces surrounding individual honeycomb cells have outline stitching. Border and frame quilted in overall herringbone stitch. 122″ × 112″.

Maker, Locality, and Period
Maker unknown. Maryland. c. 1840.

Comment
Textile printing appeared in America after the mid–18th century and quickly reached a high degree of sophistication in the shop of John Hewson, a craftsman well known for his beautiful colorfast designs. His work answered the need for printed fabrics, which were so important in the development of American quiltmaking.

Hints for Collectors
It was once thought that the best quilts were fashioned in the northeastern states. New discoveries, however, continue to alter this misconception. Prices of quilts at one time were consistently higher in the Northeast, but with the increasing number of quilt galleries across the country, the prices paid for comparable quilts are generally the same from place to place.

Price Guide Group: Circular Geometric Quilts.

Description
Pieced Mennonite quilt. 49 full and partial hexagons in printed
fabrics include blue-and-white plaids and red-and-white and blue-
and-white pinstripes. Solid fabrics include red, white, black,
blue, and gray. Each cell defined by orange hexagonal grid.
Navy-blue binding.

Materials, Quilting, and Dimensions
Cotton and silk. Diamond quilting throughout. 86″ × 70″.

Maker, Locality, and Period
Maker unknown. Pennsylvania. Early 20th century.

Comment
Grandmother's Flower Garden was a very popular pattern
during the latter half of the 19th and the early 20th centuries,
and became especially common during the Depression, when
quiltmaking was almost a necessity. The design is a variation of
the one-patch, where patches are sewn together one after the
other, eventually creating an overall design. In the example
illustrated, the patches would have been drawn with the help of a
small template in order to ensure a consistent size and shape.

Hints for Collectors
This simple geometric design lends itself well to a variety of color
schemes, which partially accounts for its continued popularity
among quiltmakers. Generally, quilts from the first half of the
20th century, even though they may be superbly crafted, bring a
much lower selling price than 19th-century quilts. Because they
are relatively inexpensive, they appeal to those who are just
beginning to form quilt collections.

Price Guide Group: Amish and Mennonite Quilts.

Private Collection.

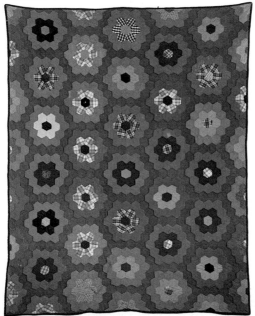

111 Grandmother's Flower Garden

Description
Pieced Amish quilt. 77 full and partial hexagons create
Grandmother's Flower Garden pattern. Colors include pink, red,
olive-green, and multicolored print fabrics. Each cell defined by
black grid. Space between cells filled with olive-green triangular
pieces that create six-pointed stars with hexagonal center. Wide
olive-green border. Red binding.

Materials, Quilting, and Dimensions
Wool. Each hexagon has fine outline stitching, with interior
parallel stitching. Outer border has diamond stitching.
77½″ × 76¾″.

Maker, Locality, and Period
Maker unknown. Indiana. c. 1880.

Comment
This pattern is also known as French Bouquet, Mosaic, or
Honeycomb and was very popular during the late 19th century.
Except for its characteristically wide Amish border and the use
of olive-green, it might easily be mistaken for a non-Amish quilt.
It is very rare to see an Amish quilt with patterned fabrics on its
face, although there are a few others in existence from Berks
County, Pennsylvania.

Hints for Collectors
Because Amish bedcovers rarely integrate printed fabrics on the
quilt top, the collector must be aware of other qualities beyond
pattern to determine the value of a quilt. Notice that the
quiltmaker's fine sense of color and intricate stitching have
transformed an ordinary quilt into an exceptional one.

Price Guide Group: Amish and Mennonite Quilts.

Private Collection.

Grandmother's Flower Garden

Description
Pieced quilt. Hundreds of hexagonal pieces in prints and solids arranged to form large central hexagon, surrounded by 4 pieced starlike motifs. Patches coordinated to form small triangles that line up to form bands of concentric frames that radiate outward. Predominantly green, blue, yellow, and brown. Green binding.

Materials, Quilting, and Dimensions
Cotton. Unquilted. 83″ × 79½″.

Maker, Locality, and Period
Maker and locality unknown. c.1870.

Comment
The Grandmother's Flower Garden pattern is created by the repetition of one geometric shape across the surface of a bedcover. It was a design popular in the late 19th century, and especially during the Depression, when many housewives were forced to return to frugal household practices. Because the design used very small pieces of fabric, every extra scrap of material could be applied to the composition of a quilt. The quilt illustrated was made during the Victorian period and is more ornate than many Grandmother's Flower Garden quilts fashioned in the 1930s.

Hints for Collectors
Quilts from the 1930s are just beginning to attract the interest of serious collectors. But since fine 19th-century examples are becoming increasingly rare and costly, many collectors are looking seriously at 20th-century quilts .

Price Guide Group: Circular Geometric Quilts.

Courtesy Museum of American Folk Art, New York City.

Quilts with Star Designs

Although the star with its many variations has traditionally been one of the most popular quilt motifs, it is not an easy design to cut or stitch. Precision is extremely important, since any inaccuracy in the cutting or piecing, however slight, will be multiplied as pieces are added and the star becomes larger. Unless the points and edges fit exactly, a star will not lie flat but will wrinkle or curl at the edges.

The simplest, most popular star pattern is an eight-pointed star that is usually composed of eight or sixteen diamond-shaped patches stitched together to form a star. In addition, there are four-pointed stars (Evening Star), five-pointed stars (Star of the West), six-pointed stars (Texas Star), and quilts made up of 20 or 30 smaller, separate stars that form one overall pattern (125). Perhaps the most common variation is the Star of Bethlehem (115), in which hundreds of diamond-shaped patches radiate outward from a central eight-pointed star to form one huge, overall star. The extremely popular Sunburst pattern (116) is constructed like the Star of Bethlehem, but it is more abstract. In it, hundreds of diamond-shaped patches extend to the edges of the bedcover. In some of the most striking star quilts, the star is composed of bold, vibrant colors set on a darker, contrasting ground (113).

Quilts in this section date from the early 19th through the mid–20th century. They often have an elaborately quilted ground and border and sometimes combine stars with other motifs such as flowers, trailing vines, or animals.

One often comes across unfinished quilt tops in such patterns as the Star of Bethlehem. Be aware that a top may have been left unfinished because the design was too badly pieced to lie flat on a bed. While the colors may be very pleasing, poor examples of a fine motif are rarely worth buying.

113 Star of Bethlehem

Description
Pieced quilt. Large eight-pointed star constructed of small diamonds on blue ground. Predominantly orange, gold, white, red, lilac, pink, brown, beige, and gray. Blue border. Blue binding.

Materials, Quilting, and Dimensions
Cotton. Area around star quilted in squares and diamonds. Border has rope design. 80″ × 77″.

Maker, Locality, and Period
Maker unknown. New England. c. 1900–10.

Comment
Constructed from the center out, this pattern requires great skill. If the diamond-shaped pieces are not cut accurately, the quilt top will curl as it is pieced together, and no amount of pulling will make it lie flat. While all Star of Bethlehem quilts combine fabrics of different colors, not all succeed in achieving the sense of vibrant color that this one has. As the colors radiate out from the center, the star appears to shimmer.

Hints for Collectors
The Star of Bethlehem design was popular as early as 1825, and continues to be popular with quiltmakers today, so in this case the pattern is no indication of age. Period fabrics and the fineness of the quilting stitches, however, are both good clues. In general the finer the stitching, the earlier the quilt. Needlewomen have always taken pride in small, precise stitches. Some of the most intricately stitched quilts have more than 14 to the inch.

Price Guide Group: Star Quilts.

Collection of Massimo Vignelli.

Star of Bethlehem

Description
Amish pieced quilt. Large eight-pointed star constructed of diamonds in orange, light green, pink, and blue. Orange frame. Blue ground. Orange binding.

Materials, Quilting, and Dimensions
Cotton. Star with parallel quilting. Ground with diamond quilting. Border with rope quilting. 76″ × 76″.

Maker, Locality, and Period
Maker unknown. Pennsylvania. c. 1920.

Comment
The Star of Bethlehem, also known as the Blazing Star, was very popular in the 19th century with Amish and non-Amish alike, and many examples have survived. The original pattern was similar to the example illustrated, with the large eight-pointed star sometimes measuring up to 8′ across. Later variations in the design included small pieced or appliquéd stars between the points of the larger star, appliquéd flowers and other naturalistic motifs, and common household objects such as scissors, spools of thread, and darning eggs. The Star of Bethlehem pattern continues to be made today.

Hints for Collectors
When choosing a quilt with a pieced star design, the construction is particularly important. As in the Sunburst pattern, a single miscalculation will destroy the symmetry of the design. Although the piecing in the example illustrated is not particularly fine, the rich color combination and intricate quilting add immeasurably to the appeal of this textile.

Price Guide Group: Amish and Mennonite Quilts.

Private Collection.

115 Star of Bethlehem

Description
Pieced quilt. Large eight-pointed star constructed of small diamonds in various pastel prints on white ground. At its center, small eight-pointed star in red-and-green print. Sunburst motif in each corner and along each side in various pastels. Red, gold, and black floral printed border. Pink binding.

Materials, Quilting, and Dimensions
Cotton. Ground with diamond quilting. 92″ × 90¾″.

Maker, Locality, and Period
Elizabeth E. Moseman. Port Chester, New York. 1849.

Comment
Composed of more than 4200 pieces, this quilt won first prize at the state fair in Bridgeport, Connecticut, in 1849. While the Star of Bethlehem alone is common, the designs inside the border, also pieced of diamond-shaped patches, are an original addition. Together they are a good example of how a new design is created by combining traditional ones. The shape of the corner motifs is especially effective because the angle at which they are set draws the eye toward the large star in the center.

Hints for Collectors
A quilt with the date written or stitched on it is especially significant for the collector or historian because it helps confirm the date of particular fabric styles and colors. An undated quilt is usually given a date 10 years later than the fabrics that were used in its construction, as it is generally assumed that the fabrics would have been saved over a 10-year period.

Price Guide Group: Star Quilts.

Courtesy America Hurrah Antiques. Collection of Chase Manhattan Bank, New York City.

Sunburst

Description
Pieced quilt. Concentric octagons constructed of diamonds in
various prints radiate from central eight-pointed star in yellow-
and-brown print, creating sunburst effect. Predominantly pinks,
browns, and blues. Brown binding.

Materials, Quilting, and Dimensions
Cotton. Unquilted. 125⅛" × 118½".

Maker, Locality, and Period
Possibly Rebecca Scattergood Savery. Philadelphia. c. 1840.

Comment
The striking visual effect of this quilt is due in part to its
sophisticated use of color. Its probable maker, Rebecca
Scattergood Savery, a descendant of a well-known Quaker
family, is known to be the maker of several other quilts,
including one almost identical to this in both pattern and fabric.
This huge bedcover would have taken a very long time to cut and
piece, and it is very likely that the maker had helpers who did
the actual stitching. The overall choice of design and fabrics,
however, would have been hers alone.

Hints for Collectors
Bedcovers in this pattern were extremely difficult to make, as
the cutting and piecing of the small diamonds had to be exact.
While the pattern was fairly popular, the quality of quilts in this
design varies greatly. Be especially careful with unquilted tops;
they may have been poorly cut or pieced and hence left
unquilted.

Price Guide Group: Star Quilts.

Courtesy Museum of American Folk Art, New York City.

Star of Bethlehem

Description
Pieced and appliquéd quilt. Large central star constructed of small diamonds in red, orange, green, and white on white ground. Half stars along each side and eight-pointed stars at each corner in red, orange, and green; all surrounded by appliquéd leaves, horses, birds, and baskets. White binding.

Materials, Quilting, and Dimensions
Cotton. Diamonds have outline stitching. Ground has diamond quilting. 78″ × 78″.

Maker, Locality, and Period
Maker unknown. Maine. c. 1870.

Comment
The large Star of Bethlehem is always constructed from hundreds of diamond-shaped patches, but the area surrounding the star may differ considerably from quilt to quilt. Frequently, a number of smaller stars or borders set off the central star, but the use of appliqué, here apparent in the baskets, animals, leaves and birds, is unusual. The combination of the large, somewhat formal star with many simple everyday objects is unexpected, but as in much folk art, it is the unusual that creates the work's unique appeal.

Hints for Collectors
A quilt that successfully integrates appliquéd motifs with a traditional pieced pattern is often more desirable than a quilt that uses only a single technique. Look for original variations that transform a common design into something special.

Price Guide Group: Star Quilts.

Private Collection.

Description
Pieced and appliquéd quilt. Large eight-pointed star constructed of elongated diamonds radiating out from small central eight-pointed star. Predominantly yellows, greens, pink, red, and white on maroon ground. Appliquéd tulips between points of star, and Princess Feather motif in each corner. Red border. Green binding.

Materials, Quilting, and Dimensions
Cotton. Diamonds with outline stitching. Ground with diamond quilting. 84″ × 82″.

Maker, Locality, and Period
Maker unknown. Pennsylvania. c. 1880.

Comment
Possibly of Mennonite origin, this quilt combines brightly colored pieced work with bold Pennsylvania German motifs, including the tulip and Princess Feather. With their strong sense of color and skillful use of bold designs, Pennsylvania quilts are distinctly different from quilts made in other areas. However, the combination of the Star of Bethlehem with large Princess Feathers is unusual, even in Pennsylvania quilts.

Hints for Collectors
When looking for antique textiles, do not overlook the obvious sources. Bedcovers were often handed down from generation to generation, and families sometimes tucked quilts away in unlikely places. Such discoveries, however, are becoming more and more difficult to make.

Price Guide Group: Star Quilts.

Courtesy Thomas K. Woodard, American Antiques & Quilts, New York City.

Description
Appliquéd quilt. 5 red eight-pointed stars; central star plain, others with 8 feathers arranged like spokes of a wheel. Feathers in blue, orange-gold, and red-and-white print. White ground. White binding.

Materials, Quilting, and Dimensions
Cotton. Feathers have outline stitching. Ground with diagonal quilting. 71½″ × 69″.

Maker, Locality, and Period
Maker and locality unknown. c. 1850.

Comment
Also referred to as Ben Hur's Chariot Wheel, or Star and Plume, the Princess Feather pattern was especially popular in the mid–19th century, although it was difficult both to cut out and to appliqué. The design appeared first on the East Coast and then moved across the country with settlers going west. Of interest because it is reversible, this bedcover has on its back a large geometric design in the same colors as the quilt top. Quilt backs were often carefully designed so that if the back were revealed it would not contrast with the side meant for viewing.

Hints for Collectors
Reversible quilts are hard to find, particularly with an attractive pattern on both sides. Interestingly, this example is appliquéd on one side and pieced on the other. Many reversible quilts are of southern origin.

Price Guide Group: Star Quilts.

Collection of Rhea Goodman.

Description
Pieced and appliquéd quilt. Eight-pointed Star of Bethlehem constructed of diamonds radiating out from small central star of brown-and-white print. Predominantly prints in light browns and pink on white ground. Multicolored triangles arranged between points of large star. Miniature Sunburst pattern in each corner in browns, pinks, white, and orange. Yellow trailing vine border with multicolored tulips and red maple leaves. Pink binding.

Materials, Quilting, and Dimensions
Cotton. Central white ground quilted in parallel lines; outer white area quilted in running feather pattern. Outer border with outline stitching and flowers, echoing motifs found on pieced designs. 74″ × 74″.

Maker, Locality, and Period
Maker unknown. Pennsylvania. c. 1855.

Comment
This quilt successfully combines both appliqué and piecing techniques. The pieced sunbursts and large central star, all bordered by a floral appliquéd trailing vine, are an unusual combination, but the maker's sense of design and color bring the diverse elements together.

Hints for Collectors
Quiltmakers generally determined their palette carefully. Since the overall scheme here is pastel, the intrusion of bright red leaves seems to be a deliberate decision to introduce contrasting color. Scrutinize the colorful portions of a bedcover carefully; if they seem inconsistent with the dominant color scheme, they may be later additions.

Price Guide Group: Star Quilts.

Courtesy America Hurrah Antiques, New York City.

121 Sunburst

Description
Appliquéd and pieced quilt. 9 sunbursts in pink, white, green, and blue-and-yellow print, with pink eight-pointed star at center of each sunburst, and small pink eight-pointed star between them. 4 appliquéd tulip blocks in pink and green fabric, arranged in square around central sunburst. White ground. Inner border pink appliqués of birds, diamonds, and full and partial stars surrounded by green and pink garland. Outer border pink with sawtooth edge. White binding.

Materials, Quilting, and Dimensions
Cotton. Ground quilted in parallel lines. Outer border with diamond quilting. Embroidered details on birds. 92″ × 92″.

Maker, Locality, and Period
Maker unknown. Probably Pennsylvania. c. 1850.

Comment
The amount of time and effort required to design and execute this Sunburst pattern is hard to imagine today. An Ohio woman, creator of a similarly intricate quilt, once remarked: "It took me more than 20 years, nearly 25, in the evening after supper when the children were all put to bed to make that quilt. My whole life is in that quilt . . . all my joys and all my sorrows."

Hints for Collectors
For anyone choosing a quilt, aesthetic value is as important as age, condition, and the quality of the needlework. Many collectors, especially those fond of modern art, are drawn to vividly colored quilts that are graphically strong.

Price Guide Group: Star Quilts.

Courtesy America Hurrah Antiques, New York City.

Description
Pieced quilt. 9 sunbursts in maroon, blue, green, and gold prints, with blue prints pieced to create swirling effect. White ground. White diamonds formed where sunbursts meet. 4 white blocks, each with Mariner's Compass pattern in white and red-and-white print. Dark green and white sawtooth border. Dark green binding.

Materials, Quilting, and Dimensions
Cotton. Central white blocks quilted in diagonal lines. Diamond-shaped white blocks have feathered circles enclosing diamond quilting. White border area with diamond quilting; chevron quilting between points of stars. 114″ × 112″.

Maker, Locality, and Period
Maker unknown. New England. c. 1850.

Comment
Few quilts are as dramatic as this one. Note especially how the blue-and-white printed fabric is used on the sunbursts to achieve the effect of movement, suggesting the Harvest Sun pattern. The use of the dark green and white sawtooth border and the dark green binding is also very unusual. Perhaps the quiltmaker intended them to be as unobtrusive as the central section is exuberant.

Hints for Collectors
The pattern of this quilt is unusual and seldom found today. It required great skill to execute; the most difficult task was to make the stars uniform, meeting exactly at the connecting points. Whenever a quilt has sawtooth borders or edges, be sure to check for wear; they are often badly frayed.

Price Guide Group: Star Quilts.

Courtesy America Hurrah Antiques, New York City.

Description
Pieced quilt. 16 full and 4 partial eight-pointed stars in Harvest
Sun pattern. Predominantly red, black, blue, and tan prints on
white ground. Red border. White binding.

Materials, Quilting, and Dimensions
Cotton. Suns with outline quilting. Ground with diamond
quilting. Border quilted in diagonal lines. 75″ × 67″.

Maker, Locality, and Period
Maker unknown. Southwestern United States. c. 1880.

Comment
There are many star variations, some composed of a number of
smaller stars in blocks, and some of one large star dominating
the entire quilt. Each design has its own name, and frequently
several names were used for the same pattern. The pattern
illustrated here was also known as Prairie Star in the Midwest
and Ship's Wheel in Massachusetts. Many star designs differ only
slightly; the sole difference sometimes is a change in the
arrangement of light and dark colors, rather than in the cutting
and piecing of patches.

Hints for Collectors
Quilts like this one are not especially rare, but striking examples
in good condition are becoming increasingly difficult to find. Once
thought of as everyday bedcovers, patchwork quilts are now
much in demand as prime examples of American folk art. Since
the Whitney Museum's 1971 exhibit "Abstract Design in
American Quilts," contemporary interest in antique quilts has
soared.

Price Guide Group: Star Quilts.

Private Collection.

Feathered Star

Description
Pieced, appliquéd, and reverse-appliquéd quilt. 15 feathered stars in grid of gold, blue, and blue-and-white check on white ground. Each eight-pointed star encloses centered one-piece square. Border has 23 appliquéd potted plants irregularly spaced and set on diagonal in corners. Plants, in same prints as stars and grid, have 2 white elliptical reverse-appliqué cutouts and 1 heart in reverse appliqué. Appliqué in upper right corner modified to fit available space. White binding.

Materials, Quilting, and Dimensions
Cotton. Star blocks have outline and floral quilting. Border has outline, floral, and heart-shaped quilting. 92″ × 74″.

Maker, Locality, and Period
Maker unknown. New England. c. 1850.

Comment
The heart quilting in the border and the reverse-appliqué hearts in the plants suggest that this textile was intended to be a bridal quilt. It was considered unlucky to use the heart motif on other quilts.

Hints for Collectors
Although the spacing of the border plants is irregular, this bedcover is very finely stitched and the reverse-appliqué work rare, so that both add substantially to its value. Reverse appliqué is accomplished by cutting a design out of the appliqué so that the ground fabric shows through, then turning the cut edges under, and stitching around the cutout area. It requires great skill with a needle and would have been attempted only by a very experienced quilter.

Price Guide Group: Star Quilts.

Courtesy America Hurrah Antiques, New York City.

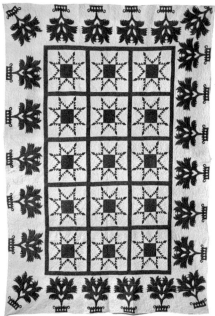

125 Eight-Pointed Star

Description
Pieced quilt. 31 full and 18 partial eight-pointed stars in blue-and-white print form overall diagonal pattern on white ground. Framed in same blue-and-white print. White inner border. Outer border same blue-and-white print. White binding.

Materials, Quilting, and Dimensions
Cotton. Lavishly quilted. Ground in center section quilted in parallel lines within stars, diamonds, and feathered ovals. Inner border with feathered quilting. Frame and outer border quilted in diagonal lines. 78″ × 68″.

Maker, Locality, and Period
Maker unknown. Midwest. Late 19th century.

Comment
Ingeniously pieced, this bedcover is constructed only of straight-edged pieces of fabric, and yet the design creates an optical illusion of circles. This effect is achieved by cutting the points of the stars longer and narrower than is common, and setting the stars diagonally.

Hints for Collectors
This is an excellent example of the quilter's art, both for its fine, elaborate quilting and for the visual effect created by the elongated stars. Such mastery of the form is rare, and the result is an extraordinary and very valuable bedcover that should be preserved under optimal conditions. Whether on display or in storage, the amount of light and moisture should be controlled, and dust as well as the oils and dirt that come from handling avoided.

Price Guide Group: Star Quilts.

Courtesy America Hurrah Antiques, New York City.

Kansas Troubles

Description
Pieced quilt. 14 full and 20 partial blocks composed of white and blue-and-white printed triangles alternating with white whole and partial squares. Sawtooth frame in blue-and-white print. White inner border. Outer sawtooth border in same print as frame. Cutouts for four-poster bed. Blue binding.

Materials, Quilting, and Dimensions
Cotton. Blocks quilted with feathered wreath and parallel lines. White border has running feather. Ground with diamond quilting. 88″ × 86″.

Maker, Locality, and Period
Maker unknown. New England. c. 1875.

Comment
In an interesting variation of the Kansas Troubles pattern, this quiltmaker has arranged the pattern on the diagonal, creating an open and satisfying design. It seems likely that the quilt was intended for a very narrow, high bed, as the drop flap at the bottom is not very wide.

Hints for Collectors
While many collectors are not attracted to quilts of only 2 colors, the superior craftsmanship and exciting design of this one make it very desirable. In addition, this quilt was originally made for a four-poster bed, which is quite rare. Usually bedcovers were adapted for such use after they were completed, often after they had been used. Altered bedcovers are easy to distinguish as they lack an overall unity of design. They also bring considerably less in the marketplace.

Price Guide Group: Star Quilts.

Courtesy America Hurrah Antiques, New York City.

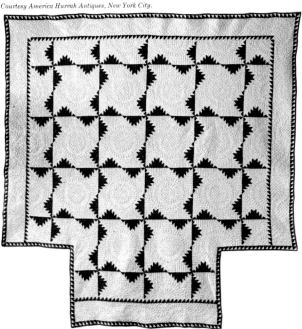

127 Columbia Star

Description
Amish pieced quilt. Black, blue, lavender, and gray diamond blocks arranged to create white six-pointed stars. Framed in blue. Inner border white. Outer border black. Light gray binding.

Materials, Quilting, and Dimensions
Cotton. Each patch with outline quilting. Borders with herringbone quilting. 86″ × 74″.

Maker, Locality, and Period
Maker unknown. Holmes County, Ohio. c. 1945.

Comment
By the 1930s, the midwestern Amish had been strongly influenced by quilt designs outside their own communities and their quilts became almost indistinguishable from non-Amish ones. The six-pointed star was a popular motif throughout the United States, and so the clue to the Amish origin of this piece is the use of their characteristically somber yet rich colors.

Hints for Collectors
The experienced collector always prefers quilts in good condition, like the one shown here. When an old quilt has holes or tears or is stained and discolored with age, it is often very difficult to clean or repair. An exceptional or rare example is sometimes worth buying in poor condition, but it should then be given to a professional conservator for corrective treatment. Since this is expensive, it is usually best not to buy quilts that need substantial restoration.

Price Guide Group: Amish and Mennonite Quilts.

Courtesy America Hurrah Antiques, New York City.

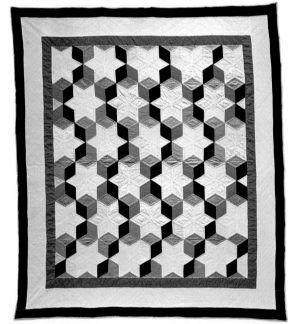

Description
Mennonite pieced quilt. Central red and green eight-pointed star surrounded by gold blocks; further surrounded by inner border of larger red and green sixteen-pointed broken star enclosed by triangular gold patches. Green and gold sawtooth frame. Border green. Red binding.

Materials, Quilting, and Dimensions
Cotton. Central eight-pointed star quilted in diagonal lines. Surrounding gold blocks quilted in parallel lines and feathered wreaths. Broken star quilted in diagonal lines. Gold triangular patches quilted in feathered wreaths. Sawtooth frame closely quilted in parallel lines. Border quilted in running feather and diagonal lines. 80″ × 80″.

Maker, Locality, and Period
Maker unknown. Pennsylvania. c. 1890.

Comment
The quilting in the piece shown here is exceptionally fine. Every possible area has been intricately stitched. The feathered wreaths found on the gold blocks here have also been successfully applied to the combination color blocks found in the corners of the central area. The very close quilting stitches, which would have taken many hours to complete, give the quilt a very interesting texture.

Hints for Collectors
Extraordinary both for its quilting and its bold pieced design, this quilt is the work of a very special quiltmaker. Not many quilters combined such fine needlework skills with a sense of design.

Price Guide Group: Amish and Mennonite Quilts.

Courtesy America Hurrah Antiques, New York City.

Description
Pieced and appliquéd crib quilt. 4 large blocks in pink, red, yellow, and maroon prints, each with large eight-pointed star constructed of yellow print triangles and central pink print square. Blocks divided by red print cross. From each star leaflike motifs extend to 3 corners of square; 4th in central corner. Wide border in green-and-yellow print with yellow print rectangles at each corner. Apricot binding.

Materials, Quilting, and Dimensions
Cotton. Quilted in parallel lines and chevrons. 44¾″ × 39½″.

Maker, Locality, and Period
Maker unknown. Pennsylvania. c. 1865.

Comment
The printed fabrics found in this crib quilt were probably mass-produced specifically for use in clothing or quilts. While it might seem that crib quilts would have been made in soft pastel colors, they in fact reflect the preferred colors of full-scale quilts of the period.

Hints for Collectors
Dating a quilt on the basis of its pattern alone is virtually impossible because many patterns have been popular since the early 19th century. Although dating a quilt by its fabrics is somewhat more reliable, it also has its limitations. If comparable, documented pieces are available an approximate date may sometimes be ascribed. Collectors should remember that even with documentation, experts allow a 10 to 20 year leeway, since many quiltmakers saved scraps for years before sewing them into a bedcover.

Price Guide Group: Crib Quilts.

Courtesy America Hurrah Antiques, New York City.

Feathered Star

Description
Mennonite pieced quilt. 16 eight-pointed red, yellow, and green feathered stars alternate with plum and white feathered squares and diamonds. Narrow frame red and green, in Streak of Lightning design. Green border. Yellow binding.

Materials, Quilting, and Dimensions
Cotton. Feathered stars, squares, and diamonds quilted in diamond pattern. Border has rope design. 84″ × 84″.

Maker, Locality, and Period
Maker unknown. Berks County, Pennsylvania. c. 1890.

Comment
Most early Mennonite quilts that were made of wool have not survived. The natural dyes in the early pieces caused the fabrics to disintegrate with time. The cotton fabric and vibrant colors in this piece indicate that it was probably made in the late 19th or early 20th century, when such fabrics became widely available.

Hints for Collectors
It is best not to hang a quilt from the same side for any length of time. Too much stress is put on the fabric, and eventually the fibers will stretch and the fabric may rip or become distorted. To be hung properly, a quilt should be stretched and mounted on all 4 sides on a frame made specifically for that quilt. The bedcover may then be easily rotated and the weight evenly distributed.

Price Guide Group: Amish and Mennonite Quilts.

Courtesy America Hurrah Antiques, New York City.

Variable Star

Description
Pieced crib quilt. 12 blocks with eight-pointed stars in blue print alternate with 13 one-piece blocks in pink, green, and white print. 2 narrow pink frames, then sawtooth frame in 2 blue prints. Border pink-and-white floral print. Embroidered initials "JTM" in center of sawtooth border on one side. Pale blue-and-white printed binding.

Materials, Quilting, and Dimensions
Cotton and polyester. One-patch blocks have quilted and stuffed feathered wreaths. Outer border with chevron quilting. 38″ × 38″.

Maker, Locality, and Period
Judith Tasker Mount. Flintridge, California. 1978.

Comment
According to the maker, it took about 250 hours to cut, piece, quilt, and stuff this bedcover. The quilted feathered wreaths were stuffed from the back, using the blunt end of a large-eyed tapestry needle to "spin small pieces of cotton bat" into the space between the quilt top and backing. While contemporary quiltmakers often use 19th-century patterns, few of these quilts have the fine stitching and time-consuming stuffed work seen in this piece.

Hints for Collectors
This quilt, with its excellent needlework, might easily be taken for a much earlier example. However, the combination of cotton and polyester fabric (identifiable by its texture and look) is a clue that it was made fairly recently.

Price Guide Group: Crib Quilts.

Courtesy Museum of American Folk Art, New York City.

Eight-Pointed Star

Description
Pieced quilt. Full and partial eight-pointed star blocks set on diagonal in variety of printed fabrics including green-and-red plaid, florals, red-and-brown stripes, and black with small red nosegays. Blocks separated by zigzag configuration in print of gray-and-brown scrolls accented with flower bouquets outlined in white. Border in same fabric. Cut out for four-poster bed. Narrow print binding.

Materials, Quilting, and Dimensions
Cotton, glazed and unglazed. Unquilted. 109½″ × 102″.

Maker, Locality, and Period
Maker unknown. New Hampshire. c. 1840.

Comment
Star patterns, some common and some one-of-a-kind, number in the hundreds. The eight-pointed star alone has many variations, including the Braced Star, with a diamond-shaped center, and the LeMoyne Star, called Lemon Star in New England, in which each point is made of 2 triangles of alternating colors. Other eight-pointed star patterns include Evening Star, Variable Star, Ohio Star, and the Lone or Texas Star. The example illustrated combines 2 different patterns: some of the stars have a single piece for the central square, and others have 2.

Hints for Collectors
Made to fit a four-poster bed, the cutouts at the bottom of this quilt were probably done sometime after the piece was finished, since they cut off part of several stars. Early repairs or changes like the cutouts seen here are less serious than more recent alterations, such as the addition of a new binding.

Price Guide Group: Star Quilts.

Courtesy Kelter-Malcé Antiques, New York City.

133 Album

Description
Pieced quilt. 85 blocks set diagonally in grid, each with six-pointed star. Each block signed. Small pen and ink drawing within stars. Stars predominantly red, blue, orange, brown, and green prints. Grid printed fabric in brown, blue, and white. Inner border gradational blue-green print with red pattern. Outer border on 3 sides printed fabric in brown, pink, and green. Green-and-yellow geometric print binding on 3 sides.

Materials, Quilting, and Dimensions
Cotton. Block quilting in central area. 82½″ × 82″.

Maker, Locality, and Period
Several quiltmakers. Philadelphia, Pennsylvania. c. 1830–50.

Comment
It is rare to find several quilts, especially early ones, by the same makers. This quilt, however, is very like another album quilt from Philadelphia and is made from similar materials. It has many of the same signatures of members of the Scattergood, Cresson, and Savery families of Philadelphia. The fabrics used—ribbon and scroll prints in reds, blues, greens, and browns, many with flower sprays—are typical of the period from 1830 to 1850.

Hints for Collectors
A quilt like this is an important historical record, both for its signatures and for the small pen and ink drawings indicative of the tastes and attitudes of the period. Despite their historical importance, early quilts can sometimes be bought for less than newer pieces with greater visual appeal.

Price Guide Group: Star Quilts.

Courtesy Ruth Bigel Antiques, New York City.

Album

Description
Pieced quilt. 49 blocks in grid, each with six-pointed star surrounding white hexagon containing signature and, in some, small pen and ink drawing. Stars predominantly dark brown, blue, green, and deep red prints. Grid of 2 multicolored printed fabrics. Inner and outer borders and binding same dark-hued prints as grid. Dated. Brown print binding.

Materials, Quilting, and Dimensions
Cotton. Stars have outline quilting. Border and grid with diamond quilting. 83¼" × 79½".

Maker, Locality, and Period
Maker unknown. Philadelphia, Pennsylvania. 1844.

Comment
Generally, album quilt blocks were made and signed by a number of different people as a remembrance, just as the pages of a photograph album would have been. Presentation quilts, given to a minister or teacher who was moving away, and Friendship quilts, worked by one's friends, were 2 common types of album quilts. The example shown, with men's and women's names and inscriptions like "Forget me not" and "Remember me," was probably made for a departing friend.

Hints for Collectors
The printed fabrics used for the stars on this quilt were cut so carefully that there are 6 small flowers per star, one in each of its 6 points. Such consistently fine workmanship, along with the detailed pen and ink drawings, mark this bedcover as a very valuable album quilt. This consistency implies that it may have been made by only one person, as album quilts sometimes were.

Price Guide Group: Star Quilts.

Courtesy Museum of American Folk Art, New York City.

Patriotic Quilts

Ever since the Revolutionary War patriotic themes and motifs have been featured on bedcovers. These spreads have portrayed love of one's country and celebrated American heroes. Quilts in this section generally date from the very early part of the 19th century to the mid–20th century.

For obvious reasons, quilts with patriotic themes became more prevalent during periods of national emergency or celebration. For example, quilts featuring the American eagle enjoyed wide popularity from the late 1780s until the 1840s and then declined, only to be revived again during the Civil War. In the 1930s when quiltmaking kits became fashionable, eagles and other patriotic motifs reappeared in stylized forms. The many bedcovers represented in this section include a Liberty Quilt, popular from revolutionary days until the late 1840s (143), a quilt that commemorates the Century of Progress Exhibition in 1933 (146), and a bedcover that documents America's role in the Second World War (145).

It was not unusual for a quiltmaker either to piece or appliqué representational motifs such as emblems, shields, or stars; sometimes a real American flag was used as the central design element (139). George Washington and Abraham Lincoln were popular historical figures and are found on early patriotic quilts, while modern quiltmakers have incorporated figures such as Franklin D. Roosevelt and Winston Churchill (145) into their designs. Patriotic slogans are another popular feature, with such phrases as "E Pluribus Unum," "Victory is Our Goal," and "Remember Pearl Harbor."

Because patriotic motifs and overall designs are not particularly complex, these quilts are often embellished with an extensively quilted ground and border. But the appeal of these bedcovers lies beyond their beauty. They can be important social documents illustrating the political sentiments of an era.

135 Flag

Description
Pieced quilt. 130 small, square, one-starred, red, white, and blue flags alternating from horizontal to vertical positions. Blue binding.

Materials, Quilting, and Dimensions
Cotton. Unquilted. 76″ × 62″.

Maker, Locality, and Period
Maker unknown. New York State. c. 1910.

Comment
Although actual flags were sometimes used for the top of a quilt, the flag motifs in this bedcover were arduously pieced by the maker. The stripes are arranged to form a kind of basketweave pattern; the placement of the stars is less consistent. For example, in the top row 3 of the vertically striped flags have the star in the lower left corner, while 2 have it in the lower right.

Hints for Collectors
Bedcovers with American flag designs are much in demand by collectors, and although the flag motif was very popular, they are becoming increasingly rare. Many date from around the time of the Centennial in 1876 or the Bicentennial in 1976, but they were also made as an expression of pride when a quiltmaker's state joined the Union. In rare instances, the number of stars included in the design indicates the number of states in the Union when the quilt was made. More often, however, the number is arbitrary.

Price Guide Group: Patriotic Quilts.

Courtesy America Hurrah Antiques, New York City.

.36 Goose in the Pond

Description
Pieced quilt. 9 blocks constructed of triangles, small nine-patch squares, and stripes creating Goose in the Pond pattern. Predominantly red and blue on white ground. Each block separated by grid of 4 red and 3 white stripes, intersecting in checkered blocks of 49 blue and white squares. Framed by red and white stripes, with blue and white nine-patch at each corner, and blue and white checkered rectangular blocks at ends of grid. White inner border. Red outer border. Red binding.

Materials, Quilting, and Dimensions
Cotton. Goose in the Pond blocks with square quilting. Remaining areas with diagonal quilting. 76″ × 76″.

Maker, Locality, and Period
Maker unknown. Ohio. c. 1895.

Comment
Although a variation of Goose in the Pond—also called Young Man's Fancy—the colors of this bedcover suggest it was meant to be patriotic. The grid is much more complicated than is common, having 7 stripes rather than the usual single stripe between the blocks. Unlike quilts created from fragments of fabric saved in the ever-present rag-bag, this quilt was undoubtedly pieced with materials bought especially for it.

Hints for Collectors
With its immediate visual appeal, this quilt would be likely to attract collectors of contemporary art. In fact, pieces with a strong graphic quality like this one have been largely responsible for the revival of interest in quilts in the 1970s and 1980s.

Price Guide Group: Patriotic Quilts.

Courtesy America Hurrah Antiques, New York City.

137 Kansas Baby

Description
Pieced and appliquéd crib quilt. Central five-pointed blue star embroidered with the word "Baby" and white floral sprigs and surrounded by 35 stars, also in white embroidery. Ground red and white stripes. Blue border with embroidered white stars. White binding.

Materials, Quilting, and Dimensions
Hand-dyed homespun cotton. Stripes quilted in parallel lines. Stars surrounded by fine outline quilting. Embroidery. 36⅞" × 36¾".

Maker, Locality, and Period
Maker unknown. Kansas. c. 1860.

Comment
A charming example of the patriotic quilt, this simple piece has many of the qualities of fine folk art. The word "Baby" has been carefully embroidered in a fine script embellished with small flowers and set on a star against a background of stripes, bringing together both the personal and the patriotic.

Hints for Collectors
This quilt is particularly desirable for its patriotic theme, its small size, and its excellent condition. While many crib quilts were made, few survived the repeated washings necessary with constant use. However, some crib quilts were made for show, to be used only on special occasions when the maker may have had visitors into her home. Show quilts often remained in good condition and are highly desirable finds.

Price Guide Group: Crib Quilts.

Friendship Flag

Description
Pieced quilt. Made in shape of flag with red and white stripes and 45 white stars on pale brown field. Embroidered place name and date also on pale brown field. Embroidered signatures in red on white stripes and border, and white on red stripes. Dated. White border. White binding.

Materials, Quilting, and Dimensions
Cotton. Brown area quilted in diagonal and parallel lines creating radiating diamond. Stripes and border quilted in diagonal lines. Embroidery. 84″ × 74″.

Maker, Locality, and Period
Maker unknown. Beatrice, Nebraska. August 18, 1899.

Comment
Probably made by one person, this quilt contains an exceptionally large number of names. It was most likely a friendship or presentation quilt, given to a teacher or minister who was moving away. While such quilts were fairly common, it is extraordinary to see so many signatures, 440 in all, suggesting that the person for whom the quilt was made was well known and important. Quilts were generally signed either with pen and ink or embroidered. As in many signature quilts, the names here all appear to have been embroidered by the same hand.

Hints for Collectors
Documented quilts like this one are usually of greatest interest to collectors concerned with history. Unfortunately, they tend to be less exciting visually than abstract designs. This example, however, is unusual in that it has both visual appeal and historic interest, a combination that makes it quite valuable.

Price Guide Group: Patriotic Quilts.

Courtesy America Hurrah Antiques, New York City.

Description
Pieced, appliquéd, and stuffed crib quilt. Appliquéd American flag slightly folded and attached to beige flagpole on white ground. Blue border scalloped on inner edge. Blue binding.

Materials, Quilting, and Dimensions
Cotton. Background quilted in large diamonds. Flagpole and rope stuffed. Flagpole has large hanging tassel. 51″ × 31″.

Maker, Locality, and Period
Maker unknown. New England. c. 1940.

Comment
A unique modern quilt, extensively stuffed and appliquéd to appear three-dimensional, this is a good example of how cleverly a quiltmaker can create a novel effect. The flag has been folded and appliquéd onto the top, and the upper part of the flagpole carefully stuffed, while the lower part hangs free of the quilt and ends in a large, knotted tassel. Slightly larger than most crib quilts, the quilt illustrated may have been used for an older child's bed, or simply as a decorative throw.

Hints for Collectors
Only recently, as 19th- and early 20th-century examples have become increasingly more difficult to find, have collectors become seriously interested in modern quilts. A highly original and playful quilt like this one is the kind of quilt worth buying and holding on to. As with furniture of the 1940s and 1950s, prices are very reasonable, and examples can still be found at yard sales and thrift shops.

Price Guide Group: Crib Quilts.

Courtesy Kelter-Malcé Antiques, New York City.

Description
Pieced and appliquéd quilt. 13 American flags, arranged in 3 rows of 3 and 2 rows of 2, each with 36 stars. 4 red, white, and blue shields, one at each end of shorter flag rows. White ground. White border. Red binding.

Materials, Quilting, and Dimensions
Cotton. Unquilted. Embroidered white stars. 84″ × 82½″.

Maker, Locality, and Period
Maker and locality unknown. c. 1900.

Comment
Quilters have used patriotic motifs to decorate their bedcovers ever since this country began. Eagles, shields, flags—sometimes giving a clue to a quilt's date in the number of their stars—were all popular symbols. Made around 1900, this bedcover expresses a feeling of pure American patriotism. Simple in concept, its orderly arrangement of flags and strong use of color suggest a military feeling. Although quilt tops are rarely devoted entirely to military themes, some depict historical figures who have been associated with American military actions. During the Second World War many victory quilts were made, often depicting the friendship among the Allied powers.

Hints for Collectors
While not to everyone's taste, a quilt like this is an important piece of Americana. It would probably appeal to anyone collecting textiles or other folk-art forms that express Americans' love of country. Collectors should seek out objects that have similar themes and motifs because they are generally considered more valuable when sold as a collection than separately.

Price Guide Group: Patriotic Quilts.

Private Collection.

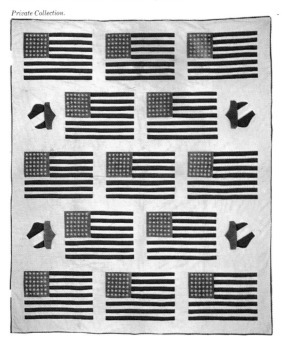

Description
Pieced quilt. Central red, white, and blue six-pointed star, surrounded by 6 smaller six-pointed stars in same colors with white predominant. In each corner, small American flag set diagonally. Date embroidered at center bottom. Frame of red, white, and blue diagonal stripes. Border white. White binding.

Materials, Quilting, and Dimensions
Cotton. Stars and flags with outline quilting in white. Ground and blue part of flags have diamond quilting. Border quilted in rope design. White stars on flags embroidered. 76″ × 76″.

Maker, Locality, and Period
Maker unknown. Ohio. 1928.

Comment
The use of a traditional pattern in combination with American flags is unusual. It is interesting to compare the carelessly stitched date and the somewhat awkwardly pieced flags with the precisely cut and pieced starbursts.

Hints for Collectors
When buying a quilt, always ask for the provenance. It may be invaluable in tracing the maker, or in finding out where and when the quilt was made. Quilts were not necessarily made in the state in which they were found. Families moved frequently, especially in the late 19th century when successive waves of people went west. If known, the name given a quilt by its maker may be a clue to period and locality, as quilt patterns frequently went by different names in different eras and areas of the country.

Price Guide Group: Patriotic Quilts.

Courtesy America Hurrah Antiques, New York City.

Eagles with Cigars

Description
Pieced and appliquéd quilt. Central eight-pointed star surrounded by 2 circles with sawtooth edges, all red on white ground. 4 yellow, red, and tan eagles with cigars in beaks surround central motif. Outstretched wings form overall diamond. 16 eight-pointed red stars, 4 surrounding central motif, 3 in each corner. Triple sawtooth border in red, yellow and beige. White binding.

Materials, Quilting, and Dimensions
Cotton. Eagles quilted in parallel lines. Outline quilting around medallions, eagles, and sawtooth border. White ground and red stars with diamond quilting. 102″ × 97″.

Maker, Locality, and Period
Maker and locality unknown. c. 1850.

Comment
The eagle was a popular motif from Revolutionary times through the mid–19th century. This particular design was sold in kit form from the mid–19th century until around the time of the Centennial and turns up fairly frequently, often with some individual touches. This example has particularly fine quilting stitches, especially on the eagles' feathers and bodies.

Hints for Collectors
Both patriotic and humorous, this quilt is especially desirable as a collector's piece. Made in fairly large numbers, it is often found in good condition, probably because it was made as a "show" quilt. The triple sawtooth border is an unusual feature, and makes this quilt large enough for a king-size bed.

Price Guide Group: Patriotic Quilts.

Courtesy George E. Schoellkopf Gallery, New York City.

E Pluribus Unum

Description
Appliquéd quilt. 5 large eagles in blue-and-white print; each grasps in its beak banner embroidered "E PLURIBUS UNUM." Eagles wear blue-and-white shield and grasp branch in right talons. Small eight-pointed blue-and-white print stars surround eagles and are scattered over top. Doves, crescents, and hearts flank central eagle. One dove, initials, and date at bottom. White binding.

Materials, Quilting, and Dimensions
Cotton. Eagles quilted in parallel lines. Shields and ground with diamond quilting. Embroidered details. 75" × 67".

Maker, Locality, and Period
Initialed LW. Pennsylvania. 1844.

Comment
The eagle was adopted as a national symbol over the objections of Benjamin Franklin, who felt the turkey far more appropriate since it signified peace and prosperity, rather than war. In the decorative arts, the eagle seems to have gone out of fashion in the 1840s, only to have been revived again during the Civil War for use on what were called Union quilts.

Hints for Collectors
Patriotic quilts enjoyed a renewed period of popularity during the 1930s; many of these quilts are dated. In cases where they are not, the age of the materials and quality of the quilting are good clues to whether the quilt is mid–19th century or much later. In general, the finer the stitching, the earlier the piece.

Price Guide Group: Patriotic Quilts.

Courtesy America Hurrah Antiques, New York City.

Framed Center Eagle

Description

Appliquéd quilt. Floral chintz appliqués on white ground. Central diamond with inner sawtooth edge encloses eagle patterned in red, green, and yellow beneath 24 five-pointed stars. Innermost square border with sawtooth edge frames central diamond and 4 abstract designs, 1 in each corner of square. Surrounded by multiple chintz borders, with sawtooth, garland, and swag motifs. Outermost border sawtooth-edged. White binding.

Materials, Quilting, and Dimensions

Cotton and chintz. Remarkable stitching and stuffed work. Diamond quilting on eagle. In central section, 8 quilted pineapple motifs as well as leaf and floral quilting. Borders with shell quilting and stuffed leaves; also acorns, stuffed grapes, and original quilting motifs. 108″ × 108″.

Maker, Locality, and Period

Maker unknown. New England. c. 1810.

Comment

Cotton chintz was scarce and very expensive in the 18th and early 19th centuries. Appliquéing small pieces of it onto a plain, often homespun, ground was an economical way to create a beautiful quilt top.

Hints for Collectors

The example illustrated is highly desirable because of its great beauty, extraordinary stitching, and age. This type of quilt is very rare, and the kind of museum-quality piece that only occasionally appears on the market.

Price Guide Group: Patriotic Quilts.

Courtesy America Hurrah Antiques, New York City.

Victory Quilt

Description
Pieced and appliquéd quilt. Central portion 8 blue Vs enclosing motifs that include 2 hands shaking, representing America and Great Britain; portraits of Stalin, Churchill, Roosevelt, and MacArthur; and children saluting the flag. Inscribed "VICTORY IS OUR GOAL" beneath eagle shown ripping apart Nazi and Japanese flags. At top, inscribed "REMEMBER PEARL HARBOR," flanked by 3 flowers. 3 dots and 1 dash above the Vs for the letter "V" (for victory) in Morse code. Inner frame red-and-white striped fabric with small five-pointed blue stars. Surrounding motifs include flags, crosses, and stars. Outer frame red. Inner border white. Outer border blue. No binding.

Materials, Quilting, and Dimensions
Cotton. Some outline stitching. Central section quilted in large and small stars. Inner frame in diagonal lines and outer frame and borders in stars. Embroidered details. 88″ × 74″.

Maker, Locality, and Period
Mrs. W. B. Lathouse. Warren, Ohio. c. 1941–45.

Comment
Mrs. Lathouse, the maker of this quilt, was a professional seamstress who came to America from Wales in 1922. A quilt like this one is important not only as a piece of textile art but also as a social document.

Hints for Collectors
Only recently have textile collectors begun to take serious notice of 20th-century quilts. Even now it is only those with handsome designs and fine quilting that command a substantial price. Original designs are usually very desirable.

Price Guide Group: Patriotic Quilts.

Courtesy America Hurrah Antiques, New York City.

Commemorative

Description
Appliquéd quilt. 3 central completed and partially completed portraits—George Washington, Franklin Delano Roosevelt and Abraham Lincoln—surrounded by various patriotic and domestic motifs. Below Washington, small ax and branch with 4 cherries. Below Lincoln, kneeling black man with unbound hands. Above portraits, 2 American flags flanking bald eagle, and beneath them a pastoral scene. Border motifs include car, zeppelin, airplane, and eight-pointed stars in each corner. Frame red. White inner border. Outer border blue with scalloped edge. Blue binding.

Materials, Quilting, and Dimensions
Cotton. Portraits surrounded by quilted double circle enclosing vine motif. Central area quilted in running double diamonds that enclose hearts, anchors, and crosses; red frame in plant motifs; white inner border in stars; blue binding in spirals. Embroidered inscriptions and details. 82″ × 66″.

Maker, Locality, and Period
Mrs. W. B. Lathouse. Warren, Ohio. 1933.

Comment
This quilt commemorated the Century of Progress Exhibition in 1933. It is unfinished, for the details of Roosevelt's face are missing. Nevertheless, this is an exceptional quilt because of its fine work and elaborately detailed motifs.

Hints for Collectors
Although quilts with patriotic themes were very popular, those that have the kind of detail seen here have usually been kept in the maker's family as prized possessions.

Price Guide Group: Patriotic Quilts.

Courtesy America Hurrah Antiques, New York City.

Thematic Quilts

These bedcovers either commemorate a specific event or
incorporate pictorial elements to create unusual patterns. In the
chronology of quilting, thematic quilts are relatively recent: they
have been made from the late 19th century to the present day.
Their construction relies on common quiltmaking techniques,
including piecing and appliquéing, simple quilting stitches,
embroidery, and, to some extent, stuffed work. The quilts shown
here depict many different subjects ranging from events in a
maker's life (149) to religious verses (153) and the alphabet (151);
the latter two types were probably used for teaching a young girl
her letters and quilting techniques. Although most of the quilts
are original designs, one example (150) was made from a kit, a
common practice in the early 20th century.

Two unusual Hawaiian pictorial quilts are also included here
(147, 148). Until sewing was introduced to the islands in 1820,
the natives relied on bedcovers made from the steeped and
beaten bark of the mulberry tree, but by 1838 Hawaiian women
were producing their own beautifully crafted quilts. Their
designs were either based on floral or fruit forms or reflected the
island's history and myths.

Another notable, although uncommon, variation that appears in
this section is a quilt that has been pieced with parts of clothing
(155). This example is particularly interesting because the
maker has used vests and ties to create an eight-pointed
star.

Some of the most fascinating textiles in this section are
contemporary quilts. During the past 20 years, artists
throughout the country have once again become interested in
making handcrafted textiles. The best contemporary artists are
both innovative and traditional. Unlike functional spreads made
in past decades, contemporary quilts are rarely intended to be
used as bedcovers, but are meant to be displayed and judged as
works of art.

My Beloved Flag

Description
Pieced and appliquéd quilt. Central scene depicts 2 figures in
native dress guarding symbol of Hawaiian monarchy, over which
float stylized curtains and a crown. On either side of crown are
words "KUUHAE ALOHA." Predominantly red, white, and blue.
Border created by joining 4 Hawaiian flags. Red binding.

Materials, Quilting, and Dimensions
Cotton. Center scene and inscription with outline stitching.
Border quilted in diamonds. 90½″ × 84½″.

Maker, Locality, and Period
Maker unknown. Hawaiian Islands. Before 1918.

Comment
On April 3, 1820, Mrs. Lucy Thurston, an American missionary,
wrote in her diary: "Kalakua, Queen dowager, was directress.
The women of rank were furnished with calico patchwork to
sew." And so began what was probably the first quiltmaking
done in Hawaii. Sewing, which was previously unknown to the
islands, evolved according to a rigid social scheme: only the
aristocratic and royal families were allowed to participate. The
rest of the island's inhabitants continued to make their clothing
and bedding by steeping and beating the bark of mulberry trees,
which produced a parchmentlike cloth called "tapa." Flag
patterns are popular quilting patterns in Hawaii. The national
flag was taken down for 2 months in 1893, and during that time
women made flag quilts as an expression of their strong national
pride.

Hints for Collectors
Early Hawaiian quilts rarely appear in the marketplace. Even
modern Hawaiian bedcovers are uncommon.

Price Guide Group: Hawaiian Quilts.

Courtesy Honolulu Academy of Arts, Honolulu, Hawaii.

148 Gardens of Eden and Elenale

Description
Appliquéd quilt. Design of 2 equal divisions. Left side 2 figures in royal court dress: crowned man dressed in red and yellow with word "ELENALE" above him faces woman in brown and red dress crowned by word "LEINAALA" and abstract pink tree. Above scene are words "KE APO O KE KAUOHA." Right side Adam and Eve in Garden of Eden, under tree bearing heart-shaped fruit in red, pink, and dark brown. Above tree angel with red wings reads from brown-and-yellow book. Crowning angel are words "MAHI NAAI O EDENA." White ground. Both sections framed by plant and floral motifs, left predominantly yellow with red accents and right predominantly red with yellow accents. Yellow binding with fringe on 3 sides.

Materials, Quilting, and Dimensions
Cotton. White ground with shell quilting. Motifs with outline stitching. 92″ × 78½″.

Maker, Locality, and Period
Maker unknown. Hawaiian Islands. c. 1910–18.

Comment
The full name of this quilt, "Na Kihapai Nani Lua 'Ole O Edena a Me Elenale," translates as "The Beautiful Unequaled Gardens of Eden and Elenale." The male figure is identified as Elenale and the female as Leinaala, the principal characters in a Hawaiian romance popular in the late 19th century.

Hints for Collectors
Early Hawaiian quilts have original and strikingly colored designs, predominantly in red and white. Templates or paper patterns frequently served as guides for the designs.

Price Guide Group: Hawaiian Quilts.

Courtesy Honolulu Academy of Arts, Honolulu, Hawaii.

Description
Appliquéd quilt. 20 blocks with red, gold, and faded green appliqués. Double block in center depicts red, gold, white, and pink mounted hunters and dogs. Large variety of common motifs (pineapple, trees, flowers, horses, hearts), unique designs (parlor lamp, hand with ringed index finger, gold anchor with stars, and oak leaves), and related hunting scenes (tied horse surrounded by 4 dogs, hunter in forest with his dog). Linked chain border of red, gold, beige, and pink. Red binding.

Materials, Quilting, and Dimensions
Cotton. Quilted in undulating lines, echoing design motifs. 88″ × 70″.

Maker, Locality, and Period
Edith Seaman. Long Island, New York. c. 1870.

Comment
While some brides' quilts have only a heart, this one has several motifs associated with marriage, including the pineapple for hospitality, the red hearts, and the hand with a wedding ring prominently displayed. As with many pictorial quilts, the images are drawn from the personal experience of the quiltmaker. We know that the 3 men on horseback were the bride's father, brother, and fiancé. One might guess that the crystal lamp was intended for the couple's new home.

Hints for Collectors
Because the origins of most quilts and the identities of most quiltmakers are unknown, any information about the maker, the provenance, or the significance of a unique design is of historic importance. Such documentation also increases the quilt's value.

Price Guide Group: Pictorial Quilts.

Courtesy America Hurrah Antiques, New York City.

Sunbonnet Sue

Description
Pieced and appliquéd quilt. 36 blocks, each containing appliquéd figure in profile wearing bonnet and carrying purse or umbrella. Each figure created from variety of solid-color and printed fabrics, including checks, plaids, and floral patterns. Predominantly brown, blue, and yellow. White ground. White border. Scalloped outer edge. Red printed binding.

Materials, Quilting, and Dimensions
Cotton. Diamond quilting across ground; rope motif in border. 76″ × 74″.

Maker, Locality, and Period
Maker and locality unknown. c. 1920.

Comment
This bedcover could have been made anywhere in the United States, for by 1920 printed patterns were widely available by mail order and in popular ladies' magazines like *Woman's Home Companion* and *The Modern Priscilla*. Bertha L. Corbett, author of *Sunbonnet Babies* (1900), has been credited with the creation of this design.

Hints for Collectors
With increasing interest in 1920s and 1930s furniture and decorative arts, quilts of this period are in turn becoming more popular. However, they can still be purchased for significantly less than their 19th-century counterparts. They are recognizable by their distinctive pastel colors, including solids in peach, turquoise, purple, pink, and yellow, as well as brightly colored prints, usually on a white ground.

Price Guide Group: Pictorial Quilts.

Courtesy America Hurrah Antiques, New York City.

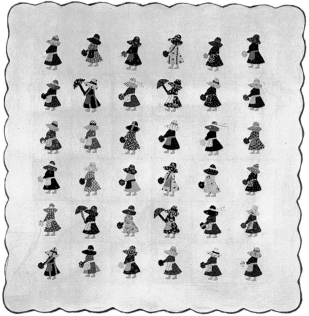

Alphabet

Description
Pieced and appliquéd quilt. White blocks set on diagonal with letters of complete alphabet in colored fabrics, alternating with diagonally set blocks of blue-and-white print. 4 lower blocks incorporate date as part of design element. 3 sides of frame contain gold stars and 4th side incorporates maker's name as part of design. Blue-and-white printed border. No binding.

Materials, Quilting, and Dimensions
Cotton. Unquilted. 88″ × 79″.

Maker, Locality, and Period
Elva Smith. New York State. 1896.

Comment
This quilt is a marvel of curious inconsistencies beginning with the reversed S in both the alphabet and the maker's name. Notice that to solve the problem of symmetry with a 26-letter alphabet, the seamstress incorporated the completion date within the central design; then, as if to amplify upon this unusual detail, she used her name for part of the star-filled frame. These inconsistencies betray the hand of a young child, perhaps learning not only the alphabet but also the art of quilting.

Hints for Collectors
The colors of this quilt remain crisp and bright; if it were not dated, it would be tempting to think that the quilt was made long after 1896. Even without its date, an experienced collector could establish its true age by examining the printed fabrics and thread.

Price Guide Group: Pictorial Quilts.

Courtesy America Hurrah Antiques, New York City.

Sampler

Description
Pieced quilt. Central rectangle with pieced initials, date, and design elements, including diamonds and small nine-patch blocks in blue-and-white printed fabric; frame of faded blue-and-white printed fabric with faded pink and blue cross motif and triangular corner pieces in pale blue-and-white printed fabric. Central frame surrounded by faded pink eight-pointed stars alternating with pale blue-and-white one-patch blocks. Outer frame consists of faded pink and blue-and-white printed fabric, with corner squares of brown-and-white printed fabric. Inner border has pieced herringbone design of blue, brown, and white printed bars on ground of pale blue-and-white. Top edge of bedcover has outer border in faded blue-and-white, while bottom and sides have solid white border. Brown-and-yellow printed binding.

Materials, Quilting, and Dimensions
Cotton. Central section teacup quilting. Inner border quilted in diamond motif; outer border quilted in undulating wave pattern. 92″ × 86″.

Maker, Locality, and Period
Initialed "H.D.B." New Paltz, New York. 1807.

Comment
It is rare to find an early 19th-century quilt documented with initials and a date. Because the details of the central design are similar to patterns found on samplers, this textile may be related to the sampler tradition.

Hints for Collectors
Beware of dates on textiles when they are associated with initials; the date may refer to the birth date of the maker or an historic event, and not to the year the bedcover was made.

Price Guide Group: Pictorial Quilts.

Courtesy America Hurrah Antiques, New York City.

153 Lord's Prayer

Description
Pieced quilt. Red hexagonal pieces on white ground spell out first part of Lord's Prayer. Text underlined with beige hexagonal lines. Scalloped edge. Red binding.

Materials, Quilting, and Dimensions
Cotton. Central portion quilted in diagonal lines. Border quilted in parallel lines perpendicular to edge of quilt. 74″ × 68″.

Maker, Locality, and Period
Maker and locality unknown. c. 1875.

Comment
Alphabet quilts provided a unique opportunity for the young seamstress to create a visually pleasing textile and learn her alphabet at the same time. Other variations include quilts with single letters, the entire alphabet, the maker's name, popular sayings, or biblical verse. The quilt illustrated is particularly fine, for the hexagons are very small, the quilting precise, and the border carefully finished.

Hints for Collectors
Collectors interested in samplers are often attracted to alphabet quilts, for both played a part in the education of children in 19th-century America. Although any form of an alphabet quilt is fairly rare, the Lord's Prayer variation is especially so, and for that reason very valuable. As with any quilt, the better the stitching and condition, the greater the value. In addition, the example shown is notable for its folk art quality, seen in the backward Ns and the way words are arbitrarily divided from one line to the next.

Price Guide Group: Pictorial Quilts.

Courtesy America Hurrah Antiques, New York City.

154

The Gingham Dog and the Calico Cat

Description
Appliquéd and pieced crib quilt. Appliquéd dog in red-and-white checked gingham with brown fabric spots; appliquéd cat in blue-and-white calico. White ground. Embroidered inscription. Blue-and-white calico border with red-and-white checked gingham corner squares. No binding.

Materials, Quilting, and Dimensions
Cotton. Large diamond quilting in central field. Dog and cat figures have embroidered faces. 34⅝″ × 28⅜″.

Maker, Locality, and Period
Maker unknown. Probably Pennsylvania. c. 1910.

Comment
The pieced crib quilt is generally a small version of a full-size bedcover, with everything reduced in scale. The appliquéd crib quilt, however, tends to have larger motifs and to be more playful and decorative. Here the visual impact of the distinctive dog and cat motif is made stronger by the blue and red outside border and the addition of an embroidered inscription.

Hints for Collectors
The blue-and-white calico used for the body of the cat and the border is typical of late 19th- and early 20th-century appliquéd quilts. They were often embellished with embroidery in an attempt to produce a bedcover that was visually striking and yet able to withstand constant use. Each part of the quilt, including the top, stitching, and colors used, is important in attempting to determine its age. While none of these parts may individually suggest a date, together they may point to a particular period.

Price Guide Group: Crib Quilts.

Courtesy Museum of American Folk Art, New York City.

155 Vest Collage

Description
Appliquéd quilt. 8 black vests sewn to off-white ground form circular pattern. 8 men's neckties in prints, stripes, and solid colors form eight-pointed star of radiating arrowlike motifs. Placement of armholes creates internal design of star, and each vest also forms arms of larger star. Off-white binding.

Materials, Quilting, and Dimensions
Cotton. Wool vests with buttons and pocket welts. Rayon ties. Center of quilt stitched with eight-pointed star. White ground with diamond quilting. 82″ × 62″.

Maker, Locality, and Period
Mrs. Lewis Rogers. Gordon, Texas. 1940.

Comment
During the late 19th and early 20th centuries, imaginative needlewomen occasionally incorporated actual pieces of wearing apparel into the design of their bedcovers. Quilts embellished with bathing suits, women's underwear, women's hats, and even women's longstockings are known. The example illustrated is out of the ordinary, however, because the vests have been appliquéd to create a common quiltmaking motif—the eight-pointed star.

Hints for Collectors
Because few quilts that integrate wearing apparel have reached the marketplace, there is no real guide to an accurate evaluation of their worth. Since the antique quilt market fluctuates with supply and demand, the price for any unique textile is determined by what a buyer is prepared to spend.

Price Guide Group: Pictorial Quilts.

Courtesy America Hurrah Antiques, New York City.

Description
Pieced quilt. 16 central blocks composed of solid gray, black, and black and white pin stripes, with blue highlights. Large intersecting grid created by 5 black and white vertical bars and 5 brown and white horizontal bars. Teal blue ground. Teal blue border. Blue binding.

Materials, Quilting, and Dimensions
Cotton. Ground quilted with large diamond motif and diagonal and parallel line quilting. 80″ × 74″.

Maker, Locality, and Period
Molly Upton. Locality unknown. 1975.

Comment
Ms. Upton's work is a good example of a new group of professionally trained artists who work with modern images through traditional media. Upton has created a work based on the aesthetic principles of Op Art, a style popular among visual artists in the Northeast during the late 1960s and early 1970s. Although we know that the quilt is flat and 2-dimensional, the open-ended grid seems to hover over the black and white blocks as they recede into the surface of the quilt.

Hints for Collectors
Although the example illustrated is a quilt, it would not be classified with antique American textiles of the 19th and early 20th centuries. Contemporary textiles are often regarded as pieces of visual art, and the market for them is related to the market for contemporary art. Prices are therefore compatible with those of paintings, rather than those of antique textiles.

Price Guide Group: Pictorial Quilts.

Private Collection.

Description
Pieced and appliquéd quilt. Central scene depicts spires of
Coutances Cathedral composed of printed and solid-color fabrics;
predominantly brown, blue, and gray. Pale blue ground. Maroon
printed frame. Navy-blue inner border. Outer border magenta.
Blue binding.

Materials, Quilting, and Dimensions
Cotton. Tufting and outline stitching. 76″ × 72″.

Maker, Locality, and Period
Susan Hoffman. New York City. 1975.

Comment
Although some contemporary quiltmakers like to recreate or
adapt traditional designs, others prefer to use the quilt top as a
painter would a canvas. In this quilt the artist has chosen to
create in fabric a picture of a favorite church, framing it with a
stained-glass-like pattern in cloth. Still, she also uses the
traditional elements of quiltmaking. In the example illustrated,
she has employed piecing, appliquéing, quilting, and even
tufting.

Hints for Collectors
Modern quilters have created all kinds of nontraditional designs,
using both representational and nonrepresentational forms. A
design like this one, done in a realistic style, must be seen from a
different perspective than the design of a typical 19th-century
piece constructed of hundreds of tiny diamonds, triangles, or
other geometric components.

Price Guide Group: Pictorial Quilts.

Collection of Sydney and Frances Lewis.

Description
Pieced and appliquéd quilt. Central scene depicts rocking chair, mirrored bureau, gray-and-white printed fabric floor, and red-and-white dotted fabric wallpaper. Surrounded by pictorial vignettes showing staircase with balustrade, windows, grand piano with black-and-red plaid top, wing chair, fireplace, and geometric carpet. Predominantly brown, red, black, pink, and blue, with many different dotted, striped, and patterned fabrics. Dark brown binding.

Materials, Quilting, and Dimensions
Satin, velvet, antique cotton and cotton blends, organdy, and wool. Machine appliquéd and quilted. 62" × 55".

Maker, Locality, and Period
Lee Farrington. Boston. 1981.

Comment
This quilt was created in the tradition of the commissioned portrait, for it was made at the request of a specific collector and depicts the interior of his home. Similar tones and a careful choice of fabrics have enabled the artist to create a unified effect even though she included a very wide range of motifs. Note the detail used in the central 5-sided area showing the bedroom. Not only are a bureau, a rocking chair, and a tall mirror shown, but so are the objects on the bureau.

Hints for Collectors
It is particularly difficult to assess the monetary worth of contemporary textiles, especially if the artist is not represented by a dealer or gallery. When encountering modern bedcovers, always inquire about their prices and you will eventually develop a sense for determining their fair market value.

Price Guide Group: Pictorial Quilts.

Private Collection.

159 Moonlit Doves

Description
Pieced and appliquéd quilt. Central portion of scene depicts avocado plant in pot on windowsill against checkerboard ground of dark green and brown-and-white print. Flanked by brown plaid tree with lime and dark green plant on left; on right by vertical strips of yellow, red, brown, and white plaids, checks, and prints. Window has arch in dark green. Partial eight-pointed star encloses 2 doves facing each other in flight. Upper portion of quilt is blue fabric with moonlike circular motifs. Triple border of pale brown, light brown, and black.

Materials, Quilting, and Dimensions
Cotton, cotton blends, and wool. Quilted and tufted. 84½″ × 84″.

Maker, Locality, and Period
Susan Hoffman and Molly Upton. Pennsylvania. 1970s.

Comment
This bedcover is part of a thematic "Pair Collection." The 2 artists collaborated in the designing, sewing, and quilting of the bedcover. Although there is a long tradition in America of collaboration on quilts—most obviously the quilting bee—it is rare to find contemporary artists working together on the same textile. Generally, one artist designs the textile, then contracts a fine seamstress to do all the sewing, piecing, and quilting.

Hints for Collectors
This quilt was meant to be hung like a painting, although it is large enough for a full-size bed. Particularly pleasing is the use of colored and patterned fabrics to reflect the colors of the objects they depict.

Price Guide Group: Pictorial Quilts.

Collection of Renée Guest.

Description
Pieced and appliquéd quilt. Scene depicts archway flanked by blue and white Doric columns with lime-green, yellow, and dark green plant capitals, and colored interior archway. Brown-and-gray plaids lead away from arch. Upper portion of scene pieced horizontally with yellows, browns, and blue bars; lower portion pieced with squares of pale blue stripes, and solid gray, tan, brown, and black. 2 potted plants in middleground, one bearing brown flowers. Predominantly blue, brown, and gray. Gray border. Pale blue binding.

Materials, Quilting, and Dimensions
Cotton, cotton blends, and wool. Pots quilted in blocks. Foreground squares quilted with diagonal lines forming X motif. 92″ × 80″.

Maker, Locality, and Period
Molly Upton and Susan Hoffman. Locality unknown. 1974.

Comment
Much of these artists' work is characterized by striking, clean design. Notice the strong geometric quality of this naturalistic image in direct contrast to more abstract work.

Hints for Collectors
While the American quilt was originally meant to be functional, few contemporary quilts are intended for use as bedcovers. Rather, many artists have taken traditional quiltmaking techniques and created works of art to be hung and enjoyed as one would fine paintings.

Price Guide Group: Pictorial Quilts.

Courtesy Mr. J. G. Upton.

Leaf, Vine, and Basket Quilts

Naturalistic motifs, such as flowers, leaves, and vines, have been favorite designs on textiles for centuries, and American quilts share this tradition. Most of the quilts in this section date from 1850, although examples with these types of motifs were created throughout the history of American quiltmaking. They were made in all parts of the continental United States as well as in Hawaii.

Generally, flowers, leaves, and baskets occupy the central portion of the quilt, while meandering, leafy vines are located in the border. The individual floral designs are stylizations of such common flowers as lilies, carnations, and roses.

Most of the quilts shown here are appliquéd, because this method is especially suited to curvilinear shapes like flowers and leaves. A design that employs forms with angular sides, such as baskets or sawtooth borders, is usually both pieced and appliquéd (176). Many of these quilts were originally constructed in blocks that were later stitched together to form the top (172, 174). The bedcovers illustrated here are also extensively quilted with complementary floral patterns, or the motifs themselves may be outline stitched to accentuate their design (172). Borders are frequently used, and they usually include a sawtooth pattern and a meandering vine (165, 175).

There also seems to be a preference for red and green fabrics. Unlike the materials used to make many other quilts, the fabrics for these naturalistic designs were often purchased especially for the quilt.

Because many of these naturalistic motifs were used throughout the country, the same design may have serveral different names. For instance, the California Rose (164) in yellow was often called the Texas Yellow Rose; the North Carolina Lily (172) was called the Wood Lily in northern New England, the Meadow Lily in Pennsylvania, and the Mountain Lily in Kentucky.

Description
Hawaiian appliquéd quilt. Yellow plant and flower motifs on white ground. An X of 4 large plant arms that meet at right angles to create central floral design. X surrounded by large wreath of leaves intersected on each side by fan of flowers. Yellow binding.

Materials, Quilting, and Dimensions
Cotton. Extensive outline stitching both outside and within motifs. 92¾″ × 86¼″.

Maker, Locality, and Period
Maker unknown. Hawaii. c. 1900–25.

Comment
This bedcover is typical of many of the quilts that were made on the Hawaiian Islands during the late 19th and early 20th centuries. Note the extensive outline stitching, the use of large floral motifs, and the simple color scheme. These Hawaiian quilts employed an unusual appliqué technique. A large piece of cloth was folded in half twice, then a design was cut out of the fabric. When the material was unfolded, the design of the appliqué emerged. Hawaiian quilts of the period were never made from scraps. Quilting was a privilege of the upper classes, and cottons were purchased for specific projects.

Hints for Collectors
Hawaiian quilts from this period are very rare. While a few have appeared in the Northeast in the past 10 years, the finest examples are already in museums. Particularly fine collections may be seen at the Honolulu Academy of Arts and the Bernice P. Bishop Museum of Hawaii.

Price Guide Group: Hawaiian Quilts.

Courtesy Bernice Pauahi Bishop Museum, Honolulu, Hawaii.

Description

Appliquéd quilt. Central square contains an X of 5 Whig Rose motifs, each motif consisting of 4 green double stems with gold and red flowers that radiate from central flower of red, yellow, and pink. Green sawtooth frame surrounded by red, yellow, and green meandering, flowering vine. White ground. White binding.

Materials, Quilting, and Dimensions

Cotton. Ground has floral quilting. 96½″ × 94¾″.

Maker, Locality, and Period

Maker unknown. Pennsylvania. c. 1870.

Comment

This pattern was originally called the Democratic Rose. It became the focal point of an argument between 2 early American political parties, the Whigs and the Democrats, each claiming the symbol for its own use. Throughout the history of American quiltmaking, the rose has been perhaps one of the most common motifs, and one dear to the quiltmaker. A quick count produces as many as 30 variations of the rose pattern. For some, the slightest change in a pattern will merit the creation of a new quilt name.

Hints for Collectors

Floral appliqués enjoyed wide popularity in the late 19th and early 20th centuries, but few of the many examples on the market have the clarity of design and color that this piece has. Such clear, bright colors are especially desirable, as is the fine cutting and skillful stitching of the individual pieces.

Price Guide Group: Floral Quilts.

Courtesy Museum of American Folk Art, New York City.

Grape Vineyard

Description
Appliquéd quilt. 6 groups of symmetrical, starlike lavender grape clusters with green vines and leaves, alternating with 6 white blocks. Grapevines join, creating diagonal lines that frame the quilted white blocks. Meandering green grapevine border with lavender grape clusters. All grapes stuffed. Corner edges rounded. White ground. Green binding.

Materials, Quilting, and Dimensions
Cotton. Grapes stuffed. White blocks quilted in circles enclosing grape and heart motifs. Quilted diagonal lines run from edge of blocks to outer edge of quilt. 92″ × 74″.

Maker, Locality, and Period
Maker and locality unknown. c. 1920.

Comment
This is a 20th-century version of an antique pattern. In the 1920s and 1930s, women's magazines began reproducing old patterns, and women everywhere repeated designs popular in the late 19th century. In the 1920s, most quiltmakers purchased fabric especially for quilts, rather than relying on remnants they had saved.

Hints for Collectors
Pastel fabrics were particularly popular with the quiltmaker between 1920 and 1940, and many quilts of the period are identifiable by their characteristic colors: pink, lavender, mint green, and turquoise. While these quilts are gaining in popularity, especially among collectors who want them for bedcovers, they are still considerably less expensive than 19th-century ones with bold, vibrant colors.

Price Guide Group: Floral Quilts.

Collection of Rhea Goodman.

California Rose

Description
Appliquéd quilt. 4 California Rose motifs; each motif consists of floral center with long stems, leaves, blossoms, and buds in red, orange, and green. Ground has red and gold stars, gold oak leaves, and red crescent-shaped motifs arranged around rose motifs. Border of red and gold flowers, crescent-shaped motifs, and gold octagons. White ground. Red binding.

Materials, Quilting, and Dimensions
Cotton. Ground quilted in diagonal lines. 82″ × 74″.

Maker, Locality, and Period
Maker unknown. New York State. c. 1860.

Comment
Color was an important factor in the creation of rose motifs. When executed in yellow, the California Rose was often called the Texas Yellow Rose. Both might be known as the Combination Rose. Rose patterns were named not only for colors and geographic locations but also for people, perhaps including quiltmakers. A list of mid-19th-century pattern names includes the Harrison Rose, Loretta's Rose, Mrs. Kretsinger's Rose, Mrs. Harris's Colonial Rose, and Sadie's Choice Rose, which is one of the oldest rose patterns.

Hints for Collectors
The rose motif was extremely popular in the 19th century, and numerous examples survive. Collectors should look for fine stitching and a strong, unusual design when purchasing a rose-pattern quilt.

Price Guide Group: Floral Quilts.

Courtesy America Hurrah Antiques, New York City.

California Rose

Description
Appliquéd quilt. 4 California Rose motifs, each block with central blossom of yellow, pink, green, and red; 4 green stems with pink and red flowers radiate from central blossoms. Blocks separated by crossing bands of off-white ground. Stylized undulating green vine border with red and yellow flower sprays. Red binding.

Materials, Quilting, and Dimensions
Cotton. Crossing bands of ground quilted in feathered vine, which meets feathered circle in center. California Rose blocks quilted in diagonal lines. 74″ × 74″.

Maker, Locality, and Period
Maker unknown. Ohio. c. 1855.

Comment
Young women often made a quilt with a rose pattern for their dower chests, but the pattern was not confined solely to the trousseau. Settlers often dedicated quilt patterns to the states where they had settled, and consequently there is a rose pattern for virtually every part of the Union. A few that were very popular include the Ohio Rose, Topeka Rose, Missouri Rose, Kentucky Rose, Virginia Rose, and California Rose. Notice that the vinelike border illustrated here is a very individual interpretation of a conventional motif. Borders were often altered by quiltmakers to express personal taste.

Hints for Collectors
The subtle hues of this quilt have been carefully coordinated to create a pleasing juxtaposition of colors. Although collecting tastes may change, a finely appliquéd quilt will always retain its commercial value.

Price Guide Group: Floral Quilts.

Courtesy America Hurrah Antiques, New York City.

Oak Leaf

Description
Appliquéd quilt. 20 blocks in Oak Leaf pattern, each composed of 4 green oak leaves that alternate with stylized gold leaves, both surrounding red four-leaf clover motif. Between oak leaf blocks, 12 small, green four-leaf clover motifs. Meandering green vine border with red and gold blossoms. In each corner, a green eagle grasping 2 broken arrows is incorporated into vine motif. White ground. Scalloped edge. Red binding.

Materials, Quilting, and Dimensions
Cotton. Border quilted in lines parallel to trailing vine. 86″ × 74″.

Maker, Locality, and Period
Maker unknown. New England. c. 1850.

Comment
An inventive quiltmaker would often take a standard pattern like the Oak Leaf, change it slightly, and combine it with her own designs to create a unique bedcover. The border design in this quilt is individual in the unusual combination of 2 common motifs, the trailing vine and the eagle. Although the eagle holding 2 broken arrows was a popular patriotic motif, it was rarely used alongside a floral pattern.

Hints for Collectors
While an original combination of common quilt motifs makes a quilt unique, such quilts are not necessarily the best textiles. In the example illustrated, however, the four-leaf clovers, eagles, and oak leaves create a very successful design.

Price Guide Group: Floral Quilts.

Courtesy America Hurrah Antiques, New York City.

167 Elaborate Patch

Description
Appliquéd quilt. 9 floral motifs, each formed by large center blossom of yellow, red, green, and white. 4 smaller red and yellow flowers with green leaves emanate from large blossom. Noncontinuous green garland border accented by red and yellow flowers. White ground. Yellow binding.

Materials, Quilting, and Dimensions
Cotton. Interiors of floral motifs quilted with outline stitching. Ground quilted in modified shell design. Border quilted in diagonal lines. 84″ × 84″.

Maker, Locality, and Period
Maker unknown. Pennsylvania. c. 1860.

Comment
Floral patterns have reigned supreme throughout most of the history of American quiltmaking. In its colors and design, the bedcover shown here is typical of many Pennsylvania quilts produced between 1850 and 1900. The garland border of this quilt does not meet at the corners. It was unusual for a quiltmaker to leave a noncontinuous border. Borders were usually very carefully thought out, not only because they had to be sewn fastidiously, but also because they contributed to the overall design and provided an area for creativity.

Hints for Collectors
Many floral quilts were produced during the second half of the 19th century. Learn to recognize the better examples, which are distinguished by their use of color, clarity of design, and fine needlework.

Price Guide Group: Floral Quilts.

Courtesy America Hurrah Antiques, New York City.

Rose Wreath

Description
Appliquéd quilt. 9 wreaths of 4 red roses and faded green leaves symmetrically arranged. Pattern echoed in meandering leaf-and-rose border. White ground. Red binding.

Materials, Quilting, and Dimensions
Cotton. Interior of each rose wreath quilted in teacup motif. Concentric diamonds quilted in diamond-shaped areas between appliquéd wreaths and between vine border and wreaths. Quilted hearts run from concentric diamond to concentric diamond. Ground between border and edges quilted in shell motif. 89½" × 89½".

Maker, Locality, and Period
Maker unknown. Midwest. c. 1850.

Comment
This quilt would probably have been quilted on a wooden frame in the home. Nearly every household in the mid–19th century owned a frame for the stitching of quilts. Generally, these frames were collapsible and could be stored when unused. In some houses, particularly in the South, quilting frames were suspended on ropes from the ceiling.

Hints for Collectors
The pattern shown here is one of a multitude of rose designs that were popular during the mid–19th century. The value of this quilt is increased by the fine quilting and the maker's simple color scheme. Prices of quilts do vary from region to region, but it is no longer true that quilts have consistently higher prices in large urban centers.

Price Guide Group: Floral Quilts.

Courtesy America Hurrah Antiques, New York City.

169 Snowflake

Description
Appliquéd quilt. 9 Snowflake patterns in blue-and-white printed fabric on white ground. Reverse appliquéd eight-pointed star cut out of center of each snowflake. Snowflakes enclosed by rope border in blue-and-white printed fabric. Blue-and-white printed clamshell pattern binding.

Materials, Quilting, and Dimensions
Cotton. Center section quilted in diamonds and large full and partial feathered medallions. Border quilted in diagonal lines of varying widths. 74″ × 74″.

Maker, Locality, and Period
Maker unknown. Ohio. c. 1865.

Comment
The fabric used in this bedcover may have been bought especially for it, because the delicacy of the blue-and-white print is particularly appropriate for the design. Moreover, the intricate quilting adds to the light and fragile appeal of this textile. The consistently high quality of the quilting on this bedcover suggests that it may have been the work of a single maker.

Hints for Collectors
Some collectors choose to collect a single type of bedcover, enabling them to become experts in a particular area. Specialization makes it somewhat easier to make wise decisions about the provenance and value of certain bedcovers. In addition, a specialized collection is often more valuable than a group of assorted quilts.

Price Guide Group: Floral Quilts.

Courtesy America Hurrah Antiques, New York City.

Rose of Sharon

Description
Appliquéd quilt. 9 large orange, red, and green flowers on white ground, each embellished with buds that emanate from central blossom. Bordered on 3 sides by green meandering vine with red and orange flowers and buds. Bottom corners cut to fit four-poster bed. White binding.

Materials, Quilting, and Dimensions
Cotton. Leaves quilted between each rosebud. Quilted flowers and oak leaves appear across surface of quilt. Top border quilted in wide band of tightly stitched diagonal lines. 90″ × 86″.

Maker, Locality, and Period
Maker unknown. Indiana. c. 1855.

Comment
This bedcover has a strong folk art quality, created by its irregular shape and boldness of color and design. Notice that the vine border does not cross the top of the quilt, and that the lower corners have been cut out to accommodate a four-poster bed. The absence of a top border would indicate that there were probably matching pillow shams that would have completed the design of the border.

Hints for Collectors
Many collectors prefer country quilts to the more sophisticated city versions, but by the end of the 19th century, quilts were made throughout America, and the distinction between rural and urban began to have little meaning.

Price Guide Group: Floral Quilts.

Private Collection.

171 Peony

Description
Appliquéd quilt. 24 stylized peonies with buds spaced evenly across central section of bedcover. Each peony of red-and-yellow and blue-and-brown printed fabrics. Bordered on 3 sides by noncontinuous trailing vine of leaves in blue-and-brown print. White ground. White binding.

Materials, Quilting, and Dimensions
Cotton. Central field quilted in floral motif and concentric diamonds. Border quilted in chevron design. 78″ × 72″.

Maker, Locality, and Period
Maker unknown. New York State. c. 1855.

Comment
The Peony pattern is really a variation of the Tulip design, which became common with westward expansion. This fine example can be given an approximate date because the printed fabrics were manufactured in the 1850s. The 3-sided border indicates that the top of the quilt would probably have been complemented by pillow shams. The shams might have continued the leafy trailing vine motif or possibly added another row of peonies. Unfortunately, it is rare to find a bedcover and its matching pillow shams. They have usually become separated over the years.

Hints for Collectors
This is a particularly desirable quilt, for the clear, well-conceived design is finely executed with attractive fabrics.

Price Guide Group: Floral Quilts.

Courtesy America Hurrah Antiques, New York City.

North Carolina Lily

Description
Pieced and appliquéd quilt. 32 white blocks set on diagonal: 20
with large red and green North Carolina Lilies, alternating with
12 white blocks of large red seven-pointed stars and smaller red
and white reverse-appliquéd stars in 4 corners of each block.
Border edged with 14 red lilies on green trailing vine, with tiny
red buds at each corner. White ground. Red binding.

Materials, Quilting, and Dimensions
Cotton. Extensively quilted with outline quilting echoing large
red stars. Border quilted in parallel lines. 86″ × 78″.

Maker, Locality, and Period
Maker unknown. New York State. c. 1855.

Comment
The lily was a very popular design motif in mid-19th-century
quilts, and the pattern acquired many different names as it
traveled across the country. It was called Wood Lily in northern
New England, Meadow Lily in Pennsylvania, North Carolina
Lily throughout the South, and Mountain Lily in Kentucky and
Tennessee. The names given quilt designs can be very confusing,
as the same pattern may have several names, depending on
where or when it was made, and no single authoritative source
for names exists.

Hints for Collectors
The tiny red stars done in reverse appliqué, a time-consuming
technique demanding great skill, the lavish amount of quilting,
and the graphic quality of the overall design combine to make
this bedcover an extraordinary and rare example.

Price Guide Group: Floral Quilts.

Courtesy America Hurrah Antiques, New York City.

173 Bird and Oak Leaf

Description
Appliquéd summer spread. 20 wreaths created by red-and-white and green-and-white printed fabric leaves and flowers. Wreaths enclose flower design with 2 buds topped by bird in green-and-white and red-and-white printed fabric. Bordered on 2 sides by meandering vine with leaves, flowers, and buds interspersed with small birds. White ground. Green-and-white printed binding.

Materials, Quilting, and Dimensions
Cotton. Unquilted. Bird eyes embroidered throughout. 88″ × 76″.

Maker, Locality, and Period
Maker unknown. New York State. c. 1860.

Comment
The lack of a vine border on 2 sides of this bedcover does not mean that it was unfinished or repaired. It is likely that the bedcover was made with a specific location in mind, perhaps a bed that sat in a corner, and that 2 of the sides would not be visible.

Hints for Collectors
There is a preponderance of red and green quilts from the 19th century. Most were crafted from new fabric sold in general stores or through mail-order catalogues. Hand-dyed fabrics of this period are seldom colorfast, so collectors must be very careful when cleaning their antique bedcovers. Professional cleaning is always preferable.

Price Guide Group: Floral Quilts.

Courtesy America Hurrah Antiques, New York City.

Description
Appliquéd quilt. 25 blocks of wreaths with red-and-white and green-and-yellow printed leaves. In each block, corners have boomerang-shaped motif in red-and-white print. Blocks contained by thin grid of green-and-yellow printed fabric. Swag border of red-and-white and green-and-yellow printed fabrics. White ground. White binding.

Materials, Quilting, and Dimensions
Cotton. Center of each wreath and border have diamond quilting. 84″ × 84″.

Maker, Locality, and Period
Maker unknown. New York State. c. 1860.

Comment
Publications like *Godey's Ladies' Book* brought new needlework techniques into the home of the quiltmaker. For almost 70 years *Godey's* enjoyed a very large readership that eagerly awaited new sewing ideas. Sample copies of *Godey's* could be had for 15¢ in 1884, and a subscription was available for $2 a year. Besides quilting patterns, *Godey's* offered lessons in cooking and dressmaking, and also music instruction.

Hints for Collectors
The boomerang motif at the corners of each block is very unusual. The swag border is made up of similarly shaped pieces that overlap. Such details, although seemingly insignificant, are important to collectors who pride themselves on having a collection that contains a large variety of quilt designs. Pieces with unique touches are, of course, especially desirable.

Price Guide Group: Floral Quilts.

Courtesy America Hurrah Antiques, New York City.

Description
Pieced and appliquéd quilt. 49 white diamond blocks alternate with diamonds of blue-and-white printed fabric. Each white diamond contains a 3-stemmed lily in red printed and black printed fabrics. Sawtooth border in red printed fabric on white ground across top of quilt. Other 3 sides have Streak of Lightning border of red printed fabric on white ground. Blue-and-white printed binding.

Materials, Quilting, and Dimensions
Cotton. White blocks quilted in parallel lines. Blue-and-white printed blocks quilted in diamonds. Blue-and-white half-blocks quilted in chevron design, as is white ground in border. 92″ × 92″.

Maker, Locality, and Period
Maker unknown. Massachusetts. c. 1850.

Comment
Although relatively few exceptional quilts are available today, bedcovers were made in very large quantities throughout most of the country during the 19th century. Historical records show that one seamstress might have produced more than 100 quilts in a lifetime.

Hints for Collectors
While there may be quilts with more elaborate designs, or with richer varieties of color, few approach the dramatic beauty of this handsome textile. The bold balance between the pieced floral blocks and the printed fabric blocks is contained by a beautiful and skillfully conceived border.

Price Guide Group: Floral Quilts.

Courtesy America Hurrah Antiques, New York City.

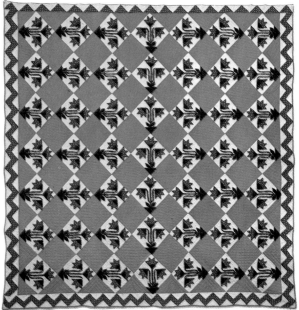

Description
Pieced and appliquéd quilt. 36 white diamond blocks alternate with 25 blue-and-white printed diamonds. Each white diamond contains a gold, blue, and red Mariner's Compass surrounded by 4 red and blue acorns. White sawtooth border. Small blue and white triangles in each corner. Blue binding.

Materials, Quilting, and Dimensions
Cotton. Blue-and-white print quilted in parallel lines and chevron pattern. 84″ × 84″.

Maker, Locality, and Period
Maker unknown. Ohio. c. 1870.

Comment
The acorn motif is relatively rare in quilting patterns. In this example it has been combined with the Mariner's Compass and creates an entirely unusual design. By the mid–19th century standard quilt patterns were widely available, but inventive seamstresses continued creating their own variations. Creative quiltmaking skills were often an important social asset, as quilts were much discussed and the inventive quiltmaker considered a pattern authority.

Hints for Collectors
Note that the fabrics used in the example illustrated are uniform in color, which may mean they came from rolls of material sold especially for quiltmaking. Such fabrics became available in the mid–19th century. The value of a bedcover, however, is determined by its design, execution, and rarity rather than whether old scraps or new fabrics were used in its creation.

Price Guide Group: Floral Quilts.

Courtesy America Hurrah Antiques, New York City.

177 Tree of Life

Description
Amish pieced quilt. 9 green trees on white diamond blocks.
Leaves of each tree composed of tiny triangles creating larger
chevron design. Tree motif alternates with black diamond blocks
quilted with white thread. Inscribed "1921 MAY 2." White frame.
Black border. Quilted with white thread. White binding.

Materials, Quilting, and Dimensions
Cotton. Extensively quilted. Central black blocks quilted in
feathered medallions enclosing concentric circles and in parallel
lines in corners. Frame quilted in rope motif. Border quilted in
feathered vine. 78″ × 76″.

Maker, Locality, and Period
Maker unknown. Ohio. 1921.

Comment
It is particularly rare to find an Amish quilt that uses white
thread on black fabric. While the Tree of Life pattern was not a
traditional Amish design, by 1921 the Amish had incorporated
many non-Amish motifs into their quilting vocabulary. Even
though the Ohio Amish were less traditional than their
Pennsylvania counterparts, if there were not such a simple color
scheme and superb quilting, few would suspect that this
bedcover was Amish.

Hints for Collectors
Although the bedcover illustrated is particularly rare, it is not as
valuable as other more classic Amish designs. Remember that
some Amish communities were less traditional than others, and
that even with a wealth of information about Amish textiles,
attribution may be difficult.

Price Guide Group: Amish and Mennonite Quilts.

Private Collection.

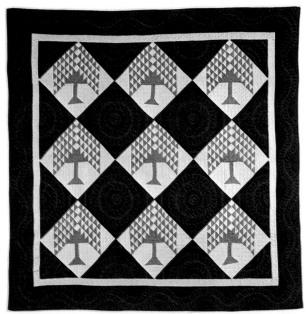

Tree of Life

Description
Pieced quilt. 20 trees in red, yellow, and tan, each made of small triangles and diamonds on white ground. Frame red. Border white. No binding.

Materials, Quilting, and Dimensions
Cotton. Tree motifs quilted in parallel and outline stitching. Ground has diamond quilting. Borders quilted in diagonal lines. 85″ × 69½″.

Maker, Locality, and Period
Maker and locality unknown. c. 1860.

Comment
The Tree of Life motif originated with 18th-century palampores, which the English imported to America from India. During the 19th century, the design changed from one large tree with many branches to, in the case of quilts, repeated geometric tree motifs placed across the surface of the bedcover. The example illustrated might also be called a variation of the Pine Tree pattern that originated in the United States during the latter part of the 18th century. Its design honored the colonists' pine tree flag.

Hints for Collectors
There are many variations of the Tree of Life pattern, including Christmas Tree, Temperance Tree, Tree of Temptation, and Tree of Paradise; some are pieced while others are appliquéd. Since thousands of 19th-century quilts are available, it is usually possible to be very selective in choosing a bedcover, even if a particular pattern is sought.

Price Guide Group: Floral Quilts.

Collection of Mr. and Mrs. Donald Morris.

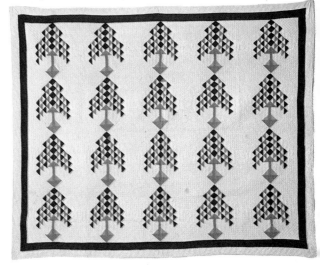

179 Baskets

Description
Pieced and appliquéd quilt. 42 green baskets, filled with green, brown, and off-white triangles, alternate with off-white diamonds. Off-white ground. Light green inner and outer sawtooth borders surround central border of red appliquéd flowers with light green stems and leaves. Green binding.

Materials, Quilting, and Dimensions
Cotton. Baskets and borders quilted in diamonds. Ground between baskets quilted in large diamond blocks enclosing feathered medallions. 80″ × 76″.

Maker, Locality, and Period
Maker and locality unknown. c. 1825.

Comment
The design of this bedcover was carefully planned, for when the quilt is placed on the bed, some baskets will appear upright from either side of the bed. Baskets were a very popular motif among quiltmakers from approximately 1850 on, as they could easily be modified to suit individual tastes.

Hints for Collectors
This example is particularly striking, for its light green and red border motifs contrast nicely with the green, brown, and off-white baskets in the central field. It is unusual to find a basket motif without a handle, and even more unusual to have the basket filled with an abstract design, as it is here. Unique details such as these are highly prized by collectors.

Price Guide Group: Floral Quilts.

Courtesy America Hurrah Antiques, New York City.

180 Basket of Flowers

Description
Appliquéd quilt. 16 baskets, each containing 3 red-and-white printed flowers with green stems and leaves. Baskets composed of solid white and red-and-white printed triangles, with red-and-white printed base. Undulating green vine border with red-and-white printed blooms and buds. Green appliquéd initials and date in center of bedcover. White ground. Red-and-white printed binding.

Materials, Quilting, and Dimensions
Cotton. Flowers and baskets quilted in fine parallel and diagonal lines. Full and partial feathered ovals quilted between baskets; each oval filled with fine diamond quilting. Border with diagonal quilting, and vine finely outlined with feathered motif. 88″ × 86″.

Maker, Locality, and Period
Initialed M Mc. New York State. 1853.

Comment
It is interesting to note how quiltmakers varied a single theme. Baskets and flower designs were very popular during the 19th century, and quiltmakers delighted in extending their repertoires. Some of the most popular basket patterns were Basket of Daisies, Carlie Sexton's Flower Basket, Mrs. Hall's Basket, Garden Gift, Colonial Basket, and Flower Basket, to name only a few.

Hints for Collectors
Assigning dates to quilts is problematic even with the more obvious examples. This quilt, based on its style alone, could reasonably be ascribed to the late 19th century, but is in fact much earlier.

Price Guide Group: Floral Quilts.

Courtesy America Hurrah Antiques, New York City.

Representational Quilts

All of these quilts have prominent realistic motifs, such as people, buildings, animals, plants, and landscapes. In most, the motifs are organized within a grid. Although a few examples are appliquéd, most are pieced. Some of the pieced quilts are built up of hundreds of small geometric patches, which when sewn together form houses or trees. Other less intricate examples consist of larger patches that make up simpler motifs such as sailboats.

Among the most charming bedcovers are those that depict the rural schoolhouses of 19th-century America. The best schoolhouse quilts have bright colors, an organized composition, and meticulous pieced work. A variation of the schoolhouse pattern combines blocks of houses with blocks of trees.

Many quilts with realistic motifs have unique designs and for that reason are in great demand today. Examples like the quilt called Dolls (185) are especially interesting, since they combine unusual motifs (in this case rag dolls) with a standard overall pattern (here blocks placed within a Streak of Lightning grid).

A few representational bedcovers were made from kits (187, 188). Although the designs were mass-produced, quiltmakers could personalize their work by choosing unusual color combinations, by exercising fine craftsmanship, and by the way in which they organized the individual blocks.

Two of the most striking pieces in this section were created by a contemporary quiltmaker (191, 192). Like many of the other bedcovers included here, these modern examples consist of blocks organized within a grid. But each of these quilts explores a theme that is worked out through the progression of its blocks; the subtle changes that occur from block to block animate the surface of the textile. Using new fabrics, such as lamé, and a new approach, contemporary artists have injected vigor into a textile form that began long ago.

181 Schoolhouse

Description
Pieced and appliquéd quilt. 20 red schoolhouses with pale green roofs arranged in 5 rows on white ground. Red binding.

Materials, Quilting, and Dimensions
Cotton. Outline stitching around schoolhouses, windows, doors, arches of towers, and under tower roofs. White boxlike stitching to delineate bricks on walls and chimneys, panel stitching on doors, and 2 rows of circles on each roof. Ground quilted with stylized flowers and leaves. 84" × 72".

Maker, Locality, and Period
Maker unknown. Pennsylvania. c. 1920.

Comment
Variations on the house theme, including schoolhouses, churches, and barns, were very popular from about 1850 through the early 20th century. Most feature side views of a schoolhouse or buildings. In this example note the detailed appliqués, such as the crosses of the windowpanes and the outlines of the doors. Other variations may be far more abstract.

Hints for Collectors
Although the example illustrated is pieced and appliquéd, quilts depicting buildings were often simply appliquéd. Always look for idiosyncratic touches on a bedcover with a repeating design. Often the quiltmaker deliberately sewed a "mistake," thought by some quilt fanciers to reflect the maker's faith in God: Only God can make a perfect thing.

Price Guide Group: Pictorial Quilts.

Courtesy Thomas K. Woodard, American Antiques and Quilts, New York City.

Little Red Schoolhouse

Description
Pieced quilt. 20 schoolhouses in red-and-white prints.
Schoolhouse windows yellow, red, and white striped fabric.
Blocks separated by green-and-yellow printed grid that also
forms border. Green-and-yellow printed binding.

Materials, Quilting, and Dimensions
Cotton. Schoolhouses have diagonal and outline quilting. Border
with vine quilting. 90″ × 78″.

Maker, Locality, and Period
Maker unknown. Pennsylvania. c. 1890.

Comment
The Little Red Schoolhouse pattern, thought to have originated
in New Jersey in the 1870s, had wide appeal during the late
Victorian period. Many variations developed, most of them based
on the arrangement of the schoolhouses. More than a dozen
variations of the house motif are known—Schoolhouse, Village
Church, Honeymoon Cottage, and Old Kentucky Home—most of
them pieced, and all of them appealing to the Victorian love of
sentiment.

Hints for Collectors
The Little Red Schoolhouse motif can be found on very crude
pieces as well as on finely made ones, with prices varying
considerably. The intricacy of the design and needlework as well
as the color and quality of the fabrics all affect value. While
trends may change and a pattern or style neglected now may
soon be much in demand, the best examples generally maintain
or frequently increase their value.

Price Guide Group: Pictorial Quilts.

Courtesy America Hurrah Antiques, New York City.

House and Tree I

Description
Pieced quilt. 25 blocks of trees in shades of green, alternating with houses in white, red, green, blue, and gold. Blocks separated by grid of blue and gold diagonal stripes, with pale green squares at each intersection. On 3 sides, double border of blue and gold diagonally striped bands and red band; at top, pink band replaces the red. Pale pink binding.

Materials, Quilting, and Dimensions
Cotton. House blocks with outline quilting. 78″ × 76″.

Maker, Locality, and Period
Maker unknown. Virginia. c. 1900.

Comment
An extraordinarily rich textile, this vividly colored piece displays its maker's individuality. None of the houses are the same; the windows, doors, chimneys, even the backgrounds, are all different. This bedcover shows the amount of thought and effort many quiltmakers put into their work.

Hints for Collectors
This is an unusual and very desirable quilt, especially for the collector who appreciates modern art. Few quilts are as vigorous or as boldly executed as this one. While many might find the colors too jarring or the piecing too bold, the example illustrated is a masterpiece of American needlework. Comparable examples would undoubtedly fetch exceptionally high prices in the marketplace.

Price Guide Group: Pictorial Quilts.

Courtesy America Hurrah Antiques, New York City.

Description
Pieced quilt. 21 blocks with houses in red, blue, green, tan, yellow, and white. Corner blocks with trees in red, green, yellow, and tan. Blocks separated by grid of red and white diagonal stripes, with blue squares at each juncture and corners. Inner border dark green, yellow, and blue diagonal stripes. Outer border dark green. Pale green binding.

Materials, Quilting, and Dimensions
Cotton. House blocks with outline stitching. 78" × 78".

Maker, Locality, and Period
Maker unknown. Virginia. c. 1900.

Comment
Diaries and journals frequently recorded the prodigious output of a single needlewoman, for example, Julia Ann Flickinger, born in 1827: "From the moment when she was old enough to wield needle and thread, she must have been an industrious piecer of quilts, for, at her death, she left over 150." The quilt illustrated was made by an unidentified master quiltmaker from Virginia; all 4 known examples of her work are now in private collections.

Hints for Collectors
Gaining access to private textile collections is very helpful. Many museums around the country also have important quilts and bedcovers. Most, however, lack the space to exhibit even a small part of their collections, so that seeing a group of textiles may require writing ahead to the curator or registrar for an appointment.

Price Guide Group: Pictorial Quilts.

Courtesy America Hurrah Antiques, New York City.

185 Dolls

Description
Pieced quilt. 23 diagonally placed white squares, each with a pieced rag doll figure dressed in red, yellow, or shades of gray and brown. Ground and border brown-and-white print. Yellow binding.

Materials, Quilting, and Dimensions
Cotton. White squares and brown-and-white ground quilted in diamonds. Figures with outline stitching. Embroidered mouths and eyes. 73½″ × 71″.

Maker, Locality, and Period
Maker unknown. Southern Missouri. c. 1900.

Comment
This bedcover is particularly striking graphically, not only because of its primary colors, but also because of the underlying Streak of Lightning pattern in brown-and-white printed fabric, that organizes the white squares into rows. Notice that this quilt has relied on a bold pattern and bright colors to achieve its visual effects rather than on fine stitching.

Hints for Collectors
Collectors with an eye for the unusual would be delighted with this bedcover. Human figures are very rare in pieced quilts, and figures with the power and charm of these are even rarer. The blank expressions and stiff poses make these 2-dimensional figures very much like the rag dolls—another form of folk art—commonly found in southern states. A one-of-a-kind quilt like this, even if in less than perfect condition, is a rare find.

Price Guide Group: Pictorial Quilts.

Courtesy America Hurrah Antiques, New York City.

Sailboats

Description
Amish pieced quilt. 35 sailboats constructed of triangles and trapezoids, in green, blue, and lavender, on variously colored grounds. 4 vertical lavender bands divide boats into rows of 7. Brown inner border surrounds blocks. Green outer border. Pale green binding.

Materials, Quilting, and Dimensions
Cotton. Boat blocks with diamond quilting. Chevron quilting in vertical stripes. Inner border with floral quilting; outer border with rope motif. 85″ × 71″.

Maker, Locality, and Period
Maker unknown. Topeka, Indiana. c. 1960.

Comment
Many contemporary Amish women have continued to make quilts in traditional Amish designs. Others, however, like the maker of this quilt, have been influenced by non-Amish quilt patterns. An illustration in a magazine like the *Ladies' Home Journal* or *Better Homes and Gardens* may very well have inspired this quilt design.

Hints for Collectors
Were it not for its somber colors, this bedcover might well be mistaken for a non-Amish quilt, because of its nontraditional, 20th-century pattern. Even in the early days the Amish were susceptible to the influence of their non-Amish neighbors, and created quilts in a much wider range of designs than the few permitted by the Pennsylvania Amish. While not as valuable as a traditional late 19th-century Amish quilt, a piece like this has great appeal because of its strong and unusually graphic design.

Price Guide Group: Amish and Mennonite Quilts.

Courtesy Museum of American Folk Art, New York City.

Elephants

Description
Pieced quilt. 4 large blocks, each with purple and orange elephant, made of pieced squares and triangles, on white ground. Elephants separated by orange grid with nine-patch orange and white block at each intersection. Inner border of purple and white stripes, with full and partial nine-patch blocks at corners and center of sides. Narrow outer border is orange. White binding.

Materials, Quilting, and Dimensions
Cotton. Individual patches have outline stitching. Grid and purple and white border have parallel line quilting. White ground bordered with parallel line quilting enclosing block quilting. 82½″ × 62½″.

Maker, Locality, and Period
Maker unknown. New York State. c. 1930.

Comment
With the start of the Depression in 1929, quilts provided an economical alternative to expensive blankets, and they were a good excuse for getting together during the long evenings. This bedcover was undoubtedly made from a kit. Some kits may only have included a pattern with suggestions for materials; more complete packages with everything needed to make the quilt, including precut quilt patches, were also available.

Hints for Collectors
This quilt, in orange and purple, uses the colors typical of 1930s quiltmaking. Although made from a kit, it has great charm. Most quilts that were made from kits are reasonably priced.

Price Guide Group: Pictorial Quilts.

Courtesy Kelter-Malcé Antiques, New York City.

Description
Pieced quilt. 9 donkeys in pink, white, and green on white ground. Divided by grid in turquoise and green, with nine-patch green and white squares at 4 intersections in central field and at each corner. Grid forms border. Yellow binding.

Materials, Quilting, and Dimensions
Cotton. Outline quilting; square quilting on white ground, grid, and border. 77½" × 77½".

Maker, Locality, and Period
Maker unknown. California. c. 1930.

Comment
When, after a period of little interest between 1900 and 1930, quiltmaking again became very popular, a number of magazines began publishing quilt designs and instructions. Daily newspapers also ran regular columns on quiltmaking, and ladies' journals advertised quilt kits with precut pieces for traditional as well as modern designs. The example illustrated was made from such a kit.

Hints for Collectors
Although many collectors consider quilts made from kits less interesting or imaginative than those with original designs, many women created unique pieces by making changes in the pattern or by adding some touch of their own. The donkeys in the example illustrated—possibly made in an election year by a strong supporter of the Democrats—were undoubtedly the product of a kit, but the placement of its figures and the colors used in this quilt make it unlike any other, and visually very pleasing.

Price Guide Group: Pictorial Quilts.

Courtesy Kelter-Malcé Antiques, New York City.

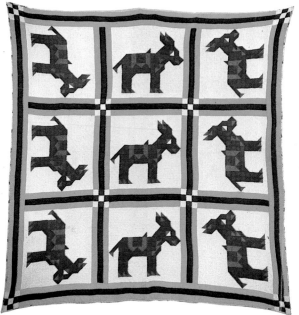

189 Dragonfly

Description
Pieced and appliquéd quilt. 12 black blocks, each with maroon, yellow, and blue dragonfly motif. Blocks enclosed by dark blue grid, with yellow squares at each intersection; grid also forms border. No binding.

Materials, Quilting, and Dimensions
Cotton. Dragonflies quilted in parallel lines and surrounded by outline quilting. Grid and border quilted in parallel lines, yellow squares in triangular motifs. 79½″ × 62″.

Maker, Locality, and Period
Maker unknown. North Carolina. c. 1875.

Comment
Although all quilts are bedcovers, this one, with its strong, heavy cotton, was undoubtedly intended for everyday use. Though the material is coarse, the motifs relatively crude, and the stitching very loose, this quilt has great appeal. Because of the quiltmaker's excellent sense of design and color, an everyday object has been transformed into a work of art. The narrow width suggests this quilt was made for a single bed, possibly a child's.

Hints for Collectors
A true country quilt, this piece has the strong graphic quality characteristic of the best American folk art. The slight irregularities in the shape of the appliqués, the loose, extensive quilting that adds texture and movement and the bold dragonfly shapes—all contribute to make this an outstanding example of a folk textile.

Price Guide Group: Pictorial Quilts.

Courtesy Kelter-Malcé Antiques, New York City.

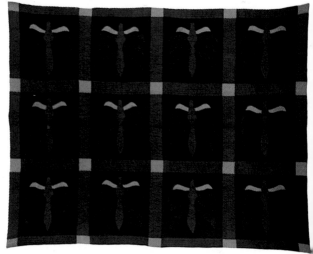

Pineapple

Description
Appliquéd and reverse appliquéd quilt. 16 white blocks, each with red, green, and white pineapple, separated by 3-part grid of red and green also forming outer border. White binding.

Materials, Quilting, and Dimensions
Cotton. Entire bedcover quilted in teacup motif. White parts of pineapples reverse appliqué. 104″ × 102″.

Maker, Locality, and Period
Maker unknown. Pennsylvania. c. 1860.

Comment
The pineapple motif, a symbol for hospitality, was popular in this country throughout the 18th and early 19th centuries. It was increasingly used on textiles after New England missionaries returned from Hawaii in the 1820s. In this quilt, the pineapple is seen on a branch, rather than in a bowl with other fruit, as was common in paintings and on album quilts. The quilting on this example was probably done by more than one quilter, as the stitching in some blocks is very tight and the circles perfectly formed, while in others the circles are loosely stitched and irregular.

Hints for Collectors
The red, green, and white combination was especially popular for quilts in the second half of the 19th century, and many examples exist. Few, however, are as charming and original as this one. The stylized pineapples, with their bushy tops, thick supporting stems, and small immature fruit, result in an attractive simplicity and directness.

Price Guide Group: Pictorial Quilts.

Courtesy America Hurrah Antiques, New York City.

Description
Pieced and appliquéd quilt. 16 stuffed blocks with sequential images of mountains, clouds, and moon. Divided by pale gray grid. Each block predominantly blue and white. Pale gray border.

Materials, Quilting, and Dimensions
Velveteen, satin, cotton, and lamé with stuffed work. Outline quilting. 82″ × 62″.

Maker, Locality, and Period
Sheila Perez. Connecticut. 1976.

Comment
During the women's movement of the late 1960s, many women artists turned to the traditional fabric mediums. Quiltmaking especially enjoyed a revival—partly because it was originally done almost exclusively by women. Here, the artist uses block construction for a narrative effect. The series of frames tells the story of the waxing and waning of the moon. Not only does the grid act as a unifying device, but it underlines the subtle transition from one time period to the next.

Hints for Collectors
Like many contemporary quilts, this one was clearly meant to be displayed as a wall hanging rather than actually used as a bedcover. The mixture of fabrics—particularly the velveteen, satin, and lamé—would not withstand everyday use. Part of the excitement of purchasing a modern quilt is being able to meet the artist and talk about the work. Most quiltmakers are happy to discuss their designs and choice of fabrics and may offer to show you other works.

Price Guide Group: Pictorial Quilts.

Collection of Mr. and Mrs. Ralph O. Glendinning.

Sunrise/Sunset

Description
Pieced and appliquéd quilt. 12 stuffed blocks with sequential
images of rising and setting sun. Divided by pale pink grid. Sun
bright gold; landscape, clouds, and sky grays, browns, yellows,
and pale greens. Pale pink border. No binding.

Materials, Quilting, and Dimensions
Cotton, silk, satin, and gold lamé. Outline quilting with rays of
sun stitched in straight lines. 68″ × 62″.

Maker, Locality, and Period
Sheila Perez. Connecticut. 1976.

Comment
This quilt was never intended to be used as a functional bedcover
but to be displayed like a painting. It is one of a series of quilts
made over a period of 3 years, exploring transitions in daily life,
such as the rising and setting of the sun or the moon. Like many
modern examples, the quilt has a polyester stuffing and uses a
variety of exotic fabrics, including gold lamé for the sun. For the
back, however, the quiltmaker employed the traditional cotton.

Hints for Collectors
Contemporary quilts can be seen in arts and crafts galleries and
crafts fairs throughout the country. Galleries usually offer
exhibitions that change every 3 or 4 weeks. If you are interested
in modern textiles, place your name on the mailing list of a local
crafts gallery. A knowledgeable and helpful dealer can be one of
the greatest assets to a collector of antique or contemporary
textiles.

Price Guide Group: Pictorial Quilts.

Courtesy Sheila Perez.

Crazy Quilts

 Crazy quilts are made of literally hundreds or thousands of pieces of fabric cut in irregular sizes and shapes and then stitched together. Early American housewives fashioned these bedcovers from scraps of fabric that they had salvaged and often saved for years. Some scholars believe that crazy quilts were the earliest quilts designed, but because they were almost entirely utilitarian, and were used faithfully until they wore out, there are too few examples remaining to verify this theory. What is certain about the crazy quilt is that it was well suited to the needs of early American homes.

The technique for constructing crazy quilts is very much like that used to make Log Cabin designs. Small pieces of fabric are sewn onto large squares (195) or long strips (199), which are then sewn together to make a top. Like Log Cabin quilts, crazy quilts were usually tufted, rather than quilted, because the stitching that held the bits of fabric together was also strong enough to secure the quilt. The design was intended to appear haphazard, or "crazy." Recognizable shapes or representational images were usually avoided, though pictorial crazys (193) and crazys that display patterns were also created. Some even combined Log Cabin and crazy blocks (200).

The quilts in this section are primarily from the Victorian period, reflecting the popularity of the form from 1870 to 1900. Although most of these Victorian quilts are made up of a variety of exotic fabrics—silks, velvets, and satins—any kind of material, from treasured hair ribbons and bits of a wedding dress to discarded neckties, was used. Many quiltmakers embellished their works with fancy embroidery stitches (202). Sometimes these stitches also held the individual pieces or blocks together.

Victorian crazy quilts were not made solely for the bedroom. Smaller examples were employed as decorative spreads or throws for sofas, stools, and other parlor furniture. To assist the seamstress in planning her quilt, many 19th-century magazines featured quilting instructions. Although crazy quilts continue to be made today, the most outstanding examples are products of the late 19th century. With their eclectic use of opulent materials and their complex, random designs, crazy quilts truly reflect the sensibilities of the Victorian age.

Description
Pieced and appliquéd quilt. 12 irregular blocks depicting land- or seascapes, including houses, gardens, and sailing ships. Predominantly blue, brown, and maroon. Deep burgundy plush velvet border. No binding.

Materials, Quilting, and Dimensions
Silk, velvet, and plush velvet. Cross- and whip stitches join blocks. Many patches elaborately embroidered. Unquilted. 74¼″ × 57″.

Maker, Locality, and Period
Celestine Bacheller. Wyoma, Massachusetts. c. 1850–1900.

Comment
It is thought that the 12 squares in this extraordinary textile are meant to depict the houses, landscapes, and seascapes in the vicinity of the quiltmaker's home on the North Shore of Boston. Using the silks and velvets typical of period crazy quilts, she has attempted a sense of perspective, not always successfully, but the result is a charming piece of folk art.

Hints for Collectors
This quilt is too expensive for most collectors, yet it sets a standard by which to judge other pieces. Many Victorian crazy quilts have as many elaborately embroidered areas as this one, but few create such a detailed and charming record of village life. In the 19th century, quilting was one of the few recognized outlets for women's artistic impulses, and what is seen here might in other times have gained expression in a painting.

Price Guide Group: Crazy Quilts.

Courtesy Museum of Fine Arts, Boston, Massachusetts.

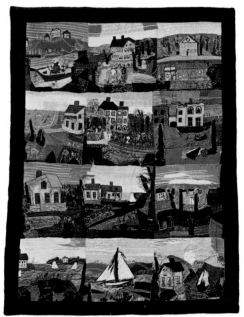

Description
Pieced and appliquéd quilt. Numerous motifs appliquéd on irregularly shaped blocks. Variety of wild and domestic animal motifs, including crane, ostrich, elephant, owl, rooster, horse, and donkey; other motifs include furniture and flowers. Unusual detail of stuffed hand (lower left) grasping embroidered, tasseled white towel. Predominantly brown, red, black, and yellow. Meandering vine with red, white, yellow, and orange flowers on black border; blooms of flowers pieced in velvet. Dated. Red binding.

Materials, Quilting, and Dimensions
Silk and velvet with stuffed work. Lavishly embroidered. Tassels. Unquilted. 80″ × 76″.

Maker, Locality, and Period
Maker and locality unknown. 1886.

Comment
Only during the Victorian period could this extravagant textile have received the amount of attention required to complete it. It was at the Philadelphia Centennial Exhibition in 1876 that a broad segment of the American population first experienced Japanese art and culture. Every aspect of American decorative arts was influenced. The numerous crane motifs in this quilt find their origin in Oriental imagery.

Hints for Collectors
Crazy quilts, once scorned as the tasteless expression of the late Victorians, are now becoming fashionable again. Tastes in collecting change quickly, and the astute collector who looks for quality in currently neglected objects may find great bargains.

Price Guide Group: Crazy Quilts.

Courtesy America Hurrah Antiques, New York City.

Description
Pieced crib quilt. 12 blocks made up of irregularly shaped patches of prints and solids. Embroidered motifs include circles, flowers, stars, leaves, triangles, a moon, and a horseshoe. Predominantly reds, browns, blues, and white. Dated. No border. No binding.

Materials, Quilting, and Dimensions
Cotton, wool, and velvet. Individual patches and blocks elaborately stitched and embroidered together. Embroidered motifs. Unquilted. 48″ × 43¼″.

Maker, Locality, and Period
Maker and locality unknown. 1902.

Comment
Crazy quilts enjoyed their greatest popularity during the 1880s and 1890s. The Victorian sensibility for richly textured, sentimental bedcovers continued in some areas of the country well into the 20th century, but by the time this quilt was made, American tastes were becoming simpler, and quilt designs more orderly.

Hints for Collectors
The collector looking for a crib quilt should carefully check the edges of small quilts. Some quilts have been cut down to accommodate smaller, more modern beds, and hide damaged areas. Do not confuse crib quilts in silk and velvet with throws and table covers, which usually have no backing and are generally smaller.

Price Guide Group: Crib Quilts.

Courtesy Museum of American Folk Art, New York City.

Description
Amish pieced quilt. 56 blocks; central blocks in modified Log Cabin pattern and in modified Fan pattern. Remaining blocks have irregular circular motif around red center patch. Predominantly red, blue, brown, tan, and black. Multiple border tan, blue, dark brown, and orange. Dated and initialed.

Materials, Quilting, and Dimensions
Cotton. Diagonal quilting in each block. Border quilted in diamond motif. Blocks embroidered together with red thread. 82″ × 76″.

Maker, Locality, and Period
Initialed F.A.P. Pennsylvania. 1892.

Comment
This is a very rare quilt because of its complex design and Amish provenance. Reclusive and unaffected by non-Amish bedcover patterns, the Amish at this time generally quilted simple geometric designs such as Sunshine and Shadow and Diamond in Square. Equally unusual is the use of embroidery on the top of this bedcover: most Amish spreads were only quilted. Typical, however, are the dark, rich colors and the skill employed in the diamond quilting on the borders.

Hints for Collectors
Note that this design is particularly restrained when compared with other crazy quilts of the same period. A spread like this would be prized by collectors of Amish, crazy, or Log Cabin quilts.

Price Guide Group: Amish and Mennonite Quilts.

Courtesy America Hurrah Antiques, New York City.

197 Block

Description
Pieced quilt. 49 blocks with central geometric designs including six-pointed stars and Baby Blocks; upper left block with nine-patch design. Predominantly red, gray, blue, and green prints. Red frame. Wide border of similar prints cut in random shapes. Plum binding.

Materials, Quilting, and Dimensions
Cotton. Outline quilting. Frame quilted with running diamond design. Some embroidery within blocks. 88″ × 84″.

Maker, Locality, and Period
Maker unknown. Pennsylvania. c. 1895.

Comment
In this atypical crazy quilt, only a few of the blocks contain embroidery, and the bedcover is quilted, not tufted. Notice the quiltmaker's imagination and restraint in her use of the six-pointed star and her choice of colored fabrics. Some star motifs are actually composed of Baby Blocks, which creates an interesting and subtle optical illusion.

Hints for Collectors
Because of the fine choice of colors and designs, this crazy quilt is particularly successful. Most other crazy quilts were lavishly embroidered, and many employed rich and lush fabrics—silk, velvet, and satin. An unusual example like this would be of interest to all quilt collectors, not just those who collect crazy quilts.

Price Guide Group: Crazy Quilts.

Courtesy America Hurrah Antiques, New York City.

Description
Pieced quilt. 49 full and partial six-pointed stars, created by piecing small black triangles to each side of hexagons. Each triangle embroidered with floral spray or blossom. Predominantly black, blue, red, and purple. Dark red border embroidered with meandering vines, leaves, and floral sprigs. Yellow binding.

Materials, Quilting, and Dimensions
Cotton and velvet. Lavishly embroidered: every triangular patch has small embroidered spray of flowers. Border embroidered with flowers, leaves, and meandering vines. Unquilted.
84″ × 78″.

Maker, Locality, and Period
Maker and locality unknown. c. 1875.

Comment
A remarkable amount of time and energy was lavished on crazy quilts and the example illustrated is certainly no exception. Long and tedious hours were spent piecing the tiny scraps into the hexagons that form the center of the six-pointed stars, and special effort was needed to piece the entire quilt. This quilt is also superbly embroidered, a task which involves many hours of work. It took literally hundreds of hours to create this textile.

Hints for Collectors
The quilt illustrated here is a prize find. All its parts, including the extensive embroidery, are in very good condition. Always carefully examine velvets and velours—if they are badly worn, the only solution is to patch or replace the fabric, which substantially reduces the quilt's value.

Price Guide Group: Crazy Quilts.

Private Collection.

Description
Pieced quilt. Trapezoids, small triangles, squares, and irregular shapes in solid and printed fabrics. Predominantly red, yellow, tan, and blue. Also included are many variations of pieced quilt patterns, such as Nine Patch and Log Cabin. Red binding.

Materials, Quilting, and Dimensions
Cotton. Some loose stitching. 87½″ × 75½″.

Maker, Locality, and Period
Maker unknown. Connecticut. c. 1890.

Comment
The term "crazy quilt" is a misnomer, because the bedcover was usually tufted rather than quilted. Crazy quilt patterns were also used for parlor throws of all sizes, shapes, and weights. The fine piecework in the example illustrated was particularly difficult to execute because small pieces of fabric tend to buckle. Notice the large variety of shapes and patterns employed. By the mid–19th century, middle-class women who could afford servants were freed from the usual Victorian household duties and could spend their leisure time at needlework. Fine needlework quilts, therefore, became a mark of affluence.

Hints for Collectors
There are still many well-made crazy quilts on the market. Try to find an example that is carefully pieced and extensively embroidered. And remember, an immense amount of time went into making such a quilt. Although sewing machines became popular in the mid–19th century, this bedcover would have been pieced entirely by hand.

Price Guide Group: Crazy Quilts.

Courtesy America Hurrah Antiques, New York City.

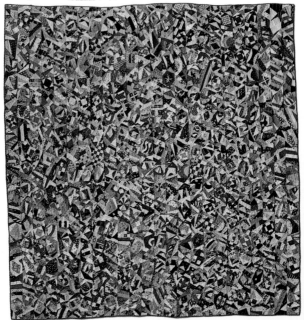

Description
Pieced quilt. Combination of Log Cabin and traditional crazy quilt designs. Red center square contains embroidered fan and basket of daisies and black-eyed Susans. Barn Raising pattern radiates outward in traditional Log Cabin blocks. Predominantly red, blue, white, and green. Inner border of wide crazy quilt blocks with randomly cut and embroidered fabrics. Outer border dark red with corner squares containing embroidered nosegays.

Materials, Quilting, and Dimensions
Silk; center square and outer border velvet. Extensive silk embroidery. Unquilted. 66″ × 54″.

Maker, Locality, and Period
Maker and locality unknown. c. 1880.

Comment
Wide velvet borders were common on crazy quilts made during the latter part of the 19th century. It is out of the ordinary, however, to see such a combination of patterns. This quilt has especially fine piecing and intricate stitches. Such bedcovers were often made from salvaged pieces of silk and velvet that had originally been purchased as dress material.

Hints for Collectors
In some quilts, the border design seems incomplete. Edges of bedcovers, especially at the head of a bed, often wore out quickly. Attempts to mask such damage sometimes involved cutting down a textile or adding a new binding—both alterations that lessen the value of any quilt.

Price Guide Group: Crazy Quilts.

Courtesy America Hurrah Antiques, New York City.

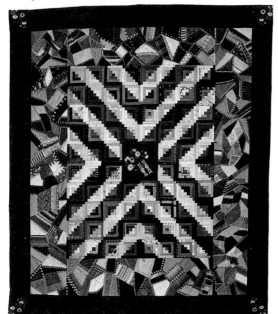

Contained Crazy

Description
Pieced quilt. Diamonds composed of randomly cut solid and printed fabrics contained by grid of white diagonal bands. Small red-and-black printed diamonds at each grid intersection. Predominantly purples, blue, brown, white, and red. Pen and ink signature. Border brown, white, black, and red floral print.

Materials, Quilting, and Dimensions
Cotton. Large diamonds with outline stitching. Diagonal bands quilted in parallel lines. 92″ × 86″.

Maker, Locality, and Period
Mary E. Gormly. New York State. c. 1880.

Comment
This quilt displays elegance and restraint. Crazy quilt patterns are generally confused arrangements of fabric, but here the white grid organizes the textile and gives it visual harmony. And the printed fabric border adds an order to this quilt that sets it apart from many other crazy quilts. Particularly fine piecing is evident in the small printed diamonds at the intersections of the grid.

Hints for Collectors
Although many crazy quilts are loosely organized into strips or squares, few are as carefully thought out as this rare example. The diagonal grid that encloses the individual pieced diamonds is an unusual detail. Regardless of how out of the ordinary a quilt may be, its value always depends largely on its beauty. In this quilt, the collector finds both characteristics.

Price Guide Group: Crazy Quilts.

Courtesy America Hurrah Antiques, New York City.

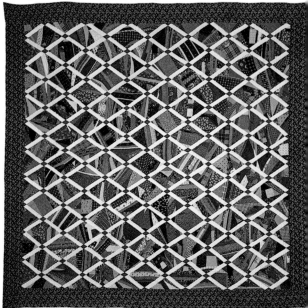

Fan

Description
Pieced and appliquéd quilt. 30 pieced and embroidered fans, symmetrically arranged. Cut pieces of solid and printed fabrics form ground between fans. Extensively embroidered motifs, including flowers, birds, butterflies, a hand mirror, and parts of human body. Predominantly yellow, pink, red, and blue. Yellow binding with ruffle.

Materials, Quilting, and Dimensions
Silk and velvet. Lavishly embroidered. Unquilted. 68″ × 56″.

Maker, Locality, and Period
Maker and locality unknown. c. 1880.

Comment
On this bedcover, rich fabrics have been employed in a complicated design, and virtually every square inch has been embroidered with fancy stitches or pictures. Note whimsical touches such as the embroidered lady's lower calf and high-heeled shoe, the tiny ladybug stitched on a small white square, and the large appliquéd yellow hand. The use of velvet to highlight some of the fans is an extraordinary feature.

Hints for Collectors
Few bedcovers as elaborate and finely worked as this one appear on the market. With its elegant embroidery and overall sense of design, it exemplifies the artistry of the Victorian era. Only 10 or 20 years ago, the decorative arts of the late 19th century were largely ignored by collectors. Today Victorian pieces are much in demand. The lesson is clear: Tastes change, and textiles that are currently undervalued may command substantial sums in the future.

Price Guide Group: Crazy Quilts.

Courtesy America Hurrah Antiques, New York City.

Coverlets

American coverlets of the 18th and 19th centuries are admired today for their beauty and skillful weaves, but in early America they were prized for their usefulness. Coverlets had to be warm, above all else, for even the most luxurious homes were drafty and poorly heated. Probably the first settlers to arrive in America brought coverlets with them along with their other household goods, but very soon they began to make bedcovers in this country. While the wealthy could continue to import textiles from Europe, the vast majority of American colonists had to be self-sufficient; most families possessed both a spinning wheel for spinning linen and woolen threads as well as a four-harness loom for weaving. Learning how to spin and weave was an essential part of a child's education.

The first woven coverlets in America were produced by women on handlooms in the home. By the beginning of the 19th century, however, male professional weavers began to arrive from England, Ireland, Scotland, France, and Germany, attracted by the promise of ample employment and political and social stability. Many of these weavers settled in the Northeast, and others moved on to the Midwest. Like the folk painter, the 19th-century weaver led an itinerant life, traveling from town to town in quest of those who might require his services. Upon arrival in a new location, he would advertise in the local newspaper and set up his loom wherever he could find lodgings. A client would select a pattern from the weaver's book, and it would be woven with slight variations. Some weavers established themselves in a permanent location where the population was of sufficient size to support a weaver on a regular basis. Often the weaver who had a shop also wove carpets to special order.

Although several kinds of coverlets are known from the late 18th and early 19th centuries, only four basic types remain today: the

Detail of a Double Weave coverlet. Collection of Rowenna Pounds.

Overshot, the Double Weave, the Summer and Winter, and the Jacquard.

Overshot

Made on four-harness looms, Overshot coverlets are among the earliest American woven bedcovers. The name "overshot" describes the weaving technique. The horizontal, or weft, threads were allowed to skip, or "overshoot," three or more vertical, or warp, threads at a time, giving the coverlet a thick but loosely woven appearance. Because of this loose weave, Overshot coverlets tended to wear out easily. The warp threads were generally made of natural, undyed cotton, and the weft of dyed wool. The cotton added strength to the textile while the wool gave warmth. Overshot coverlets made after 1830 used a colored warp as well as multicolored wefts. Patterns usually combine stripes, squares, and diamonds, using a "floating" weft of colored thread over the plain background. Because of the narrow loom frame, these coverlets were always made of two pieces and seamed through the middle. In the South it was believed that an uneven seam would turn away evil spirits and insure good luck for the person who used the spread.

Double Weave

The second principal type of coverlet is the Double Weave, sometimes called the Double Cloth. It was woven on handlooms as well as fully and partially mechanized looms. Although Double Weaves are thought to have been made as early as 1725, surviving examples date from 1800 to 1900. Double Weave coverlets have two sets of warps and two sets of wefts, simultaneously producing two separate layers of cloth that are interwoven at predetermined intervals. The layers of cloth can actually be pulled apart. Many modern upholstery fabrics are woven in the same way and are called "pocket-weave." The

Detail of an Overshot coverlet. Courtesy Ruth Bigel Antiques, New York City.

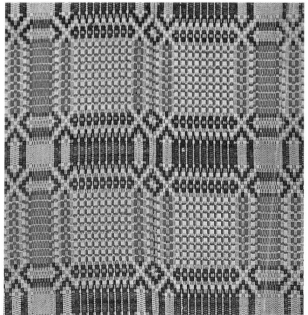

pattern on one side of the Double Weave is repeated on the reverse side, usually in a lighter color. For this reason Double Weaves are often confused with Summer and Winter coverlets, which are also reversible but only of a single thickness.

Summer and Winter

The Summer and Winter coverlet seems to have originated in Pennsylvania in the early 19th century. The professional weavers who emigrated from Germany created most of the surviving Summer and Winter coverlets on looms with five or more harnesses. Similar in construction to the Overshot coverlet, the Summer and Winter spread differs in that the supplementary weft never goes over more than three warp threads at a time. It is therefore more tightly woven. The name Summer and Winter refers to the fact that the pattern on one side is reversed on the other; the lighter-colored side was meant for summer display and the darker one for use in winter. Overshot, Double Weave, and Summer and Winter coverlets were usually woven in geometric patterns, sometimes with design motifs similar to those on quilts. Specific coverlet patterns were named, although, just as with quilts, names varied greatly from region to region.

Jacquard

The fourth coverlet form is the Jacquard, a term referring to a coverlet made on a loom that was fitted with a special mechanical device known as the Jacquard attachment. This device was introduced in France by the weaver Joseph Jacquard in 1801 and brought to America in the 1820s. Not only did the Jacquard attachment greatly increase the speed for making a coverlet, it also organized the warp and weft threads according to holes on a series of cards that resemble old-fashioned player piano rolls or today's computer punch cards.

Detail of a Jacquard coverlet. Private Collection.

These cards activated the loom and thereby dictated the pattern. The Jacquard attachment could also be added to existing looms used to make Double Weave coverlets. But this attachment was difficult to operate and was therefore used only by professional weavers.

For the first time, it was possible to create large, unseamed coverlets with complicated curvilinear patterns and elaborate borders. So distinctive are these border designs that some collectors specialize in different types, such as eagles, urns, rosettes, and buildings. In one corner of the Jacquard coverlet, the weaver usually included his name, the name of the destined owner, and often the town, state, and date of weaving. Because of this signature block, we have more precise information about Jacquard coverlets than any other type. Although some handweavers also wove their names into their coverlets, to do so was time consuming and rarely attempted. Many weavers named their patterns, although just as with quilts and other bedcovers, the same pattern could be given different regional names.

Colors and Dyes
Although the pattern designs differed, all four types of coverlets tended to use a limited color range, which is quite distinct from the multihued palette seen in quilt fabrics. The more restricted spectrum was partly due to the dyes available for the wool threads.

By far the most popular dye was indigo-blue, originally imported from India but also derived from a wild plant that grew in the southern states. Red dye was produced from imported Asian madder root or South American cochineal, made from the dried bodies of small insects. At first these imported dyes were sold by itinerant peddlers in the Northeast, and later in general stores throughout the country. Other colors came from homemade

Detail of a Jacquard coverlet. Private Collection.

vegetable dyes, such as brown from the bark of red oak or hickory, and yellow from peach leaves, goldenrod, or black-eyed Susans.

Weaving Mills

By the mid–19th century, coverlets had begun to be produced in weaving mills on fully mechanized looms. Most of these factories were located in the industrial Northeast and parts of the Midwest. While their size varied, they were usually created by several weavers banding together or a father-and-son team that had hired additional helpers.

Initially the weaving factories specialized in the production of textile materials and the manufacture of carpets. But soon the popularity of woven bedcovers encouraged many to expand their operations to include coverlets. One such factory was Cockfair Mills, founded in Indiana in 1816. Originally this mill did only carding and fulling of cotton, but later on converted to weaving. Cockfair employed seven men and, like most mills, used water-powered looms.

Numerous smaller operations existed, such as the Franklin Woolen Factory in Ohio, which employed three men. Yet in 1850, with only a small staff, Franklin was able to produce 500 coverlets and 1500 yards of carpets, valued at about $3700. Prices for coverlets varied from region to region, although the differences were slight. The Franklin Woolen Factory sold its coverlets for about $6, while those at the Globe Factory in Pennsylvania brought $4.

Like the itinerant weavers before them, the mills devised their own signature blocks or trademarks to be incorporated into the design of a bedcover. Signature blocks often included the name of the factory, the maker, and the date, while trademarks were generally confined to linear designs or representational motifs

Detail of a Jacquard border. Courtesy Museum of American Folk Art, New York City.

like flowers. During the Civil War, however, most weaving factories turned to the manufacture of blankets for the military and ceased coverlet production.

The hand-weaving industry never recovered, except for a fleeting revival of interest in coverlets around the time of the Philadelphia Centennial celebration in 1876. Only in parts of Appalachia, Ohio, Indiana, and Illinois has the tradition lived on to a minor extent. In these areas, coverlets with simple geometric designs are still being woven on old handlooms. It is not difficult, however, to distinguish these new coverlets from those made in the 19th century. Not only will the antique textile show more wear, but the fabric will feel softer. New coverlets tend to feel crisp.

Detail of a Jacquard signature block. Courtesy Ruth Bigel Antiques, New York City.

Description
One-piece Jacquard coverlet. Central medallion has large twelve-pointed red and white star flanked by 2 elaborate scrolls. Multiple frames of leaf and floral motifs, leaf figures in corners, and white running diamond border. Inner border geometric and floral design. Outer border trailing vine with large flowers on 3 sides; no border at top. Signed and dated in lower corner blocks. Red fringe on 3 sides.

Materials and Dimensions
Cotton and wool. 92″ × 80″.

Maker, Locality, and Period
John Seibert, Jr. or Sr. Lehigh County, Pennsylvania. 1848.

Comment
Coverlets made by professional weavers were often signed and dated. In fact, a signature usually indicates that a piece was made by a professional. Both John Seiberts, Jr. and Sr., are known to have been active weavers in Lowhill Township, Lehigh County, Pennsylvania, in the 1840s. Several signed examples of their work are extant, but whether father or son made this coverlet is not known. Woven in one piece, with a Jacquard attachment, this bedcover is an excellent example of what was technically possible with the attachment when coupled with a fully mechanized loom.

Hints for Collectors
This bedcover is in extraordinarily fine condition. The red remains brilliant and all the strands of fringe are intact. It is also well documented, which is important in determining authenticity, especially when a coverlet looks as new as this one does.

Price Guide Group: Jacquard Coverlets.

Private Collection.

Centennial Design

Description
One-piece Jacquard coverlet. Central eight-pointed blue star surrounded by smaller blue stars on white field, floral wreath, scalloped border, larger floral wreath, elaborate scroll border, and field of blue diamonds. In each corner, eagle with spread wings clasps shield and arrows. Frame of white running diamonds. Inner border has leaf and floral motifs, with wreath in 2 lower corners. Zigzag outer border. Blue fringe on 3 sides.

Materials and Dimensions
All wool. 86″ × 78″.

Maker, Locality, and Period
Maker unknown. Pennsylvania. c. 1876.

Comment
The American eagle was a very popular design motif in the 19th century. Its use in coverlet decoration declined in the 1840s, but was revived during the Philadelphia Centennial of 1876. The coverlet illustrated, with its eagles and shields, is a good example of work in the Centennial period. The popularity of woven bedcovers waned after 1850 except for the few made around the time of the Philadelphia exposition. By the turn of the century they had disappeared from American households.

Hints for Collectors
Coverlets from this period were until recently thought to be garish. With the increasing interest in early American textiles, however, and the current vogue for quilts, collectors are also beginning to appreciate these textiles.

Price Guide Group: Jacquard Coverlets.

Courtesy Jay Johnson, America's Folk Heritage Gallery, New York City.

Floral Medallions

Description
Two-piece Jacquard coverlet. 2 full and 2 partial large floral medallions, each with central oval medallion. White pattern on blue ground. Border has pairs of eagles crowned by stars that form arches; building between eagles at 2 sides as well as pairs of pillars and eagles at 3 sides. Phrases in corner blocks.

Materials and Dimensions
Cotton and wool. 99½″ × 76″.

Maker, Locality, and Period
Maker unknown. New York State. c. 1840.

Comment
It was common for professionals to weave their name as well as that of the buyer into one or more corner blocks, but phrases or sayings were sometimes substituted. Of these, moral or religious phrases are by far the most popular. This coverlet bears the unusual motto: "AGRICULTURE AND MANUFACTURES ARE THE FOUNDATION OF OUR INDEPENDENCE," most likely expressing the maker's view of his growing country.

Hints for Collectors
A coverlet like the example illustrated may be of special interest to a collector because its motto expresses an attitude typical of the age. The pattern seems to continue off the top of the bedcover, creating an unbalanced design. Because this appears to have been the weaver's intention, it does not diminish the value of the piece.

Price Guide Group: Jacquard Coverlets.

Collection of William C. Ketchum, Jr.

Medallion and Stripe

Description
Two-piece Jacquard coverlet. 24 full and partial floral medallions in dark blue and white, connected by floral stripes and separated by white trailing vines. Dark blue and white fringe on 3 sides.

Materials and Dimensions
Cotton and wool. 90″ × 76″.

Maker, Locality, and Period
Maker and locality unknown. c. 1850.

Comment
Coverlets like this could have been made in the Midwest as well as the Northeast, for by the mid–19th century, many patterns were widely published. Since more people were able to travel across the United States, styles in the decorative arts spread quickly.

Hints for Collectors
Until recently coverlets like the example illustrated were much less popular among collectors than the earlier Overshot or Summer and Winter types. But, as more collectors become interested in coverlets and the earlier types become increasingly rare, mid-19th-century examples, especially those in fine condition, are now sought after as well. Also, the 1970s and 1980s have brought a reevaluation of Victorian design, and collectors are now paying more attention to this previously neglected decorative style. As a result, such coverlets are likely to increase in value.

Price Guide Group: Jacquard Coverlets.

Private Collection.

E Pluribus Unum

Description
One-piece Jacquard coverlet. 70 blue eagles holding branch, each surrounded on 3 sides by motto "E PLURIBUS UNUM." Border has horses and small potted plants; row of geometric designs on top and bottom edge. Each corner has floral motif. White ground. Blue and white fringe on bottom.

Materials and Dimensions
Cotton and wool. 87″ × 71″.

Maker, Locality, and Period
Maker unknown. Pennsylvania. c. 1840.

Comment
With its complex design, curvilinear forms, and absence of a center seam, this coverlet was certainly woven with a Jacquard attachment on a large fully mechanized loom. Such a complicated bedcover could not have been made on a handloom or even a half-mechanized loom.

Hints for Collectors
For most collectors handwoven coverlets are more desirable than those made on mechanized looms. Yet some collectors are drawn to these machine-woven coverlets because of their more intricate designs. In the example illustrated the pattern and colors are particularly pleasing; the inscription and eagles are true Americana. Eagles are one of the most common coverlet motifs, along with flowers, birds, willow trees, and buildings. Notice the contrasting border with horses and potted plants in this well-preserved coverlet.

Price Guide Group: Jacquard Coverlets.

Courtesy America Hurrah Antiques, New York City.

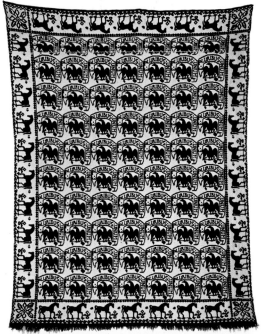

Tiles with Eagle Border

Description
One-piece Double Weave Jacquard coverlet. Alternating rows of
tile and floral motifs in white. Border on 3 sides; stylized eagles
and columns on left and right, eagles and diamonds on bottom.
Signed and dated in lower corner blocks. Blue binding.

Materials and Dimensions
Cotton and wool. 87½″ × 76″.

Maker, Locality, and Period
Possibly P. M. Morehouse. Locality unknown. 1837.

Comment
The blue and white coverlet remained popular in England as well
as America until the introduction of synthetic dyes in the late
19th century. Before this time dyes were scarce. One way to
produce the color blue was by soaking it out of the indigo paper
used to wrap imported loaves of cane sugar. Many homes still
had an indigo tub on the back of the stove until the early 20th
century, even though synthetic indigo was available
after 1890.

Hints for Collectors
Blue and white coverlets like the one shown are quite common,
although not all are signed and dated. As with any textile, such
documentation adds to its value. Since this is the only coverlet
extant with the name P. M. Morehouse on it, it is not known
whether the name refers to the coverlet's maker or the person
for whom it was made.

Price Guide Group: Jacquard Coverlets.

Courtesy Greenfield Village and Henry Ford Museum, Dearborn, Michigan.

Floral Wreath

Description
One-piece Jacquard coverlet. 20 large floral wreaths in dark blue on white alternate with rows of stylized bird motifs. Small blue leaves and flowers between larger motifs. Bordered on 3 sides with leaf and floral motifs edged by narrow band of geometric shapes. Bottom corner squares have leaf medallions. Blue binding at top and bottom.

Materials and Dimensions
Cotton and wool. 88½″ × 78½″.

Maker, Locality, and Period
Maker and locality unknown. c. 1850.

Comment
In the mid–19th century a blue and white coverlet with a lavish, undulating design would have been considered very fashionable. As in all Victorian decorative arts, coverlet design was rich in detail. A coverlet like the example illustrated, despite its complicated pattern, would have been made quickly, for with the Jacquard attachment, such designs were easy to execute. In fact, a fine coverlet could be produced in only a single day.

Hints for Collectors
Always inspect a coverlet carefully for any alterations made after it was first woven. Restoration of small tears does not substantially affect the value of a spread, but a major change, such as cutting a coverlet down from its original size, would lessen its worth.

Price Guide Group: Jacquard Coverlets.

Courtesy Ruth Bigel Antiques, New York City.

Description

Two-piece Jacquard coverlet. 20 motifs of Double Rose pattern in white, interspersed with floral designs and small eight-pointed stars. Border on 3 sides in grape-and-leaf pattern above running diamond. Lower corner blocks signed. Dated within diamonds in lower corners. Dark blue fringe on sides and off-white fringe on bottom.

Materials and Dimensions

Cotton and wool. 96″ × 82″.

Maker, Locality, and Period

William Lowmiller. Lycoming County, Pennsylvania. 1845.

Comment

This coverlet, woven on a handloom with a Jacquard attachment, was made in 2 sections and then sewn together—notice the thin white line running down its center. Early handloomed Jacquard coverlets, like this one, are rare, as mechanized looms were in general use by the 1820s. After the Civil War, mass production stifled any attempt to revive the art of making coverlets except by mechanical means.

Hints for Collectors

Blue and white were the most popular colors used for early coverlets, and they remain very popular among collectors today. If the white appears dirty, remember that age may be a factor or that undyed cotton appears cream-colored rather than pure white. Cotton was usually not dyed because colors tended to fade, while wool held them remarkably well.

Price Guide Group: Jacquard Coverlets.

Private Collection.

211 Double Rose with Bird and Rosebush Border

Description
Two-piece Jacquard coverlet. 20 full and partial Double Rose patterns in red alternate with 25 large full and partial floral and bird motifs in red and blue. Bird and rosebush motif border on 3 sides in red and blue. 2 corner blocks signed and dated. Red and blue fringe on sides, beige fringe on bottom, and top hemmed in blue.

Materials and Dimensions
Cotton and wool. 94″ × 80″.

Maker, Locality, and Period
Gabriel Rauser. Delaware County, Ohio. 1843.

Comment
Many American coverlets made on a handloom with the Jacquard attachment were signed in one or both of the corner blocks. Gabriel Rauser, whose name appears on this coverlet, worked in Ohio in the mid–19th century. In some cases, the name on a coverlet represented the person it was made for, and occasionally both the weaver's name and the buyer's name were included.

Hints for Collectors
Although professional weavers worked from pattern books, they prided themselves on their individuality. The floral and double bird motifs illustrated here were very popular in Ohio during the mid–19th century, yet there are an amazing number of variations. Because coverlets were often signed and dated, it is possible to compare the work of one weaver with that of another. Signed coverlets are considered more valuable than the unsigned work of a comparable weaver.

Price Guide Group: Jacquard Coverlets.

Private Collection.

Double Rose with Bird and Rosebush Border

Description
Two-piece Jacquard coverlet. 54 full and partial Double Rose motifs in blue and red alternate with red and blue stars. Bordered on 2 sides with red and blue roosters above row of small stylized flowers. Border on bottom has red and blue rosebushes and birds. Corner blocks signed and dated. Red and blue fringe on 2 sides, white fringe on bottom.

Materials and Dimensions
Cotton and wool. 90″ × 71½″.

Maker, Locality, and Period
F. Yearous. Ashland County, Ohio. 1853.

Comment
The Double Rose pattern, popular in Philadelphia as well as the Midwest, was fairly common, but the example illustrated is an original variation. Note the repetition of the red and blue Double Rose motif in a smaller version in blue, creating continuous running diagonals of double roses and stars in red and blue.

Hints for Collectors
Coverlet weavers took great pride in creating their own variations of published patterns, which they often renamed. As with quilt patterns, the names given coverlet designs changed over the years and from one region to another. Examining the patterns on a number of coverlets is a good way of familiarizing yourself with the more common ones, making it possible to recognize unique or effective variations.

Price Guide Group: Jacquard Coverlets.

Courtesy Ruth Bigel Antiques, New York City.

213 Modified Oak Leaf with Oak Tree Border

Description
One-piece Jacquard coverlet. 24 full and partial white oak leaf medallions, each with 4 modified oak leaves. Separated by small white stars and white floral medallions with curling leaves. Lower 2 corners signed and dated. Bordered on 2 sides with white oak trees; bottom border has white floral motif crowned by narrow blue and white band with linear design, and below, band of red and white running diamonds. Red and blue fringe in wide stripes on 3 sides, 4th side hemmed.

Materials and Dimensions
Cotton and wool. 93½″ × 70½″.

Maker, Locality, and Period
Probably Jacob Hausman, Sr. Berks County, Pennsylvania. 1845.

Comment
It was not uncommon during the mid–19th century for more than one member of a family to be a coverlet weaver. In Europe such skills were often passed on from father to son, and to some extent this tradition continued in America. Jacob Hausman, Sr., who lived in Lobachsville, Berks County, Pennsylvania, had 5 sons, all of whom were coverlet weavers. One son was named Jacob, Jr., but the date on the coverlet suggests it was the work of the father.

Hints for Collectors
Comparing the coverlets of one weaver with the work of another is useful, not only to discern an individual weaver's style, but also to trace the popularity of specific patterns and the history of a particular community of weavers.

Price Guide Group: Jacquard Coverlets.

Courtesy Ruth Bigel Antiques, New York City.

Floral Medallion

Description
Two-piece Jacquard coverlet. 5 rows of 4 red, dark blue, and white floral medallions alternating with rows of elaborate diamond-shaped leaf motifs with curved sides. Floral and leaf border on 3 sides. Medallion in 2 corner blocks. Off-white fringe on bottom.

Materials and Dimensions
Cotton and wool. 85½″ × 68″.

Maker, Locality, and Period
Maker and locality unknown. c. 1850.

Comment
Made of 2 loom widths sewn together, this coverlet is an example of a transitional design that was popular after the geometric Summer and Winter and Double Weave types were in style. They preceded the elaborate, full-size factory-woven Jacquards of the late Victorian period. By mid-century, synthetic dyes were readily available in America, vastly expanding the range of possible colors. They could be purchased at stores or ordered through the mail.

Hints for Collectors
When buying a coverlet always become familiar with its history, if possible, including information about the previous owners, the maker, or where it was found. Although it takes time, write down the information and keep a file on each object in your collection. One detail often leads to another, and as new information is discovered, the collector may be able to determine the origins of similar textiles.

Price Guide Group: Jacquard Coverlets.

Courtesy Ruth Bigel Antiques, New York City.

215 Snowflake Medallion with Hemfield Railroad Border

Description
Two-piece Jacquard coverlet. 20 full and partial snowflake medallions in white, interspersed with 3 types of variant medallions on dark blue and brown. White side borders have double row of railroad motifs; single row of same design on top and bottom. Pair of profiles encircled by words "HEMFIELD RAILROAD" in each corner. Red and white and dark blue and white fringe on 3 sides, 4th side hemmed.

Materials and Dimensions
Cotton and wool. 90¼″ × 81″.

Maker, Locality, and Period
Probably Daniel Campbell, William Harper, Martin Burns, George Coulter, or Harvey Cook. Pennsylvania or West Virginia. c. 1840–50.

Comment
The Jacquard attachment for the handloom was expensive and difficult to work; consequently it was used almost exclusively by commercial weavers. The pattern of the example illustrated was too complicated to make on an old handloom. It commemorates the opening of the Hemfield Railroad, but the location of the railroad is unknown. The profile figures in the corner blocks are thought to represent T. McKennan, the president of the railroad.

Hints for Collectors
The piece illustrated is one of only 5 known examples of this very rare coverlet pattern. Its mysterious history, brilliant colors, and original two-color fringe make this coverlet extremely valuable.

Price Guide Group: Jacquard Coverlets.

Courtesy Museum of American Folk Art, New York City.

Tiles Design

Description
Two-piece Jacquard coverlet. 12 full and partial circular shapes in white on black and with concentric diamonds and floral motif in center. White floral motifs on orange-red squares between ovals. Each square enclosed by curving diamond-shaped outline whose sides form oval around each circular motif. Orange-red, black, and white fringe on 3 sides, 4th side hemmed.

Materials and Dimensions
Cotton and wool. 84″ × 74″.

Maker, Locality, and Period
Maker and locality unknown. c. 1850.

Comment
Many European weavers, who were trained to operate the Jacquard loom attachment, emigrated to the United States from England, Scotland, France, and Germany, and moved to the less industrialized Midwest, where there was more opportunity to work. The coverlet illustrated, very similar in its design to ingrain carpeting, may have come from Indiana. Many of the most active weaving families of Scotland resettled there, and may have helped produce the double cloth carpets that were dyed in the fiber, or "in the grain"; hence the name ingrain.

Hints for Collectors
Although several checklists of coverlet weavers have been published, as well as handbooks of coverlet techniques and catalogues of museum collections, much research remains to be done on woven bedcovers. The collector who reads the literature and knows what is available in his or her particular area may know more about coverlets than many antiques dealers.

Price Guide Group: Jacquard Coverlets.

Private Collection.

217 Tile Design with True Boston Border

Description
Two-piece Jacquard coverlet. 20 dark blue and white eight-pointed stars and 30 full and partial medallions connected by floral stripes. Border at bottom an intricate floral pattern; side border composed of rows of buildings known as True Boston Border. Dated in both lower corners. Dark blue and white fringe at bottom.

Materials and Dimensions
Cotton and wool. 98″ × 77″.

Maker, Locality, and Period
Maker unknown. Possibly from Cockfair Mills. Harmony, Indiana. 1848.

Comment
Most coverlets woven on a handloom with a Jacquard attachment were made in 2 pieces and sewn together down the middle. In the example illustrated, the seam is easy to see because the coverlet is slightly discolored where it has been sewn. Indiana coverlets typically have fringe on 1 side—occasionally on 3—and 3-sided borders with 2 signature blocks at the bottom. Note that the lower 2 corners have what appears to be the Cockfair Mills trademark—cross-hatched corner blocks with dates. Cockfair Mills was founded in 1816 and, using water-powered looms, specialized in weaving.

Hints for Collectors
Attributing a coverlet to a particular weaver solely on the basis of its pattern is not possible. Pattern books were widely used and original designs often copied.

Price Guide Group: Jacquard Coverlets.

Private Collection.

218 Sunburst Medallion with Potted Rose and Bird Border

Description
Two-piece Jacquard coverlet. 12 sunburst motifs in cream-color on black, red, and faded olive-green, separated by dark blue stripes with rows of leaf and floral motifs. Bordered on 3 sides with alternating potted roses and birds. Black, red, dark blue, and olive-green fringe on 2 sides; beige fringe on bottom.

Materials and Dimensions
Cotton and wool. 90″ × 76″.

Maker, Locality, and Period
Maker and locality unknown. c. 1850.

Comment
As the 19th century progressed, coverlet designs became more and more complicated, eventually giving way to the grandiose designs of the Victorian period. The example illustrated is stylistically a transitional piece: the center retains the overall geometric feeling of handloomed pieces, but the borders are filled with flowing, organic forms in a style not found earlier. To a certain extent the simple designs of handloomed coverlets resulted from the limitations of the loom, for the flowing lines seen in the border of this piece would not have been possible without the Jacquard attachment.

Hints for Collectors
In general, Jacquards woven on partially mechanized looms are more desirable in the marketplace than those woven on fully mechanized looms. As the earlier coverlets become increasingly rare, however, collectors are refocusing their attention on fine Jacquards that are completely machine woven.

Price Guide Group: Jacquard Coverlets.

Private Collection.

219 **Floral Medallion with Rose Border**

Description
Two-piece Jacquard coverlet. 24 red, dark blue, green, and white floral medallions, each separated by a blue, red, yellow, and white eight-petaled flower. Bordered on 2 sides by modified red, yellow, green, and blue tulips. Bottom border has blue, red, and green stylized trees. Running diamond band below trees. Lower 2 corners signed and dated. Red, dark blue, green, and yellow fringe on 3 sides.

Materials and Dimensions
Cotton and wool. 103⅜" × 84".

Maker, Locality, and Period
Charles Wiand. Allentown, Pennsylvania. 1844.

Comment
Shortly after the Jacquard attachment was introduced into America, a large number of professional weavers from the British Isles and Europe came to the United States, bringing with them the knowledge of how to operate the new half-mechanized looms. Some settled in the Northeast, but others moved to Indiana, Illinois, Iowa, or Ohio, frequently in small towns where there was a need for their skills. These weavers often wove their name, initials, or trademark, along with the date, into one or more corner blocks of a coverlet, as seen in the example illustrated.

Hints for Collectors
As a rule, more complicated, flowing designs generally appear later in the 19th century. It is not possible, however, to date coverlets on style alone.

Price Guide Group: Jacquard Coverlets.

Courtesy Museum of American Folk Art, New York City.

Double Oak Leaf with Oak Tree Border

Description
Two-piece Jacquard coverlet. 24 full and partial squares composed of Double Oak leaves in white on red, black, and olive-green. Oak leaves are separated by red, black, white, and olive-green floral grid. Bordered on 3 sides with oak trees and tulips above red, black, and green running diamond motif. 2 lower corner blocks signed and dated. Red, black, and olive-green fringe on 3 sides.

Materials and Dimensions
Cotton and wool. 94″ × 83″.

Maker, Locality, and Period
J. Lantz. Lancaster or Northampton County, Pennsylvania. 1837.

Comment
By 1837 coverlet weaving had become a profitable business, and many immigrant weavers were well established in their communities. Many towns, however, were not large enough to support a full-time professional, and weavers had to work as farmers or storekeepers as well. Even in hamlets such materials as cotton and wool were readily available to coverlet makers. Cotton yarn was spun by machine in eastern factories and transported to all parts of America.

Hints for Collectors
In contrast to the 19th-century quiltmaker, who was for the most part an anonymous homemaker, the weaver was a skilled craftsman and often quite well off. Coverlets were highly prized and often signed in the weave: the example illustrated has the names of the weaver and the person who ordered it and the date in each of the 2 corner blocks.

Price Guide Group: Jacquard Coverlets.

Private Collection.

Double Oak Leaf with Tulip Border

Description
Two-piece Jacquard coverlet. 24 full and partial squares, each with red and blue Double Oak leaf pattern on beige ground. Oak leaves separated by red and blue floral grid. Bordered on 3 sides by oak trees and tulips. 2 corner blocks signed and dated. Dark blue fringe on 3 sides; 4th side hemmed.

Materials and Dimensions
Cotton and wool. 96″ × 82″.

Maker, Locality, and Period
Benjamin Hausman. Allentown, Pennsylvania. 1838.

Comment
The half-mechanized Jacquard loom attachment revolutionized the coverlet industry, making weaving easier and much faster. A coverlet might have taken weeks to complete with a handloom, but with even a partially mechanized loom—prepared the night before—it could be made in a day. The number of harnesses, or frames, that could be used also increased dramatically, making possible more complex and varied designs. But by the time the Civil War ended, tastes had changed significantly, and coverlets were never again as much in demand as they had been between 1830 and 1850.

Hints for Collectors
After 1890 most dyes used were commercially produced and reasonably colorfast, yet many coverlet makers chose to dye their thread with natural pigments, which were not always permanent. In the coverlet illustrated, the colors have remained bright, but the fringe is very worn. This makes the coverlet slightly less valuable.

Price Guide Group: Jacquard Coverlets.

Private Collection.

Star and Diamond

Description
Two-piece Summer and Winter coverlet. 260 eight-pointed stars alternate in rows of red and dark blue set on white; between stars are rows of blue, gold, and red diamonds. Bordered on 2 sides in red, blue, and gold modified herringbone patterns; border at bottom modified stars. Corner blocks red and blue diagonal stripes. Red, blue, and gold fringe on sides, white fringe at bottom.

Materials and Dimensions
Cotton and wool. 104½″ × 70¼″.

Maker, Locality, and Period
Maker and locality unknown. c. 1820.

Comment
Classified here as a Summer and Winter coverlet, this example could also be called a Multiple Shaft coverlet, which is a kind of bedcover made with as many as 18 shafts, or harnesses, for the pattern and 2 for the ground.

Hints for Collectors
Coverlets similar to the example illustrated were also made in Canada during the early 19th century. In general, Canadian coverlets are less expensive than their American counterparts since they are less in demand. Collectors should be aware that Canadian coverlets are often sold as though they were of American provenance. If a coverlet is Canadian, a collector generally should not pay as much for it.

Price Guide Group: Overshot and Summer and Winter Geometric Coverlets.

Courtesy Ruth Bigel Antiques, New York City.

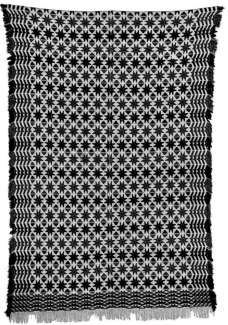

Star and Diamond

Description
Two-piece Summer and Winter coverlet. 180 whole and 6 half stars alternate with rows of red-white-and-blue diamonds set on beige field. Stars woven so they create an interlocking series of circles. Bordered on 3 sides by 4 rows of partial stars and red and blue fringe. Top edge bound and partially fringed.

Materials and Dimensions
Cotton and wool. 102″ × 84″.

Maker, Locality, and Period
Maker and locality unknown. c. 1820.

Comment
Although professional weavers also made Double Weave, Overshot, and Summer and Winter coverlets, it is more likely that the example illustrated was made at home on a handloom. The Star and Diamond was a traditional pattern, and would have been readily available through the mail. While the design is regular across the lower half of the coverlet, it becomes irregular in the middle of the upper half because 2 differently woven widths of cloth were sewn together.

Hints for Collectors
Most Summer and Winter coverlets were woven with a cotton warp and a wool weft, as in the example illustrated, but some were also made entirely of wool or linen. Those made only of cotton, however, are extremely rare; some cotton "coverlets" may, in fact, have been used as tablecloths.

Price Guide Group: Overshot and Summer and Winter Geometric Coverlets.

Courtesy George E. Schoellkopf Gallery, New York City.

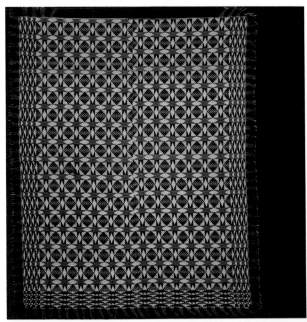

Star and Diamond

Description
Two-piece Summer and Winter coverlet. 100 red-and-white and
purple eight-pointed stars with 4 small white diamonds alternate
in horizontal rows with larger diamonds of red-and-white and
purple. Borders at top and bottom have thin triangular motifs.
Borders at sides have modified pine trees. Rows of small red,
white, and blue triangles in corner blocks. Fringe at bottom.

Materials and Dimensions
Cotton and wool. 88″ × 66″.

Maker, Locality, and Period
Maker and locality unknown. c. 1820.

Comment
The term "Summer and Winter" is thought to have originated in
North America, and refers to the reversible design of such
coverlets. It is believed that the darker side was used in winter,
and the lighter in summer. The design is exactly the same on
both sides, but the colors are reversed. The term "Summer and
Winter" is somewhat confusing, however, as Double Weave and
Jacquard coverlets also have the same positive/negative effect.

Hints for Collectors
While coverlets like the example illustrated are popular in the
Midwest, they are still available at surprisingly low prices in the
Northeast, where textile collectors are much more interested in
antique quilts. As is often the case with 19th-century coverlets,
the fringe has all but worn away, and this example has a lower
value than a perfect one.

Price Guide Group: Overshot and Summer and Winter
Geometric Coverlets.

Courtesy Jay Johnson, America's Folk Heritage Gallery, New York City.

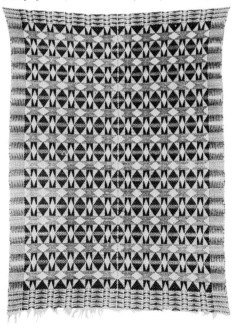

225 Snowflake and Flowers

Description
Two-piece Summer and Winter coverlet. Horizontal rows of red and white flowers and small snowflakes alternating with blue and white large and small snowflakes. Bordered on 3 sides by modified floral motifs in red, white, and blue. No fringe or binding.

Materials and Dimensions
Cotton and wool. 80″ × 73″.

Maker, Locality, and Period
Maker and locality unknown. c. 1820.

Comment
Although many coverlets were made at home on a handloom, others were made by itinerant weavers, who would set up shop in a small town and weave coverlets in partial exchange for wool and local products. The bedcover patterns were chosen in consultation with the buyer from the book of patterns the weaver brought with him. Coverlet patterns, called "drafts," were intricately detailed notations which recorded the exact construction of each coverlet. The weaver had only to be careful not to repeat the same pattern in the same town.

Hints for Collectors
Except for some in private hands, there are few comprehensive collections of coverlets in America today. The most important resource for those interested in American coverlets is the Art Institute of Chicago; for Canadian coverlets, the Royal Ontario Museum.

Price Guide Group: Overshot and Summer and Winter Geometric Coverlets.

Courtesy Jay Johnson, America's Folk Heritage Gallery, New York City.

Snowball with Pine Tree Border

Description
One-piece Summer and Winter coverlet. Horizontal rows of 102 gray snowball motifs set on bluish gray field, each enclosed in block with small white square at each corner. Bordered on 2 sides with pine tree motifs. Mauve binding.

Materials and Dimensions
Cotton. 103″ × 84″.

Maker, Locality, and Period
Maker and locality unknown. Late 19th century.

Comment
The first cotton factory was established in Massachusetts in the 1780s; many others quickly followed. With the ready demand, large cotton plantations in the South were busy providing raw materials for factories in the North. The mechanical spinning of yarn revolutionized coverlet making, and cotton available at a reasonable price soon replaced linen, which was grown at home and required a long and arduous process to turn into yarn. The coverlet illustrated is rare because both warp and weft are cotton. In most coverlets, cotton yarn was combined with wool, which took the dye more easily.

Hints for Collectors
This textile is referred to as a coverlet, but its narrow width suggests it may have been intended for use as a table covering. While most bedcovers in this style were made between 1810 and 1830, in certain rural areas they were made until the late 19th century.

Price Guide Group: Overshot and Summer and Winter Geometric Coverlets.

Collection of William C. Ketchum, Jr.

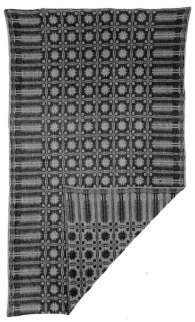

227 Snowball with Pine Tree Border

Description
Two-piece Double Weave coverlet. Blocks of 4 white snowball motifs with interlocking grid surround 9 small modified snowballs set on dark blue field. Framed by series of modified Xs and Os. Pine Tree border on 4 sides in white and dark blue interlocking at corners.

Materials and Dimensions
Cotton and wool. 86″ × 70″.

Maker, Locality, and Period
Maker and locality unknown. c. 1820.

Comment
Although new coverlet patterns were constantly being designed, they were based on a limited number of motifs. Different patterns could be created by grouping motifs together, separating them from other motifs, or weaving them in a variety of colors. The Snowball pattern worked especially well in the essentially geometric designs produced by the Double Weave technique, as did the Pine Tree border. A number of variations of this border were made, including the one illustrated—3 pine trees grouped together in each motif.

Hints for Collectors
Even though Double Weave coverlets were usually made by professional weavers, they were seldom signed or dated because of the technical difficulty of doing so on a handloom. The few that were are extremely rare and coveted by serious collectors. They are worth considerably more in the marketplace than undocumented examples, provided they are in good condition.

Price Guide Group: Double Weave Geometric Coverlets.

Courtesy Ruth Bigel Antiques, New York City.

Snowball with Pine Tree Border

Description
Two-piece Summer and Winter coverlet. 48 red snowball motifs enclosed in blocks with 2 small red squares at each corner, except for blocks that are adjacent to border. Bordered on 3 sides by red pine tree motifs interlocking in corners. Red and blue fringe on 3 sides; 4th side hemmed.

Materials and Dimensions
Cotton and wool. 91½″ × 76″.

Maker, Locality, and Period
Maker and locality unknown. c. 1830.

Comment
Summer and Winter coverlets were constructed in the same way as the Overshot type, except that the supplementary wefts in the Summer and Winter never jumped more than 3 warp threads at a time. Made on a handloom, a Summer and Winter coverlet pattern was essentially the same back and front, with only the colors reversed. Unlike the later Jacquard types, such coverlets were not signed.

Hints for Collectors
Summer and Winter coverlets are among the most sought after of the various coverlet types; their simplicity of design makes them particularly appealing to contemporary collectors. In general, however, coverlets have not achieved the wide popularity and value that quilts have—although at the time they were made, coverlets were worth much more.

Price Guide Group: Overshot and Summer and Winter Geometric Coverlets.

Courtesy Henry Ford Museum, The Edison Institute, Dearborn, Michigan.

Description
Two-piece Double Weave coverlet. 143 eight-pointed red stars in dark blue diamonds that are enclosed by pale brown diamonds forming overall diagonal grid. Alternate diamonds have beige scroll-like floral design on dark blue field. Framed on 2 sides by modified pine trees, alternately pale brown and deep red on dark blue ground. Frame at bottom has stylized trees in deep red on dark blue. Border on sides alternating beige and pale brown scrolls on dark blue. Border at bottom abstract geometric design in same colors. Red and blue and beige and blue fringe on 3 sides.

Materials and Dimensions
Cotton and wool. 87″ × 78″.

Maker, Locality, and Period
Maker unknown. Probably Pennsylvania. c. 1835.

Comment
In unusually fine condition, this coverlet has retained almost all its fringe and its rich, warm colors, which were probably made with home dyes. The blue would have come from the wild indigo plant, the red from the madder plant, and the pale brown from any of several natural sources, among them red oak or hickory bark. Although this bedcover looks very much like one made on a handloom, it was probably made on a half-mechanized loom with a Jacquard attachment.

Hints for Collectors
Because collectors in the Northeast have been slow to recognize their artistic and historical value, handwoven bedcovers can still be found tucked away in antiques shops or for sale at country auctions.

Price Guide Group: Double Weave Geometric Coverlets.

Collection of Rowenna Pounds.

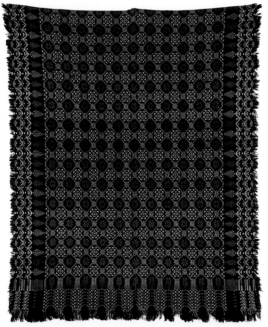

Pine Bloom

Description
Two-piece Overshot coverlet. 36 tan and white whole and partial squares separated by red and white horizontal bands with pine bloom motif at juncture with tan and white vertical bands. White fringe at bottom.

Materials and Dimensions
Cotton and wool. 97″ × 68½″.

Maker, Locality, and Period
Maker and locality unknown. c. 1810.

Comment
The term "Overshot" comes from the weaving process. In an Overshot coverlet, made with 4 shafts, or harnesses, a supplementary weft "overshoots" the foundation, a technique easily recognized by examining the weave. The extra weft is fairly loose and can be picked up with one's fingernail; for this reason the weft threads generally show wear before the rest of the coverlet. As the early handlooms were far too narrow to weave a textile this wide in one piece, a coverlet was woven in 2 sections and sewn together down the middle. In this example the juncture of the 2 pieces is easily seen, for the motifs in the center differ from those on either side.

Hints for Collectors
Bedcovers in the Overshot weave are among the rarest of 19th-century coverlets. Surprisingly, the persistent collector can still find a few early Overshot coverlets in good condition at reasonable prices. The lack of fringe on 2 sides of the example illustrated does not affect its value.

Price Guide Group: Overshot and Summer and Winter Geometric Coverlets.

Courtesy Ruth Bigel Antiques, New York City.

Description
Two-piece Summer and Winter coverlet. 195 large squares, each constructed of 4 small squares in shades of peach, blue, and gray and cut diagonally by diamond grid of small dark blue squares. Border on 3 sides in geometric pattern of peach, blue, and gray. Fringe in same colors on 3 sides, blue binding on 4th side.

Materials and Dimensions
Cotton and wool. 80″ × 78″.

Maker, Locality, and Period
Maker and locality unknown. c. 1820.

Comment
An interesting aspect of this early coverlet is the similarity of its design to quilt patterns of the same period. It is easy to see the One-Patch pattern in the dark blue squares, as well as echoes of the Log Cabin design in the construction of the individual blocks.

Hints for Collectors
This coverlet is particularly fine, not only because of its excellent condition but also because its colors are quite unusual. Fringe was sometimes added to a coverlet after it was woven, but in many cases it was simply an extension of the warp or weft threads, as seen here. Always examine the fringe on a coverlet carefully to make sure it is original; fringe that has been replaced is much less desirable. The monetary value of antique quilts has risen steadily over the past 10 years, but woven bedcovers are still undervalued.

Price Guide Group: Overshot and Summer and Winter Geometric Coverlets.

Courtesy America Hurrah Antiques, New York City.

Description

Two-piece Double Weave coverlet. 126 blocks with pale green snowflake motifs on red field, enclosed by red grid with small green Xs and Os. 1 white square at corners of each block. Bordered on 3 sides by red, pale green, and white geometric designs and fringe.

Materials and Dimensions

Cotton and wool. 84″ × 76″.

Maker, Locality, and Period

Maker and locality unknown. c. 1825.

Comment

The Double Weave coverlet was made with 2 warps and 2 wefts, creating 2 separate layers. Because it required enough thread to weave 2 layers of cloth simultaneously, it was more expensive than the Overshot, but also much heavier, warmer, and more durable. Coverlets like the example illustrated would have been woven by either itinerant weavers or, in the larger communities, local weavers.

Hints for Collectors

The European coverlet weavers who came to America in the 1820s and 1830s went to Canada as well, and many designs were produced in both countries. A coverlet of almost identical design to the one shown here, for example, is now in the King's Village Historical Settlement in New Brunswick, Canada, and is known to have been made in that province between 1810 and 1835.

Price Guide Group: Double Weave Geometric Coverlets.

Collection of William C. Ketchum, Jr.

Other Bedcovers

Because 19th-century pieced or appliquéd quilts attract the most attention today, collectors often forget that these textiles were fairly late developments in the history of American bedcovers. Bed rugs, embroidered textiles, linsey-woolseys, and whitework appeared in colonial America, while stenciled spreads were fashionable in the early 19th century.

Bed Rugs

Early inventories and letters indicate that bed rugs were among the first bedcovers used in the colonies. These thick woolen textiles, closer in appearance to carpets than to other types of bedcovers, were a necessity in the cold bedchambers of the early settlers. Many bed rugs were imported from Europe, but most of the few remaining today were made in the colonies, following Old World designs.

Produced in homes throughout New England, where winters are very harsh, bed rugs generally have large-scale designs that cover the surface of the bedcover. One of the most common designs was the clamshell pattern, often executed in shades of blue and white. Also popular were large-scale floral designs, many of which were similar to common crewelwork patterns. Most bed rugs were initialed and dated by their makers.

Linsey-Woolseys

The earliest type of quilted spreads used in the colonies were probably linsey-woolseys, although there are no records proving that they were brought here by the first settlers. They were heavy, durable bedcovers made of homespun wool-and-linen cloth sewn to a linen or wool backing. The top was usually glazed to give it a sheen.

Unlike the later pieced quilts that depend on the arrangement of hundreds of small patches for their designs, the beauty of linsey-woolseys comes from their vivid solid colors, such as various

Detail of an embroidered bedcover. Courtesy Henry Ford Museum, The Edison Institute, Michigan.

shades of red, watermelon pink, deep blue, and indigo, as well as their lavishly quilted patterns, including large flowers, hearts, leaves, and feathers. Although most linsey-woolseys were made of several large pieces of colored cloth with only one or two seams, pieced examples have also been found.

Known to have been made in Pennsylvania, New York, and New England throughout the 18th and early 19th centuries, linsey-woolseys were greatly undervalued until fairly recently. But as an appreciation of the various kinds of early textiles has grown, they have become highly prized.

Embroidered Bedcovers

The term "crewel" comes from the name of a European town where fine embroidery wools were manufactured. Crewel embroidery done in the colonies, however, utilized loosely twisted cotton or silk as well as woolen thread. Early settlers from almost every country incorporated their own particular embroidery styles and motifs in their bedcovers: German immigrants, for example, often depicted tuliplike flowers, while the English favored Prince of Wales feathered crests. As their ties to Europe weakened, colonial women depended less and less on design books from abroad, and by the second half of the 18th century, their embroidery designs had become freer and less confined than those done in Europe.

Besides choosing and then drawing the pattern, a needlewoman had to select the stitches and colors to be used on the bedcover. The number of different stitches sewn on any one textile depended on the skills of its maker. Satin, split, stem, star, cross-stitch, French, and Roumanian stitches were among the most popular. As for thread colors, only shades of blue were utilized at first, but the subsequent mastery of natural dyes other than indigo allowed for different hues.

Detail of a stenciled bedcover. Courtesy Smithsonian Institution, Washington, D.C.

Whitework

During the late 18th and early 19th centuries, all-white quilts were extremely popular, particularly as bridal gifts. Like linsey-woolseys, these whitework bedcovers were elaborately quilted with fine stitches in floral, fruit, or feather designs, which were stuffed to stand out in relief. In stuffed work, the filler was added after the top and backing had been stitched together with elaborate designs: from the back the threads were carefully pulled apart so that small pieces of cotton could be inserted. These quilted spreads required much skill and time, and a seamstress would not undertake such an effort until she felt particularly qualified to do so.

Candlewick spreads, often also all white, are not quilted but embroidered or woven. Woven candlewicks were made only for a short period around 1820, and have designs of stylized trees, flowers, or geometric motifs, usually arranged in a central medallion. These raised designs were created during the weaving process by making certain loops longer than others.

Embroidered candlewicks generally have realistic motifs, sewn with thick cotton cording in a variety of raised stitches, such as outline, stem, and satin stitches. Often the same stitch was sewn with threads of varying thicknesses; large tufts were created by using heavier cording and shearing the loops.

Candlewick spreads are not very common, so that when they do turn up, they frequently go unrecognized and thus may be inexpensive. Machine-embroidered candlewicks have been made since the 19th century; they can be recognized by the regularity of design and evenness of texture not found on hand-embroidered examples.

Stenciled Bedcovers

Stenciled fabrics—tablecloths, scarves, as well as bedcovers—were produced during the brief period from about 1820 to 1840,

Detail of a stuffed-work quilt. Courtesy America Hurrah Antiques, New York City.

particularly along the eastern seaboard. Delicate and colorful, with an airiness unmatched by other textiles, stenciled bedcovers were usually made of lightweight, unlined cotton and were intended to be used as summer spreads. Because of their short-lived popularity, however, the number of stenciled spreads surviving today is small.

Floral designs were the most common, although birds, baskets of fruit, and trees were also used. Housewives traced and cut their own stencils until mass-produced patterns became readily available in about 1835. The actual stenciling was done with cotton balls soaked in dye, which were applied to the fabric through the holes in the cutouts. Some dyes were particularly hard to work with, tending to run and blur or else fade quickly. Spreads were finished with border designs or occasionally with hand-knotted fringe. A few rare stenciled examples were quilted, and in some instances even incorporated patchwork.

Detail of a glazed worsted quilt. Courtesy America Hurrah Antiques, New York City.

233 Clamshell Bed Rug

Description
Bed rug in 3 shades of blue and off-white. Central rectangle with clamshell pattern bordered on 3 sides by teardrop shapes. At top center, 2 branches of leaves beneath dark blue floral form in which initials and date have been stitched. 3-sided border of double waving-and-pointed lines, with clamshell motif repeated in rounded lower corners.

Materials and Dimensions
Wool on undyed wool. 3 widths seamed together. Uncut pile. 88½″ × 87″.

Maker, Locality, and Period
Initialed ERG, for Greer family. Near Norwich/New London, Connecticut. 1790.

Comment
In early America, indigo-blue dye was readily available and became, along with the color of undyed wool, the most common shade for bed rugs. Rugmakers of the period not only dyed their wool but also raised the sheep, spun the sheared wool, and then wove it into material for the rug's foundation. Unlike many later hooked rugs, bed rugs were not made from scraps, but were well thought out pieces, both in design and color.

Hints for Collectors
European bed rugs were imported into the American colonies, but few, if any, have survived. Of the bed rugs known today, almost all are believed to be of American origin.

Price Guide Group: Bed Rugs.

Courtesy The Brooklyn Museum, Brooklyn, New York.

Description
Center composed of 4 hearts facing a blossom, with another blossom on top of each heart, all enclosed in circle with scalloped edge. Circle surrounded by floral motifs, horses, and birds in shades of orange, yellow, and green on ground of mixed blues. Orange and yellow frame with scalloped interior edge. Wide blue inner border with single flower motif on each side in shades of orange, yellow, and green. Top flower flanked by initials "CT" and date; top and bottom flowers flanked by 2 round forms; side flowers next to single round form. Outer border repeats scallop design. Lower corners cut to accommodate four-poster bed.

Materials and Dimensions
Wool on undyed linsey-woolsey. 3 widths seamed together. 91″ × 84″.

Maker, Locality, and Period
Catherine Thorn. Ipswich, Massachusetts. 1724.

Comment
One of the earliest known bed rugs to have survived, this piece is thought to have been made for the trousseau of the maker's sister. The background color in most early rugs is not a consistent shade. Generally wool was dyed at home, and in the process the maker might underestimate the amount of yarn she would need and have to dye another batch, which often turned out to be a different shade.

Hints for Collectors
This early rug's design, probably the invention of the maker, is very rare. Neither a rug nor a bedspread, the bed rug is a unique form. Few have survived, and any found today, provided they are in at least fair condition, are quite valuable.

Price Guide Group: Bed Rugs.

Courtesy Wenham Historical Association, Wenham, Massachusetts.

235 Bed Rug

Description
Abstract center design in X shape forms base for 4 flowers on aqua stems in different sizes and shapes, 2 bearing fruit. Initials "RP" and date at top in red flanked by 2 flowers. Large rectangular inner border encloses central motifs and has interior edge of stacked scallop shapes. Surrounding central area on 3 sides are undulating double vines of fruit and flowers. Predominantly red, yellow, green, and light and dark blue. Faded black ground. Scallop-motif outer border on 3 sides. Bottom corners rounded.

Materials and Dimensions
Wool on wool homespun. 3 widths seamed together. Uncut pile. 93½" × 90".

Maker, Locality, and Period
Rachel Packard. Jericho, Vermont. 1805.

Comment
A family document explains that the yarns for this brilliantly colored bed rug were spun, woven, dyed, and made into a bedcover by Rachel Packard when she was 71 years old. Very carefully planned and worked, it has several different textures and weights of yarn: the ground—now a faded black—is made of finely spun yarn, while the brighter colored motifs are somewhat coarser.

Hints for Collectors
This rug, currently in a museum collection, is a superb example of the form. Its maker had a rare combination of artistic talent and needleworking skills that enabled her to execute her design and create a marvelous piece of textile art.

Price Guide Group: Bed Rugs.

Courtesy Henry Ford Museum, The Edison Institute, Dearborn, Michigan.

236 Floral Bed Rug

Description
Floral designs in warm shades of beige, yellow, green, light red, and blue. Large center flower framed by trailing vine and flanked by 2 large flower clusters, which are set horizontally. Large blossoms in each corner; bottom 2 flowers surrounded by trailing vines. Teardrop-motif border on 3 sides; 4th side has irregular scallop shapes with inscription, "SARA DENNY," and "ES". Bottom corners rounded.

Materials and Dimensions
Wool on linen. Cut and uncut pile. 97″ × 87″.

Maker, Locality, and Period
Initialed E.S. for Sara Denny. Locality unknown. c. 1800–25.

Comment
Most bed rugs were generally initialed and dated by their makers, although occasionally the initials or name may indicate the person for whom the rug was made. Interestingly, this piece is inscribed very close to the top, with "SARA DENNY" in 2 different-size letters. It is thought that this bed rug was made for Sara Denny because the initials "ES" also appear on the textile. Notice that large areas of the rug are worked in brighter colors, which may mean that the rug was completed at a later date or, more probably, that it was extensively restored.

Hints for Collectors
There is a quality to this rug, both in the design and lettering, that suggests it may have been made by a fairly young girl.

Price Guide Group: Bed Rugs.

Courtesy Shelburne Museum, Shelburne, Vermont.

237 Crewelwork Spread

Description
Crewelwork spread with floral designs arranged to form a
central square with inconsistent border motifs. Central motif
has 4 large leaflike shapes emanating from center oval.
Predominantly shades of green, blue, red, and yellow. White
ground. Inner border alternating leaves and stylized grape
clusters connected by thin trailing vine. Outer border flower,
fruit, and leaf forms.

Materials and Dimensions
Linen crewel embroidery and cotton. Embroidery on all motifs.
101″ × 98″.

Maker, Locality, and Period
Clarissa Stohard Seyo. Near New Paltz, New York. 1728–48.

Comment
An exceptional example of crewelwork, this bedspread took 20
years to make (although time would have been taken out for
other projects as well), which suggests the amount of careful
work that went into such a piece. A bedcover like this, however,
would most likely have been a labor of love and quite possibly the
major needlework accomplishment of a woman's life.

Hints for Collectors
In a set of bed hangings (or bed furniture, as they are often
called), the spread usually was the piece to wear out first, so that
most of the hangings that remain today are valances. Such pieces
are irreplaceable, and should be stored or displayed where both
temperature and humidity can be controlled.

Price Guide Group: Crewel Coverlets and Blankets.

Courtesy the Colonial Williamsburg Foundation, Williamsburg, Virginia.

Crewelwork Spread

Description
Crewelwork spread with floral design on white ground. Flowers in shades of yellow, red, and blue, with brown connecting branches and blue-green leaves. Bottom corners cut out for four-poster bed. Green binding.

Materials and Dimensions
Crewel embroidery on cotton with linen warp. Twill woven. 78¾" × 56".

Maker, Locality, and Period
Mary Thurston Fifield and Mary Fifield. Boston. c. 1711–14.

Comment
This elaborately "workt," or embroidered, bedcover from the early 18th century closely resembles English crewelwork of the same period and was probably part of a set of bed hangings, which would have included 3 valances, a head cloth, 2 narrow side curtains, 2 large side curtains, the spread, and pieces for the bed rail. Such a large amount of hand-embroidered cloth took a very long time to make, and we know that the example illustrated was made by a mother and daughter team over the course of several years. The bed furnishings had to serve 2 purposes: decoration, because the master bed was usually in the parlor and exposed to public view; and warmth, because the curtains were pulled shut against cold drafts in poorly heated rooms.

Hints for Collectors
Because of their age and the amount of wear that bedcovers endured, few complete sets of bed hangings exist today.

Price Guide Group: Crewel Coverlets and Blankets.

Courtesy Museum of Fine Arts, Boston, Massachusetts.

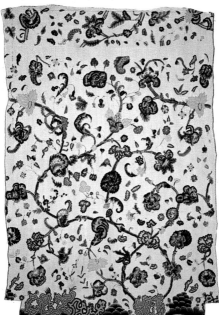

Description

Bedcover: Top and center field with large-scale floral design on off-white ground. Trailing vine border encloses 6 flower motifs. Drops, which are separated from central field by blue double strips, have trailing vines incorporating floral design similar to that in center. Predominantly shades of blue, red, pink, green, and yellow. Bottom corners cut out for four-poster bed. Dark blue binding. Irregularly sculpted edges. Valances: several varieties of trees in shades of green and brown with tan bark, and grapevines with light and dark blue grapes, all set on hilly, green earth. White ground with poetic inscriptions. Dark blue binding. Irregularly sculpted edges.

Materials and Dimensions

Crewel embroidery on linen homespun. 79″ × 73½″.

Maker, Locality, and Period

Mary Bulman. York, Maine. c. 1745.

Comment

The pieces illustrated are part of one of the finest complete sets of 18th-century American bed hangings in existence today. It is believed that Mary Bulman designed and worked the entire set herself, in part while her husband was serving as a surgeon in Nova Scotia during the siege of Louisburg. He died at Cape Breton in 1745, and her sorrow is reflected in the lines she chose to embroider, taken from Isaac Watts's poem "Meditation in a Grove": "I'll carve our passion on the bark/ And every wounded tree/ Shall drop and bear some mystic mark/ That Jesus Dy'd for me/ The swains shall wonder when they read/ Inscrib'd on all the grove/ That heaven itself came down and bled/ To win a mortal's Love." Since most sets of bed furniture were divided up when their makers died, this complete set is a rarity.

American crewel was usually embroidered on a rough homespun

Courtesy Old Gaol Museum, York, Maine.

that was made both in the home and by craftsmen specifically for embroidery. Early crewelwork was often worked in shades of indigo-blue and had a loose, overall design. Along with changes in design came the development of several new embroidery stitches, such as feather, seed, outline, and French knot. As with the set shown here, most of the early pieces of crewelwork that come down to us now are in the form of hangings from bed sets. Although crewelwork was a cherished possession and pieces were rarely thrown away, bed spreads were in constant use and would most likely be the first to wear out. Lacking a complete set the maker may have stored the rest of the bed furnishings away and so many of these pieces remain in virtually the same condition they were in when first used.

Hints for Collectors

As typical examples of American needlework, this bedcover and valances have a lighter, more open feeling than their European counterparts. A set as rare as this one would be found almost exclusively in a museum collection rather than on the commercial market. For today's collector, valances that have been well cared for make excellent period additions to linsey-woolsey bedcovers. The 2 may be very effectively displayed together.

Price Guide Group: Crewel Coverlets and Blankets.

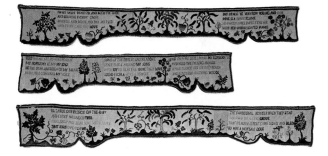

Description
Central section has 2 blue, scrolled, pillarlike forms made of blue
strapwork, which are joined at top and bottom by more
strapwork. At top of each pillar and at foot of central field is
small flowering tree; tree at bottom has yellow bird on perch.
Pillars wrapped with trailing floral vine in shades of rose, blue,
green, yellow, beige, and white, ending in scrollwork at bottom,
which is decorated with 2 small conifers and trailing leaves and
flowers. Side and foot panels have delicate floral border at edges
of center section. Trailing floral vine motif along bottom edge of 3
sides in same colors as center section. White and off-white
ground. Green binding along sculpted edges. Bottom corners cut
out for four-poster bed.

Materials and Dimensions
Crewel embroidery and appliquéd strapwork on linen homespun.
112″ × 78½″.

Maker, Locality, and Period
Maker and locality unknown. c. 1725–50.

Comment
This spread is part of one of the very few complete sets of bed
hangings that have survived. Originally the property of Thomas
Hancock, a Boston merchant and shipowner, the set was passed
down to his nephew John Hancock. The bedcover is a superb
example of strapwork (which is applied coach braid, also used as
trimming on European clerical robes) and floral embroidery.

Hints for Collectors
Spreads were prized family possessions and would have been
passed down from one generation to the next until they were no
longer presentable.

Price Guide Group: Crewel Coverlets and Blankets.

Courtesy the Henry Francis du Pont Winterthur Museum, Winterthur, Delaware.

Crewelwork Spread

Description
Central section of spread has 2 dark blue trailing vines of flowers running parallel from top to bottom. Floral embroidery red, pink, yellow, brown, green, and blue on off-white ground. Side and bottom panels with trailing vine motif in same colors. Irregularly sculpted edges. Bottom corners cut out for four-poster bed.

Materials and Dimensions
Crewel embroidery on linen homespun. Central field has diaper-pattern weave. 87″ × 72″.

Maker, Locality, and Period
Maker unknown. Massachusetts. c. 1740.

Comment
American crewelwork was done on coarse linen, sometimes woven in the home and sometimes woven by professional weavers who made cloth especially for such work. Beginning in the 17th century, English manufacturers produced fine, loosely twisted woolen thread in many different colors. American women, however, whose access to crewel thread was limited, used whatever they could get for embroidery, including cotton and silk.

Hints for Collectors
American crewelwork is characterized by a more open style of design than English crewelwork. It was often playful and individualistic, with attempts at creating realistic, lifelike images rather than stylized ones.

Price Guide Group: Crewel Coverlets and Blankets.

Courtesy Henry Ford Museum, The Edison Institute, Dearborn, Michigan.

242 Embroidered Wool Coverlet

Description
Central rectangle with 8 large red, blue, and black abstract floral designs in 2 columns surrounded on 3 sides by large, winding, scroll-like vine emanating from heart at base. Vine bears small flowers and similar floral motifs around center of coverlet. Beige ground. Initialed and dated. Bottom corners cut out for four-poster bed. Black fringe binding on 3 sides.

Materials and Dimensions
Embroidery on wool. Twill woven. 82″ × 72″.

Maker, Locality, and Period
Initialed AL. Locality unknown. 1832.

Comment
Embroidery on wool became popular in about 1850, and remained so throughout the Victorian period. This coverlet is typically American because one stitch dominates, and it tends to create a general coarsening effect. While very different in feeling from an 18th-century embroidered coverlet, this striking piece, with its simple yet bold design and coloring, is very appealing.

Hints for Collectors
At the time it was made, this piece would not have been valued as highly as the earlier and more elaborate crewelwork on linen spreads. But with the growing scarcity of embroidered coverlets this piece is even more valuable today, and a welcome addition to any collection of American textiles.

Price Guide Group: Crewel Coverlets and Blankets.

Courtesy Henry Ford Museum, The Edison Institute, Dearborn, Michigan.

Embroidered Bedcover

Description
Abstract central design has smaller circles enclosed in large circle, surrounded by triangles that create starlike outer edge. Above, stylized flowering tree with linear designs in its interior, flanked by insects, floral pinwheels, and pairs of men and women; below, 2 facing birds on branch with their beaks touching; below birds are 2 pairs of men and women. Flowering branches flank central design from top to bottom. Bordered on 3 sides by large, nearly circular forms, each enclosing linear design. Lilies set between circles on one side; on other side and bottom, oak leaves in blue thread. Large star similar to central design in 2 bottom corners. White ground. Edged on 3 sides with white string net fringe.

Materials and Dimensions
Wool and cotton embroidery on linen homespun. Handmade cotton fringe. 92″ × 71″.

Maker, Locality, and Period
Maker unknown. Eastern U.S., probably Pennsylvania. c. 1815.

Comment
This bedcover has been described as a "courtship spread." Notice that there is a progression, from right to left, beginning with the first couple who stand some distance apart, and culminating with the elderly couple, the man leaning on a cane. Probably these figures represent the 5 stages of life of the couple.

Hints for Collectors
Whimsical, humorous, and sentimental, this textile is the kind of piece one comes across very rarely.

Price Guide Group: Crewel Coverlets and Blankets.

Courtesy America Hurrah Antiques, New York City.

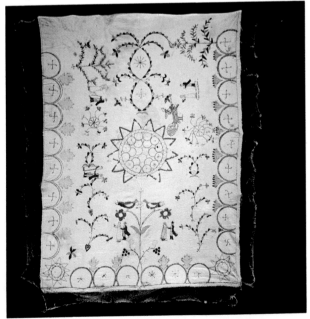

244 Embroidered Bedcover

Description
5 different kinds of flower baskets, randomly placed around sides of bedcover. Flowers in shades of red, blue, yellow, pink, and white, with brown leaves and stems, spilling out to cover much of purple ground. Brown ropelike meandering border on 3 sides, with small floral sprays in areas between curves and edge of cover.

Materials and Dimensions
Embroidery on pieced wool. 96″ × 80″.

Maker, Locality, and Period
Maker and locality unknown. c. 1770.

Comment
This fanciful and charming bedcover looks as much like twinkling stars in the night sky as it does baskets of spilled, embroidered flowers. Except for those in the bottom corners, which are almost alike, each basket is different in size, shape, and texture, and each holds a different kind of flower. Notice the delightful, yet restrained use of color in the overall design.

Hints for Collectors
Very different in feeling from embroidered bedcovers with a ground of white or off-white, embroidered spreads with a black or purple ground are often more whimsical and quaint. An early piece like this, with an unusual freehand design, jewel-like colors, and in excellent condition, is quite rare and of considerable value.

Price Guide Group: Crewel Coverlets and Blankets.

Courtesy Henry Ford Museum, The Edison Institute, Dearborn, Michigan.

Stenciled Quilt

Description
6 blue latticework baskets, filled with pink, yellow, and blue fruit and blue leaves, arranged along either side of 5 branches of fruit in blue, pink, and yellow. Trailing grapevine border in blue and pink surrounds central field on 3 sides. At top, short grapevine broken in middle by fruit branch. White ground.
No binding.

Materials and Dimensions
Cotton with stuffed work. Stenciled. Ground quilted in diamonds. 85" × 74½".

Maker, Locality, and Period
Maker and locality unknown. c. 1820–40.

Comment
While most stenciled spreads look fairly similar, this one stands out because of its blue baskets composed of dots and fruit in ice cream colors. In addition, the proportions are strikingly large, with only 6 baskets and a large, leafy grapevine covering most of the surface. Combined, they give the design a very naive quality.

Hints for Collectors
This stenciled bedcover is unusual both for its design and because it is quilted. Most stenciled spreads were limited to floral designs, occasionally in combination with fruit. This piece, however, has only fruit motifs, including the grapevine border that repeats the stenciled dots of the baskets in its leaves and fruit. The quilting is unusual because stenciled covers were generally light and unlined, to be used in summer.

Price Guide Group: Stenciled and Printed Spreads.

Courtesy Kelter-Malcé Antiques, New York City.

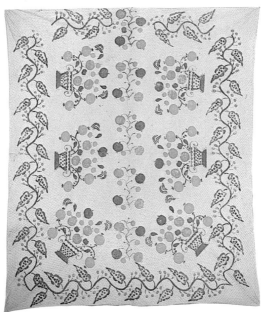

Stenciled Bedcover

Description

32 floral designs in 6 rows running down length of bedcover. 2 central rows, each made up of 2 large baskets of fruit and flowers alternating with smaller sprays of fruit and flowers. Flanking center rows, a row of alternating sprays of fruit and flowers. Outermost rows have flower sprays only. Bordered on 3 sides with floral trailing vine. Predominantly rose, yellow, orange, and greens. White ground. Bottom corners cut out to accommodate four-poster bed.

Materials and Dimensions

Cotton. Stenciled. 86″ × 81½″.

Maker, Locality, and Period

Lucinda Howland, with stenciled decorations done by a neighbor. Broome County, New York. c. 1830.

Comment

Stenciled spreads were made at home, often with home-cut stencils fashioned from a variety of materials, including thick oiled paper, tin, thin pieces of wood, and cloth dipped in beeswax to stiffen it. Several different dyes could be used to color spreads, but each had drawbacks. Although dye mixed with gum arabic would not run under the edge of the stencil, it faded quickly. Oil, ground pigment, and stencil mordant (a substance used to set the dye) were more lasting, but tended to run when washed.

Hints for Collectors

While any stenciled spread is rare, the best ones are generally made by combining several different motifs. Stenciled spreads were made to last for only a short period of time, so most examples in good condition are valuable.

Price Guide Group: Stenciled and Printed Spreads.

Courtesy Cortland County Historical Society, Cortland, New York.

Stenciled Bedcover

Description
Urn overflowing with flowers fills top central field; a bird sits among flowers. 3 floral urns, with 2 smaller birds in each, surround larger urn on 3 sides. Numerous smaller motifs placed over top of cover, including flowers, bird-topped floral sprays, and floral clusters. Feathered star in each corner. Predominantly red, blue, green, and golden yellow. White ground. Bordered on 3 sides with trailing flower and leaf design. Edged on 3 sides with hand-knotted fringe. White binding.

Materials and Dimensions
Cotton. Stenciled. Handmade cotton fringe. 91⅜" × 86".

Maker, Locality, and Period
Maker unknown. New England. c. 1825–35.

Comment
Probably designed as a spread for summer use, this lightweight cover would have required a large number of stencils for its many different designs. As stenciling became more popular, manufacturers began cutting stencils and selling patterns, and housewives no longer had to take the considerable amount of time needed to make their own. Many commercial patterns required only one stencil for an entire motif, rather than the 4 or 5 stencils used in earlier times, thus making the finished designs look less handmade.

Hints for Collectors
This spread was obviously made by an expert at stenciling, as the piece has not only been carefully painted but cleverly designed as well.

Price Guide Group: Stenciled and Printed Spreads.

Courtesy Museum of American Folk Art, New York City.

Description
Central field with 12 irregularly spaced rose wreaths, with a single blossom between each wreath. Meandering vine border echoes floral wreaths, with single red or blue flower between larger blossoms. Blue, red, and green, with lighter blue, red, and green highlights. Off-white ground. White binding.

Materials and Dimensions
Cotton. Stenciled. Block quilting throughout. 84″ × 76″.

Maker, Locality, and Period
Maker unknown. New Jersey. c. 1835.

Comment
Unusual both for its very deep colors and because it is quilted, this bedcover is different from the typical stenciled spread. Its maker may have been someone who liked appliquéd quilts but lacked the skill or time to make one. The rose wreath was a common decorative motif, used on many articles in colonial and federal homes; there are as many as 50 different variations.

Hints for Collectors
This stenciled piece is very valuable. Great care has been taken in every detail; even the tiny serrated edges of the leaves are cleanly cut and precise. Just like appliquéd quilts, which had to be carefully cut and pieced, stenciled spreads required great accuracy or the detail was lost during the application of color. Stenciled spreadmakers had a further worry—how to deal with colors that could run and ruin the clean edge of a stencil.

Price Guide Group: Stenciled and Printed Spreads.

Courtesy America Hurrah Antiques, New York City.

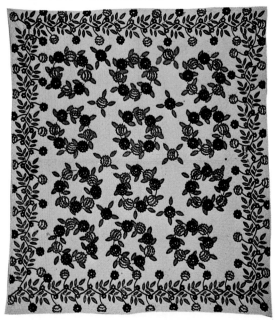

Stenciled Bedcover

Description
Central field composed of 4 rows of 3 rose wreaths, with a
nosegay of roses between each wreath. Wreaths have open
roses, buds, leaves, and tiny rose-colored flowers. Flowers are
shades of red, and leaves are shades of green. Meandering rose
vine with small flowers forms border. White ground. White
binding.

Materials and Dimensions
Cotton. Stenciled. 95¼″ × 76¼″.

Maker, Locality, and Period
Maker and locality unknown. c. 1825–35.

Comment
A common feature of stenciled spreads is a border design that
repeats the same motifs in the central field. Because this
bedcover uses a single pattern in 2 colors, and thus a relatively
small number of stencils, it would have been fairly easy to
complete once the technique was mastered. The spread is much
less elaborate and original than others made during the first half
of the 19th century.

Hints for Collectors
Many stenciled spreads are in good condition when they are
found, and this piece is a typical example of its kind. Not as
inspired or lively a piece of work as some of the other stenciled
textiles, the spread still possesses a charm common to most
finely stenciled bedcovers. Notice that the motifs are very
similar to those used on pieced and appliquéd quilts.

Price Guide Group: Stenciled and Printed Spreads.

Courtesy Smithsonian Institution, Washington, D.C.

Stenciled Bedcover

Description
Central field has large flowering tree in urn sitting on stand and crowned by floral sprays, leaf motifs, and off-white unfilled area at top. Below stand, 3 rows of urn and floral motifs. Each side of spread has 3 rows of urn and floral motifs, some with bird perched among flowers. Small, single blossoms appear between larger motifs. Predominantly blue, green, rose, and shades of yellow. Off-white ground. Small flowers and leaves on short vine segments border 3 sides. Bottom corners cut out to accommodate four-poster bed.

Materials and Dimensions
Cotton. Stenciled. 104″ × 103″.

Maker, Locality, and Period
Emily Morton. Thorndyke, Maine. 1826.

Comment
Popular between 1820 and 1840, stenciled spreads have a characteristically American look. Although the designs appear simple, they required a variety of skills from the maker. Initially, paint or dye was applied over a cutout stencil that incorporated motifs generally limited to flowers, leaves, baskets, fruit, and birds. Each color required a different stencil and had to be applied separately and then allowed to dry. If done well, each design had precise edges.

Hints for Collectors
Although it was made from a stencil, the design is full of movement, a characteristic not easy to achieve with a precut pattern. As a result, this spread is especially valuable.

Price Guide Group: Stenciled and Printed Spreads.

Courtesy Abby Aldrich Rockefeller Folk Art Center, Williamsburg, Virginia.

"Tree of Life" Palampore

Description
Tree of Life motif in shades of red, brown, yellow, blue, and purple on white ground. Tree surrounded by intricate floral sprays and branches. Side and foot panels echo central design, with foot panel also incorporating realistic green and brown earth base. Panels joined to top of spread with yellow trim. Foot panel has smaller sides with different floral design predominantly in pinks and light purples. Handmade yellow and brown fringe binding on 3 sides. Fringe binding on foot panel extended with yellow braid. Bottom corners cut out to accommodate four-poster bed.

Materials and Dimensions
Chintz and cotton. 84″ × 47″.

Maker, Locality, and Period
Maker unknown. Probably India. c. 1775–1800.

Comment
Chintzes made in India were imported to England for clothing, draperies, and bed hangings, and became so popular that the English began making their own. The palampore illustrated was probably imported from India via England. The top border of this spread has been cut to allow for the addition of a bolster.

Hints for Collectors
Even though this bedcover has been cut and altered—the trimming and fringe are later additions—it is still very rare. Most chintz bedcovers that wore out were cut up and the usable scraps salvaged for other bedcovers.

Price Guide Group: Stenciled and Printed Spreads.

Courtesy Henry Ford Museum, The Edison Institute, Dearborn, Michigan.

Hewson Print Cotton Bedcover

Description
Central medallion with tall classical urn filled with flowers and surrounded by birds, butterflies, and flowering branches. Framed by dense band of small single- and double-stemmed flowers. Frame enclosed by square of evenly placed floral bushes, some with perching bird. Predominantly brown, beige, rose, green, and blue. White ground. Wide floral border similar to frame but with outside edges printed on 3 sides to imitate fringe and tassels.

Materials and Dimensions
Printed cotton. 106¼″ × 103¼″.

Maker, Locality, and Period
Maker unknown. Probably Philadelphia. c. 1780–1810.

Comment
John Hewson was an English textile printer who moved in 1773 to Philadelphia, where he worked until 1810. His floral prints, similar to English chintzes of the period, were characterized by flower-filled urns, birds, and butterflies. Hewson printed some of his designs so that they ran all the way around the 4 sides of a bedcover in a continuous fashion. This was a new feature and different from the vertically printed designs common to other fabrics sold by the yard.

Hints for Collectors
Only about a dozen of Hewson's works have turned up, and consequently they are very valuable. Besides the example shown here, just one other complete spread is known. Other Hewson pieces may one day be discovered; in fact, as recently as 1971 a well-preserved quilt with a Hewson center was found in Massachusetts.

Price Guide Group: Stenciled and Printed Spreads.

Courtesy The Henry Francis du Pont Winterthur Museum, Winterthur, Delaware.

Embroidered Homespun Linen Coverlet

Description
Pieced central square with flower surrounded by floral wreath and randomly placed flowers and insects; 4 flowers define corners of square. Central square surrounded by concentric frames: 1st with snakelike border with flowers and insects, interrupted at each corner by bird perched on branch; 2nd with undulating vine with flowers and insects, interrupted at corners by alternating squares of dragonflies and vegetable motifs; 3rd frame wide border incorporating insects and birds and unidentified motifs, with rough-hewn urns of flowers and insects at each corner. Corners at upper left and lower right outlined with scalloped embroidery. Predominantly red, gold, pink, brown, and yellow. White ground. Signed and dated. Bordered by red embroidered undulating line, interrupted by small corner blocks with embroidered motifs.

Materials and Dimensions
Crewel embroidery on linen homespun. 108″ × 108″.

Maker, Locality, and Period
Annis Clark. Locality unknown. November 24, 1818.

Comment
Despite the maker's naively conceived forms and less than accomplished needlework, her coverlet has a well-balanced composition.

Hints for Collectors
This wonderfully quaint piece of needlework is clearly American. English needlework of the period generally had fewer open spaces as well as a more formal overall design.

Price Guide Group: Crewel Coverlets and Blankets.

Collection of Cora Ginsburg, New York City.

254 **Embroidered Checked Blanket**

Description
Squares of blue and red embroidered abstract motifs, including hearts, flowers, stars, diamonds, and linear designs, all separated by blue grid. Small navy-blue square patches articulate intersections of gridwork. Off-white ground. Dated. Blue embroidered running loop design on 3 sides and part of 4th create inconsistent border.

Materials and Dimensions
Embroidery on wool. 2 pieces seamed together. 94½″ × 83½″.

Maker, Locality, and Period
Maker and locality unknown. 1833.

Comment
This cover was made by stitching 2 widths of material together and is typical of embroidered blankets made at about the middle of the 19th century. Many homespun blankets were embroidered with geometric and abstract designs like those on the squares shown here. By 1850 the elaborate crewelwork of the previous century was no longer being done, except in very rare instances, and most needlework utilized only one stitch, making it far less difficult and time consuming.

Hints for Collectors
This type of charming country textile was mostly made in New York and Pennsylvania and has become increasingly difficult to find. Wool, unless it has been stored with great care, frequently suffers from moth damage, and while repairs are possible, they are expensive. In order to restore the original appearance of a damaged blanket, repairs should be done professionally.

Price Guide Group: Crewel Coverlets and Blankets.

Courtesy Kelter-Malcé Antiques, New York City.

255 Pieced and Stenciled Quilt

Description
Nine-patch blocks alternating with large stenciled blocks, creating overall checkerboard pattern. Each nine-patch block contains squares of multicolored prints, including flowers, pinstripes, stripes, and checks, that alternate with white squares. All stenciled blocks with rose spray on white ground, except for blocks on 3 sides of border, which contain baskets holding single large rose and smaller flowers. Rose sprays set diagonally in different directions; baskets face inward. 1 block devoted to signature and date. Predominantly rose, yellow, blue, and green. Narrow yellow binding.

Materials and Dimensions
Cotton. Pieced and stenciled. Diamond quilting throughout. 86½" × 73".

Maker, Locality, and Period
Mary Ann Hoyt. Reading, Pennsylvania. May 15, 1834.

Comment
While most stenciled spreads were made between 1820 and 1840, the addition of pieced nine-patch squares on this quilt make it very rare. Piecing, quilting, and stenciling radically alter the appearance of a stenciled spread. Most stenciled bedcovers were unquilted and made of only one layer of lightweight cotton, to be used during the summertime only.

Hints for Collectors
Even the tiniest details of the rosebuds and the leaf edges are distinguishable. Besides its unusual and successful combination of techniques, this piece is special because of the subtle arrangement of colors and prints in its patchwork blocks.

Price Guide Group: Stenciled and Printed Spreads.

Courtesy The Henry Francis du Pont Winterthur Museum, Winterthur, Delaware.

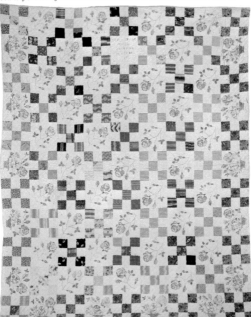

Description
25 Variable Star blocks set diagonally to create diamonds. Each eight-pointed star pieced in various combinations of black, red, tan, and marine-blue. Star blocks alternate with red-and-brown checked diamond blocks. Beige, brown, and black rectangles create border on 3 sides of quilt. Top edge has narrow marine-blue and beige border.

Materials and Dimensions
Cotton homespun, wool, and glazed linen. Quilted in diagonal lines. 88″ × 84″.

Maker, Locality, and Period
Maker unknown. Massachusetts. c. 1820.

Comment
This quilt is typical of the reasonably simple design a functional bedcover might have. The Variable Star is one of the oldest quilt patterns and is here worked skillfully. Near the lower right and left corners are patches that interrupt the design of 2 of the star motifs and the border. Sometime during the history of this bedcover they were probably added to repair or reinforce weak areas of the fabric.

Hints for Collectors
This pieced quilt would be a valuable addition to any collection, both for its age and also because utilitarian bedcovers from the early 19th century are rare. It was made from odds and ends of material and is primitive looking and very charming.

Price Guide Group: Linsey-Woolseys.

Courtesy Kelter-Malcé Antiques, New York City.

Description
4 large eight-pointed star blocks, pieced in shades of brown on beige ground. Each star block surrounded on 2 sides by narrow beige and brown border creating cross motif. Central blocks framed by light and dark brown band. Beige border with light and dark brown patches on left and right sides. Dark brown binding.

Materials and Dimensions
Unglazed worsted wool homespun. Quilted in diagonal lines and diamonds. 68″ × 68″.

Maker, Locality, and Period
Maker unknown. New England. c. 1820.

Comment
By 1820 linsey-woolseys and woolen homespun quilts were quite common, but were slowly losing their popularity to cotton patchwork quilts. Pieced spreads like this one often have a homespun backing in a durable twill-woven fabric, and were frequently quilted in white rather than matching thread, which was used for quilts in a solid color.

Hints for Collectors
This quilt is an example of a bedcover created mainly for everyday use, and yet the maker still found time to create a design in her quilting. Few utilitarian quilts have survived, and it requires some knowledge of textiles to recognize this type of bedcover.

Price Guide Group: Linsey-Woolseys.

Courtesy America Hurrah Antiques, New York City.

Description
Central field arranged in solid-color squares of red, dark blue, gray, tan, yellow, and brown. Squares separated by grid of overlapping bars of fabric, with small yellow and red squares at intersections. Bottom corners cut out to accommodate four-poster bed. No recognizable border.

Materials and Dimensions
Worsted wool homespun. Quilted in melon pattern. 88" × 88".

Maker, Locality, and Period
Maker unknown. New Hampshire. c. 1820.

Comment
This quilt was probably made of pieces salvaged from worn-out linsey-woolsey covers, but it has a carefully considered design. The small yellow squares were all placed so that when the bedcover was used, they would show off the top of the bed, with a neat row of red blocks and blue rectangles running along the 2 sides. Linsey-woolseys with similar designs were evidently quite common in certain areas, but seem not to have been very durable, as small repairs often show up on these woolen quilts.

Hints for Collectors
This pieced bedcover has an unusually striking design for a linsey-woolsey, and was probably made for a specific four-poster bed, as the cutouts seem to be an integral part of the design. It is in very good condition and particularly beautiful, attributes that make it both rare and valuable.

Price Guide Group: Linsey-Woolseys.

Courtesy America Hurrah Antiques, New York City.

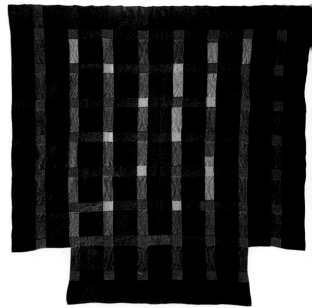

Description
Indigo-blue glazed wool bedcover. Quilted diamond blocks set in diagonal rows each contain elaborate floral and feather quilted motif set against ground of quilted parallel lines. Hemmed edges.

Materials and Dimensions
Glazed worsted. Floral, feather, and parallel line quilting. 78″ × 72″.

Maker, Locality, and Period
Maker unknown. New England. c. 1800.

Comment
This type of glazed, finely woven wool is often called "calimanco," but "glazed worsted" is the more accurate name. Calimanco actually refers to types of satin-weave wool used in the 18th century but rarely found today. The sheen of these glazed fabrics was created by one of several methods, including rubbing the cloth with a smooth stone or giving it an application of egg white and water, also called overdyeing, before the fabric was quilted. The latter method was preferred, as rubbing a stone on the wool can weaken the fabric.

Hints for Collectors
This exceptional example of a glazed worsted bedcover, with its original glaze intact, is in superb condition. The large designs are set off by the carefully quilted ground, and the diamond shapes are stitched in contrasting textures. This sort of block arrangement created by quilting alone is a very unusual pattern.

Price Guide Group: Linsey-Woolseys.

Courtesy America Hurrah Antiques, New York City.

Quilted Linsey-Woolsey Bedcover

Description
Royal-blue central rectangle created by piecing several strips of cloth. Wide dark blue border on 3 sides. Blue binding.

Materials and Dimensions
Glazed linsey-woolsey. Quilting in diamond pattern. 98″ × 92″.

Maker, Locality, and Period
Maker unknown. Connecticut. c. 1800.

Comment
The term "linsey-woolsey" is commonly used today to describe heavy, quilted wool bedcovers. Its broader definition, however, is any coarse cotton or linen fabric woven with wool. The term is derived from the Middle English word "lynsy," a corruption of "Lindsay," the village in England where such cloth was first made. This linsey-woolsey bedcover is so appealing because of its colors—the vibrant royal-blue surrounded by deep midnight-blue.

Hints for Collectors
Notice that the quilt's simple rectangular design and wide border resemble those in Amish bedcovers. Although its diamond quilting is much less elaborate than many similar pieces, the rarity and age of this bedcover make it quite valuable. In the past, linsey-woolsey bedcovers have been generally ignored by collectors. But with the steadily increasing prices of other spreads, collectors are reassessing their past indifference to these beautiful quilts.

Price Guide Group: Linsey-Woolseys.

Kelter-Malcè Antiques, New York City.

Description
Large light blue square surrounded by deep pink border that is wide on 3 sides and narrow on 4th. Pink binding.

Materials and Dimensions
Glazed wool. Central portion and border quilted in 4 large tuliplike flowers facing central abstract floral design. Feather quilting connects tulips to smaller floral figures. Corners have abstract quilting designs. Diagonal-line quilting throughout. 90″ × 90″.

Maker, Locality, and Period
Maker unknown. Pennsylvania. c. 1800–10.

Comment
Other early wool bedcovers have large design elements—like the flowers and leaves in the example illustrated—that stand in contrast to the narrow diagonal quilting of the ground. The design here is especially interesting as the quilted forms are not confined to a color area but cover the entire surface of the quilt. Linsey-woolseys appeared in many colors but most are indigo blue, since it would not show soil marks as easily as some lighter colors do, and was readily available in early American households.

Hints for Collectors
More woolen quilts have survived from the 18th century than bedcovers made from other fabrics because of their durability and the fact that so many were made. With the turn of the century, this kind of elaborate needlework became much less popular.

Price Guide Group: Linsey-Woolseys.

Courtesy America Hurrah Antiques, New York City.

262 Woven Candlewick Spread

Description
Center flower and wreath surrounded by 4 floral urns and 4 pine tree motifs set inside triple stepped diamond. Framed by crenellated square that encloses stylized flower and pine tree motifs. Further framed by variously patterned concentric squares: a repeating flower motif along large sawtooth square with a pine tree in each corner; a double-sawtooth frame; and a border of pine trees on a raised double line, with eight-pointed stars floating in each corner. Initialed at top left. All white.

Materials and Dimensions
Candlewicking in woven cotton. 85″ × 79¾″.

Maker, Locality, and Period
Initialed AFX. New York State. c. 1825–50.

Comment
Candlewicking was a technique used in the early 19th century to decorate bedspreads and pillow shams. Either woven or embroidered, these bedcovers were decorated with a coarse white cording, or "roving," similar in appearance to candlewicks. Woven candlewick spreads, like the one illustrated here, were probably made only in America in about 1820, and only for a short period of time. Embroidered candlewicking lasted much longer and continues to be done today, although by machine.

Hints for Collectors
This typical example of the woven candlewick spread is in excellent condition and has not yellowed (a common occurrence with white pieces). Interestingly, it has the same motifs—pine trees, eight-pointed stars, and stylized flowers—found in both appliquéd and pieced quilts.

Price Guide Group: Whitework.

Courtesy Museum of American Folk Art, New York City.

Description
Central medallion format with large floral urn sitting on square area. Foot of urn flanked by initials and date. Central medallion surrounded by scallops within narrow square border. Large swags and tassels frame central medallion. Each swag encloses large fruit basket. Narrow quilted border. All white.

Materials and Dimensions
Cotton. Central medallion contains stuffed floral urn on square area quilted in diamonds; flowers are quilted and stuffed. Quilted scalloped frame surrounded by diamond quilting. Large border swags and tassels quilted and stuffed, and stuffed fruit basket fills area within each swag. Fine line quilting throughout. Narrow outer border quilted in swags and circles. 90″ × 88″.

Maker, Locality, and Period
Initialed LCB. New York State. 1861.

Comment
All-white quilts require more expertise with a needle than any other quilt form. They reached their height of popularity in the years between 1800 and 1850. This quilt is one of 2 very similar bedcovers; both have extraordinary stitching and elaborate designs; they are superb examples of this type.

Hints for Collectors
This quilt is a textile masterpiece, with extremely detailed stitching usually associated with late 18th- and early 19th-century pieces.

Price Guide Group: Whitework.

Courtesy America Hurrah Antiques, New York City.

Description
Center with latticework basket filled with fruit and loosely
framed by 4 grape clusters. Inner border meandering grapevine.
Outer border continuous line of leaflike forms. Edged on 3 sides
with netted handmade fringe. All white. White binding.

Materials and Dimensions
Cotton and muslin. Quilted basket filled with stuffed fruit and
surrounded by stuffed grape clusters. Quilted meandering vine
border with stuffed grapes and leaves. Outer border has quilted
leaflike forms. Finely quilted ground. Cotton handmade netted
fringe on 3 sides. 33″ × 28″.

Maker, Locality, and Period
Maker unknown. New England. c. 1825.

Comment
In a pieced or appliquéd quilt the design depends on color,
fabrics, and the overall optical effect of the patches or appliqués.
In an all-white spread, however, the design is created solely by
the quilting and stuffed work. To do the stuffed work, the quilter
carefully spreads apart the coarse threads of the backing and
stuffs tiny bits of cotton (other stuffing materials may be used)
underneath the top to pad or raise the design.

Hints for Collectors
This bedcover has superb needlework and is an unusual size for
an all-white piece, which makes it doubly rare. It was probably
used only on very special occasions, as a child's bedcover used
any more frequently would never have remained in such good
condition.

Price Guide Group: Whitework.

Courtesy America Hurrah Antiques, New York City.

Embroidered Candlewick Pillow Sham

Description
Large eagle under crown and stars and partially framed by banner with words "E PLURIBUS UNUM." Eagle holds sheaf of wheat in its right claw and branch in left. Surrounded on 3 sides by trailing vine. Signature and date across top. Bordered on 3 sides with lace and fringe. All white.

Materials and Dimensions
Cotton. Embroidered and sheared eagle. All other motifs and words embroidered. Hand-crocheted lace and hand-knotted fringe. 61″ × 29½″.

Maker, Locality, and Period
Anne D. Miller. New York State. April 10, 1832.

Comment
Embroidered candlewicking became very popular around 1825. Notice that the depiction of the eagle is unusual, especially with its long, skinny legs and claws set at odd angles to the body. Different from a woven candlewick piece, in which all the threads are uniform in size, this piece with its high pile was made with various thicknesses of candlewicking thread that were pulled up to a certain height and then cut, producing the soft looking surface of the eagle's body.

Hints for Collectors
An unusual pillow sham of hand-embroidered candlewicking, this piece was made to cover a bed. It is a good example of 19th-century needlework techniques, and its eccentric eagle makes it a charming piece of folk art as well.

Price Guide Group: Whitework.

Courtesy Jay Johnson, America's Folk Heritage Gallery, New York City.

Rugs

Until well into the 18th century, few Americans had rugs or carpets. Only the wealthiest families could afford to import handmade Oriental rugs or machine-made carpets from Europe. Floors were generally kept bare or covered with clean sand swept into attractive patterns.

Early Rugs

The earliest rugs produced in America were intended for the bed and were made by sewing yarns through a heavy woolen foundation. They had elaborate designs and were often dated and signed with the maker's initials.

Toward the end of the 18th century, imported carpets became more widely available. The most common were known as Turkish and Persian carpets, named after the countries where their patterns originated. Flat, two-ply Scottish carpets were also very popular throughout New England, as were painted canvas floor cloths. Another alternative was simply to paint floors in geometric designs or patterns that imitated those that were common on carpets.

It was not until the 1830s that American manufacturers began producing room-size woven carpets in any quantity. Even so, most early 19th-century rugs were small and made either at home or by itinerant or local weavers. The earliest were multicolored striped rugs and rag carpets made from cloth strips. The strips were woven in patterns that later became common on hooked rugs.

Appliquéd and embroidered rugs were also fashioned at home during this period. Time-consuming to create and somewhat fragile, they were primarily showpieces to be displayed on tables and chests. One of the most well-known and elaborate embroidered rugs is the Caswell carpet. Worked in the 1830s and composed of 76 embroidered wool squares, each with a different design, plus a rectangular section used to cover the hearth in

Detail of a hooked rug. Private Collection.

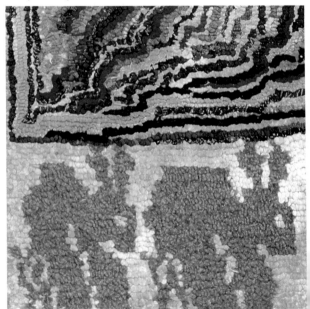

summer, it was made by a Vermont woman from wool she sheared herself, then spun and dyed expressly for use in the carpet.

Yarn-Sewn and Shirred Rugs

Between 1800 and 1840 yarn-sewn rugs began to be made in the home. Using a continuous running stitch, yarn was pulled up through a loosely woven base so that loops were left on top to form the rug's pile.

Around 1830, shirred rugs also became common. Actually a type of appliquéd rug, these were fashioned by gathering a strip of cloth, rather than yarn, on a thread and sewing that shirred strip, or "caterpillar," to a foundation. Although most rugs were made with caterpillar, or chenille, shirring, bias shirring is also known. In bias shirred rugs, one-inch-wide strips of cloth cut on a bias are folded in half and the fold stitched down so that the two ends form the pile.

Since most yarn-sewn and shirred rugs date from the 1830s or 1840s, they are very rare today. Colored with vegetable dyes, in original, often primitive designs, most have faded with age to soft, warm tones. They are surprisingly lightweight and, because of their fairly thin foundations, much more flexible than the later hooked rugs.

Braided and Hooked Rugs

By the end of the 19th century, few homes were without rugs of some kind; many were braided or hooked. It is thought that braided rugs—easier and less time-consuming to make than hooked rugs—first appeared around 1830. The simplest to make of all scrap-bag rugs, they require no drawing or designing abilities on the maker's part. Once the long, narrow strips are braided together, all that remains is to sew them in coils into an oval or circular shape. The Shakers were especially skilled at

Detail of a hooked rug. Private Collection.

making braided rugs, and created some of the most handsome examples known, many with concentric rings of color instead of the usual random color patterns.

Throughout the second half of the 19th century hooked rugs were very common; some experts feel that they are one of the few indigenous American folk arts. Although similar techniques probably originated in Europe, evidence suggests that the hooking done in this country had its origin in the rough mats that sailors made with rags and a common shipboard tool. That tool later evolved into a special hook used only for rugmaking.

The earliest hooked rug designs tend to be fairly primitive and often depict familiar objects, like flowers, houses, or a favorite animal. Geometric designs, which required little drawing ability to sketch, were also favored for hooked rug patterns.

Prestenciled Patterns

In the 1850s, burlap became readily available in this country and provided an inexpensive, convenient backing material for rugs. Partly as a result, hooked rugmaking soared in popularity. Edward Sands Frost, a Maine tin peddler who produced his own tin stencils, began selling rug-size pieces of burlap stamped with his own designs. Many rugs made after 1868 were based on Frost's patterns. Their symmetrical designs, which include elaborate floral arrangements, carefully posed animals, and scrollwork or geometric borders, distinguish them from the less predictable compositions found in original designs. Other manufacturers also sold printed patterns.

Although commercial patterns undoubtedly contributed to the decline of original hooked rug designs, they also made it possible for women with little artistic ability to design their own rugs in patterns that pleased them. Occasionally, rugmakers adapted printed patterns by choosing new color combinations or by modifying the design.

Detail of a yarn-sewn rug. Courtesy America Hurrah Antiques, New York City.

Modern Rugmaking

Although hooked rugmaking had declined in popularity by 1900, the 1910s and 1920s saw a revival of the technique, particularly in craft cooperatives. Situated in rural areas of New England and Canada, the cooperatives met the demands of a public increasingly interested in American handicrafts. During the 1930s, hooked rugs were avidly collected, and several books were written on the subject.

Interest in handmade American rugs as an art form soared again in the 1970s. Currently handmade rugs are popular with collectors, and, compared with other period textiles, are very reasonably priced.

Hooked, braided, yarn-sewn, and shirred rugs are all collected today; the last two types are by far the rarest and most expensive. Thousands of hooked rugs, and even greater numbers of braided ones, were made, and many fine examples are yet to be discovered. Rugs with unusual color schemes or ingenious designs, preferably in good condition, are well worth seeking out and buying.

Detail of a braided rug. Private Collection.

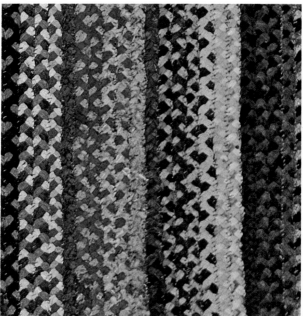

Pictorial Rugs

Like other folk artists, early rugmakers, many from Maine and the Canadian Maritime provinces, created rug designs based on their houses, farm animals, and favorite landscapes. A housewife would draw a pattern on a linen or homespun foundation, often using a piece of charcoal. Frequently a scene would lack perspective: in a farm scene, a rooster might be taller than a barn, and a flower the tallest of all. These early rugs, produced from about 1830 to 1850, are generally considered the most charming as well as the most primitive.

The colors have faded on most early 19th-century rugs because early vegetable dyes were not colorfast. Luckily, some rugs retained their original hues because they were stored and never used. Many reveal distinct, bright primary colors, while others have more subtle earth tones.

Prior to the 1860s, when patternmakers began printing and selling rug patterns stenciled on burlap, the designs of handmade rugs were original. Even after prestenciled patterns became fashionable, some women continued to create their own designs —often of the same subjects as the commercial patterns but rendered very differently. Generally, however, rugs made after 1875 followed kit patterns that even indicated color schemes. Many of the early kits were the products of Edward Sands Frost, whose rug patterns were often inspired by rugs that he had seen along his peddler's route. Since his metal stencil patterns tend to be stiff and lifeless, these qualities are helpful in distinguishing rugs made on commercial patterns. Despite the uniformity of manufactured patterns, some rugs made from kits are especially appealing—generally because the rugmaker took liberties with the prescribed colors or added other small changes of her own.

Most rugs hooked on a prestenciled pattern will be more symmetrical than those from original patterns. In addition, the primitive or naive quality so pronounced in original pictorial rugs is usually absent, and realistic forms, rather than fanciful or humorous ones, predominate. Many mass-produced designs have a somber quality totally lacking in the freer, but often less technically correct, original examples. As a rule, rugs made on commercial patterns are less interesting and less desirable than original designs.

With the recent revival of interest in collecting hooked and other handmade rugs, many contemporary rugmakers have started to create their own naive designs. These modern rugs can be distinguished from earlier 19th-century rugs by their strong, new-looking colors and evenly textured pile, in which all the loops are raised to the same height.

Lion Design Hooked Rug, Frost Pattern

Description
Stenciled Edward Sands Frost pattern #176. Tan and brown lion seated on ground of irregularly shaped designs in grays, olive-green, browns, and beige. Purple background with spray of flowers on each side of lion. Pink, purple, and red flowers with black-veined, gray leaves and red stems. Purple border matches background. No binding.

Materials and Dimensions
Wool on burlap. 46″ × 25″.

Maker, Locality, and Period
Maker and locality unknown. Pattern by Edward Sands Frost & Co., Biddeford, Maine. Design c. 1868–1900.

Comment
Edward Sands Frost, a Maine tin peddler, made his own rug stencils and stamped his designs on burlap. He began selling them door to door in 1868, and by the time he sold his business in 1876, he had made 750 zinc stencils, from which 180 designs could be printed. Preprinted rug patterns, which were soon copied by a number of other companies, enabled hooked-rug makers with little drawing ability to make a rug simply by filling in the spaces between the lines with the designated color. Today, designs from Frost's original stencils are printed and sold by Greenfield Village and the Henry Ford Museum in Dearborn, Michigan.

Hints for Collectors
Hooked rugs made on a prestenciled pattern are easy to distinguish from original designs because they are usually symmetrical. Although lions were a popular subject, the Frost lion is easily identified by the formal pose and the tall, stiff flowers on either side.

Price Guide Group: Pictorial Hooked Rugs.

Courtesy Henry Ford Museum, The Edison Institute, Dearborn, Michigan.

Lion Design Hooked Rug

Description
Original design. Beige and white lion outlined in black. Eye and tongue shocking pink. Background in striations of various colors, with several shades of blue predominant. Inner notched border maroon and dark blue. Outer border beige. No binding.

Materials and Dimensions
Wool and cotton on burlap. 44″ × 28″.

Maker, Locality, and Period
Maker unknown. Ohio. Late 19th century.

Comment
Lion designs were extremely popular for hooked rugs, and several companies sold patterns with lions on them. Although the maker of this rug may have been influenced by other patterns, there is a spunkiness to this animal that sets it apart from stenciled lions, which generally have little vitality. The striated background and keyhole border are quite sophisticated for an original design.

Hints for Collectors
The strong design, the spikelike mane of the lion, and the geometric border all combine to give this rug character and make it a real prize. The collector should check the condition of both the foundation and the pile with any hooked rug, as dry, brittle pieces falling out indicate the fibers are deteriorating. If this is the case, the rug is not worth buying because it will soon disintegrate.

Price Guide Group: Pictorial Hooked Rugs.

Courtesy Museum of American Folk Art, New York City.

268 Modern Noah's Ark Hooked Rug

Description
Original design. Central square with animals walking down winding road toward Ark. Scene with blue ocean, white waves, a tree with red and blue birds, flecked olive-tweed grass, green palm tree and pines, and scarlet flowers. 2 human figures at lower right. Purple border with large black-and-white speckled eagle at each corner and bowl of fruit or flowers at middle of each side. No binding.

Materials and Dimensions
Wool on burlap. 88″ × 80″.

Maker, Locality, and Period
Rubens Teles. New York City. 1980.

Comment
With its naive biblical scene, American eagles, and traditional fruit and flower compotes, this rug might easily be mistaken for a 19th-century rug. However, wool yarn was rarely used for an entire rug after 1850, and before 1850, light linen or homespun would have been used for the backing rather than the burlap used on this rug.

Hints for Collectors
Since the Bicentennial, hooking rugs has become very popular. Although few contemporary rugs are of interest to the collector, a piece like this, which closely resembles a naive painting, is an exception. The border designs and the central scene are the work of a contemporary artist well aware of traditional folk motifs.

Price Guide Group: Pictorial Hooked Rugs.

Courtesy Jay Johnson, America's Folk Heritage Gallery, New York City.

Blackhawk Design Hooked Rug

Description
Original design. Name "BLACKHAWK" appears in tan on blue background across top. Below, tan, white, and brown American eagle on purple background, with blue strip at lower right. Eagle above rectangular block in purple tweed with cutout for bottom of eagle design. In center, a multicolored block in red, black, gray, purple, brown, and white. Below, row of 3 cocoa-colored animals, possibly rabbits, each with pink eye, on light gray background. Border striped triangles in black, white, blues, tan, and wine-red, on black background. No binding.

Materials and Dimensions
Cotton and wool on burlap. 40½″ × 25″.

Maker, Locality, and Period
Maker unknown. New England. c. 1875–1900.

Comment
The unique group of motifs on this rug—an eagle, some whimsical animals, and the name Blackhawk—probably had special significance for its maker. Blackhawk was a famous racehorse in the last decades of the 19th century, but why the name was hooked into this rug remains a mystery. The multicolored block of curving lines in the center of the rug is known as a "hit-or-miss" design.

Hints for Collectors
Many one-of-a-kind rugs were made during the late 19th century, and their value lies primarily in their individual appeal. The rug illustrated was hooked after stenciled rug patterns had become common.

Price Guide Group: Pictorial Hooked Rugs.

Private Collection.

Rabbit Design Hooked Rug

Description
Original design. 2 pairs of rabbits, each pair divided by a green stalk. Red and pink flowers outlined in green between rabbit pairs. Pink background. Irregular scalloped magenta frame on black background. No binding.

Materials and Dimensions
Wool and cotton on burlap. 53″ × 31″.

Maker, Locality, and Period
Maker unknown. Pennsylvania. 1890–1900.

Comment
Thousands of hooked rugs were made from 1850 to 1900, but many lacked visual appeal. By the 1890s, stenciled rug patterns were sold by a number of companies, and the quality of the designs had deteriorated considerably. A whimsical, turn-of-the-century hooked rug like the one illustrated here is rare today. The irregularity of the pattern—the pink background conforms to the scalloped border in some places and is straight in others—indicates that the rug is an original design.

Hints for Collectors
Rugs made from stenciled patterns are generally less valuable and sought after than an original design, although some collectors specialize in acquiring rugs made from early patterns. The lively quality of the smiling rabbits and the inventive use of color in this rug definitely make it a fine example of an original, freehand pattern.

Price Guide Group: Pictorial Hooked Rugs.

Courtesy America Hurrah Antiques, New York City.

Tabby Cat Design Hooked Rug

Description
Original design. Striped black, gray, and white cat with yellow
eyes on gray rug against purple background; framed by scalloped
circle edged with tan and set on brown and black square. Inner
scalloped border beige. Hexagon border of blue, purple, pink,
and tan blocks outlined in brown and edged in pink on one side.
Outer border black. No binding.

Materials and Dimensions
Wool and cotton on burlap. 35″ × 35″.

Maker, Locality, and Period
Maker unknown. Probably New England. c. 1875–85.

Comment
A popular story tells how a woman in Nova Scotia had her
husband hold her cat down on a piece of burlap so she could
outline it with a pencil and create a design for her rug. That the
cat on this rug was subjected to the same treatment is unlikely;
the primitive quality of the design suggests that it was drawn
freehand.

Hints for Collectors
A naive design like this one often indicates a fairly early rug.
Any rug with a burlap backing, however, was almost certainly
made after the late 1850s, when burlap commonly replaced linen
or hemp. Occasionally, a rug made after 1860 does turn up with a
homespun backing, so the backing alone is not enough to date a
piece. To see if a rug has faded check the back, where the colors
should approximate their original hues.

Price Guide Group: Pictorial Hooked Rugs.

Courtesy America Hurrah Antiques, New York City.

Description
Original design. Black dog outlined in white, with orange and white eye, collar, and chain. Dog's chain attached to 3-rail white fence; entire scene set on tan rectangle outlined by red, yellow, and orange line. Rectangle with areas of darker tan and with name "NED" (upper left) and "1900" (upper right), both in purple. Border at top and bottom with brown scrolls outlined in white or yellowish-white and surrounded by red and blue areas. Border at sides with single white scroll on dark yellowish-brown background. In each corner, red hearts outlined in white with pale blue centers. No binding.

Materials and Dimensions
Cotton on burlap. 41″ × 21¾″.

Maker, Locality, and Period
Maker unknown. Carroll County, Maryland. Dated 1900.

Comment
Although hooked rugs frequently have a date worked on them, that date may not indicate when the rug was made. Often rugs commemorated a special occasion of some kind. Here, 1900 may be the year the dog became a family pet.

Hints for Collectors
This animal rug with its childlike perspective—note the very large dog and the very small fence—is a good example of original folk art. Hooked with fairly large loops, it has an uneven texture that accentuates the large, slightly irregular scrolls. In a rug made from a printed pattern, the scrolls would be perfectly shaped.

Price Guide Group: Pictorial Hooked Rugs.

Collection of Morgan Anderson.

Grenfell Hooked Rug with Puffins

Description
Grenfell Mission design. 3 puffins, each perched on tip of an iceberg. Black bodies with white breasts and orange feet, beaks, and eyes. Beige and tan striped icebergs; blue and turquoise striped ocean; beige sky with 2 black stripes. Gray-beige border with dark brown at bottom edge. No binding.

Materials and Dimensions
Thinly cut strips of cotton and wool on burlap. 25½″ × 20″.

Maker, Locality, and Period
Maker unknown. Labrador or the Canadian Maritime Provinces. c. 1920–30.

Comment
Puffins and polar bears are motifs frequently found on rugs made in Labrador and sold through the Grenfell Mission there between 1900 and 1930. The patterns were created by designers at the mission, and the rugmakers were supposed to work the patterns in prescribed colors. Frequently, however, individuals followed their own imaginations, and 2 rugs made from the same pattern may be very different. Most of those sold by the mission bear the label "Grenfell Industries, New Foundland, Labrador." In the first 2 decades of the 20th century, a number of craft cooperatives were established, many of them by mission societies, in diverse areas of the country, such as New England and the Appalachian Mountains.

Hints for Collectors
Of the rugs made and sold at missions and co-ops, those from Grenfell are generally the finest and most distinctive. Grenfell rugs are hard to find, however, and are more likely to be seen in Maine and Canada than elsewhere.

Price Guide Group: Pictorial Hooked Rugs.

Courtesy America Hurrah Antiques, New York City.

Description
Original design. 2 roosters in shades of gray and black, with
yellow beaks, blue eyes, pink and white tweed combs, and white-
striped tail feathers. Background in irregular patches of rust,
olive-green, tans, browns, and orange. Striped border of white,
pink, brown, purple, and green with yellow or green blocks at
corners. No binding.

Materials and Dimensions
Wool and cotton on burlap. 39″ × 22″.

Maker, Locality, and Period
Maker unknown. New England. c. 1890.

Comment
Many hooked rugs have borders, some with scallops or scrolls
and others with geometric designs, but few are bordered as
cleverly as this. The narrow stripes and corner squares imitate
the incised decoration typical of Victorian furniture. Design
elements like this that were used only during a specific period
can help date the piece and are especially useful on a hooked rug,
since many hooked-rug patterns were used over long periods of
time.

Hints for Collectors
This rug is in good condition, but many hooked rugs have holes in
them or torn bindings. New bindings can be attached without too
much expense, but more extensive repairs ought to be done by
an expert and can be costly. To fix a hole correctly, a new piece
of burlap must be sewn to the old foundation, and the missing
loops reworked through that. Merely reattaching loose pieces,
which is quicker, is only a temporary solution, for they will
loosen again shortly.

Price Guide Group: Pictorial Hooked Rugs.

Courtesy America Hurrah Antiques, New York City.

Rooster Design Hooked Rug

Description
Original design. 2 black roosters with red combs, eyes, and
wattles and yellow-edged legs flanking 2 yellow chicks standing
on half an eggshell. Between roosters, white flower on red and
pink background. Birds on white background outlined in gray
and black. Around central design, irregularly shaped patches of
tan, brown, and blue framed diagonally at each corner by red and
pink stripes. Black triangles in corners. No binding.

Materials and Dimensions
Wool and cotton on burlap. 43″ × 26½″.

Maker, Locality, and Period
Maker unknown. York, Pennsylvania. c. 1895.

Comment
Before the Civil War, rugs took their colors from the original
tones of the scraps used to make them, or from scraps tinted
with homemade dyes from native plants, wood barks, or berries.
Toward the end of the 19th century, synthetic coal-tar and
aniline dyes were introduced for home use, and rugs began to
appear in new, vibrant shades. Early synthetic dyes, however,
faded quickly when exposed to light, so that the colors of many
Victorian rugs are different today from what they once were.
The rug shown here, found wrapped in old newspapers, retains
its original brilliance.

Hints for Collectors
Barnyard animals were popular as designs for pictorial rugs and
patternmakers even offered prestenciled patterns of roosters and
chicks. This rug, however, with its tiny, irregularly shaped
chicks and sturdy roosters, is clearly the product of someone's
imagination.

Price Guide Group: Pictorial Hooked Rugs.

Courtesy America Hurrah Antiques, New York City.

Description
Original design. Central horse of red and red tweed set on rectangular area in predominantly drab olive. Background in abstract shapes of browns, black, and drab olive, with random loops of purple-and-red tweed. Smaller horse in each corner: 2 beige or white, 1 gray, and 1 red tweed. Black binding.

Materials and Dimensions
Cotton on burlap. 37½″ × 17½″.

Maker, Locality, and Period
Maker unknown. Probably Pennsylvania. c. 1850–1900.

Comment
Made from bits and pieces of both solid colors and flecked tweed cotton, this is a real scrap-bag rug. The limited resources available to the maker, however, were no detriment to her creativity. The heavy-legged red horse with its single tweed leg and body stands out against the background, creating a dramatic figure. The irregularity of the background adds to the naive quality of this piece and helps enhance the 4 smaller horses in the corners.

Hints for Collectors
This pictorial rug is an outstanding piece of folk art. The large central horse and small corner horses are typical of the kind of repetition and balance often seen in folk paintings. Here the horse figure seems especially well suited to the rug's long, narrow shape.

Price Guide Group: Pictorial Hooked Rugs.

Private Collection.

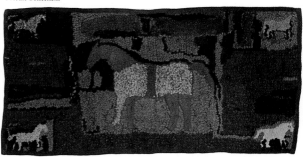

Horse Design Hooked Rug

Description
Original design. Gray and black striated horse with beige and white eye and beige hooves set on rectangular background of undulating stripes in tan and white. Corners of rectangle red, yellow, blue, white, and tan stripes. "1880" in red, surrounded by black (lower left). Multicolored zigzag border. Multicolored binding.

Materials and Dimensions
Wool and cotton on burlap. 53″ × 36″.

Maker, Locality, and Period
Maker unknown. Pennsylvania. Dated 1880.

Comment
Of the many animal designs used on hooked rugs, horses are some of the most common. Few, however, are as lively as this one. The use of striated color on both horse and background creates a feeling of movement that is further intensified by the jagged border pattern.

Hints for Collectors
Pictorial hooked rugs are in great demand today, and one with a charming original design like this is a prize. Although most rugs of this quality have already made their way to shops specializing in folk art, one occasionally turns up at a country auction or fleamarket, usually in need of a good cleaning. Provided the piece is not full of holes—the work of mice or moths—a design like this one is well worth buying.

Price Guide Group: Pictorial Hooked Rugs.

Courtesy America Hurrah Antiques, New York City.

Description
Original design. Red bull outlined in black with blue eye, gray front hooves, and brown and red tail. Upper part of background beige; lower part gray. Bull stands on patch of brown above full-length strip of turquoise. Mottled blue-and-brown border. Black binding.

Materials and Dimensions
Wool, felt, and cotton on burlap. 37″ × 25″.

Maker, Locality, and Period
Ethel Bishop. Maine. 1979.

Comment
This huge, solid red figure could as easily appear in a folk painting as a hooked rug. While animal rugs often picture a favorite dog or cat, a bull is more exotic.

Hints for Collectors
New or old, a rug like this is a fine piece of folk art. Many contemporary rugs are uninspired and ordinary. Few are as well conceived and eye-catching as this one. Rugs with a simple, primitive design tend to be either fairly early examples or contemporary ones, and only a few date from the late 19th and early 20th centuries. The early rugs can usually be identified by examining their condition: the back will be brighter than the front, and the pile is often worn down and soft. The collector should learn to distinguish between modern rugs and earlier primitive examples. A modern rug can still be worth buying and enjoying, but for far less money than a 19th-century one.

Price Guide Group: Pictorial Hooked Rugs.

Private Collection.

Grenfell Hooked Rug with House

Description
Grenfell Mission design. Blue-green house with lighter patch at one end; light brown roof, chimney, and trim; and white windows and doors. Olive-green lawn with white picket fence. Pale blue fir trees at left side and in back of house. Gray sky across top, and pink ground to left of fence. No binding.

Materials and Dimensions
Thinly cut strips of wool, cotton-knit jersey, and dyed, unraveled burlap on burlap. 20½″ × 13″.

Maker, Locality, and Period
Maker unknown. Labrador or the Canadian Maritime Provinces. c. 1920–30.

Comment
Dr. Wilfred Grenfell, who went to Labrador with a British hospital ship in the 1890s, stayed there and established the Grenfell Mission. He then organized rugmaking into a cottage industry, and helped promote and sell the distinctive rugs of the region. These rugs are unlike any others. Hooked from very thin strips of material, the loops are pulled through every opening in the weave of the burlap, creating a tightly woven, very durable rug with a smooth surface that looks almost like needlepoint.

Hints for Collectors
While not all rugs of this type were actually sold through the mission, any of the pale-colored, tightly hooked rugs from the area are known as Grenfell. They are easily identifiable with or without the characteristic "Grenfell Industries, New Foundland, Labrador" label.

Price Guide Group: Pictorial Hooked Rugs.

Courtesy America Hurrah Antiques, New York City.

Description
Original design. Red house with dark blue roof, chimneys, window and door frames, and path. Green tree with black trunk. Blue-gray mottled background with blue-gray border, wider at sides than top and bottom. No binding.

Materials and Dimensions
Wool and cotton on burlap. 26½″ × 20″.

Maker, Locality, and Period
Maker unknown. New York State. c. 1900–20.

Comment
Primitive designs, like the fine example illustrated here, were sometimes taken from a child's drawing and redrawn to rug size. The thick loops of cloth indicate that the rug was probably made quickly. This tends to make the pile less durable than that of a more tightly hooked rug. The bold colors and distorted proportions are typical of the more interesting folk rugs. Because of these graphic qualities and the rug's small size, it is especially suitable for hanging.

Hints for Collectors
Some rugs featuring houses are very realistic; others like this one are pure folk art based on fantasy buildings. Although the materials used to make this rug date from the early 20th century, the building depicted is a stereotype that could have existed in practically any period. The rug's excellent condition and vivid colors suggest it was hardly used, which increases its market value.

Price Guide Group: Pictorial Hooked Rugs.

Collection of William C. Ketchum, Jr.

House Design Hooked Rug

Description
Original design. Beige house with attached carriage barn.
Trimmed in brown with blue at windows and doors, red
chimneys, beige driveway, and yard in browns. Background in
browns and lavender. Border in abstract shapes of pink, red,
blue, brown, and white. Black binding.

Materials and Dimensions
Wool and cotton on burlap. 58½″ × 35½″.

Maker, Locality, and Period
Maker unknown. New York State or New England. c. 1880.

Comment
Some rugmakers were good at drawing a design, others had a
natural sense of color, but few combined both skills as well as
this artist. Although this rug was made in the 1880s, its
multicolored abstract border has a particularly modern look.
Hooked rugs frequently pictured the maker's most prized
possession. The power of this design conveys how proud its
owner must have been of her home.

Hints for Collectors
Houses are a common motif on pictorial hooked rugs, but the
interesting composition of this one makes it a rare example. The
late 19th-century architecture is typical of New England, a fact
that helps establish the date and locality. A rug of this quality is
expensive, but with today's huge demand for figural rugs, it is
well worth the price, provided the rug is in good condition.

Price Guide Group: Pictorial Hooked Rugs.

Courtesy America Hurrah Antiques, New York City.

Yarn-sewn Rug with Floral and House Design

Description
Original design. Large central flower with blue leaves and stems and orange flowers and buds. Randomly placed triangles, flowers, and leaves in blue, orange, beige, and black. 2 orange houses with blue doors and blue and beige windows at bottom center. Blue background with irregular patches of beige and orange. Triple border: 2 black stripes enclosing 1 beige stripe. Blue binding.

Materials and Dimensions
Wool on madder-dyed linen. 29¼" × 17¼".

Maker, Locality, and Period
Maker unknown. New England. c. 1800.

Comment
Yarn-sewn rugs were probably the earliest hooked-type rugs made. Most were stitched in New England or Canada between 1800 and 1840. A length of two-ply yarn was sewn through a foundation of homespun linen or an old grain sack with a loose, continuous running stitch, leaving loops on the surface. The loops were then pulled up from the foundation and usually clipped to form the rug's pile. The rows of loops following the contours of the flowers and houses add both movement and texture to the rug illustrated.

Hints for Collectors
Most yarn-sewn rugs are fairly primitive in design. Few are as exceptional as this one. The huge overhanging flower, the helter-skelter placement of different shapes, the small houses, and the intense colors make this a wonderful piece of folk art. Almost any yarn-sewn rug in reasonably good condition is valuable, since a small number have survived.

Price Guide Group: Floral Hooked Rugs.

Courtesy America Hurrah Antiques, New York City. Collection of Jonathan Holstein.

283 Yarn-sewn and Chenille-shirred Rug with House

Description
Original design. Red house with blue doors and windows and white roof. Left side, tan house between 2 blue trees. Right side, blue trees lining roadway. Surrounding land, road, and sky in blues and white. Frame of chenille shirring: 2 rows of beige within several rows of brown. Wide border pink, red, and black roses with blue stems and leaves set on black background with patches of brown. No binding.

Materials and Dimensions
Wool on linen. 60″ × 46″.

Maker, Locality, and Period
Maker unknown. New England. c. 1830.

Comment
This rug is a fine example of 2 early rugmaking techniques: yarn sewing and shirring. In yarn sewing, the yarn is sewn through the foundation with a running stitch; the loops formed by the stitches are pulled up through the backing to form a pile. In shirring, often called chenille shirring, strips of wool, 1–1½″ wide, are sewn down the center with a running stitch and then gathered into folds by pulling the thread. The resulting "caterpillar" is then sewn to the foundation.

Hints for Collectors
To identify the yarn-sewn and shirred areas of a rug, look at the back. Where it has been yarn-sewn, rows of large, even stitches will appear. In the shirred areas, only the tiny thread stitches that attach the shirred cloth to the backing will show.

Price Guide Group: Pictorial Hooked Rugs.

Courtesy America Hurrah Antiques, New York City.

Hooked and Painted Rug with Waterfall

Description
Original design. Water blue and white; Niagara Falls and water below in blue and white stripes. Turquoise trees; blue sky; green hills outlined in black; beige dam. Oil paint applied on top of pile. Mauve binding.

Materials and Dimensions
Wool, cotton, and oil paint on burlap. 38″ × 20″.

Maker, Locality, and Period
Maker and locality unknown. c. 1920–30.

Comment
With blue, white, and turquoise paints applied to the surface, this pictorial rug is unique. Possibly the rugmaker was dissatisfied with the colors of the rug's fabrics and decided to alter them with paint. Whatever her motivation, the rug is an interesting example of the kind of ingenuity often found among rugmakers. Niagara Falls was a popular tourist spot in the 1920s and 1930s and thousands of people visited it every year. Although many amateur artists painted the scene, it is unusual to find it as the subject of a hooked rug.

Hints for Collectors
This rug is of special interest to the collector because of its unusual execution and subject matter. Clever experimentation with design, color, materials, or technique always makes a piece more valuable. Here the carefully thought-out design and realistic depiction of water make this rug an authentic piece of folk art.

Price Guide Group: Pictorial Hooked Rugs.

Courtesy America Hurrah Antiques, New York City.

Car Design Hooked Rug

Description

Original design. Black car with royal blue doors, red trim, whitewall tires, and black wheel spokes set on pale blue background. Green, pink, and yellow inner border at top and bottom. Outer border in stripes of light purple and pale pink, with multicolored flecks at top. The make of the car, "HUDSON," in black on lower section. Black binding.

Materials and Dimensions

Cotton, wool, and velvet on burlap. 34″ × 26″.

Maker, Locality, and Period

Maker and locality unknown. c. 1920–40.

Comment

The pale pink, blue, and purple, as well as the 1920s model car, date this rug to the Depression years. An earlier rugmaker might have shown a favorite dog or cat, but the creator of this rug chose to picture the family car, obviously a prized possession. The smallest details have been carefully worked into the rug, right down to the gold hood ornament.

Hints for Collectors

Pictorial hooked rugs, especially those with the charm and originality of this one, are very popular and bring consistently high prices. If you find a 50-year-old rug, try flexing the back to make sure the burlap is not brittle and dry. Should small pieces fall out, it means that the backing will not hold up and the rug is not worth buying.

Price Guide Group: Pictorial Hooked Rugs.

Courtesy America Hurrah Antiques, New York City.

Simple Simon Design Hooked Rug

Description
Probably variation of stenciled design. Black silhouettes of
Simple Simon carrying pie, from which ribbon of steam rises, and
toadstool-like shape with triangular top. Orange moon outlined in
black with yellow eyes and mouth, and yellow stars outlined in
black. 2 moundlike areas at bottom, 1 light orange, 1 darker
orange. Horizontal bands of dark purple, tan, and lighter purple
form top half of background, with bottom half tan. Irregular
black border. Black binding.

Materials and Dimensions
Wool on burlap. 36″ × 24″.

Maker, Locality, and Period
Maker unknown. Connecticut. c. 1930.

Comment
The rather sophisticated human figure in this design suggests
that it may have been based on a prestamped pattern, although
it bears no resemblance to other known patterns. Whether or not
the design is original, the figure, with its raised front foot and
sense of motion, gives the rug a very realistic quality. The
purples and pale orange (especially when combined with black)
are typical of the 1930s.

Hints for Collectors
Offbeat and modern, this rug has its own particular charm and
will appeal to anyone interested in 1930s styles and taste. Rugs
from the 1930s and 1940s can still be found at yard sales and
thrift shops. Examine them carefully; even such relatively new
examples may be in poor condition.

Price Guide Group: Pictorial Hooked Rugs.

Courtesy Museum of American Folk Art, New York City.

Centennial Design Hooked Rug

Description
Stenciled design, probably by Edward Sands Frost. Red, white, and blue shield framed by the word "CENTENNIAL" in red across top, and dates "1776–1876" in pink outlined by light purple at bottom. Beige background. Border of irregularly shaped stars in purple, pink, and beige on black background. No binding.

Materials and Dimensions
Wool on burlap. 42″ × 31½″.

Maker, Locality, and Period
Maker and locality unknown. c. 1876.

Comment
The American Centennial of 1876, like the Bicentennial of 1976, inspired many rugmakers to depict patriotic motifs in their work. The semicircular shape of this rug, probably intended for use as a doormat or in front of a fireplace, is found less frequently than the more common rectangle. The great majority of hooked rugs were made in rectangular shapes, possibly because old grain sacks were used as backings. But a number of rugs in this semicircular shape are known to exist.

Hints for Collectors
As a piece of original Americana, this rug is the type often sought by collectors. It documents the pride aroused in Americans by the hundredth birthday of their country. The bright, almost garish reds, pinks, and purples are typical of the colors found in Victorian rugs after commercially made, synthetic dyes were introduced for home use. Today, of course, the colors appear more muted.

Price Guide Group: Pictorial Hooked Rugs.

Courtesy Museum of American Folk Art, New York City.

Rugs with Floral and Geometric Designs

 Floral and geometric rug designs have always appealed to American rugmakers. Floral patterns were perhaps the more demanding, since they required some drawing skill. Almost anyone with a basic sense of design could work out a pleasing geometric pattern using straight lines or circles, which could be traced from a cup and saucer. No doubt this simplicity contributed to their popularity.

Some of the more interesting geometric designs are based on circles, among them the very old clamshell pattern with its many variations (310). Using only overlapping, variously colored circular forms, the talented rugmaker was able to create an intricate design, as pleasing to us in the 20th century as it would have been in earlier times. Generally, the most successful patterns are those in which the rugmaker has been able to use a particular form with some consistency. For example, in two of the oblong rugs included here (312, 313), the long, narrow concentric rectangular shapes emphasize the shape of the rug.

In the second half of the 19th century, patternmakers began selling prestenciled hooked-rug patterns on burlap foundations. Distinguishing between simple rugs made from original designs and those hooked on prestenciled patterns is often very difficult, especially with geometric rugs. Very complicated geometric patterns, however, such as those with cubes or three-dimensional figures, were often prestamped.

Floral rugs in the early 19th century usually had one or two large, boldly colored flowers and were often surrounded by elaborate scrolls and flowered borders. Original floral patterns are very desirable, especially the early primitive designs made before 1850, which are generally yarn-sewn or shirred on a linen foundation. From the 1860s to the end of the 19th century, floral designs became increasingly more elaborate: large sprays of realistic looking flowers were often surrounded by oval borders with scrollwork or large leaves (292, 293). Occasionally, rugmakers combined floral and geometric designs, creating rugs that are especially attractive (289, 309).

Description
Original design. Central black flower stem with 4 black branches and 5 yellow and white flowers with black centers on blue-green background. Tan and white cloudlike forms outlined in gray above and below central flower. Multiple-frame border tan, browns, blue, and maroon. Corners of inner frame cut diagonally to form beige triangles edged on one side with beige, red, black, gray, and maroon stripes. Brown and black outer frame. No binding.

Materials and Dimensions
Cotton on burlap. 13″ × 9½″.

Maker, Locality, and Period
Maker unknown. New England or Pennsylvania. c. 1850–1900.

Comment
This small rug was probably used as a table or chest covering. The wide, loosely hooked loops of material and the primitive design suggest it may have been made by an inexperienced rugmaker, possibly someone who had seen a floral rug in a friend's house and attempted to make a similar one. Much of its charm lies in its simplicity.

Hints for Collectors
A very small or very large hooked rug is unusual and generally more expensive than a typical 3′ × 5′ rug of comparable quality. Should you find a loosely woven rug like the one illustrated, remember that the thick loops will not stand hard wear and the rug is best hung on a wall or displayed on a table.

Price Guide Group: Floral Hooked Rugs.

Collection of William C. Ketchum, Jr.

289 Yarn-sewn Rug with Floral and Geometric Design

Description
Original design. Central pink, gold, and beige flower with blue-green leaves and stem. Two-tone brown background with multicolored triangle at each side. Blue-green frame with pink diamonds at corners. Triple border: double blue-and-white inner border surrounding central design, blue-green middle border, and blue-green outer border with scalloped inner edge in tan. No binding.

Materials and Dimensions
Wool on linen. 12″ × 8″.

Maker, Locality, and Period
Maker unknown. New England. Early 19th century.

Comment
Throughout the 17th century and part of the 18th, rugs were used primarily to cover tables or chests. They continued to be used as table covers into the early 19th century, even as rugs became common on floors. This miniature yarn-sewn rug was probably used to cover a table or stool. Sewn with bits of different colored wool and yarn, a small piece like this gave the rugmaker a chance to use her ingenuity. The brown tip of the flower stem suggests that she ran short of blue-green wool.

Hints for Collectors
This early yarn-sewn rug is especially valuable because of its size. Its value is further enhanced because it is in good condition. Very few pieces with their vivid colors, pile, and foundations intact have survived.

Price Guide Group: Floral Hooked Rugs.

Courtesy America Hurrah Antiques, New York City.

Floral Design Hooked Rug

Description
Probably original design. 4 central flowers, 3 in purples and 1 orange, with 2 red and 2 orange buds, on gray-green stems with gray-green leaves. Beige background framed by irregularly shaped vine of tan leaves veined in black on wide black border. No binding.

Materials and Dimensions
Wool on burlap. 45½″ × 27″.

Maker, Locality, and Period
Maker unknown. New England. c. 1870–90.

Comment
This general design—a floral center surrounded by leaves and a border—was extremely common during the late 19th century. Most floral rugs were worked on a printed pattern in which all the leaves were exactly the same size and shape and the flowers symmetrically placed in a central oval. Such precision and balance are lacking here and suggest that the rugmaker drew her own design, similar to but less perfect than those she had seen on commercial patterns. However, the naive quality of this design makes it, in many ways, more appealing than prestamped patterns.

Hints for Collectors
The vividly colored flowers and childlike leaves give this rug a charming primitive quality. As in any piece of good folk art, the personality of the craftsperson comes through and increases the value of the work.

Price Guide Group: Floral Hooked Rugs.

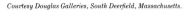

Courtesy Douglas Galleries, South Deerfield, Massachusetts.

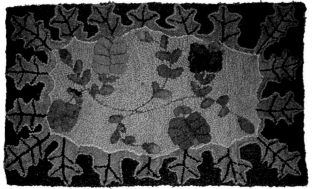

291 Floral Design Hooked Rug

Description
Original design. Central floral spray of 3 red roses with smaller
flowers and leaves, outlined in beige and set in irregular blue
patch on beige and light blue oval. Initials "M.E.H.N." and date
"1868" at opposite ends of central spray. Blue and brown border
decorated with red and beige sprays of rosebuds and leaves, and
large red double rose at either end of oval. Greenish-gray
binding.

Materials and Dimensions
Wool and cotton on burlap. 46″ × 32½″.

Maker, Locality, and Period
Maker unknown. New England. Dated 1868.

Comment
A few hooked rugs were made before 1850, generally on
foundations of loosely woven linen or homespun hemp. By the
late 1850s, however, inexpensive burlap sacking was being
imported from the East Indies in large quantities, and rug
hooking became a common pastime. Many rugs in the 1850s and
1860s were made from old burlap feed sacks that measured
46″ × 40″ when opened and laid flat. These are very nearly the
dimensions of this rug. The number of rugs of similar size
suggests how frequently these sacks were used as backing for
hooked rugs.

Hints for Collectors
Its primitive design and thick loops mark this rug as fairly old.
The 1868 date, however, is not necessarily the date it was made.
Rugs often included dates in commemoration of an event that
had taken place much earlier.

Price Guide Group: Floral Hooked Rugs.

Courtesy America Hurrah Antiques, New York City.

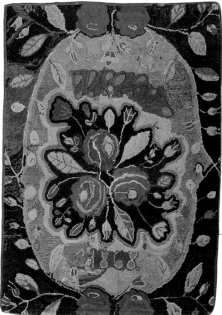

292 Floral Design Hooked Rug, Frost Pattern

Description
Stenciled Edward Sands Frost pattern #12. Central spray of roses in red, pink, and purple, with red buds and two-tone tan and green leaves. Petal edges and leaf veins outlined in black. Maroon background. 2 pairs of scroll-like leaves with black veins on sides: 1 leaf red and purple and 1 leaf tan and gold in each pair. Border of 3 rows of 2-colored stripes: tan and black, red and pink, and tan and brown. No binding.

Materials and Dimensions
Wool and cotton on burlap. 34½" × 21".

Maker, Locality, and Period
Maker unknown. Cincinnati, Ohio. Pattern by Edward Sands Frost & Co., Biddeford, Maine. Design c. 1885.

Comment
Typical of late 19th-century rugs in both color and design, this piece exemplifies the Victorian love of vivid, sometimes garish colors and large-scale designs. It is made on a Frost pattern and follows it almost exactly, the only change being an extra design in the border. While many rugmakers followed the printed pattern to the letter, others made small changes of design or color, either to suit their own tastes or to use up small bits of unmatched materials.

Hints for Collectors
A good example of a late 19th-century pattern-based rug, this one has all the characteristic qualities: a balanced formal design, a large, realistic floral spray, scroll-like leaves, and an overall lack of spontaneity.

Price Guide Group: Floral Hooked Rugs.

Private Collection.

Floral Design Hooked Rug, Frost Pattern

Description
Stenciled Edward Sands Frost pattern #60. Central oval with 3 large roses and rosebuds, daisies, and other flowers in red, pink, blue, and purple on beige background. Enclosed by rust-colored scrollwork oval. Triangular sprays of red roses and buds at each corner. Wine-colored background surrounds scrollwork. No binding.

Materials and Dimensions
Wool on burlap. 46¾" × 28½".

Maker, Locality, and Period
Maker and locality unknown. Pattern by Edward Sands Frost & Co., Biddeford, Maine. Design c. 1868–1900.

Comment
Frost designed hundreds of floral patterns, all of them with rather elaborate compositions. In most, the flowers were worked in subtle gradations of color, in an attempt to make them look realistic. In contrast, floral rugs in original designs tend to use only one or two primary colors, and to be very simply conceived.

Hints for Collectors
Rugs hooked on printed patterns and the few unhooked, stenciled burlap rug backings that still exist are of interest mainly to specialized collectors. Patterns made by Frost were stamped "E. S. Frost and Co., Biddeford, Me," but even without their mark, Frost rugs are easily recognized by their formal, realistic floral sprays and their symmetrical scrollwork borders. Today Frost's designs are printed and sold by Greenfield Village and the Henry Ford Museum in Dearborn, Michigan.

Price Guide Group: Floral Hooked Rugs.

Courtesy Henry Ford Museum, The Edison Institute, Dearborn, Michigan.

Floral Design Hooked Rug

Description
Adapted Edward Sands Frost pattern #2. Center with orange-pink roses and other flowers in blues, pinks, and pastels. Leaves several shades of green. Beige and white striated background. Large scroll designs in tans and browns outlined in gold, gray, browns, and black. Brown and black border, with pink and red roses and leaves of turquoise, greens, and gold at each corner. Brown binding.

Materials and Dimensions
Cotton on burlap. 77″ × 35″.

Maker, Locality, and Period
Edna Styles. Readfield, Maine. Late 19th century.

Comment
Although based on a Frost pattern, this design has been altered slightly by the maker. In the printed pattern, there are 2 separate sprays of rosebuds at either end of the floral center. Here the maker has replaced them with flowers of her own and enlarged the central design. While the scrollwork resembles that on the printed pattern, it has an almost freehand look and is outlined rather haphazardly in black.

Hints for Collectors
A rug based on a pattern but changed slightly is primarily of historical interest. Here neither the design nor the colors are particularly attractive, and the overall feeling is stiff and formal. Like many rugs made on a pattern, this one lacks some of the charm of an original design.

Price Guide Group: Floral Hooked Rugs.

Private Collection.

Floral Design Shirred Rug

Description
Original design. Ring of 12 diamonds, each with blue center, surrounded by concentric diamonds of red, white, blue, red, and pale green on brown background. Garland of blossoms, buds, and leaves in reds, blues, pinks, apricot, turquoise, and greens. Background of blocks in black, browns, and gray-blue. "AUGUSTINE W. PHILLIPS" in light brown across bottom. No binding.

Materials and Dimensions
Primarily wool on homespun. 64″ × 56″.

Maker, Locality, and Period
Maker unknown, possibly Augustine W. Phillips. Probably New England. c. 1830.

Comment
In its size and prominent signature, this rug is similar to the 18th- or early 19th-century bed rugs, used to cover the bed rather than the floor. Bed rugs were usually dated and signed with the maker's name. The design generally covered most of the surface, leaving little undecorated space. The stylized flowers and two-tone leaves are common in early designs.

Hints for Collectors
An early rug like this, especially one in such excellent condition, is extremely rare and valuable. Most pieces of this age and quality are in museums or historical society collections. While few people can own such pieces, studying them will give the collector a good sense of the characteristics of early rugs.

Price Guide Group: Floral Hooked Rugs.

Courtesy America Hurrah Antiques, New York City.

296 Appliquéd and Embroidered Table Rug with Floral Design

Description
Original design. 24 blocks, each appliquéd and embroidered with spray of flowers. Pink, yellow, red, blue, beige, white, and purple flowers, including pansies and bellflowers, each with green leaves and stems. Background blocks predominantly black; some khaki. Scalloped border in blue, gray, and khaki embroidered in red. No binding.

Materials and Dimensions
Cotton appliqué and wool embroidery on wool. 44″ × 30″.

Maker, Locality, and Period
Maker unknown. New England. c. 1835–40.

Comment
A rug like this, with its appliqué and embroidery worked on individual blocks that were stitched together, has more in common with an appliquéd quilt than a hooked rug. Against a black background, however, the flowers look quite different than they would against the usual white ground of a quilt. While much heavier than a quilt, this piece is still lighter than a rug intended for floor use.

Hints for Collectors
This unusual rug is in good condition and would make a fine addition to any collection. Rugs made before 1850 are fairly rare, since many homes had no textile floor coverings well into the 19th century. Made for a tabletop or chest, rugs like this were never walked on. Therefore, they are usually in good condition.

Price Guide Group: Floral Hooked Rugs.

Courtesy America Hurrah Antiques, New York City.

Appliquéd and Embroidered Table Rug with Floral Design

Description
Original design. 32 tan and black blocks in checkerboard pattern appliquéd and embroidered with birds, flowers, and baskets of flowers in red, yellow, blue, green, tan, and brown. Flower stems embroidered in white; flowers, baskets, and other designs outlined with white stitches. Motifs executed in pairs, with single flower basket in corner squares. Border appliquéd with hearts, flowers, and leaves in same colors. No binding.

Materials and Dimensions
Cotton appliqué and wool embroidery on wool. 68″ × 37″.

Maker, Locality, and Period
Maker unknown. New England. c. 1835–40.

Comment
Referred to as rugs, lightweight appliquéd pieces like this were never meant to be used on the floor. The example illustrated is long and narrow and may well have been intended to cover a low storage chest. Heavily embroidered with white thread around the appliqués, this piece is an interesting combination of 2 techniques, embroidery and appliqué.

Hints for Collectors
An early handmade rug, this primitive piece with its delicate embroidery and whimsical design is the kind of rug one seldom finds. Few such elaborate early 19th-century rugs were made, and of those, even fewer exist today. Not within the means of most collectors, a piece like this is very expensive.

Price Guide Group: Floral Hooked Rugs.

Courtesy America Hurrah Antiques, New York City.

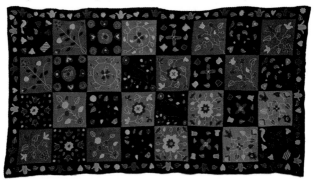

298 Geometric Abstract Design Hooked Rug

Description
Original design. Central rectangle with irregular rows of clover-leaf designs in tans, reds, and grays with concentric outlines in blue, gray, and brown. Wide frame of abstract designs in brown, blue, and gray outlined in yellow and black on sand-colored background. Border of tan and gray squares outlined in red alternating with S shapes in 2-tone gray on black background. Black binding.

Materials and Dimensions
Wool on burlap. 87″ × 78″.

Maker, Locality, and Period
Maker unknown. New York State. c. 1900–10.

Comment
This rug is a good example of how American Indian designs influenced early 20th-century rugmaking. Only the central square with its concentrated sense of movement suggests the texture and look of a hooked rug; the outer borders resemble those used on a woven Indian blanket or Near Eastern woven rug.

Hints for Collectors
Most hooked rugs measure 2′ × 3′ or 3′ × 5′, so this one is unusually large, perhaps intended as a room-size carpet. Its size, shape, and abstract design make it quite rare and valuable. The palette of this rug, as well as its motifs, show the beginnings of the developing Art Deco movement. The designs are very unusual for a rug of this period, when most rugmakers were still working with rather stiff floral designs, many of them on prestamped patterns.

Price Guide Group: Geometric Hooked Rugs.

Private Collection.

Geometric Design Hooked Rug

Description
Original design. Central eight-pointed star in red, gray, green, white, and shades of brown and blue. Leaf at each corner in pink, lilac, green, peach, red, gray, and black. Background is random geometric pattern of blue, purple, brown, black, and tan. No binding.

Materials and Dimensions
Cotton on burlap. 41″ × 25″.

Maker, Locality, and Period
Maker unknown. New England. c. 1880–90.

Comment
The random pattern of multicolored fabric hooked in straight lines and used here for the background is called hit-or-miss, confetti, rickrack, or long line. Common to both New England and Canada, but most frequently found in New Brunswick, it gives the rugmaker a chance to use odd scraps of fabric. The thriftiest rugmakers sometimes bought remnants and scraps from woolen mills or clothing factories, and this rug might easily have been made from such leftover materials.

Hints for Collectors
Although these scrap-bag rugs have their own particular charm, they do not appeal to everyone and can sometimes be bought quite cheaply. The backing as well as the loops that form the pile should be soft and flexible with no dry pieces flaking or falling out.

Price Guide Group: Geometric Hooked Rugs.

Private Collection.

300 Shaker Braided Rug

Description
Original Shaker design. Central pattern of alternating red and gray-green wedges surrounded by concentric rings in different designs. Beige and brown ring around center, then 4 rows of 3-strand braids. Multicolored outer ring. Border double row of 3-strand braiding. No binding.

Materials and Dimensions
Cotton and wool. Diameter 44″.

Maker, Locality, and Period
Maker unknown. New York State. Late 19th century.

Comment
A common Shaker product, braided rugs like this were used by the Shakers and sold in Shaker-run shops to people outside their community. The creation of these rugs allowed their makers the opportunity to use small scraps of fabric by sewing them into long, narrow strips, and then braiding several together. Many types of small rugs, including knitted and crocheted examples, were made, and frequently a rug combined more than one method of construction. Most Shaker rugs were made in concentric rings of color that radiated out from the center and had several rows of braiding around the edge.

Hints for Collectors
This rug has retained its vivid colors. In many examples, however, the shades have faded and taken on a softer look. While pieces that retain their original brightness are generally more valuable, slightly faded rugs have their own charm and are even preferred by some collectors.

Price Guide Group: Braided and Rag Rugs.

Courtesy Museum of American Folk Art, New York City.

Braided and Appliquéd Penny Rug

Description
Original design. Central oval in tans and browns with 8 stitched-down "pennies," each composed of rust-colored circle on top of gray circle over maroon, then white, and then red circle. Central oval surrounded by concentric ovals in browns, gray, red, dark blue, blue-and-tan braided together, and gray. Brown scalloped border. No binding.

Materials and Dimensions
Wool and cotton. 40″ × 32″.

Maker, Locality, and Period
Maker and locality unknown. c. 1850–1900.

Comment
This piece combines braiding and a variation of appliqué in which small circles, or "pennies," in graduated sizes are laid one on top of the other and stitched down through the center. In some cases all the layers are stitched through to lie flat against the surface; in others only an X is stitched through their centers so that the edges are left free. Experts believe that originally the cloth circles were traced around large 19th-century pennies—thus the name penny rug.

Hints for Collectors
Very popular in the late 19th century and early part of the 20th, penny rugs come in a variety of shapes: hexagons, rectangles, diamonds, and even octagons. On most pieces the entire surface is covered with pennies. This rug is very unusual because it combines the penny style with braiding, and is considerably more valuable than a rug made only in the penny style.

Price Guide Group: Braided and Rag Rugs.

Courtesy Douglas Galleries, South Deerfield, Massachusetts.

302 Shaker Braided Rug with Ingrain Carpet Center

Description
Original design. Oblong piece of ingrain carpet in brown, yellow, and red edged in black surrounded by concentric ovals of red, blue, green, and red, each braided in several colors to create a shaded effect. Brown braided border. No binding.

Materials and Dimensions
Cotton and wool. 54″ × 36″.

Maker, Locality, and Period
Maker unknown. Sabbathday Lake, Maine. c. 1880.

Comment
All braided rugs are made essentially the same way. Long fabric strips are seamed to make tubes that are braided together, wound into either an oval or round shape, and then stitched at the edges. The colors of most braided rugs are entirely random, dependent on the fabrics at hand. What makes Shaker braided rugs distinctive are the concentric rings of shaded color, as shown in this handsome example. Notice the old piece of carpet used for the center of this braided rug—this technique was common in Maine Shaker communities.

Hints for Collectors
The central piece of machine-made carpeting in this rug adds historical significance and helps date the piece. Any rug that combines store-bought carpet, or any fabric not commonly found in a handmade rug, with a technique like braiding is uncommon, and for that reason of interest to the collector.

Price Guide Group: Braided and Rag Rugs.

Private Collection.

Description
Original design. Central rectangle with random pattern in tans, red, brown, white, and blue surrounded by striped blue and white rectangle. Concentric frames of red, tan with some black tweed, and red again. Tan and blue frames surround red. Border with diagonal stripes in black, browns, and brown tweed. No binding.

Materials and Dimensions
Wool and cotton on burlap. 46″ × 25″.

Maker, Locality, and Period
Maker unknown. Maine. c. 1850–1900.

Comment
Probably a scrap-bag rug, this geometric design shows how cleverly the 19th-century rugmaker used whatever fabric was on hand to create an interesting pattern. Note the selection of colors for the rectangles surrounding the hit-or-miss center. A rug like this would not only have provided warmth, it would have added color and texture to the surroundings. This sort of concentric rectangular design, with a slightly different center pattern, was very common and easy to work, requiring only the ability to hook in a straight line.

Hints for Collectors
Geometric rugs are still being made today and fit easily into both modern and traditional decorating schemes. As most designs are very common, look for those with pleasing colors that are in good condition. Reject any that would need more than a new binding.

Price Guide Group: Geometric Hooked Rugs.

Private Collection.

Shaker Shag Rug with Geometric Design

Description
Original design. Shaggy texture. Concentric rectangles—blue, red, blue-and-white, and olive—surround central rectangle with abstract design of multicolored yarns. No binding.

Materials and Dimensions
Unraveled hand-knit or machine-knit wool on burlap. 25¾″ × 18½″.

Maker, Locality, and Period
Maker unknown. Possibly community in New York, Maine, New Hampshire, Massachusetts, Indiana, Ohio, or Kentucky. Late 19th or early 20th century.

Comment
Some experts believe that shag rugs like this one were sewn by the women of Shaker communities in Maine, but no one is absolutely certain. Shag rugs are made by sewing the intact end of partially unraveled strips of either hand-knit or machine-knit woolens to a foundation. The loose, unraveled ends of the yarn create the shaggy surface.

Hints for Collectors
Needlewomen outside the Shaker communities also made shag rugs, but the technique was never widely used and few examples of these rugs exist. While an odd piece may turn up occasionally, it will be of interest primarily to the collector who specializes in various types of hooked rugs. The small size of the rug illustrated makes it rare and increases its value.

Price Guide Group: Geometric Hooked Rugs.

Courtesy Museum of American Folk Art, New York City.

Geometric Design Hooked Rug

Description
Original design. Pale gray central rectangle surrounded by 14 bands in mauve, reds, grays, tans, mulberry, and black. Brown-and-black border. No binding.

Materials and Dimensions
Cotton on burlap. 40″ × 19½″.

Maker, Locality, and Period
Maker unknown. Maine. c. 1850–1900.

Comment
Geometric patterns are among the earliest designs known and have been found on Middle Eastern and Oriental carpets since the 16th century. Easier than drawing flowers or other figures, geometrics require only that the rugmaker follow the straight lines of the burlap foundation to create a square or rectangle. The success of the design depends almost completely on the colors and fabrics chosen.

Hints for Collectors
Although pictorial rugs generally cost more, good geometric designs have been increasing in value steadily. The rug illustrated, with its rich colors and clean, abstract design, is an especially good example of the form and is probably less expensive than a pictorial rug of comparable size and quality. Be sure that any rug you buy lies flat, because one that curls or buckles has a flaw in its construction or has deteriorated with age and is less valuable.

Price Guide Group: Geometric Hooked Rugs.

Private Collection.

Hooked Rug with Central Medallion

Description
Stenciled pattern. Central Oriental motif in tan, blue, beige, and purplish-blue outlined in gray. Rose-beige background enclosed by blue rectangular frame with steplike corners. Multiple concentric frames of same shape in browns, tans, blues, and purples. Striped L-shaped outer corners in same colors. Brown striped border. No binding.

Materials and Dimensions
Cotton on burlap. 43½″ × 24½″.

Maker, Locality, and Period
Maker unknown. New England. c. 1850–1900.

Comment
Although Edward Sands Frost was among the first to print and sell rug designs on burlap, many quickly followed. In the 1880s and 1890s, Sears Roebuck's and Montgomery Ward's mail-order catalogues listed a number of patterns including so-called Turkish or Oriental designs similar to the one illustrated here. The appearance of printed patterns in the second half of the 19th century is often cited as the reason for a decline in the originality and charm of hooked rugs, but patterns made it possible for a woman with no drawing skill to make a simple rug.

Hints for Collectors
Plain rugs like this one are not hard to find and are often inexpensive. Sometimes they will be slightly worn and have a raveled edge, as in this example, but a new binding is easily attached.

Price Guide Group: Geometric Hooked Rugs.

Private Collection.

Description
Adapted stenciled pattern. Center diamond in blue and gray hit-or-miss pattern outlined in tan and black. Surrounding area abstract floral design of purple, gray, black, and tan. Triple borders of concentric rectangles in brown, tan, and black. Black twill binding.

Materials and Dimensions
Cotton and wool on burlap. 39″ × 22½″.

Maker, Locality, and Period
Maker unknown. New York State. c. 1900–20.

Comment
Many rugs made from patterns similar to this one have elaborate center medallions. It would appear that the maker of this piece found the central motif too difficult or time-consuming and chose to replace it with the much simpler hit-or-miss, or rickrack, center. It was not unusual for rugmakers to modify or simplify designs both for their own convenience and to make use of materials on hand. Such variations were not always successful, but the ones that worked were usually much more visually exciting than the original stenciled patterns.

Hints for Collectors
The colors in this rug have faded to pleasant, muted tones. To see how much brighter and stronger the colors were originally, examine the underside of a rug. In most cases, the colors produced by aniline dyes seem, to today's viewer, unpleasant and garish. In this case, it is fortunate that the aging process has produced a faded, but appealing color scheme.

Price Guide Group: Geometric Hooked Rugs.

Collection of William C. Ketchum, Jr.

Floral Design Hooked Rug

Description
Probably stenciled pattern. Scrolled floral design in beige with brownish-red tips. Dark brown background. Black and brown border. No binding.

Materials and Dimensions
Cotton on burlap. 52″ × 29″.

Maker, Locality, and Period
Maker unknown. New England. Late 19th century.

Comment
This design is quite simple for a hooked rug, and was probably made from a pattern. From about 1870 on, many companies sold preprinted rug patterns. Other small industries were spawned by the popularity of hooked rugmaking, including E. Ross and Company from Toledo, Ohio. Ebenezer Ross was the inventor of a mechanical "punch-hook," one of several kinds of mechanical hooks invented at the end of the 19th century. Rugs made with a punch-hook were worked from the underside. While this sped up the process of making a rug, it also created a very even pile that was less interesting than the textured pile created by the ordinary rug hook, which resembles a crochet hook.

Hints for Collectors
The simple curvilinear design of this rug is attractive, but neither rare nor particularly remarkable. A piece like this is worth purchasing only if it is moderately priced and in good condition.

Price Guide Group: Floral Hooked Rugs.

Courtesy Douglas Galleries, South Deerfield, Massachusetts.

Art Deco Design Hooked Rug

Description
Original design. 2 pink and blue flowers with green and white stems and leaves on black central diamond. Pink diamond surrounds black one. Border single row of black diamonds alternating with pairs of multicolored triangles. Blue triangles at inside corners. Peach squares with flower at outside corners. Narrow lavender border. No binding.

Materials and Dimensions
Cotton on burlap. 43″ × 26″.

Maker, Locality, and Period
Maker unknown. Carroll County, Maryland. c. 1930.

Comment
During the 1920s, Americans enjoyed a renewed interest in indigenous handicrafts, including hooked rugs. Collectors bought and sold large numbers of 19th-century rugs, and people throughout the country began to make rugs again, but this time they reflected the Art Deco aesthetic. Rugs were executed with stepped or pyramid-shaped patterns in pastel colors including lavender, pink, turquoise, and mint green, often set against a black background. As handmade rugs became fashionable, magazines began featuring them in elegant interiors and department stores used them in their window and store displays.

Hints for Collectors
A number of rugs from the 1920s and 1930s survive today. Like the rug illustrated, the better examples have original, lively designs with the diamond patterns not quite perfect or slightly irregular flowers.

Price Guide Group: Floral Hooked Rugs.

Private Collection.

310 Geometric Design Hooked Rug

Description
Clamshell pattern forms 3 contiguous diamonds; each with red circle at center surrounded by beige ring, surrounded by brown and beige overlapping circles. Larger diamonds constructed of red and beige circles, brown and gray circles, and blue and white circles radiating out from center, linked by purple and beige circles in outer rows. Background is overall clamshell design in rust and browns. Brown border. Blackish-brown binding.

Materials and Dimensions
Wool and cotton on burlap. 71″ × 31″.

Maker, Locality, and Period
Maker unknown. Probably New England. c. 1885.

Comment
The clamshell pattern is one of the oldest curvilinear designs, long popular in quiltmaking as well as in rugmaking. Also called fish scales, it is frequently found on rugs from the Maritime Provinces of Canada and the New England seacoast. The design is said to have been brought to Prince Edward Island, Canada, by an English minister, although it probably originated hundreds of years before that. Each shell is formed by tracing the edge of a cup or saucer and it is one of the easiest forms to make.

Hints for Collectors
Clamshell pattern rugs, particularly in colors as striking as these, are not easy to find. Many were made in dull tans and browns, and few have a design within the pattern like the example shown here.

Price Guide Group: Geometric Hooked Rugs.

Courtesy America Hurrah Antiques, New York City.

Geometric Design Hooked Rug

Description
Original design. Oblong rug with black, gray, pink, purple, and orange concentric rectangles superimposed on beige, pink, and purple rings. Black background. On each side, 3 pyramids composed of zigzag stripes in gold, pink, cocoa, orange, tan, and lavender; all facing center. No binding.

Materials and Dimensions
Wool on burlap. 43″ × 28″.

Maker, Locality, and Period
Maker unknown. New York City. c. 1930.

Comment
With its skyscraperlike stepped pyramids, this rug reflects the influence of Aztec and Mexican architecture on Art Deco design. Many rugs of the 1920s and 1930s have geometric designs, but their characteristic pastel colors give them a very different look from 19th-century geometrics, which were usually done in either earth tones or primary colors. The dark background is also rare in early geometrics, although it is fairly common in Art Deco rugs.

Hints for Collectors
Art Deco rugs can still be found in thrift shops and at yard sales, often for very little money. However, with the current interest in Art Deco furnishings, prices are increasing rapidly. Some rugs are original designs like the one illustrated, but others are based on prestenciled patterns.

Price Guide Group: Geometric Hooked Rugs.

Courtesy Jay Johnson, America's Folk Heritage Gallery, New York City.

312 Geometric Design Hooked Rug

Description
Original design. Bull's-eye of red and tan concentric rings on beige diamond. Diamond has double frame of tan surrounded by brown and black, set in rectangular frame of browns and black with red triangles at inside corners. Border at sides single row of Log Cabin squares, widening to double row at top and bottom. Squares in beiges, browns, reds, blues, and gold, outlined in black. Black binding.

Materials and Dimensions
Cotton and wool on burlap. 40″ × 29″.

Maker, Locality, and Period
Maker and locality unknown. c. 1890–1900.

Comment
The combination of 2 geometric designs—the large-scale bull's-eye and the smaller Log Cabin blocks—makes this rug both interesting and unusual. Rug patterns, especially geometric ones, were frequently based on quilt patterns. The Log Cabin design used here for the border imitates the quilt pattern of the same name so popular in the late 19th century.

Hints for Collectors
Although pictorial rugs with landscapes, houses, or figures have generally been the most popular, geometrics are becoming more and more prized. A bold, original design like the one illustrated is very desirable; the maker has successfully created a striking rug that stands out as an exceptional example of its kind.

Price Guide Group: Geometric Hooked Rugs.

Courtesy America Hurrah Antiques, New York City.

313 Log Cabin Style Hooked Rug

Description
Original design. Diagonal rows of dark-toned, multicolored blocks alternate with rows of lighter-colored blocks. Each block composed of 10 or more L-shaped bands to right of and below small square enclosing dots or small abstract design. Dark-colored squares in red, black, yellow, purple, and green; lighter ones in white, lavender, gray, turquoise, tan, pink, and red. Brown binding.

Materials and Dimensions
Wool and cotton on burlap. 72″ × 39″.

Maker, Locality, and Period
Maker unknown. Probably New England. c. 1920–30.

Comment
The design illustrated is very similar to that of a Log Cabin quilt. But the dots in the small squares are very unusual; few rugmakers would have taken the time to hook these very small areas in different colors.

Hints for Collectors
Because the same geometric designs have been used for a long time, a rug like this is difficult to date. A Log Cabin pattern, however, is almost certainly post-Civil War, since the design had no marked popularity earlier. Other clues for dating a rug are the width of the fabric strips and the evenness of the pile. Rugs made after 1850 were usually made with machine-woven fabric, producing a tighter weave. Today the fabric for hooked rugs is almost always cut with a mechanical cutter to exactly the same width, creating a rug with a very even pile.

Price Guide Group: Geometric Hooked Rugs.

Courtesy America Hurrah Antiques, New York City.

314 Flame-stitch Pattern Hooked Runner

Description
Original design. Stepped V-shaped design in fuchsia, pinks, reds, grays, white, tan, browns, blues, and black, repeated several times to form traditional flame-stitch pattern. Black frame of uneven width. Beige border lacks hooking. No binding.

Materials and Dimensions
Wool and cotton on burlap. 138″ × 18½″.

Maker, Locality, and Period
Maker unknown. Probably New England. c. 1885.

Comment
The flame stitch, a common pattern in 18th-century embroidery, has been adapted here to create an unusual stairway or hall runner. The rugmaker gave the traditional pattern an entirely new look by enlarging the usually small-scale design. Set off by pale tans and grays, the strong black, pink, and red steplike Vs stand out as if they were hooked higher than the other Vs, although all the loops are actually pulled up to exactly the same height.

Hints for Collectors
Runners are fairly hard to find and examples in good condition are scarce. Despite their rarity, the long, narrow dimensions make them less in demand than a typical 3′ × 5′ rug, and prices are comparable. While a portion of a rug is always less valuable than a complete one, an attractive piece of a runner in good condition might be salvaged, bound, and hung on a wall.

Price Guide Group: Geometric Hooked Rugs.

Courtesy America Hurrah Antiques, New York City.

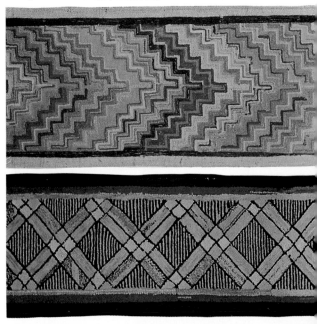

Geometric Design Hooked Runner

Description
Original design. Overlapping striped diamonds in blue, gray, orchid, and tan, with patches of tweed separated by narrow black line. Corner of each diamond has small full and partial four-patch blocks in tan, white, and red. Background narrow black lines on tan. Uneven frame: red and tan, changing to gray, white, and red. Black or dark brown border. No binding.

Materials and Dimensions
Wool and cotton on burlap. 212½" × 14".

Maker, Locality, and Period
Maker unknown. Probably New England or Canada. c. 1880–1900.

Comment
Used as a stairway or hall runner, this long, narrow rug has an unusual geometric pattern. Hooked runners in general are rare, and most were made in the striped hit-or-miss design. Although slightly more than 17' long, the example illustrated is still shorter than some. Runners have been found as long as 25'.

Hints for Collectors
Despite its relative rarity, a rug like this will be comparably priced to other hooked rugs. Its value depends on good design, color, condition, and age. The soft shades, unusual design, and interesting borders of this rug make it a particularly good example of its type.

Price Guide Group: Geometric Hooked Rugs.

316 Rickrack Pattern Hooked Rug

Description
Original design. Multicolored abstract design black, white, beige, red, and gray. Black border. Black binding.

Materials and Dimensions
Wool and cotton on burlap. 59″ × 33″.

Maker, Locality, and Period
Maker unknown. New England. c. 1890–1910.

Comment
Similar to the confetti, or hit-or-miss design, this pattern is a wavy rickrack variation sometimes called agate. A pattern that resembles marble, it is generally used as a background rather than overall design. More often a rug like this was created from the colors and fabrics on hand, making a design as one went along. Simple to work, this design can be very effective when it uses enough light colors to make it stand out.

Hints for Collectors
Although thousands of rag-bag rugs were made, few are as successful as this one. The blend of colors and the strong sense of movement are quite sophisticated for an essentially utilitarian rug. These rugs are not to everyone's taste and can sometimes be bought quite reasonably. Because rag-bag rugs were made for everyday use, many of those that are sold today show wear, which can be substantial. Fresh colors and a foundation that is intact make even an ordinary example worth buying. A rug that interprets the essentially random rickrack pattern as successfully as the one illustrated here is always a find.

Price Guide Group: Geometric Hooked Rugs.

Courtesy Douglas Galleries, South Deerfield, Massachusetts.

317 Woven Shaker Rag Rug

Description
Original design. Various shades of green and brown woven in zigzag effect. Brown binding.

Materials and Dimensions
Cotton. 50½″ × 39½″.

Maker, Locality, and Period
Maker unknown. Hancock Shaker Village, Massachusetts. Late 19th or early 20th century.

Comment
Since the first Shaker communities of the early 1800s, handmade rugs have been sold outside the community as a means of livelihood. Today they are still woven at the Sabbathday Lake community in Maine. Traditionally the work was completed by the Shaker women, or "sisters," but occasionally the "brethren" also worked as weavers.

Hints for Collectors
Plain and sturdy, this rug is primarily of historical interest as an example of the sort of textiles Shakers have produced for generations. Although it is most appropriate for a room containing other Shaker textiles and furniture, such an unobtrusive design would go with most furnishings. Like almost everything made by the Shakers, this rug can take a good deal of hard wear. Many collectors prefer more decorative examples with pictures, and consequently, woven Shaker rugs like the one illustrated are moderately priced and can be purchased fairly readily.

Price Guide Group: Braided and Rag Rugs.

Courtesy Hancock Shaker Village, Hancock, Massachusetts.

Samplers and Needlework Pictures

In the earliest colonial days, needlework was a necessity for all textiles in daily use, including clothing, underwear, towels, linens, and bed coverings. Every woman knew the basic needlework skills and either made these utilitarian items herself or taught family members, servants, or slaves how to make them. These included not only sewing and embroidery, but also spinning and knitting. Although plain sewing was vital, needlework was never strictly confined to clothing and linens. Unadorned rooms were transformed into elegant ones with all types of elaborate needlework, including samplers, embroidered pictures, fire screens, and seat covers.

The rising merchant class demanded beautifully embroidered clothing as well. Needlewomen embellished waistcoats, petticoats, wedding gowns, and even aprons and slippers. An accomplished seamstress commanded the respect of the community and her work was always in demand.

Schools

Many of the smaller pieces of needlework that remain from the 18th and early 19th centuries were made by young girls at school. They were intended as a "sample" of needlework stitches that a young child fashioned while learning embroidery skills. In this they differed from their prototype, the 16th-century European sampler. The latter was a long piece of fabric on which a seamstress had embroidered standard stitches for her reference later on. It was rolled up and stored away until she needed to refresh her memory about how to execute a particular stitch.

In America, working a sampler was deemed an essential part of a genteel education for a girl. Elementary embroidery skills were acquired at home or through a neighborhood dame school—a school similar to today's kindergarten. They were established by English women of "good breeding" and were intended for well-

Detail of an alphabet sampler. Courtesy Museum of American Folk Art, New York City.

to-do pupils. Even small boys sometimes learned to sew and knit in the dame schools. Later a pupil might receive further instruction at a boarding school, seminary, or academy. Children whose parents were less affluent were taught plain needlework at home.

One of the first needlework schools in America belonged to a Mistress Mary Turfrey, wife of the commander of Fort Mary, who advertised her courses in the Boston newspapers of 1706. From this early date to 1835, newspapers in New York and Philadelphia as well as down the eastern seaboard to Baltimore and Charleston carried advertisements for needlework schools offering every kind of stitch and embroidery instruction imaginable.

Although many of the small needlework pieces available today were worked by young girls in schools, women of all ages also devoted much of their leisure time to needlework at home.

Designs and Materials

Most American samplers from the 18th and 19th centuries contain embroidered alphabets, numerals, verses, pictures, or combinations of these elements. Frequently samplers record the names of their makers, the town or city and county in which they lived, the date of their birth, and the date the piece was finished. Often a teacher's name also appears. Because of this precise information, many samplers can be positively dated and attributed to schools, unlike other textiles, such as rugs and quilts, whose exact dates are generally unknown and whose makers are usually anonymous.

The earliest American samplers were tall and narrow. Usually they were 18 to 29 inches long and only 7 to 9 inches wide.

In most American samplers from this period, the ground fabric on which the design was sewn was linen. Occasionally other materials were used, including a fine wool called tammy, as well

Detail of a pictorial sampler. Courtesy Sotheby Parke Bernet, Inc., New York City.

as tiffany gauze, and linsey-woolsey. The numerals, letters, or designs were at first fashioned with linen or silk threads, but examples made after 1840 primarily used wool. On occasion, samplers and silk embroideries were further embellished with watercolor painting, fabric appliqués, mica, beads, gold, silver, spangles, and silk ribbons and rosettes. Engravings were sometimes also added to a sampler's surface.

For the simplest samplers, the young pupil followed the teacher's instruction on how to plan and execute the design, using a basic counting method, known as the counted-thread technique. Other samplers displayed designs that were drawn freehand and then transferred, or pounced, from paper to fabric.

Some elaborate needlework patterns were also imported from England throughout the 18th and 19th centuries, and teachers occasionally ordered these for their students. From one surviving newspaper advertisement it is known that rented patterns were also available and apparently in great demand. Many pictorial designs were copied from engravings, which were purchased from booksellers or selected from favorite novels. Some teachers promoted their own designs, however, and sold them to pupils for a nominal fee. Women skilled in pattern design advertised their talent in newspapers.

It is especially difficult to distinguish between American and English samplers made before 1750. The designs in the horizontal bands and the stitches are often similar; in addition well-known motifs and patterns, such as the Tudor Rose, acorn, carnation, and the fleur-de-lis were used both here as well as abroad. But by mid-century, American sampler designs took on a distinct appearance, displaying a more naturalistic style as well as a greater variety of stitches. The formal, stylized horizontal bands popular in the early 18th century were gradually replaced by more pictorial designs. Narrow borders began to enclose the

Detail of a pictorial sampler. Courtesy Sotheby Parke Bernet, Inc., New York City.

top and sides, until gradually the border increased in width to cover a large part of the design. With the advent of the Federal period patriotic images such as the eagle, flag, and such figures as Liberty became popular, and by the 19th century houses, animals, landscapes, and even public buildings were relatively common subjects.

Predrawn Patterns

By the middle of the 19th century needlework patterns, along with quilt patterns, began to appear in popular magazines. *Godey's Ladies Book*, as well as *Miss Leslie's Magazine* and *Miss Peterson's Magazine*, encouraged the widespread use of brightly colored, predrawn patterns that were known as Berlin work because the first commercial designs were imported from Germany. Patterns were printed on sturdy paper and the colors to be stitched were hand-painted onto the designs. Thousands of Berlin-work patterns were printed and sold along with instructions for decorating tables, pillows, and footstools, and for creating fancy needlework pictures. As late as the 1920s and 1930s women's magazines advertised predrawn sampler patterns that included simple mottoes, usually to be executed in a cross-stitch and other relatively easy stitches.

Since the Bicentennial, American needlework has become increasingly appealing to collectors, an interest prompted in part by the focus on all American handicrafts as well as a greater number of major exhibitions and museum shows throughout the country.

Detail of a verse sampler. Courtesy America Hurrah Antiques, New York City.

Description

Decoration at top 5 rows of eight-pointed red and blue stars separated by 3 rows of red and blue geometric designs, topped by white fringe and name. Bottom decoration 1 row of red and blue stars above date, 1 row of trees and birds in red and blue below, and white fringe along bottom hem. Inscribed "ELISABETH DILLIER" at top and "1832" at bottom, in red.

Materials, Stitching, and Dimensions

Cotton on linen. Cross-stitches. 50″ × 19″.

Maker, Locality, and Period

Elisabeth Dillier. Lancaster County, Pennsylvania. 1832.

Comment

In the 19th century, the decorated show, or hand, towel usually hung on the door on top of the guest towel. Called the "Paradenhandtuch," it was first common in Germany and later in Pennsylvania, where many Germans settled. Besides being ornamental, the decorated show towel was considered a symbol of cleanliness. The same stylized motifs were used in America and abroad, including trees, baskets of fruit, tulips, birds, hearts, and stags. This type of needlework reached its height of popularity in America during the 1830s and 1840s.

Hints for Collectors

The rarest Pennsylvania German show towels date before 1820. Early examples are frequently worked in cotton on linen and are usually longer and thinner than towels made during the next 2 decades. Later examples tend to be decorated with wool thread.

Price Guide Group: Samplers.

Courtesy America Hurrah Antiques, New York City.

17th-century Band Design Sampler

Description
Wide and narrow horizontal bands with grape clusters, acorns, Tudor roses, and S motifs in muted green, blue, tan, yellow, and cream color. Inscribed "That GOD IS MINE ASSUREDLY I KNOW BECAUSE MY BLESSED JESUS MADE HIM SO/SARAH STONE /1678" in green and tan.

Materials, Stitching, and Dimensions
Polychrome silks on closely woven linen ground. Stitches are satin, cross-stitch, backstitch, double-running, eyelet, detached buttonhole, long-armed cross-stitch, and Montenegrin cross-stitch. 16¾" × 7⅞".

Maker, Locality, and Period
Sarah Stone. Salem, Massachusetts. 1678.

Comment
The muted coloring of the example illustrated is typical of early American needlework. Designs with flowers in horizontal bands using a variety of stitches were inspired by prototypes made in England and on the Continent. Samplers of this type rarely had border designs. Like most samplers, this one was sewn by a child, the daughter of Robert Stone and Sara Shafflin, who was 11 years old when she made it.

Hints for Collectors
Collectors are unlikely to find a sampler as early as the one shown here, because 17th-century samplers are rare in America and difficult to distinguish from English work. Other American samplers from this period include the Lora Standish and Mary Hollingworth examples in Massachusetts, displayed at the Pilgrim Hall Museum in Plymouth and the Essex Institute in Salem.

Price Guide Group: Samplers.

Courtesy Sotheby Parke Bernet, Inc., New York City.

320 Miniature Sampler

Description
Formally balanced design with pairs of black dogs, yellow carnations, yellow hearts, and olive-green birds; cream-colored potted plant and white and indigo diamonds. Inscribed "Elizabeth Calver" in blue and black lettering, framed by olive-green fret design. Undated.

Materials, Stitching, and Dimensions
Probably silk on gauze. Lettering in cross-stitch; designs in cross-stitch and satin stitch. 6¼″ × 4⅛″.

Maker, Locality, and Period
Elizabeth Calver. England. Early 19th century.

Comment
Many delightful little samplers found in this country were actually made in England. As in the example illustrated, the workmanship is usually excellent and the design simple and formally balanced. Some English samplers are worked in a single color and bear the name of the school that the maker attended. American samplers may also have the teacher's name.

Hints for Collectors
Relatively plain, small samplers like the one seen here are fairly common at flea markets, estate sales, and antiques shops. Their miniature scale probably appealed to children who were eager to complete needlework exercises quickly. Today these tiny examples are especially attractive when they are displayed in groups.

Price Guide Group: Samplers.

Collection of Mr. and Mrs. Jerry Grossman.

Alphabet Sampler

Description
4 alphabets and numerals 1–8. 3 uppercase alphabets with 1 in
script and 2 in block letters; lower case alphabet also block type.
Letters cream-colored, blue-green, brown, black, blue, and
greenish-gray. Inscribed "MARIA KIES" at top and "M.C. Laurens.
July 24 A.D. 1819" at bottom.

Materials, Stitching, and Dimensions
Silk on closely woven linen. Eyelet stitch and cross-stitch.
8″ × 6⅛″.

Maker, Locality, and Period
M. C. Laurens. Locality unknown. 1819.

Comment
This is the most typical kind of alphabet sampler, with its 4
alphabets and basic numerals. The first name on the sampler,
Maria Kies, may be the name of the maker's teacher or perhaps
the name of a child who started the work but did not complete it.
The name found next to the date is usually the name of the
maker.

Hints for Collectors
Researching the history of a sampler and its maker can be
fascinating. Look for information in local census records, city
directories, family genealogies, and local vital statistics records,
where births, marriages, and deaths are listed. Sometimes
samplers are sold with family histories. Occasionally it is also
possible to trace events in the maker's life by consulting a family
Bible in which important dates were chronicled.

Price Guide Group: Samplers.

Collection of Mr. and Mrs. Jerry Grossman.

322 Alphabet Sampler

Description
4 alphabets: 1 lowercase block letters, 2 uppercase block letters, and 1 uppercase script. Numerals 1–19. Border at side with Greek key or fret design. Border at top and bottom arcaded strawberry designs. 10 cross bands separate alphabets, numerals, and inscription. Two-chimney building at lower right, and basket filled with flowers at left. Predominantly blue, tan, brown, green, black, and cream-colored. Inscribed "Sampler work by elizabeth Haris in the 14 Year of her age in Clement Bear County of Anapolis 1 March A.D. 1836 under the tuition of Mis Sarah Gridle."

Materials, Stitching, and Dimensions
Multicolored silks and olive-green wool on linen. Stitches are cross-stitch, Queen's, Holbein, eyelet, Roumanian couching, and stem. 21¾" × 10".

Maker, Locality, and Period
Elizabeth Harris. Annapolis County, Maryland. 1836.

Comment
Although 17th-century samplers are noted for their tall, narrow proportions, this sampler and others made in the late 18th and early 19th centuries have similar elongated shapes. The sampler illustrated is especially desirable because examples from the South and Midwest are rare.

Hints for Collectors
Note that the 2 chimneys on this sampler have lost their thread; possibly they were sewn in wool that deteriorated. Since the rest of the sampler is in good condition, the value is affected only slightly.

Price Guide Group: Samplers.

Collection of Glee F. Krueger.

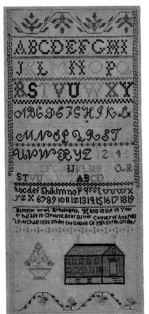

323 Alphabet Sampler

Description
2 alphabets in small and large uppercase block letters. Horizontal bands of triangles and small blocks separate large alphabet, and fret separates alphabet from inscription and numerals 1–9. Pictorial area in 3 tiers below geometric design, each tier composed of houses and trees in small and large scale. Predominantly blues, greens, browns, black, rusts, and grays. Inscribed "HANNAH STAPLES BORN SEPTEMBER THE 14, 1776." Dated 1795.

Materials, Stitching, and Dimensions
Silk on linen. Cross-stitch and eyelet stitch. 10¾" × 10½".

Maker, Locality, and Period
Hannah Staples. Possibly New York or Connecticut. 1795.

Comment
In the 18th century, sampler shapes gradually became shorter and more square. Despite the square shape of the example illustrated, its horizontal bands and lack of border connect it to earlier work. The stylized trees and houses, however, would have seemed modern in 1795. Other desirable qualities seen in this example are the fresh colors and pleasant design.

Hints for Collectors
Samplers as old as this one may have small stains. In such cases, it is wise to take them to a reputable restoration service to eliminate any problems and improve appearance. To frame a sampler, first sew the textile to a prewashed cotton backing, then mount it on a 100 percent rag mat board. Spacers should be used between the glass and the sampler to guard against pressure on stitches and circulate air.

Price Guide Group: Samplers.

Description
Central area at top 2 uppercase alphabets in script and block letters and 1 lowercase alphabet with numerals 1–7. At bottom red house flanked by tree and tree-size rose bush. Predominantly red, white, black, blue-green, and brown. Grapevine border. Inscribed "Wrought by Martha Southwick. Dublin. Aged 13. 1836." above house and "Be virtuous if you would be happy" below house.

Materials, Stitching, and Dimensions
Silk on linen. Stitches are satin, stem, split, chain, outline, and cross-stitch. 16¾″ × 15¼″.

Maker, Locality, and Period
Martha Southwick. Dublin, New Hampshire. 1836.

Comment
This 19th-century sampler includes the typical stylized house, possibly modeled after the maker's own home. The sampler is distinguished from ordinary works, however, by its delightful colors and grapevine border, a strawberry border being more usual.

Hints for Collectors
This sampler is prized for its rich red and sparkling white colors; the freshness of the piece is one of the first qualities one notices. Samplers that have not been framed and were stored away from light are more likely to retain their original brilliant color than framed examples. This sampler once belonged to 2 prestigious collections: those of Mrs. Thomas A. Lawton and Theodore H. Kapnek.

Price Guide Group: Samplers.

Courtesy America Hurrah Antiques, New York City.

Description
Strawberry border on 3 sides encloses wide central area with partial alphabet; verse; landscape of blue house, picket fence, trees, flowers, and flying birds; and 2nd verse. Area at bottom with strawberry vines, potted plant, basket of berries, rose, and pair of birds. Predominantly pink, blue, tan, yellow, cream-colored, brown, and green. Verse entitled "Retirement" reads, "Come sweet Retirement, lend thy smile,/ And lead me to thy pleasant bower,/ There let me rest from care and toil,/ And share reflections' sober hour./ How fair is the rose! what a beautiful flower!/ In summer so fragrant and gay!/ But the leaves are beginning to fade in an hour,/ And they wither and die in a day."

Materials, Stitching, and Dimensions
Silk on linen. Stitches are cross-stitch, Queen's, satin, split, slanting Gobelin, and upright Gobelin. 17¾″ × 17½″.

Maker, Locality, and Period
Lydia Fawcett. Salem, Ohio. 1835.

Comment
According to family records, Lydia Fawcett, a Quaker, was 13 when she made the sampler illustrated. She was born November 3, 1822; married Hutchins Satterthwaite in Salem, Ohio, April 29, 1846; and died there March 16, 1889.

Hints for Collectors
In addition to researching dates, collectors like to trace the origins of sampler verses. Many interesting verses that appear on early American samplers can be found in *American Samplers*, by Ethel Stanwood Bolton and Eva Johnston Coe.

Price Guide Group: Samplers.

Collection of Glee F. Krueger.

326 Family Record Sampler

Description
Top central area record of 10 children of James Towner and Mary Akin of Patterson, New York; names, birth dates, and marriage date in brown script. Pairs of birds and flower pots at corners surrounding record. Verse, signature, and date in middle of sampler. Area at bottom has yellow-green church, bright yellow house, black fence, and green and brown trees below sky dotted with small birds and butterflies in various colors. Floral border yellow, cream-colored, and green. Verse inscription in brown script: "Yet ev'ry cross a mercy is/ A blessing every thorn/ That tells us here is not our bliss/ We were for nobler born."

Materials, Stitching, and Dimensions
Silk on linen. Stitches are satin, fishbone, Queen's, tent, laidwork, and cross-stitch. 17¼″ × 16¾″.

Maker, Locality, and Period
Mary L. Towner. Patterson, New York. 1835.

Comment
Family record samplers are very common in America, and were sewn in England as well. They usually include the names of all descendants, and sometimes the birth and death dates of those deceased appear with their names or initials stitched on small tombstones near weeping willows.

Hints for Collectors
It is unusual to find such a brightly colored family record as the one illustrated here. Generally the genealogy covers most of the available space and is worked in a black or dark brown thread. The addition of the bright town scene makes this register sampler especially desirable.

Price Guide Group: Samplers.

Collection of Glee F. Krueger.

Description
Frame encloses 2 uppercase block and script alphabets, 1 lowercase block alphabet, numerals 1–9, and verse. Wide floral border at top and sides. Bottom has 12 stylized green trees flanking yellow house, and inscription. Letters black; designs blue, green, yellow, pink, and white. Inscribed "Wrought by Mary French AD 1826" and "Mary N. Moody Instrs." Verse inscription: "Beauty with all its gaudy show/ Is but a Painted bubble/ Fame like a shadow flies away/ Titles and dignity decay/ Naught but religion can display/ Toys that are free from trouble."

Materials, Stitching, and Dimensions
Silk on linen. Stitches are cross-stitch, outline, herringbone, satin, buttonhole, straight, and upright Gobelin. 18″ × 17⅞″.

Maker, Locality, and Period
Mary French. New England; possibly Francestown, New Hampshire, or Massachusetts. 1826.

Comment
With its wide proportions and cheerful yellow house, this simple sampler is an engaging, handsomely stitched piece. The sampler employs several typical 19th-century stitches, such as the upright Gobelin, buttonhole, and the popular cross-stitch.

Hints for Collectors
In judging a sampler, it is important to notice whether or not it has characteristics that distinguish it from others of its type. Here the dramatic border and good use of color make this an especially appealing piece. Since the maker, teacher, and date appear on the sampler, it is worth researching further to determine the textile's exact provenance.

Price Guide Group: Samplers.

Collection of Glee F. Krueger.

328 Alphabet Sampler

Description
Linked diamond frame encloses 2 block and 1 script uppercase alphabets, numerals 1–9, and inscription. Wide pictorial border with 2 large dressed figures at sides, nest of baby birds at top, and scene at base of 2 ladies seated under willowlike trees with two-story house and more trees between them. Large female figure padded. Predominantly blue, brown, white, pink, yellow, black, and tan. Inscribed "August 19th 1824. Eveline Freeman Wheeler Age 9 Morristown Love Peace."

Materials, Stitching, and Dimensions
Silk on linen. Stitches are cross-stitch, herringbone, outline, tent, punchwork, satin, split, straight, rice, and French knot. 17½" × 15½".

Maker, Locality, and Period
Eveline Freeman Wheeler. Morristown, New Jersey. 1824.

Comment
The 2 large, dressed figures in the border set this 19th-century sampler apart from those with the usual pictorial format. The female is padded, and a blue bead was used for the eye of the seated figure at the lower left. In the 18th and 19th centuries, needlewomen both here and abroad added beads, mica, spangles, metal threads, and ribbon borders to their samplers and silk embroidery.

Hints for Collectors
A sampler with architectural elements and figures, as in the example illustrated, usually commands great interest and a higher price than one without these features.

Price Guide Group: Samplers.

Alphabet and Family Record

Description
Alphabet, verse, signature, and family record enclosed in central frame surrounded by wide floral border. 2 block and 1 script uppercase alphabets and 1 lowercase alphabet. Pictorial border with large red and white roses and green foliage on sides, grape clusters at corners, and 4 striped fruit baskets at bottom and top. Verse inscription: "The twineing texture of this thread/ May speak of me when I am dead/ But grace not art survives the tomb/ And gives the soul immortal bloom." Inscribed "Wrought by Elizabeth Dole Aet. 10 yrs. born March 23d, 1835."

Materials, Stitching, and Dimensions
Silk on unbleached linen. Stitches are cross-stitch, eyelet, stem, satin, and outline. 27" × 24½".

Maker, Locality, and Period
Elizabeth Dole. Possibly New York or New England. 1845.

Comment
The placement of the family register at the bottom of this sampler is unusual; generally the genealogy dominates the central part of the sampler. Most family records include the marriage date of the parents and the births of the offspring. Some also list death dates or the children's marriages.

Hints for Collectors
The cheerful, naturalistic border of bright red roses makes this family record especially appealing. Most samplers of this type are fashioned only in dark, somber colors.

Price Guide Group: Samplers.

Courtesy America Hurrah Antiques, New York City.

330 Alphabet and Verse Sampler with Watercolor

Description
Inscription, verse, floral motifs, and 1 block and 1 script uppercase alphabet and 1 lowercase alphabet enclosed in sawtooth frame. Wide pictorial border with 2 American eagles and a blue-and-white checkered flower basket at top, single flowers at sides, and scene of sheep grazing near a small house at bottom. Designs predominantly brown, olive-green, blue, and cream-colored; letters in brown and black. Verse inscription: "As thus my hand with artful aim/ Confirms the useful needles fame/ So may my actions every part/ Be aimd alone to mend my heart." Inscribed "Wrought by Mary B. Gove aged 13 Dec. 15 1827/ P. H. Chase Instructress." Watercolor landscape added to bottom of sampler.

Materials, Stitching, and Dimensions
Silk on linen. Stitches are cross-stitch, seeding, straight, satin, buttonhole, French knot, stem, and outline. 17″ × 16″ (without painting).

Maker, Locality, and Period
Mary Breed Gove. Weare, New Hampshire. 1827.

Comment
Baskets of flowers were frequent sampler motifs, but the crisp blue-and-white checks used here on the container lend an individualistic zest. The teacher named in the sampler was the maker's first cousin, Phebe Hoag Chase.

Hints for Collectors
Although the design is not unusual, the addition of a watercolor painting done by the sampler maker is rare. The inclusion of 2 American eagles in the border also contributes to the work's desirability.

Price Guide Group: Samplers.

Courtesy Sotheby Parke Bernet, Inc., New York City.

331 Verse Sampler

Description
Elaborate 3-sided wide floral border and trailing grapevine frame verse at top and inscription at bottom. Sawtooth border at very bottom. 2 intertwined hearts at center with inscription "Love and Friendship" and rose wreath encircling hearts. Letters blackish-brown. Designs predominantly green, blue, cream-colored, yellow, pink, and orange. Top verse: "Fragrant the Rose is But it Fades in time/ The Vilets Sweet but quickly Past the prime/ White lilies hang there heads and Soon decay/ And whiter Snow in minutes melt away/ Such and So withering are our early Joys/ Wich time and Sickness Speedily destroys." Bottom verse: "Mary A. Slusser is my name/ and with my needle i worked the Same/ So that the world may Plainly see/ what care my Parents took of me." Inscribed "M A Slusser worked this sampler in her 10th year Feb. the 10th 1832 Mary Cross tutor."

Materials, Stitching, and Dimensions
Silk on linen. Stitches are satin, stem, buttonhole, Queen's, straight, daisy, and Florentine at base. 19¾″ × 16¾″.

Maker, Locality, and Period
Mary A. Slusser. Possibly New Hampshire. 1832.

Comment
Samplers were often made by children as presents. In this instance, the young seamstress is honoring her parents.

Hints for Collectors
Lovely samplers with floral borders, like the example shown here, are usually easier to find and less expensive than elaborate ones with people, buildings, and animals.

Price Guide Group: Samplers.

Courtesy America Hurrah Antiques, New York City.

332 Pictorial Sampler

Description
Arcaded strawberry vine border surrounds framed center.
Inscription at top separated from pictures below by sawtooth
edge and row of hearts and diamonds. Large double-handled
flower container at center surrounded by variety of motifs,
including lion, parrot, sheep, yellow house, tulips, rose, Spies of
Canaan, well with bucket, and apple or fruit tree. Predominantly
yellow, rose, green, white, red, and blue. Inscribed "Margaret
Rote Her Sampler Elizabeth BACK March 8, 1809" and "Finished
by Eliza back aged 10 Sep' 4."

Materials, Stitching, and Dimensions
Silk on linen. Stitches are cross-stitch, eyelet, satin, stem, and
split. 21¼" × 17".

Maker, Locality, and Period
Margaret Rote and Elizabeth Back. Probably Pennsylvania or
New Jersey. 1809.

Comment
This is a rare sampler because 2 children worked on it and the
completion date is noted. The varied motifs depicted here are
associated with both American and English work. The biblical
story of the spies of Canaan (Joshua and Caleb) first appeared on
foreign samplers and samplers from Boston as early as 1747. The
well and the bucket are seen frequently on examples from
Pennsylvania and New Jersey.

Hints for Collectors
Despite several Anglo-American motifs, the strawberry border
here is typically American. Small diamonds and hearts are also
perennial favorites used to fill empty spaces.

Price Guide Group: Samplers.

Courtesy America Hurrah Antiques, New York City.

333 Map Sampler

Description
Embroidered map of England and Wales. Each shire outlined in black silk with cream-colored, pink, yellow, or blue silk added. Names of countries, shires, seas, and channels in blackish-brown. Small multicolored sailing ship and yellow symbol of Britannia in corners. Border yellow rope motif. Signed.

Materials, Stitching, and Dimensions
Silk twist on unbleached linen. Names worked in cross-stitch; lines and designs in backstitch, stem, outline, and straight stitches. 12¾″ × 11¾″.

Maker, Locality, and Period
Sally Drake. America or possibly England. Early 19th century.

Comment
Many English samplers are beautifully executed on silk, using either silk or silk chenille thread. There are also simple maps on linen, similar to the one shown here, that could have been made in the United States or abroad. English map samplers date from 1780 to 1825, while American examples date back as early as 1775. Although the example illustrated was found in Salem, Massachusetts, it is not necessarily from that area. The careless needlework suggests that it may be American because English schoolchildren were usually much more meticulous.

Hints for Collectors
Dated maps with known provenance are the most desirable examples of this kind, but since American map samplers are rare, an undated map sampler is worthy of consideration.

Price Guide Group: Samplers.

Collection of Glee F. Krueger.

334 Pictorial Sampler

Description
Wide border of naturalistic berries surrounds framed center of grassy expanse with 2 trees, roses, eight-pointed star, and inscription framed by sawtooth circle. Predominantly green, russet, cream-colored, and yellow-green. Inscribed "Sarah Lee. 1811."

Materials, Stitching, and Dimensions
Silk , possibly on wool. Stitches are chain, cross-stitch, daisy, outline, and satin. 19¾" × 16½".

Maker, Locality, and Period
Sarah Lee. Possibly Massachusetts, Pennsylvania, New Jersey, or a southern state. 1811.

Comment
A sampler such as this one probably has a wool ground. Much of the border area has deteriorated, which is a common problem with wool. Tammy, a wool ground used extensively in Wales and England, was also exported to the United States and used in sampler work from about 1790 to 1825. To determine whether the ground is wool, look for selvages (specially woven edges) and blue lines woven into them.

Hints for Collectors
Holes in a sampler diminish its value. Despite its condition, however, the airy, well-organized design on the sampler illustrated makes it a worthy collectible, especially if proper care is taken to have it cleaned, restored, mounted, and framed.

Price Guide Group: Samplers.

Courtesy America Hurrah Antiques, New York City.

Pictorial Sampler

Description
Country scene with trees, houses, flower pots, a horse, dog with doghouse, sheep with lambs, and 3 figures. Top tier contains sprigs of flowers in deep arcades, with date at center. Predominantly greens, brown, blue, black, and white. Flat green satin ribbon on all sides. Initialed "KA FA TW."

Materials, Stitching, and Dimensions
Silk on wool (tammy). Stitches are cross-stitch, chain, French knot, backstitch, daisy, and straight. 12¼" × 11¼".

Maker, Locality, and Period
Maker and locality unknown; possibly Chester County, Pennsylvania, or England. 1795.

Comment
This beguiling scene could be English. During this period there was a great similarity between American and English samplers, and attempting to determine origin from the style and motifs is difficult without a name or similar example to use as a guide. Ribbon borders, for example, may be found on samplers from England or the Continent, but Pennsylvania and New Jersey pieces also often have ribbon borders. Wool appears as a ground in Pennsylvania samplers made from about 1790 to 1825, but generally wool was more commonplace abroad.

Hints for Collectors
A sampler of this quality and early date is quite difficult to find today. Surviving examples of this type are occasionally available through major auction houses. The familiar images of everyday life, such as gossiping women, a dog in a doghouse, and a sheep with lambs, give this sampler a naive charm and universal appeal.

Price Guide Group: Samplers.

Courtesy Sotheby Parke Bernet, Inc., New York City.

336 Pictorial Sampler

Description
Scene featuring grounds of Mount Vernon. Black groom holds
reins of prancing white horse; 2 ladies with parasols stroll
nearby, and weary fieldhand carries cut grain and a sickle. Pony
runs toward Potomac River with small dog at his heels.
Predominantly white, green, blue, yellow, and red. Inscribed at
top "MOUNT VERnon the Seat of the late Gen¹. G. Washington,"
and in a cartouche beneath, "Catharine Schrack Her Work Aged
14 Years. April 3, Philad. 1815."

Materials, Stitching, and Dimensions
Silk and silk chenille on linen. Stitches are cross-stitch, straight,
satin, outline, daisy, encroaching satin, and couching.
18½″ × 18½″.

Maker, Locality, and Period
Catharine Schrack. Philadelphia. 1815.

Comment
In the piece illustrated, Catharine Schrack used Samuel
Seymour's engraving of an etching by William Birch from the
series "Country Seats of the United States of 1808." A
comparison of the etching, engraving, and needlework shows
which elements were borrowed from Seymour and which ones
came from Birch. Catharine added the sun.

Hints for Collectors
A sampler with an American scene always commands a high
price, and this one is especially unusual because of the silk
chenille, usually seen in silk embroidery instead of samplers.
This example was part of the collection of Theodore H. Kapnek.

Price Guide Group: Samplers.

Pictorial Sampler

Description
Arch and columns frame central panel with 4 tiers. 1st tier of
clouds framing 2 cherubs and heart with birds; 2nd tier verse
above fruit trees, birds, dogs, and brick house; 3rd tier 2 couples
with black dog, black sheep, and shade trees; 4th tier
strawberries. Wide floral border at top and sides; inscription
along bottom. Predominantly green, blue, brown, pink, cream-
colored, and black. Verse reads, "May spotless innocence and
truth my every action guide and guard my unexperienced youth
from arrogance and pride." Inscribed "LYDIA GLADDINGS WORK
PROVIDENCE October 1796."

Materials, Stitching, and Dimensions
Silk on unbleached, coarse linen canvas. Border and strawberries
Queen's stitch; stitches elsewhere are cross-stitch, diagonal
pattern darning, Roumanian couching, Queen's, rice, tent,
outline, satin, stem, and chain. 12¼″ × 12″.

Maker, Locality, and Period
Lydia Gladding; attributed to the Balch School. Providence,
Rhode Island. 1796.

Comment
This elaborate sampler with excellent composition and rich color
is typical of the work of students from the distinguished Balch
School, run by Miss Polly (Mary) Balch in Providence, Rhode
Island, from about 1785 to 1848. Several of the samplers from the
school depict buildings in Providence.

Hints for Collectors
Needlework attributed to the Balch School has interested
collectors for more than half a century. Many of these samplers
are owned by museums and historical societies.

Price Guide Group: Samplers.

Courtesy Sotheby Parke Bernet, Inc., New York City.

338 Pictorial Sampler

Description
Central panel framed on 3 sides by strawberry vines. Goddess of Youth stands below willow near brick building and other trees, with American eagle and shield, verse, inscription, baskets of fruit, star, and hearts overhead. Face, arms, and slippers of goddess painted, and spangles in hair. Grapevine and hearts encircle central inscription. Border of pink quilled silk ribbon with corner rosettes. Predominantly green, brown, yellow, blue, red, and cream-colored. Verses read, "Love The Lord and He Will Be/A Tender Father Unto The" and "1830 This Work in Hand/My Friends May Have/When I Am Dead/And in My Grave." Inscribed above eagle "Matilda Filbert Her Work in the 12th year of Her Age."

Materials, Stitching, and Dimensions
Silk and silk chenille on linen. Stitches are cross-stitch, Queen's, couching (silk chenille on tail feather of eagle), satin, daisy, tent, slanting Gobelin, and buttonhole. 22¾" × 17".

Maker, Locality, and Period
Matilda Filbert. Berks County, Pennsylvania. 1830.

Comment
The figure illustrated is known as "Liberty in the Form of the Goddess of Youth Giving Support to the Bald Eagle." The sampler design was based on the engraving by Edward Savage of Philadelphia, dated June 1796.

Hints for Collectors
A painted face or one of applied painted paper, as seen here, is uncommon in samplers, but this technique was frequently used in silk embroidery. This sampler and 2 others with figured portraits belonged to the collection of the late Theodore H. Kapnek.

Price Guide Group: Samplers.

Courtesy Sotheby Parke Bernet, Inc., New York City.

339 Mourning Sampler

Description

Central panel with seated female figure under willow holding lidded urn. Face painted and hair applied. Butterfly above urn. Frame of meandering floral vine. Wide inner border of small squares with flowers, birds, and inscription. Outer border of green silk ribbon with applied gold braid and metal strips. Letters blackish-brown; designs predominantly brown, green, blue, yellow, and cream-colored. Verse at bottom reads, "And must this body die this mortal frame/decay and must those active limbs of/mine be mouldring in the clay. And there/for to remain untill Christ doth please to come." Inscribed "Barbara A. Baner a Daughter of Joseph and Esther Baner was Born in York March the 20 in the year of our Lord 1793 and made this sampler in Harrisburgh in Mrs. Leah Meguier School A.D. 1812."

Materials, Stitching, and Dimensions

Silk on fine gauze. Stitches are cross-stitch, satin, stem, outline, buttonhole, seeding, slanting Gobelin, encroaching satin, punchwork, straight, and flat. 18½" × 17¾".

Maker, Locality, and Period

Barbara A. Baner; school of Mrs. Isaac (Leah) Meguier. Harrisburg, Pennsylvania. 1812.

Comment

Since the needlework illustrated is dated 1812, it may have been a mourning piece for a war casualty. The butterfly in the sky often symbolized immortality.

Hints for Collectors

This design, with a central block surrounded by smaller units, is typical of both American and English work. Ribbon borders are often present in samplers from New Jersey and Pennsylvania.

Price Guide Group: Samplers.

Courtesy Sotheby Parke Bernet, Inc., New York City.

340 Silk Mourning Picture

Description
Oval border encloses 2 mourning figures at tomb. 3 cherubs fly in sky to right of trees with waterfall and house in distance. Faces of figures, cherubs, and other details painted in watercolors. Braid edging around oval; added spangles on costumes. Letters painted blue. Predominantly green, brown, ocher, blue, and white. Plinth on tomb inscribed "Sacred To the Memory of my beloved Parents, Moses & Mary Ann Jenkins" with verse below "Pour your due sorrow/O'er the silent Urn,/But still with Hope/And moderation mourn."

Materials, Stitching, and Dimensions
Silk and silk chenille on white silk. Stitches are split, satin, and stem, and couching of chenille and metal. 15¼″ × 14½″.

Maker, Locality, and Period
Daughter of Moses and Mary Ann Jenkins. Locality unknown; America or England. Early 19th century.

Comment
Painted faces and other details were often created by the child who embroidered the piece, although many teachers offered to paint them for a small charge. Sometimes the pupil's family even engaged a professional artist.

Hints for Collectors
When evaluating a sampler, it is important to note unusual elements. In this instance, the striped suit of the gentleman mourner is livelier than the plain black that is usually seen, and the design includes a colorful waterfall. The blue lettering is also uncommon; generally the lettering was printed on paper pasted to the surface, painted in dark brown or black, or stitched in fine silk.

Price Guide Group: Needlework Pictures.

Courtesy Jay Johnson, America's Folk Heritage Gallery, New York City.

Silk Mourning Picture

Description
Circular scene showing a family mourning around elaborately decorated tomb. New England town in distance on left. Applied swatch of green velvet, silver braid, watercolor and printed paper on tomb. Predominantly yellow, white, blue, green, brown, and black. Wide black border. Plinth inscribed "IN MEMORY OF Mrs Azulab Collins, died Oct. 1, 1805, Aged 38. When such friends part Tis the survivor die!" Inscribed on reverse side "So. Hadley July 15, 1807."

Materials, Stitching, and Dimensions
Silk on silk. Stitches are couching, split, French knot, seeding, satin, and daisy. 17½″ × 17″.

Maker, Locality, and Period
Maker unknown; attributed to school of Miss Abigail Wright (c. 1803–1809). South Hadley, Massachusetts. 1807.

Comment
This is one of the most elegant American silk mourning pictures, with its choice of stitches, exquisite design, and overall sense of delicacy. About 12 silk memorials are known, bearing similar characteristics and designs. However, this one is actually inscribed as being from South Hadley, and thus has become the basis for attributing the others.

Hints for Collectors
In learning to attribute silk memorials and samplers, it is helpful to compare them with published illustrations and museum pieces to see the subtle differences. Although most have the same design elements, characteristics of those from certain schools are readily discernible with practice.

Price Guide Group: Needlework Pictures.

Courtesy Museum of American Folk Art, New York City.

Modern Thread Painting

Description
Scene with convict in striped prison suit trapped on roof with unwieldy bag of money. House engulfed in flames blocking his escape and police with lasso on roof. Bright pink ground with pink, blue, white, yellow, red, and black stitches.

Materials, Stitching, and Dimensions
Cotton and silk embroidery on polyester. Freestyle stitchery. 32½″ × 26½″.

Maker, Locality, and Period
Mary K. Borkowski. Dayton, Ohio. 1968.

Comment
The artist, a third-generation quilter, has drawn on life experiences and stories for many of her quilt designs and nearly 90 thread paintings. This piece, entitled "Trapped," emphasizes the theme of greed. Texture is created by layering many threads. The artist does not rely on any particular stitch but experiments broadly to achieve the desired effects. The realistic-looking flames combine yellow and red threads in a swirling pattern.

Hints for Collectors
Many beginning collectors find that early American embroideries are beyond their financial limits. An attractive alternative is to seek appealing work by contemporary embroiderers. Always look for good workmanship, pleasing color, texture, and design. In the example illustrated, note the clearly defined lines in the house and the dramatic color contrast of the figures and flames.

Price Guide Group: Needlework Pictures.

Courtesy Museum of American Folk Art, New York City.

Embroidery on Paper

Description
Large, cut watermelon with brown-handled knife. Watermelon placed on scalloped doily. Wedge of melon nestling in foreground. Predominantly blue, white, yellow-green, and brown. Signed and dated.

Materials, Stitching, and Dimensions
Silk embroidery on paper. Stitches are satin, straight, outline, and buttonhole. 8¾" × 7⅓".

Maker, Locality, and Period
Eda Brown. Locality unknown. 1848.

Comment
The subject of the watermelon with cut pieces and a knife was often depicted in 19th-century American still lifes. This needlework example is a refreshing, simple treatment of the theme. Although a number of handsome embroideries were worked on paper in the 18th century, considerably more were sewn in the mid– and late 19th century. Some were made with silks worked directly through the paper; others also had a supporting layer of linen below the paper ground. Many paper embroideries have been found in Pennsylvania and Maine.

Hints for Collectors
Occasionally a number of charming embroideries on paper will surface at auctions, antiques shows, estate sales, and some flea markets. These embroideries are not to be confused with the punched or perforated paper embroideries seen with great frequency toward the end of the 19th century. Punched paper embroideries are moderately priced and readily available.

Price Guide Group: Needlework Pictures.

Courtesy Kelter-Malcé Antiques, New York City.

Quilt Pattern Guide

There are thousands of quilt patterns, some unique and others variations on traditional designs. In many quilts, the same motif is repeated in each pattern block, while in others two or more motifs may be used. Sometimes a single pattern may cover the entire quilt surface; still other patterns are created by changing the fabric color within each block. For example, in Log Cabin quilts both the placement of light and dark fabrics within each block and the arrangement of the blocks determine the overall quilt design.

Block Patterns

Whig Rose

Rose of Sharon

North Carolina Lily

Tree of Life

Maple Leaf

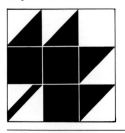

Peony

Robbing Peter to Pay Paul

Flying Geese

To help you recognize some of the most common pattern motifs, 36 block designs and 15 overall patterns are illustrated. To show how color arrangement affects the pattern, 5 Log Cabin patterns are shown as both individual blocks and overall designs.
Because quilt patterns have had long and widespread popularity, the same design is often known by different names. Conversely, the same name may be given to dissimilar patterns. The most common name appears here; alternate names are included in the text.

Rose Wreath

Foliage Wreath

Basket

Basket

Bear's Paw

Goose Tracks

Double Pinwheel

Pinwheel

Block Patterns

Greek Cross

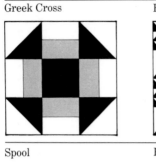

Birds-in-the-Air

Spool

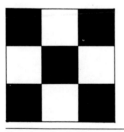

Bow Tie

Nine Patch

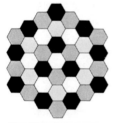

Double Nine Patch

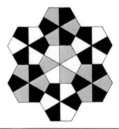

Grandmother's Flower Garden

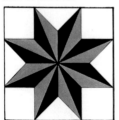

Colonial Garden

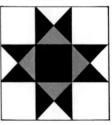

Star of the East

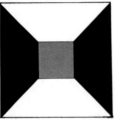

Variable Star

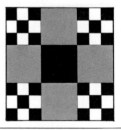

Flying Geese

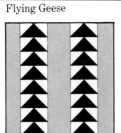

Wild Goose Chase

Roman Cross

Tumbling Blocks

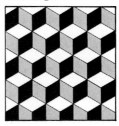

Drunkard's Path

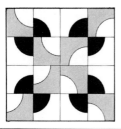

Snowball

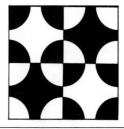

Dresden Plate

Mariner's Compass

Feathered Star

Harvest Sun

| **Log Cabin Blocks** | **Log Cabin Overall Patterns** |

Straight Furrow

 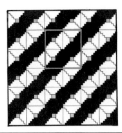

Streak of Lightning

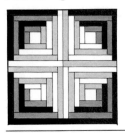 

Barn Raising

Light and Dark

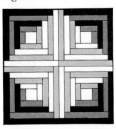 

Courthouse Steps

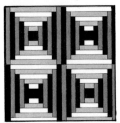 

Overall Patterns

Double Irish Chain

Irish Chain

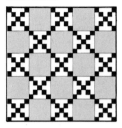

Ocean Waves

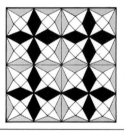

Broken Dishes

Kaleidoscope

Evening Star

Double Wedding Ring

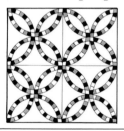

Sunburst

Star of Bethlehem

Lone Star or Texas Star

Quilting Stitches Guide

The true measure of a fine quilt is often determined by the quality of its quilting stitches. In the 19th century, quiltmakers prided themselves on the number of quilting stitches per inch, and the most skilled were able to sew 14 or more. Illustrated are 16 running motifs that are often used on borders, followed by 20 quilting designs that might appear anywhere on the quilt.

Border Stitches

sawtooth

running diamond

running double diamond

woven squares

interlaced diamonds

diamond and rope

rope

running shell

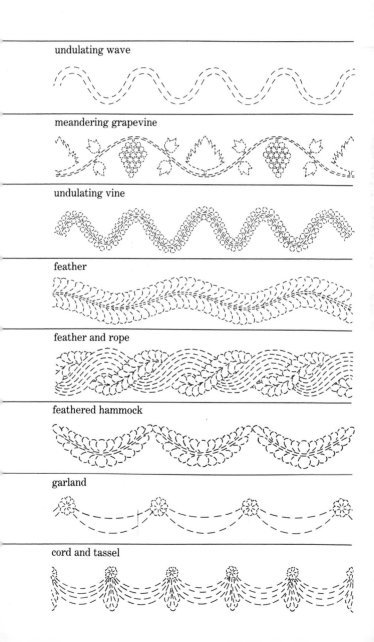

undulating wave

meandering grapevine

undulating vine

feather

feather and rope

feathered hammock

garland

cord and tassel

Stitches

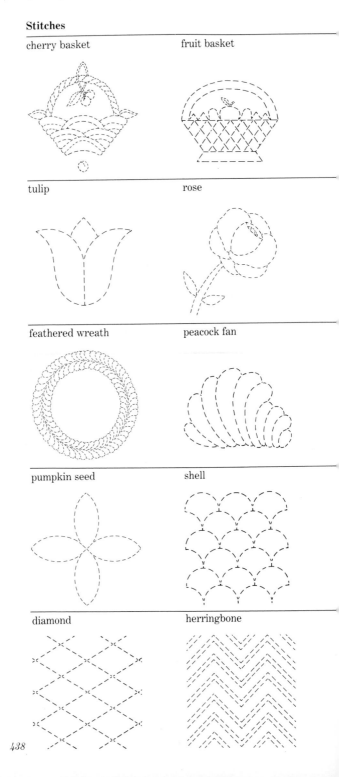

cherry basket

fruit basket

tulip

rose

feathered wreath

peacock fan

pumpkin seed

shell

diamond

herringbone

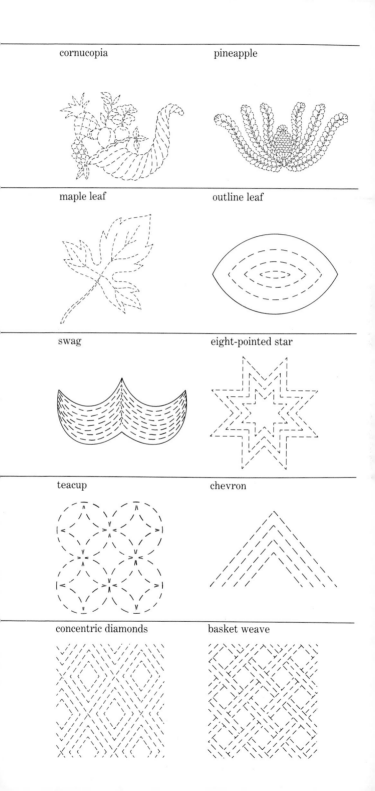

cornucopia

pineapple

maple leaf

outline leaf

swag

eight-pointed star

teacup

chevron

concentric diamonds

basket weave

Coverlet Pattern Guide

Coverlets display a variety of overall patterns. Overshot, Double Weave, and Summer and Winter coverlets have simple geometric designs. Jacquards usually have repeated curvilinear motifs, which often include tiles, flowers, or animals. Border patterns may differ considerably from the overall design, especially in Jacquards. Ten of the most characteristic border designs are illustrated.

Overall Patterns

animal motifs

geometric designs

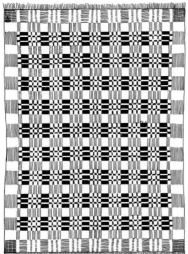

floral motifs

tiles

Border Patterns

bird and rose

tulip

grapevine

trees with picket fence

Boston town

eagle and fox

flowering bush

Hemfield Railroad

cruciform

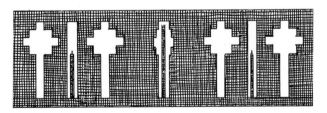

pine tree

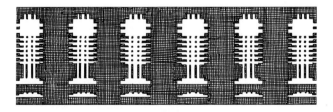

Sampler and Needlework Stitches Guide

Samplers and needlework pictures involve numerous stitches ranging from the most basic cross-stitch employed by every school child to the intricate stitches attempted only by an accomplished seamstress. Knowing the different stitches will add to your appreciation of needlework and help you evaluate the quality of a piece. Illustrated are 26 common stitches used in American needlework.

Embroidery Stitches

backstitch

double-running stitch

outline stitch

split stitch

buttonhole stitch

detached buttonhole stitch

Roumanian couching

chain stitch

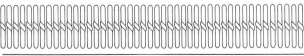

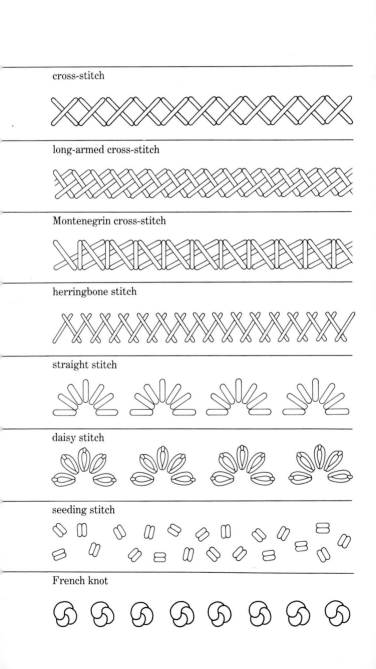

cross-stitch

long-armed cross-stitch

Montenegrin cross-stitch

herringbone stitch

straight stitch

daisy stitch

seeding stitch

French knot

Embroidery Stitches

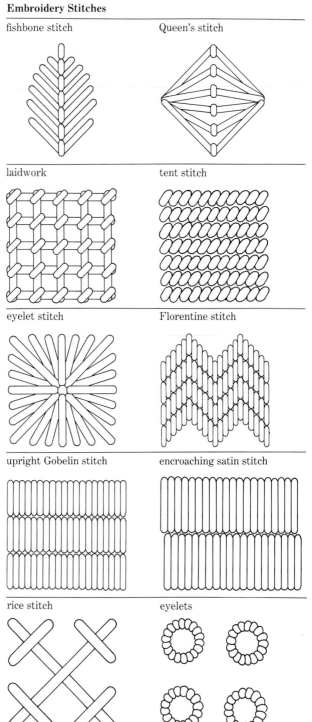

fishbone stitch

Queen's stitch

laidwork

tent stitch

eyelet stitch

Florentine stitch

upright Gobelin stitch

encroaching satin stitch

rice stitch

eyelets

Bibliography

Bishop, Robert, and Coblentz, Patricia
New Discoveries in American Quilts
New York: E. P. Dutton, Inc., 1976.

Bishop, Robert, and Safanda, Elizabeth
A Gallery of Amish Quilts: Design Diversity from a Plain People
New York: E. P. Dutton, Inc., 1976.

Bolton, Ethel Stanwood, and Coe, Eva Johnston
American Samplers
The Massachusetts Society of Colonial Dames of America
Massachusetts: Thomas Todd Printers, 1921
Reprinted New York: Dover Publications, 1973.

Burnham, Harold B. and Dorothy K.
'Keep Me Warm One Night': Early Handweaving in Eastern Canada
Toronto and Buffalo: Toronto Press with the Royal Ontario Museum, 1972.

Callister, Herbert J., and Warren, William L.
Bed Ruggs 1722–1833
Hartford, Connecticut: Wadsworth Atheneum, 1972.

Channing, Marion L.
Textile Tools of American Colonial Homes
Marion, Massachusetts: Published by the author, 1969.

Chase, Patti, and Dolbier, Mimi
The Contemporary Quilt: New American Quilts and Fabric Art
New York: E. P. Dutton, Inc., 1978.

Colby, Averil
Patchwork Quilts
New York: Charles Scribner's Sons, 1965.

Davison, Mildred
American Quilts from the Art Institute of Chicago
Chicago: The Art Institute of Chicago, 1966.

Emery, Irene
The Primary Structures of Fabrics: An Illustrated Classification
Washington, D.C.: The Textile Museum, 1966.

Finley, Ruth E.
Old Patchwork Quilts and the Women Who Made Them
Philadelphia and London: J. B. Lippincott, 1929
Reprinted Newton Centre, Massachusetts: Charles T. Branford Co., 1970.

Frost, Edward Sands
Hooked Rug Patterns
Dearborn, Michigan: Greenfield Village and Henry Ford Museum, 1970.

Hall, Carrie A., and Kretsinger, Rose G.
The Romance of the Patchwork Quilt in America
Caldwell, Idaho: Caxton Printers, Ltd., 1935
Reprinted New York: Bonanza Books/Crown Publishers, Inc., n.d.

Hall, Eliza Calvert
A Book of Handwoven Coverlets
New York: Little, Brown and Co., 1912 (1925 edition).

Hanely, Hope
Needlepoint in America
New York: Charles Scribner's Sons, 1969.

Harbeson, Georgiana Brown
American Needlework: The History of Decorative Stitchery and Embroidery from the Late 16th to the 20th Century
New York: Coward-McCann, 1938; New York: Bonanza Books, 1961.

Hedlund, Catherine A.
A Primer of New England Crewel Embroidery
Sturbridge, Massachusetts: Old Sturbridge Village Booklet Series, 1963.

Heisey, John W.
Checklist of American Coverlet Weavers
Williamsburg, Virginia: Colonial Williamsburg Foundation, 1978.

Khin, Yvonne M.
The Collector's Dictionary of Quilt Names & Patterns
Washington, D.C.: Acropolis Books, Ltd., 1980.

Kopp, Joel and Kate
American Hooked and Sewn Rugs: Folk Art Underfoot
New York: E. P. Dutton, Inc., 1975.

Krueger, Glee F.
A Gallery of American Samplers: The Theodore Kapnek Collection
New York: E. P. Dutton, Inc., in association with the Museum of
American Folk Art, 1978.

Krueger, Glee F.
New England Samplers to 1840
Sturbridge, Massachusetts: Old Sturbridge Village, 1978.

Leene, J. E. (ed.)
Textile Conservation
Washington, D.C.: The Smithsonian Institution Press, 1972.

Little, Nina Fletcher
Floor Coverings in New England Before 1850
Sturbridge, Massachusetts: Old Sturbridge Village Booklet Series, 1967.

Montgomery, Florence M.
Printed Textiles: English and American Cottons and Linens 1700–1850
New York: A Winterthur Book/The Viking Press, 1970.

Morris, Barbara
Victorian Embroidery ("Victorian Collector Series")
New York: Thomas Nelson and Sons, 1962.

Orlofsky, Patsy and Myron
Quilts in America
New York: McGraw-Hill Book Co., 1974.

Ries, Estelle H.
American Rugs
Cleveland, Ohio: The World Publishing Co., 1950.

Safford, Carleton L., and Bishop, Robert
America's Quilts and Coverlets
New York: E. P. Dutton, Inc., 1972.

Stevens, Napua
The Hawaiian Quilt
Honolulu: Service Printers, 1971.

Swan, Susan Burrows
Plain and Fancy: American Women and Their Needlework, 1700–1850
New York: A Rutledge Book/Holt, Rinehart and Winston, 1977.

Swygert, Mrs. Luther M., ed.
*Heirlooms from Old Looms: A Catalog of Coverlets Owned by The
Colonial Coverlet Guild of America and Its Members*
Chicago: Mrs. Harold E. Sanke, 1955.

Waring, Janet
Early American Stencils
New York: Dover, 1937 (1968 edition).

Woodard, Thomas K., and Greenstein, Blanche
Crib Quilts: And Other Small Wonders
New York: E. P. Dutton, Inc., 1981.

Antiques Publications

The following publications often feature articles on American textiles.

Americana Magazine
29 West 38th Street
New York, New York 10018

The American Collector
Drawer C
Kermit, Texas 79745

American Collector's Journal
Box 407
Kewanee, Illinois 61443

American Craft Magazine
401 Park Avenue South
New York, New York 10016

American Heritage Magazine
10 Rockefeller Plaza
New York, New York 10020

Antique Guide
Box 504
Morristown, New Jersey 07960

Antique Monthly
P.O. Drawer 2
Tuscaloosa, Alabama 35401

Antiques and Arts Weekly
5 Church Hill Road
Newtown, Connecticut 06470

Antiques and Collectibles
230 Arlington Circle
East Hills, New York 11548

The Antiques Dealer
1115 Clifton Avenue
Clifton, New Jersey 07013

Antiques Inc.
22000 Shaker Boulevard
Shaker Heights, Ohio 44122

Antiques Journal
Box 1046
Dubuque, Iowa 52001

Antiques Observer
3545 Chain Bridge Road, Suite 8A
Fairfax, Virginia 22030

Antiques U.S.A.
P.O. Box 974
Kermit, Texas 79745

The Antique Trader Weekly
Box 1050
Dubuque, Iowa 52001

Art & Antiques
1515 Broadway
New York, New York 10036

Art & Auction
250 West 57th Street
New York, New York 10019

The Clarion
Museum of American Folk Art
49 West 53rd Street
New York, New York 10019

Collector's Journal
421 First Avenue
Vinton, Iowa 52349

Collectors News
Box 156
Grundy Center, Iowa 50638

Colonial Homes
1700 Broadway
New York, New York 10019

Early American Life
Box 1831
Harrisburg, Pennsylvania 17105

Hobbies, The Magazine for Collectors
1006 South Michigan Avenue
Chicago, Illinois 60605

Long Island Heritage
29 Continental Place, Box 471
Glen Cove, New York 11542

The Magazine Antiques
551 Fifth Avenue
New York, New York 10017

Maine Antique Digest
Box 358
Waldoboro, Maine 04572

New York Antique Almanac
Box 335
Lawrence, New York 11559

New York-Pennsylvania Collector
4 South Main Street
Pittsford, New York 14534

Ohio Antiques Review
P.O. Box 538
Worthington, Ohio 43085

Quilters Newsletter
Box 394
Wheat Ridge, Colorado 80033

Spinning Wheel Magazine
1981 Moreland Parkway
Annapolis, Maryland 21401

Tri-State Trader
P.O. Box 90
Knightstown, Indiana 46148

Glossary

Album quilt A quilt made up of blocks, each usually contributed by a different woman, and presented as a gift to a departing friend or community figure; usually appliquéd with representational motifs. Blocks may be signed or initialed.

Aniline dye A brilliant synthetic, as opposed to natural or vegetable, dye first introduced in the late 19th century.

Appliqué To sew a piece of fabric onto a larger cloth ground.

Backing The bottom layer of a quilt or quilt block.

Baste To sew with long loose stitches that temporarily hold the fabric in place; basting stitches are removed after the final stitching is completed.

Batting Cotton, wool, or other fiber used as the center quilt layer to provide warmth.

Bed furniture Various matching bedcovers and hangings including spreads, skirts, curtains, valances, and head cloths.

Bed rug A thick, heavy wool-pile bedcover crafted by working a running stitch of wool yarn through a coarse homespun backing; the yarn may be secured by knotting, and loops of pile are sometimes trimmed; most common in the 18th century.

Berlin work Various types of needlework executed on printed canvas patterns in the 19th century; many patterns originated in Berlin.

Binding The strips of cloth or fabric tape used to finish the edges of a quilt or hooked rug.

Block The basic unit of many patchwork quilt tops; usually square.

Braided rug A floor covering made from strips of fabric, usually wool, sewed into tubes, turned inside out, braided, and stitched together in a coil, sometimes with a burlap backing.

Broderie perse An 18th-century appliqué technique in which motifs such as flowers and animals are cut out of chintz or another printed fabric and sewn onto a foundation, usually white, and then quilted and embroidered.

Calico A cotton fabric printed with small-scale figured patterns.

Candlewick spread A bedcover, usually white and often made of cotton, with raised designs either embroidered in a running stitch or woven with a heavy thread called candlewick, with the pile sometimes clipped; popular in the early 19th century.

Central medallion A large appliquéd, woven, or pieced motif, often floral; popular on bedcovers in the late 18th and early 19th centuries.

Challis A soft, thin, printed or design-woven fabric, usually of silk and worsted.

Chintz A plain-weave cotton fabric, usually floral printed and glazed.

Copperplate cloth A cotton or linen fabric with monochromatic scenes machine printed with an engraved copper plate; most common in the late 1700s in England and France.

Counterpane Any bedcover; usually but not necessarily a quilt.

Coverlet A woven bedcover, popular in 19th-century America, usually made of wool and cotton.

Crazy quilt A quilt composed of patches cut from many fabrics in irregular shapes and various sizes; often embellished with embroidery; in the late 19th century, usually made of rich fabrics such as silk, satin, velvet, and brocade.

Crewelwork Needlework using two-ply, loosely twisted wool yarn usually worked on linen; in early America, done with whatever thread was available, in free-flowing, usually floral designs.

Crib quilt A small quilt, usually done in a scaled-down version of a full-sized pattern and often made by children.

Dimity A ribbed or figured cotton fabric, often used in quilts.

Double weave coverlet A reversible coverlet consisting of 2 layers woven simultaneously; the layers are interwoven where the pattern changes; also referred to as a double cloth coverlet.

Embroidery Needlework in which a design is worked in plain or fancy stitches with threads of colored silk and wool.

Face Usually the side of a textile meant to be seen; "warp-face" means that the warp, rather than the weft, is dominant.

Floor cloth A heavy, woven canvaslike material, usually painted with floral or geometric designs and then varnished; used as a floor covering in the late 18th and early 19th centuries.

Foundation The base fabric of a sampler, needlework picture, or rug, often loosely woven, into which yarn or thread is worked.

Frame A square or rectangular border enclosing the central section of a textile. Also, adjustable square or rectangular structure over which a quilt is stretched for stuffing and quilting.

Gingham A cotton fabric of two or more colors with a woven checked or striped design.

Hawaiian quilt An appliquéd quilt with an overall design consisting of large, intricately cut appliqués, usually representing fruit, flowers, and foliage; the entire surface may be quilted along the contours of the designs; made in Hawaii in the 19th century.

Homespun A loosely woven fabric, usually of wool or linen, handloomed from handspun yarns.

Hooked rug A floor covering consisting of strips of fabric hooked through a foundation that may be linen or hemp, but more often burlap.

Indigo dye Dark blue vegetable dye, especially that extracted from indigo and woad plants; originally imported from India.

Jacquard coverlet A large, typically unseamed coverlet woven with the use of a specially mechanized loom attachment; characterized by its use of curvilinear, often representational motifs and intricate borders.

Linsey-woolsey A coarse, often glazed, material woven with a linen or cotton warp and a wool weft; linsey-woolsey bedcovers usually consist of an upper layer of linsey-woolsey, a central layer of wool, and a bottom layer of homespun linen, all basted together with thread of a matching color.

Motif A recognizable design element, such as a heart or a star.

Natural dye A dye extracted from a plant or an animal.

Needlework picture A decorative textile made by stitching silk or occasionally metal thread onto a silk foundation; often depicts rural, biblical, or mourning scenes; sometimes also painted with watercolors.

Overshot coverlet A coverlet in which supplementary weft threads skip, or overshoot, 3 or more warp threads to create a thick, loosely woven cloth; always woven in 2 pieces and seamed through the middle.

Palampore A richly colored and patterned cotton spread, often depicting the Tree of Life, imported to England from India during the 18th century.

Pictorial Depicting a recognizable object or scene.

Pieced Sewn together at edges of fabric.

Pile The cut or uncut loops of yarn or thread that form the surface of a textile.

Pillow sham A decorative quilted, appliquéd, or pieced pillow cover, usually made to match a spread or other bed furnishings.

Plain weave The simplest form of textile weave, in which the weft thread passes alternately over and under each warp thread.

Provenance The origin of a textile, often determined by tracing the collections through which it has passed.

Quilt A bedcovering consisting of top, backing, and filling; the 3 layers are usually joined together by quilting or tufting.

Quilting Stitches that bind quilt layers together and provide decoration.

Rag rug A floor covering woven from strips of rags.

Resist dyeing A method of decorating fabric in which a wax design is painted over part of the cloth, which is then immersed in dye; when the wax is removed, the undyed portion is exposed; the process is repeated for multicolored fabrics.

Reverse appliqué An appliqué technique in which a portion of an appliqué is cut out, exposing the ground fabric to view.

Roller-printed cloth A fabric printed by engraved metal cylinders rather than copper plates.

Sampler Decorative needlework, typically embroidered in various stitches with alphabets, numbers, family names and dates, mottoes, or pictorial elements, to demonstrate skill.

Selvage, or selvedge The warp edges of a woven or flat-knitted textile, finished to prevent raveling.

Sets Strips or blocks of material sometimes used to join together the sections of a quilt.

Shed The opening between warp threads through which the shuttle carrying the weft threads passes.

Shirred rug A thick floor covering in which gathered, pleated, knitted, or bias-cut strips are tacked or sewn to a burlap or linen foundation forming a pile.

Shuttle   A weaving tool that holds the weft threads as they are passed among the warp threads.

Stenciled spread   A lightweight, usually single-layered cotton spread decorated with stenciled designs—primarily flowers, fruit, birds, and trees; paint or dye is applied through stencils and allowed to dry, and the process repeated for each color; popular in the first half of the 19th century.

Stuffed work   Quilted designs that are stuffed from the back with cotton batting.

Stump work   Elaborately colored embroidery from the 17th century, with stuffed designs and scenes in high relief; also known as raised work.

Summer and winter coverlet   A closely woven coverlet with a reversible pattern, the light side thought to be displayed in summer, the dark in winter.

Summer spread   A quilt top that was intentionally left without filling or a backing, used as a bedcover.

Tabby   A plain-weave fabric; also plain silk taffeta.

Template   A pattern made of paper, cardboard, or thin metal that is traced onto fabric to ensure accuracy in cutting out a design.

Trapunto   A type of stuffed work originally used in Italy; occasionally found on American quilts.

Tufting   Joining the layers of a quilt by pulling lengths of thread or yarn up from the backing and knotting them together at the top.

Turkey work   Needlework made by knotting worsted yarn on canvas or other heavy cloth in imitation of Oriental rugs.

Twill   A basic textile weave made by carrying weft or warp threads over groups of 2 or more threads, and staggering these groups to form an overall surface pattern of fine diagonal ribs.

Valance   A short decorative drapery that hangs from a bed or canopy frame to conceal its structure.

Warp   Stationary threads that run the length of a loom and through which the horizontal weft passes.

Weave   To form cloth on a loom by interlacing weft threads through the warp threads.

Weft   Threads that are passed horizontally over and under the warp.

Whitework spread   A textile decorated with white thread on a white ground.

Worsted   Yarn which has been spun of combed wool; also the tightly knit material woven of worsted yarn.

Yarn-sewn rug   A floor covering made by sewing yarn in a continuous running stitch through a closely woven foundation and leaving loops of yarn on the surface to form the pile; the loops are usually clipped.

Price Guide

In the last few decades the prices of fine textiles have risen startlingly: In the 1930s an exquisite handmade quilt could be purchased at a fashionable antiques shop for as little as $8.50; the same bedcover may bring as much as $30,000 today! Alas, bargains are no longer commonplace; yet, with persistence, the knowledgeable collector can find good, reasonably priced examples.

The key to making wise selections is familiarity with the textiles and their current market values. "Finds" may occur in unlikely places, including auction houses. In the fall of 1980, an important collection of American antique textiles was sold at auction in New Hampshire. Many of the country's major dealers and collectors were there. Although most objects brought very high prices, one piece—a rare, machine-woven, blue-and-white candlewick spread signed by its maker and dated 1837—fetched only $85.00. Even the experts failed to recognize its importance. The buyer, a midwestern dealer, added the bedcover to his inventory at a price of $650 and took it to an antiques show in New York City. There a museum curator recognized its value and acquired it. Today it is one of the most prized examples of Americana in the museum's permanent collection and is valued at $6,500. This is not an isolated incident: Valuable pieces do occasionally pass unappreciated through major auctions, in part because of the diversity of textiles. No two textiles are identical, and the vast number of variations is precisely what makes collecting textiles so demanding and so exciting.

Organization of the Price Guide
The divisions within this price guide are based on marketplace categories. For example, all Amish quilts are grouped together. This differs from the organization of the picture-and-text entries, which are arranged visually, although each such entry refers you to the relevant price guide group.

Valuable Features
Because many textiles are unique, learning the price of any one example is rarely instructive. It is much more helpful to understand the general characteristics that determine price, such as effective use of color. Consequently, each category in this price guide has a section describing valuable features to let the buyer know what to look for; plates illustrating these features are indicated.

Price Range
The prices given here represent the general range that may be encountered anywhere from an ordinary store in the country to a fashionable antiques shop. In each category, price ranges are given for several representative examples. Occasionally an example listed is extraordinarily rare and is priced higher than the general range.

Ordinarily, textiles are less expensive in the Midwest and the South than on either coast, where competition among serious collectors can be keen and international buyers are likely to shop. The most expensive sources of textiles are fine specialty shops, where the stock tends to be very selective and the proprietors are recognized experts. The overriding considerations are whether a textile is beautiful and expertly constructed. If it is neither, its age, condition, and even historical significance do not make it especially desirable.

This Price Guide was written by William C. Ketchum, Jr.

Quilts

Since the 1920s, when a few collectors began to purchase fine quilts, prices have risen steadily. However, it is only within the last 15 years that certain types, such as Amish, Mennonite, early appliquéd, and album quilts, have brought prices in the thousands of dollars. Even though many fine quilts are costly, collectors of modest means may still find reasonably priced bedcovers. Pastel pieced quilts from the Depression years seem undervalued at prices ranging from $75 to $350, as do most Victorian crazy quilts at prices from $200 to $500. However, the trend is generally upward, since it is likely that types neglected today will eventually be affected.

Album and Sampler Quilts

Plates
13, 14, 15, 16, 17, 18, 19, 20, 21, 22, 23, 24

Description
These quilts are relatively uncommon. Made for special occasions or as gifts, many have not reached the market. The finest and most original of these quilts will command five-figure prices. 20th-century examples are rare yet relatively inexpensive.

Examples of Valuable Features
Original design: Baltimore Album (14), Betrothal Album (15), Album (22). Skillful quilting: Baltimore Album (14), Album (23). Strong colors: Baltimore Album (20).

Price Range
19th century–1920: $1000–20,000. 1920–present: $500–1500.

14 Baltimore Album $10,000–12,500
15 Betrothal Album $25,000–35,000
16 Friendship Album $7500–9000
18 Album $3500–4000
24 Sampler Album $4500–5000

Prices for the following plates are unavailable: 13, 17, 19–23.

Amish and Mennonite Quilts

Plates
25, 26, 27, 28, 29, 33, 34, 35, 40, 43, 47, 48, 51, 52, 53, 54, 55, 56, 57, 63, 70, 75, 76, 78, 81, 85, 100, 103, 105, 107, 110, 111, 114, 127, 128, 130, 177, 186, 196

Description
The bold geometric quilts made in the Amish and Mennonite settlements from Pennsylvania to Indiana are among the most desirable and expensive of all textiles. Most highly prized and costly because of their strong colors, extraordinary quilting, and originality are Amish examples from Lancaster County, Pennsylvania, and Holmes County, Ohio. Relative bargains are 20th-century quilts from Amish and Mennonite areas.

Examples of Valuable Features
Strong colors and color relationships: Split Bars (27), Ocean
Waves (47), Sunshine and Shadow (51), Circle (100). Skillful
quilting: Bars (26). Bold design: Bars (25), Concentric Squares
(29), Double Square (56).

Price Range
19th century–1900: $800–5500. 1900–40: $500–4500. 1940–
present: $150–750.

- 28 Square $1250–2000
- 40 Jacob's Ladder $1500–2200
- 48 Ocean Waves $1800–2600
- 55 Diamond in Square $1800–2250
- 107 Double Wedding Ring $2000–2500
- 110 Grandmother's Flower Garden $1500–2000
- 111 Grandmother's Flower Garden $1800–2000
- 177 Tree of Life $2500–3000
- 186 Sailboats $2000–2500

Prices for the following plates are unavailable: 25–27, 29, 33–35,
43, 47, 51–54, 56, 57, 63, 70, 75, 76, 78, 81, 85, 100, 103, 105, 114,
127, 128, 130, 196.

Circular Geometric Quilts

Plates
89, 90, 91, 93, 94, 95, 96, 97, 98, 99, 101, 104, 108, 109, 112

Description
The difficulties of accurately cutting and piecing circular
geometric designs, such as the Pinwheels pattern, make
successful examples particularly prized by knowledgeable
collectors. Among the best of such quilts there are few bargains.
However, pastel pieces from the 1930s, which are of little
interest to most collectors, are relatively inexpensive, especially
those that are not particularly well cut and sewn.

Examples of Valuable Features
Skillful cutting and stitching (surface must lie flat): Pinwheels
(104). Strong colors: Bull's Eye (90).

Price Range
19th century–1920: $250–2500. 1920–present: $200–1500.

- 89 Mariner's Compass $2200–2500
- 90 Bull's Eye $1250–1500
- 94 Mariner's Compass $1000–1200
- 95 Mariner's Compass $1000–1200
- 101 Snowball $1250–1500
- 112 Grandmother's Flower Garden $1250–1500

Prices for the following plates are unavailable: 91, 93, 96–99, 104,
108, 109.

Crazy Quilts

Plates
193, 194, 197, 198, 199, 200, 201, 202

Description
Vast numbers of crazy quilts were made during the late 19th century. Some were of wool or cotton. Most, however, were of silk and velvet; many of these have deteriorated and have practically no value. Rare examples showing realistic scenes made up of crazy quilt patches are extremely expensive. Elaborate crazys bring a good price, as do Amish examples with striking designs, but the majority are ignored by collectors and remain undervalued.

Examples of Valuable Features
Bold, graphic design: Pictorial (193), Block (197). Well-executed detail, including embroidery and other embellishment: Pictorial (194), Block (197), Fan (202).

Price Range
19th century–1920: $300–3000. 1920–present: $200–900.

193 Pictorial $25,000–35,000
198 Contained Crazy $1800–2200

Prices for the following plates are unavailable: 194, 197, 199–202.

Crib and Cradle Quilts

Plates
32, 42, 60, 72, 73, 82, 83, 84, 92, 102, 106, 129, 131, 137, 139, 154, 195

Description
Extremely popular because their small size allows them to be hung like paintings, crib and cradle quilts range widely in quality. A crib quilt must be a true miniature—a scaled-down version of a full-size quilt—rather than a segment of a full-size quilt. Collectors should understand that there are numerous fakes made from pieces of full-size quilts.

Examples of Valuable Features
Authentic miniature in scale: Kansas Baby (137). Skillful quilting: Northumberland (129). Original binding: Unique Circular Design (92), Kansas Baby (137).

Price Range
10%–15% more costly than a full-size quilt of the same pattern.

32 Four-Patch Variation $1500–2500
42 Bear's Paw $1500–2000
60 Flying Geese $1800–2200
72 Bow Tie $350–500
82 Courthouse Steps $1250–2000
83 Courthouse Steps $1500–2000

Prices for the following plates are unavailable: 73, 84, 102, 129.

Floral Quilts

Plates
1, 2, 3, 4, 5, 6, 7, 8, 9, 10, 11, 12, 162, 163, 164, 165, 166, 167,
168, 169, 170, 171, 172, 173, 174, 175, 176, 178, 179, 180

Description
This group offers the greatest variety of designs found among
American bed coverings. Such flowers as roses, tulips, and lilies
have been popularly depicted for at least 200 years. Since this
category is so broad, it also encompasses a wide variety of
prices, ranging from inexpensive, simple 1930s rose designs to
costly, highly sophisticated appliquéd patterns that were
made c. 1800.

Examples of Valuable Features
Original design: Floral (2), Hearts and Cats (8), Peony (171).
Skillful quilting: Whig Rose (162), Basket of Flowers (180).
Strong colors: Acorn and Mariner's Compass (176), Tree of Life
(178).

Price Range
19th century–1920: $400–5000. 1920–present: $200–2000.

Prices for the following plates are unavailable: 1–4, 6–12, 164–
176, 179, 180.

Hawaiian Quilts

Plates
147, 148, 161

Description
After American missionaries introduced them to quiltmaking,
the Hawaiians developed their own unusual designs and a
distinctive method of construction. Not well-known on the
mainland, these quilts are much admired locally for their rarity
and quality. Practically no 19th-century examples exist outside
museum collections. When pieces made before 1900 reach the
market, they bring very large sums.

Examples of Valuable Features
Distinctive construction technique: Floral (161). Pictorial
elements: My Beloved Flag (147) and Gardens of Eden and
Elenale (148). Fine needlework: Floral (161).

Price Range
19th century–1900: $5000–50,000. 1900–present: $500–2000.

147 My Beloved Flag $15,000–25,000
148 Gardens of Eden and Elenale $35,000–50,000
161 Floral $2000–3000

Log Cabin Quilts

Plates
77, 79, 80, 86, 87, 88

Description
Deceptively simple in appearance, Log Cabin quilts depend on
the skillful balancing of light and dark fabrics for their effect.
The most outstanding examples display patterns that resemble
abstract paintings. Less successful efforts are usually moderately
priced.

Examples of Valuable Features
Dramatic use of light-dark fabrics: Windmill Blades (87). Unusual
variations on the pattern: Log Cabin (80).

Price Range
19th century–1920: $350–2500. 1920–present: $250–1200.

79 Barn Raising $1500–2000
86 Streak of Lightning $1500–2000
88 Windmill Blades $1200–1800

Prices for the following plates are unavailable: 77, 80, 87.

Other Geometric Quilts

Plates
30, 31, 36, 37, 38, 39, 41, 44, 45, 46, 49, 50, 58, 59, 61, 62, 64, 65,
66, 67, 68, 69, 71, 74

Description
There are various geometric quilts with square and rectangular
patterns available. In general these are popular with collectors
because their rectilinear design gives them a modern look. Well-
executed examples with bold colors fetch the highest sums, but it
is possible to obtain modestly priced 20th-century pieces.

Examples of Valuable Features
Strong colors and bold color relationships: Bittersweet XII (58).
Good proportions: Flying Geese (59). Unusual or well-designed
borders: Birds-in-the-Air (61).

31 Trip Around the World $1250–1500
36 Four-Patch Check $2000–2500
37 Double Nine-Patch $2000–2500
38 Wild Goose Chase $1500–1800
39 Storm at Sea $1500–1800
41 Cross and Crown $1500–1800
46 Puss-in-the-Corner $850–1000
50 Geometric Design $2250–2500
58 Bittersweet XII $1250–1500
69 Cookie Cutter $2250–2500
71 Geometric Design $2000–2500

Prices for the following plates are unavailable: 30, 44, 45, 49, 59, 61, 62, 64–68, 74.

Patriotic Quilts

Plates
135, 136, 138, 140, 141, 142, 143, 144, 145, 146

Description
Though still made today, quilts featuring flags, eagles, and other patriotic motifs were most popular in the late 1800s. Unusual or historically important examples will bring high prices. On the other hand, those made with actual flags are of little value to serious collectors.

Examples of Valuable Features
Stylized pictorial motifs: E Pluribus Unum (143). Overall design: Flags (140).

Price Range
19th century–1920: $500–12,000. 1920–present: $250–2500.

140 Flags $850–1600

Prices for the following plates are unavailable: 135, 136, 138, 141–146.

Pictorial (figural) Quilts

Plates
149, 150, 151, 152, 153, 155, 156, 157, 158, 159, 160, 181, 182, 183, 184, 185, 187, 188, 189, 190, 191, 192

Description
Pictorial quilts are relatively uncommon and any good example will bring a substantial price, with the finest selling in the five-figure range. There are few inexpensive pieces in this category. Even pastel quilts of modest skill from the 1930s will cost several hundred dollars. A fine 19th-century example that tells a story is valued as a work of art.

Examples of Valuable Features
Good proportions with unusual design: Greek (160), Dolls (185). Variety of fabrics employed: Rooms II (158), Moonlit Doves (159). Documented history: Wedding Gift (149).

Price Range
19th century–1920: $500–20,000. 1920–present: $200–6500.

156 Geometric Construction $1800–2000
157 Spires, Coutances Cathedral $1800–2200
158 Rooms II $1800–2200
159 Moonlit Doves $1800–2200
160 Greek $1800–2200
181 Schoolhouse $1800–2500
187 Elephants $1500–1800
188 Donkeys $1500–1800
189 Dragonfly $1500–2000
191 Night Scenes $1250–1500
192 Sunrise/Sunset $1250–1500

Prices for the following plates are unavailable: 149–153, 155, 182–185, 190.

Star Quilts

Plates
113, 115, 116, 117, 118, 119, 120, 121, 122, 123, 124, 125, 126, 132, 133, 134

Description
There are many variations of the star motif, ranging from a single large star covering most of the quilt surface to assorted patterns created from dozens of large and small stars. All such quilts are popular with collectors, but because so many were made, prices remain moderate. Somewhat more expensive, priced from $850 to $3500, are "embellished" star quilts—those bordered with appliqués.

Examples of Valuable Features
Bold, graphic design: Sunburst (116), Star of Bethlehem (118). Skillful cutting and piecing: Star of Bethlehem (115), Harvest Sun and Mariner's Compass (122).

Price Range
19th century–1920: $500–2500. 1920–present: $250–1500.

113 Star of Bethlehem $1250–1500
116 Sunburst $2200–2500
118 Star of Bethlehem $2200–2500
119 Princess Feather $1800–2000
123 Harvest Sun $1500–2200
132 Eight-Pointed Star $1800–2200
133 Album $2200–2500
134 Album $2200–2500

Prices for the following plates are unavailable: 115, 117, 120–122, 124–126.

Coverlets

Woven on looms, coverlets are heavy bed coverings. In the marketplace they may be grouped into two general categories: those which are made in geometric patterns, including Overshot, Double Weave, and Summer and Winter, and those known as Jacquards, which have curvilinear elements and representational motifs. Generally, Jacquards are more expensive. Those that command the highest prices usually have interesting border designs, makers' names, and dates. All-wool or all-cotton coverlets are also higher priced than those made of both fibers. Although some bedcovers, like quilts, have brought high prices within the last 15 years—escalating as much as 400% since the late 1970s—coverlets remain good buys and worthwhile investments.

Double Weave Geometric Coverlets

Plates
227, **229**, 232

Description
Heavy and reversible, this type of coverlet can be recognized because its two layers can be separated with the fingers.

Examples of Valuable Features
Interesting color combinations: Snowflake (232). Bold design: Snowflake (232).

Price Range
$200–1500.

227 Snowball with Pine Tree Border $850–1250
229 Star with Pine Tree Border $950–1500
232 Snowflake $850–1250

Jacquard Coverlets

Plates
203, 204, 205, 206, 207, 208, 209, 210, 211, 212, 213, 214, 215, 216, 217, 218, 219, 220, 221

Description
Introduced to this country in the early 19th century, the Jacquard loom attachment allowed the weaver to produce textiles with recognizable floral and pictorial elements. All Jacquards bring a fair price; yet compared with quilts, they seem underpriced. The highest sums are paid for those with unusual borders and central medallions. The marks of known weavers also add to the value of these pieces.

Examples of Valuable Features
Unusual borders: Floral Medallions (205), Floral Wreath (209), Floral Medallion (214). Pictorial elements: Floral Medallions (205), Medallion and Stripe (206). Dates and names: E Pluribus Unum (207), Double Rose with Bird and Rosebush Border (211).

Price Range
$300–5000.

203 Central Medallion $500–800
204 Centennial Design $800–1200
205 Floral Medallions $800–1200
206 Medallion and Stripe $800–1200
208 Tiles with Eagle Border $800–1200
209 Floral Wreath $800–1200
210 Double Rose with Grape and Leaf Border $800–1200
211 Double Rose with Bird and Rosebush Border $800–1250
212 Double Rose with Bird and Rosebush Border $800–1200
213 Modified Oak Leaf with Oak Tree Border $800–1200
214 Floral Medallion $800–1200
215 Snowflake Medallion with Hemfield Railroad Border $5000–8500
216 Tiles Design $800–1200
217 Tile Design with True Boston Border $800–1200
218 Sunburst Medallion with Potted Rose and Bird Border $750–1000
219 Floral Medallion with Rose Border $950–1500
220 Double Oak Leaf with Oak Tree Border $950–1200
221 Double Oak Leaf with Tulip Border $950–1200

The price for the following plate is unavailable: 207.

 # Overshot and Summer and Winter Geometric Coverlets

Plates
222, 223, 224, 225, 226, 228, 230, 231

Description
Although these include the earliest American coverlets, they are relatively underpriced. Overshot examples in more than two colors, unusual materials, or with a rare date or initials will bring more, but most are extremely reasonable in price and offer the collector a real bargain. Costlier are the reversible Summer and Winter coverlets.

Examples of Valuable Features
Unusual materials: Snowball with Pine Tree Border (226).
Interesting color combinations: Star and Diamond (224), Pine Bloom (230).

Price Range
$500–1500.

222 Star and Diamond $850–1200
223 Star and Diamond $900–1400
224 Star and Diamond $900–1400
225 Snowflake and Flowers $700–1000
226 Snowball with Pine Tree Border $700–1000
228 Snowball with Pine Tree Border $850–1200
230 Pine Bloom $750–1000

The price for the following plate is unavailable: 231.

Other Bedcovers

Bed coverings other than quilts and coverlets were also used in America. Some, like bed rugs and early crewelwork spreads and blankets, are rare and very expensive. Whitework quilts seldom bring less than $1000. Others were made in such quantity that they are both easily found and relatively inexpensive; for example, embroidered candlewick spreads sell for $100 and up.

Bed Rugs

Plates
233, 234, 235, 236

Description
Less than 60 of these rare handmade bed coverings are known to exist, most of them in public collections. Made in New England from the late 17th century to the early 19th century, bed rugs were widely used; unfortunately, most appear to have been destroyed by moths or decay. Yet, one was recently discovered at a small rural auction!

Examples of Valuable Features
Pictorial elements and original design: Bed Rug (234). Strong colors: Clamshell Bed Rug (233). Dates and initials: Bed Rug (235).

Price Range
$10,000–30,000.

233 Clamshell Bed Rug $10,000–20,000
234 Bed Rug $12,000–20,000
235 Bed Rug $12,000–15,000
236 Floral Bed Rug $15,000–20,000

Crewel Coverlets and Blankets

Plates
237, 238, 239, 240, 241, 242, 243, 244, 253, 254

Description
Practiced largely in the 18th and early 19th centuries, crewel embroidery was a time-consuming task, and few examples remain today. Most common are crewelwork bedspreads or coverlets. Blankets with crewelwork are less often seen. Both types are expensive and hard to find.

Examples of Valuable Features
Unusual design: Crewelwork Spread (237), Crewelwork Spread and Valances (239), Embroidered Bedcover (244). Pictorial elements: Embroidered Bedcover (243).

Price Range
Coverlets or spreads: $5000–20,000. Blankets: $250–5000.

237 Crewelwork Spread $8500–12,000
238 Crewelwork Spread $7000–9000

239 Crewelwork Spread and Valances $100,000–150,000
240 Strapwork and Crewelwork Coverlet $8500–9500
241 Crewelwork Spread $3500–4500
242 Embroidered Wool Coverlet $5000–6500
244 Embroidered Bedcover $6500–7500
253 Embroidered Homespun Linen Coverlet $7500–8500
254 Embroidered Checked Blanket $2500–5000

The price for the following plate is unavailable: 243.

Linsey-Woolseys

Plates
256, 257, 258, 259, 260, 261

Description
These heavy, glazed woolen bedcoverings were made in great numbers from the late 18th to early 19th century, and quite a few have survived. However, demand for them has increased dramatically in the last few years, and prices are rising sharply.

Examples of Valuable Features
Unusual colors: Glazed Wool Quilt (261). High glaze: Indigo Glazed Worsted Quilt (259). Unusual piecework (most were whole cloth): Pieced Worsted Quilt (258).

Price Range
$500–6000.

256 Variable Star $3000–4500
260 Quilted Linsey-Woolsey Bedcover $3000–4500

Prices for the following plates are unavailable: 257–259, 261.

Stenciled and Printed Spreads

Plates
245, 246, 247, 248, 249, 250, 251, 252, 255

Description
Most stenciled cotton spreads were made from 1820 to 1840. Relatively lightweight, few have survived. Prices for those remaining are high, with design being the most important consideration in establishing a market value.

Examples of Valuable Features
Good design: Stenciled Quilt (245), Stenciled Bedcover (250). Well-designed borders: Stenciled Bedcover (250). Strong colors: Stenciled Bedcover (249).

Price Range
$2000–10,000.

245 Stenciled Quilt $4000–5500
246 Stenciled Bedcover $4500–6000

The price for the following plate is unavailable: 248.

 # Whitework

Plates
262, 263, 264, 265

Description
White-on-white textiles include extremely simple quilts, complex pillow shams, stuffed work, and spreads embellished with candlewick. Ordinary pieces are inexpensive, while elaborate ones, especially if dated or bearing names, can be quite costly.

Examples of Valuable Features
Skillful quilting: Stuffed-Work Quilt (263). Unusual design: Embroidered Candlewick Pillow Sham (265). Dates and names: Embroidered Candlewick Pillow Sham (265).

Price Range
White-on-white quilts: $100–10,000. Candlewick spreads—geometric: $200–800; pictorial: $500–2500.

Prices for the following plates are unavailable: 263, 264.

Rugs

There are several types of American rugs, all of which are beginning to attract the attention of collectors. Desirable hooked rugs with well-executed pictures from the 19th century may bring several thousand dollars, but simple floral patterns can be found for as little as $35. Simple braided rugs remain inexpensive (from $50) while rare shirred, yarn-sewn, appliquéd, and embroidered examples can bring five figures when they come on the market—Shaker shag, braided, and rag rugs are beginning to command high prices.

Braided and Rag Rugs

Plates
300, 301, 302, 317

Description
Braided or rag rugs were once made in nearly every home. Although most examples found today are rather ordinary, they are much in demand along with country furnishings. More interesting and more costly are rugs made with carpet or hooked centers or those produced in the Shaker communities. The Shakers also made rag rugs of which the most desirable are those that are highly decorative; plainer examples are relatively inexpensive.

Examples of Valuable Features
Unusual design: Braided and Appliquéd Penny Rug (301). Strong colors: Shaker Braided Rug with Ingrain Carpet Center (302).

Price Range
19th century–1950: $50–950.

300 Shaker Braided Rug $850–950
301 Braided and Appliquéd Penny Rug $500–650
302 Shaker Braided Rug with Ingrain Carpet Center $100–185
317 Woven Shaker Rag Rug $75–125

Floral Hooked Rugs

Plates
282, 288, 289, 290, 291, 292, 293, 294, 295, 296, 297, 308, 309

Description
Often patterned after contemporary European or Near Eastern carpets, the floral hooked rug became a stereotype in the late 19th century. As a result only the most unusual and the earliest examples are of any interest to experienced collectors. The most expensive florals include rare, room-sized rugs, which may fetch up to three times as much as smaller examples. Other costly pieces are shirred, appliquéd, and embroidered; rugs with outstanding color and design bring ten times more than plain examples. However, even damaged yarn-sewn rugs are valuable because they are rarely for sale. As a group, compared with the pictorials and geometrics, florals are underpriced.

Examples of Valuable Features
Non-symmetrical design: Floral Design Miniature Hooked Rug
(288), Floral Design Hooked Rug (291), Appliquéd and
Embroidered Table Rug with Floral Design (297). Color from
vegetable rather than chemical dyes: Floral Design Hooked Rug
(291). Strong colors: Appliquéd and Embroidered Table Rug with
Floral Design (296). Various textiles employed: Floral Design
Miniature Hooked Rug (288).

Price Range
19th century–1920: $35–1200.

288 Floral Design Miniature Hooked Rug $1000–1200
290 Floral Design Hooked Rug $300–400
292 Floral Design Hooked Rug, Frost Pattern $350–500
293 Floral Design Hooked Rug, Frost Pattern $500–650
294 Floral Design Hooked Rug $350–500
308 Floral Design Hooked Rug $150–225
309 Art Deco Design Hooked Rug $800–1000

Prices for the following plates are unavailable: 282, 289, 291,
295–297.

Geometric Hooked Rugs

Plates
298, 299, 303, 304, 305, 306, 307, 310, 311, 312, 313, 314, 315, 316

Description
Geometrics are increasing in popularity because they are easily
integrated into the modern home. The patterns in these rugs are
based on various combinations of squares, circles, rectangles,
and other geometric forms. The best and most costly examples
are those that combine strong colors with bold design—like
abstract paintings—as well as those that are room-size or yarn-
sewn. Shag rugs produced in Shaker communities are rare but
are of interest to the collector specializing in hooked rugs.

Examples of Valuable Features
Bold design and good proportions: Geometric Design Hooked
Rug (312), Log Cabin Style Hooked Rug (313). Strong colors:
Geometric Design Hooked Rug (311), Flame-stitch Pattern
Hooked Runner (314). Room-size rugs: Geometric Abstract
Design Hooked Rug (298).

Price Range
$50–1000.

298 Geometric Abstract Design Hooked Rug $1500–1850
299 Geometric Design Hooked Rug $500–650
303 Geometric Design Hooked Rug $175–300
304 Shaker Shag Rug with Geometric Design $150–200
305 Geometric Design Hooked Rug $150–200
306 Hooked Rug with Central Medallion $150–200
307 Hooked Rug with Diamond Center $125–175
311 Geometric Design Hooked Rug $400–700
316 Rickrack Pattern Hooked Rug $150–225

Prices for the following plates are unavailable: 310, 312–315.

Pictorial (figural) Hooked Rugs

Plates
266, 267, 268, 269, 270, 271, 272, 273, 274, 275, 276, 277, 278, 279, 280, 281, 283, 284, 285, 286, 287

Description
The rugs in this category are the most popular types of hooked rugs and generally the most costly. They feature anything from a simple cat or dog to a village scene or an early automobile or sailing ship. The highest priced examples are usually those which resemble a folk painting, or those that are room-size, shirred, or yarn-sewn.

Examples of Valuable Features
Original design: Grenfell Hooked Rug with Puffins (273), Rooster Design Hooked Rug (275).

Price Range
19th century–1920: $200–4000. 1920–present: $50–900.

266 Lion Design Hooked Rug, Frost Pattern $1500–2000
267 Lion Design Hooked Rug $850–1000
268 Modern Noah's Ark Hooked Rug $1500–2000
269 Blackhawk Design Hooked Rug $500–850
272 Dog Design Hooked Rug $1500–2000
276 Horse Design Hooked Rug $600–750
278 Modern Bull Design Hooked Rug $175–200
280 House Design Hooked Rug $1500–2000
284 Hooked and Painted Rug with Waterfall $1000–1500
286 Simple Simon Design Hooked Rug $300–350
287 Centennial Design Hooked Rug $150–300

Prices for the following plates are unavailable: 270, 271, 273–275, 277, 279, 281, 283, 285.

Samplers and Needlework Pictures

Smaller than most other textiles considered here, samplers and needlework pictures were often schoolgirls' work. The most common samplers are those that incorporate an alphabet and sometimes the numbers 1–10. Show or hand towels, which may be considered a type of sampler, are also included in this category. The price of a sampler depends upon the presence of the maker's name and the date as well as such pictorial elements as houses, people, animals, or trees, and whether it was made in America, possibly at a girls' school known for fine needlework. Needlework pictures can be very personal but are generally stylized in composition. Best known are mourning pictures. Modern needlework pictures reflect a very broad range of subject matter and free experimentation with stitchery. Quality of design and stitching are paramount here.

 ## Needlework Pictures

Plates
340, 341, 342, 343

Description
Though rarer than samplers and often more complex to create, needlework pictures are not as much sought after, probably due to their classical themes, which many find unappealing. However, almost any 19th-century example will bring 5 figures. Generally less expensive, modern needlework pictures deal with a wide variety of themes.

Examples of Valuable Features
Beautiful design: Silk Mourning Picture (340). Skillful needlework: Silk Mourning Picture (340), Silk Mourning Picture (341), Embroidery on Paper (343).

Price Range
$150–7500.

340 Silk Mourning Picture $1500–3500
341 Silk Mourning Picture $15,000–25,000
342 Modern Thread Painting $2000–2500
343 Embroidery on Paper $150–1800

 ## Samplers

Plates
318, 319, 320, 321, 322, 323, 324, 325, 326, 327, 328, 329, 330, 331, 332, 333, 334, 335, 336, 337, 338, 339

Description
Prices for samplers have risen sharply in the past 5 years despite the fact that there are many English and European examples on the market, which are often hard to distinguish from American pieces. A spectacular pictorial sampler will bring over $20,000, but a plain, unidentified alphabet sampler without pictorial elements is still worth about $150.

Examples of Valuable Features
Pictorial elements: Family Record Sampler (326), Pictorial
Sampler (335), Pictorial Sampler (338). Documented provenance:
Alphabet Sampler (328), Mourning Sampler (339). Well-designed
borders: Alphabet Sampler (324), Family Record Sampler (326).

Price Range
$150–20,000.

319 17th-Century Band Design Sampler $8000–10,000
320 Miniature Sampler $175–300
321 Alphabet Sampler $125–300
322 Alphabet Sampler $1200–2500
323 Alphabet Sampler $3000–4000
325 Verse Sampler $1800–5500
326 Family Record Sampler $1800–4500
327 Alphabet and Verse Sampler $1500–6000
330 Alphabet and Verse Sampler with Watercolor $7500–9500
333 Map Sampler $1200–3000
335 Pictorial Sampler $20,000–22,000
336 Pictorial Sampler $20,000–23,000
337 Pictorial Sampler $15,000–16,000
338 Pictorial Sampler $35,000–38,000
339 Mourning Sampler $12,000–13,000

Prices for the following plates are unavailable: 318, 324, 328, 329,
331, 332, 334.

Picture Credits

Index

Numbers refer to color plates.

Staff

Prepared and produced by Chanticleer Press, Inc.
Publisher: Paul Steiner
Editor-in-Chief: Gudrun Buettner
Managing Editor: Susan Costello
Project Editors: Mary Beth Brewer, Jane Opper
Associate Editor: David Gibbin
Assistant Editor: Lori Renn, Cathy Peck
Art Director: Carol Nehring
Art Assistants: Ayn Svoboda, Jan Barthold
Production: Helga Lose, John Holliday
Picture Library: Joan Lynch, Edward Douglas
Symbols: Paul Singer, Tuula Fischer
Drawings: Dolores R. Santoliquido
Design: Massimo Vignelli

The Knopf Collectors' Guides to American Antiques

Also available in this unique full-color format:

Chairs, Tables, Sofas & Beds
by Marvin D. Schwartz

Chests, Cupboards, Desks & Other Pieces
by William C. Ketchum, Jr.

Glass Tableware, Bowls & Vases
by Jane Shadel Spillman